Report of the Royal Commission on the Economic Union and Development Prospects for Canada

Report

Royal Commission on the Economic Union and Development Prospects for Canada

VOLUME ONE

Minister of Supply and Services Canada

COVER DESIGN: Will Rueter
INTERIOR DESIGN: Brant Cowie

Available in Canada through authorized bookstore agents and other bookstores or by mail from
Canadian Government Publishing Centre
Supply and Services Canada
Ottawa, Canada K1A 0S9

Also available in French

Printed in Canada

Catalogue No. Z1-1983/1-1E

ISBN 0-660-11851-3 (Vol. 1)

ISBN 0-660-11850-5 (Set)

Canada: $45.00 (Set)
Other countries: $54.00 (Set)
Price subject to change without notice.

Royal Commission on the Economic Union and Development Prospects for Canada

Commission royale sur l'union économique et les perspectives de développement du Canada

TO HER EXCELLENCY
THE GOVERNOR GENERAL IN COUNCIL

MAY IT PLEASE YOUR EXCELLENCY

We, the Commissioners appointed by Order in Council dated 5th November 1982 as revised and amended on 25th November 1982 and 25th January 1983 to inquire into and report upon the long-term economic potential, prospects and challenges facing the Canadian federation and its respective regions, as well as the implications that such prospects and challenges have for Canada's economic and governmental institutions and for the management of Canada's economic affairs: Beg to submit to Your Excellency this Report.

Donald S. Macdonald, Chairman

Clarence L. Barber

Laurent Picard

Albert Breton

Michel Robert

M. Angela Cantwell Peters

Daryl K. Seaman

E. Gérard Docquier

Thomas K. Shoyama

William M. Hamilton

Jean Casselman-Wadds

John R. Messer

Catherine T. Wallace

August, 1985

P.O. Box/CP 1268
Ottawa, Canada
K1P 5R3

Canada

CONTENTS

Detailed Contents lists appear at the beginning of each chapter.

VOLUME ONE

FOREWORD *xi*

ACKNOWLEDGEMENTS *xv*

PREFACE *xvii*

PART I A NEW PERSPECTIVE *1*

1 **Canada: State, Society and Economy** *3*
2 **Global Outlook** *73*

Conclusions and Recommendations 208

PART II CANADIAN OPPORTUNITIES IN AN OPEN WORLD *211*

3 **Retrospective** *213*
4 **Canada in the Global Economy: The Present Situation** *231*
5 **Canada and the General Agreement on Tariffs and Trade** *277*
6 **Freer Trade with the United States** *297*

Conclusions and Recommendations 378

VOLUME TWO

PART III GROWTH AND EMPLOYMENT *1*

Introduction *3*
7 Economic Performance and Prospects *5*
8 Economic Growth, Investment, Technology, Management and Entrepreneurship *71*
9 Industrial Policy *131*
10 Short-Term Stability and High Employment *267*
Conclusions and Recommendations *379*

PART IV NATURAL RESOURCES AND ENVIRONMENT *393*

Introduction *395*
11 Resources and Canadian Economic Development *401*
12 The Natural Resource Sectors *415*
13 The Environment, Society and the Economy *505*
Conclusions and Recommendations *529*

PART V HUMAN RESOURCES AND SOCIAL SUPPORT *535*

Introduction *537*
14 The Evolution of Policy: Major Trends and Issues *543*
15 Work and Pay: The Functioning of Labour Markets *583*
16 Immigration Policy *657*
17 Labour/Management Relations *669*
18 Education and Training *733*
19 The Income-Security System *769*
20 Social Services *805*
Conclusions and Recommendations *814*

VOLUME THREE

PART VI THE INSTITUTIONAL CONTEXT *1*

Introduction *3*
21 The Institutions of National Government *33*
22 Federalism and the Canadian Economic Union *97*
23 Citizens, Communities and the Federal State *273*
24 The Canadian Constitutional System and Unresolved Community Issues *325*

Conclusions and Recommendations 385

COMPENDIUM OF CONCLUSIONS AND RECOMMENDATIONS *409*

SUPPLEMENTARY STATEMENTS *483*

APPENDICES *557*

Appendix A – Orders in Council and Exchange of Letters with the Prime Minister 559

Appendix B – Schedule of Written Submissions 575

Appendix C – Schedules of Government Consultations and Participants in Public Hearings 599

Appendix D – The Collected Research Studies 677

Appendix E – Staff of the Commission 691

ACRONYMS *695*

FOREWORD

The Royal Commission on the Economic Union and Development Prospects for Canada was established in the fall of 1982, in the aftermath of one of the most turbulent periods of Canadian history. On the economic side, Canada was just emerging from the worst recession since the 1930s. For much of the previous decade, the country had endured unprecedented levels of inflation. But other countries, too, struggled as we did with those economic problems. In addition, however, we conducted intensive, often divisive, domestic debates over enormously complicated and difficult issues such as energy policy, our new Constitution and, especially, the question of whether Quebec would remain a part of Canada. In that setting, the central question that we Commissioners were asked to consider was: Can we not do better in the future? Our response to this question is a resounding "Yes!"

Certainly, our nation has faced difficulties, both economic and political, but our extensive meetings with Canadians across the country have reaffirmed our view of Canada as a mature, tolerant and well-governed country. We are deeply convinced that Canada possesses many valuable opportunities for satisfying achievement. To attain that achievement, however, Canadians must face the necessity to make changes in policies and in institutions that offer, at least, the comfort of familiarity. We must venture into untried ways that will demand open-mindedness, courage, innovation, and determination. This Report sets out in some detail the changes which, in our view, offer Canadians the best opportunity of fulfilling our national potential.

While we have indicated a number of directions in which we think it likely that the future will take us, including the increasingly competitive international environment and the prospects of more modest growth than the economy experienced in the golden age of the 1950s and 1960s, we have not attempted to predict the future in detail. Anyone who has had responsibility for policy making since the beginning of the 1970s would recognize that such precise prediction is unrealistic. Assured of change, but uncertain about its exact direction, the most productive policy prescription we can urge is that as individuals and through our institutions, Canadians must maintain maximum flexibility in order to adapt to that change as it occurs.

Looking back over the perspective of 35 years, beyond the economic difficulties of the immediate past, this Commission sees Canada as having attained a quite remarkable record of economic success. We believe, however, that the circumstances which brought about that success will not continue; indeed, they have already altered, both globally and domestically. The differences which are emerging in our economic experience will have to be matched by differences in economic and social policies.

While the economy was an important focus for Commissioners' concern, we were also asked to consider how Canada's political institutions function, and by what means their functioning can be improved so that our nation can achieve better economic performance. Political institutions are created in order to manage conflict, for conflict is inevitable – between individuals, between firms, between regions, and between nations. The role of institutions is to channel that conflict so that our differences do not prevent us from attaining the goals we have in common. While we Commissioners believe that Canada's political institutions have adjusted well to the strains of the past decade, we consider that they can be made to work even better.

Our nation has been favoured in its evolution by the friendly support of larger allies and of a strong neighbour. Predictably, because Canada has not been a leader in important enterprises, Canadians have too often fallen into the habit of accepting a foreign lead or adopting a foreign opinion before fully thinking through what is appropriate for *us* in *our* circumstances. This attitude has been dubbed the "colonial mentality". As the late Vincent Massey once wrote in his well-known work *On Being a Canadian*: "We have never suffered from being too sure of ourselves." Again, he wrote:

> *We are one of the few countries in the world which can strengthen its nationality without threatening or offending anyone else. A stronger national sense would only help us the better to perform our national task. It need never conflict with an international outlook.*

In this Report we advocate for Canada a full involvement in the broader world. We must have confidence in ourselves. Indeed, we echo the words of Emily Murphy: "Lean on no one. Find your own centre and live in it, surrendering it to no person or thing."

In compiling this Report, Commissioners have set out an extensive agenda for change. Some aspects of change will be imposed upon us; others we shall seek to create ourselves as we move to meet the future. Ultimately, and most weightily, the burden of that change must be borne by individuals. To move from the usual, the accustomed, the habitual into the untried, the new, the innovative has always been, at least in part, a painful experience. Government institutions and policies can and should help to cushion the shock. For all that, it remains a shock. And it must be borne.

On the other hand, the rewards for Canada of changing outmoded patterns are enormous. We Canadians enjoy incomparable advantages, not only in the country we inhabit, but in the kind of society in which we live, and with the kind of institutions we have in place. By viewing change as an opportunity rather than a threat, by moving to meet or initiate it, by adopting a positive will to use it to our advantage, we can not only improve our circumstances at home, but we can also make a significant contribution to a world in which too many others still lack many of the advantages that we Canadians enjoy.

DONALD S. MACDONALD
Chairman
May, 1985.

ACKNOWLEDGEMENTS

The Royal Commission on the Economic Union and Development Prospects for Canada and the publishers wish to acknowledge with gratitude the permission of the following publishers and individuals to reprint in this Report material from their works:

American Association for the Advancement of Science; Bank of Canada; André Blais, Université de Montréal; Brookings Institution; Butterworth; Canadian Council on Social Development; Canadian Economics Association, *Canadian Journal of Economics*; Canadian Political Science Association, *Canadian Journal of Political Science*; *Canadian Public Policy – Analyse de Politiques*; Canadian Pulp and Paper Association; Canadian Sociology and Anthropology Association, *Canadian Review of Sociology and Anthropology*; Canadian Tax Foundation; Carnegie Endowment for International Peace; Conference Board of Canada; Donald J. Daly, York University, *Data Resources Review*; Decima Research Limited; Du Pont of Canada Inc.; Exxon Corporation; *Financial Post*; Food and Agriculture Organization of the United Nations; Christopher Freeman, University of Sussex; *The Globe and Mail*; Government of British Columbia, Premier's Office; Harvard University, Graduate School of Business Administration; Her Majesty's Stationery Office; Institute for Research on Public Policy; International Monetary Fund; *International Perspectives*; The Japan Times; John Laskin for the late Bora Laskin; Institute of Public Administration of Canada, *Canadian Public Administration*; George Lermer, University of Lethbridge; Methuen; Minister of Supply and Services Canada; Native Council of Canada; New York Times Syndicate; Ontario Economic Council; Ontario Manpower Commission; Organisation for Economic Co-operation and Development; Oxford University Press (Toronto); Parliamentary Guide; Parliamentary Reporting and Distribution Directorate, Canadian House of Commons; Pergamon Press; André Piatier, École des Hautes Études en Sciences Sociales, Paris; The Honourable Senator Michael Pitfield; Princeton

University Press; Private Planning Association of Canada (C.D. Howe Institute); *Public Interest*; Queen's University, Centre for Resource Studies; Queen's University, Industrial Relations Centre; Random House, *Review of Economics and Statistics*; Paul Samuelson, Massachusetts Institute of Technology; United Nations; United States Government Printing Office; University of California at Berkeley; University of Toronto, Institute for Policy Analysis; University of Toronto Press; University of Western Ontario, *Business Quarterly*; University of Windsor, *Windsor Yearbook of Access to Justice*; John Wiley and Sons Canada Limited; The World Bank; Yale University Press.

PREFACE

The Royal Commission on the Economic Union and Development Prospects for Canada was established by Order in Council (PC 1982-3438) and publicly announced on November 5, 1982. Under the chairmanship of the Honourable Donald S. Macdonald, this Commission was required to investigate and report on "the long-term economic potential, prospects and challenges facing the Canadian federation and its respective regions, as well as the implications that such prospects and challenges have for Canada's economic and governmental institutions, and for the management of Canada's economic affairs." (The terms of reference appear in Appendix A.)

In addition, this Commission was to recommend "the appropriate national goals and policies for economic development" and "the appropriate institutional and constitutional arrangements to promote the liberty and well-being of individual Canadians and the maintenance of a strong competitive economy." Commissioners were asked, in carrying out this mandate, to examine such matters as Canada's labour market and capital requirements; trends in productivity; standards of living and social progress; regional opportunities, constraints and aspirations; ways to improve relations among governments, business, labour and other groups; the allocation of fiscal and economic powers among levels of government; the way that Canadians are represented in national institutions, and how they might be better represented.

The mandate recognized that while Canadians have had an almost unbroken run of prosperity since the Second World War, our economic successes will not continue merely by maintaining past policies. The Commission was charged with assessing whether the Canada we know today, built as it has been upon the incremental changes of the past, is well positioned for the major challenges ahead. Because Canada is going to have to adapt to meet a much more competitive world environment, the Commission's role was also to look at Canada's position in that broader context.

Given the scope and complexity of Commissioners' mandate, it was clear at the outset that only a broad approach would serve. Thus, our investigation proceeded simultaneously along a number of paths. We began by initiating a series of private consultations, soliciting written submissions, conducting public hearings, and establishing a massive research program. All of these activities took us half way through the period of our mandate. At this point, we released a discussion paper, launched a second round of more precisely focused hearings, held further consultations, and sponsored specialized symposia and seminars. Then, in the fall of 1984, Commissioners withdrew from the public arena to reflect on the vast body of knowledge and opinion we had acquired and to come up with the best definition of what Canada might become in the twenty-first century.

The Early Stages

Within a short time of his appointment, the Chairman invited the premiers and government leaders of all provincial and territorial administrations to meet with this Commission. Commissioners were most fortunate in obtaining publicly the views of many provincial premiers and of members and officials of their governments, and we are indebted to them for their frank and full contribution. (Appendix C-1 provides the schedule of provincial and territorial participation in all phases of this Commission.)

We also wish to express our gratitude to the federal government whose briefs and presentations at our public hearings were immensely helpful. Without exception, all our inquiries of federal government departments and agencies were met with careful consideration and the utmost co-operation. (The list of briefs and representations from the federal government appears as Appendix C-2.)

Similarly, we wish to express our thanks to local and regional government officials who brought to our deliberations an enthusiasm for dealing with local economic development concerns and a desire to play a larger role in national public policy making. (Appendix C-3 provides the schedule of local and regional government participation.)

In the spring of 1983, this Commission began a round of private consultations. In this four-month series of informal meetings, the Chairman and other Commissioners met with 138 public- and private-sector groups representing business, manufacturing, finance, labour, resources, agriculture, education, research, municipalities, volunteers and aboriginal communities. This consultation process gave Commissioners an opportunity to meet informally with more than 1200 of Canada's leaders and provided a forum for an early exchange of views on the many complex issues included in our mandate.

Yet another aspect of this Commission's investigation entailed a series of seminars in the summer of 1983, organized in order to encourage debate and develop public understanding of the issues involved in our inquiry. These orientation sessions benefited from the vigorous participation of 31 national business associations, 51 national volunteer organizations, and numerous executive officers of major companies, financial institutions and other private sector groups.

In the early stages of our mandate, Commissioners were eager to inform the public of our task and to elicit their support and assistance in conducting our inquiry. We set out to do this by means of an information booklet, of which 300 000 copies were distributed. In this, our first publication, we highlighted our terms of reference and our calendar of activities, and issued a specific invitation to members of the public to inform us in writing of their views and suggestions.

Public Consultations

This Commission's first foray into the field of public consultation took the form of community or town-hall meetings arranged by universities across the country. Twelve such workshops were held in all ten provinces. This approach to stimulating public interest in the work of a Royal Commission proved to be a successful and rewarding experience. Responsive audiences in every city established these meetings as important forerunners of our fall hearings. Commissioners are much obliged to the participating universities for their efficient organization and handling of these events.

In the fall of 1983, Commissioners journeyed across the country, holding hearings on 59 days in 27 cities and towns and five Arctic communities. We were heartened by the considerable interest our public hearings attracted. Indeed, requests for appearances were so numerous that Commissioners, on occasion, had to sit in panels in order to cover two locations simultaneously. Even under that arrangement, we could not accommodate all those who wished to make a representation. In all, 1827 intervenors made 759 presentations to this Commission in its first round of hearings. In addition to the live testimony presented directly to Commissioners, a total of 1164 briefs were filed with this Commission in the first round. (A schedule of written submissions appears in Appendix B, and a list of intervenors is presented by location and date in Appendix C-4.)

As we Commissioners began our hearings, our concern was for the future and how to find the course on which the second-largest country on earth might steer into that future. This Commission wishes to acknowledge that the submissions we received and the testimony we heard in the course of our hearings represent a contribution of inestimable value to that quest. Commissioners are deeply grateful to the many Canadians from all walks of life who took the time and, in many instances, made the effort to travel a great distance in order to contribute the information, the views and the proposals upon which our Report is based. We wish to emphasize the great importance of this contribution to our task.

All the submissions which this Commission received and the transcripts of the public hearings, which comprise 96 volumes, together with all other materials generated by our investigation are housed in the Public Archives of Canada, in Ottawa. As is customary, we have also provided the Library of Parliament with a complete set of these documents. In addition, the briefs and transcripts are available on microfilm, for a fee, at Micromedia Limited, Toronto.

Mid-way through our mandate, Commissioners released *Challenges and Choices*, a discussion paper designed to report to Canadians on the pulse-taking odyssey we had just completed. This document was also intended to focus attention, and launch a public debate, on the central issues that had emerged from the first phase of our work. Basic challenges were grouped into eight areas: jobs and costs, trade and industrial development, productivity, education and training, resources and the environment, social support, intergovernmental relations and the economic union, and national institutions. In fact, these groupings led to the agenda for our Final Report.

Our second round of hearings followed in the spring of 1984 in five cities over 15 days. More than 250 people participated in these lively and stimulating sessions that focused on the major challenges identified in the first round of hearings. Canadians from labour, business, the volunteer sector, indeed all walks of life, met together in a round-table format to share their views with one another and with the Commission, and to grapple with the range of difficult policy choices inherent in the resolution of the major challenges of our time. (A list of participants in the Public Debates appears in Appendix C-5.)

To complement the focused character of these public debates, Commissioners held an Open Forum on the evening of our last day in each location. In all five cities, attendance ranged from 100 to 150 people, and, once again, Commissioners were gratified by the lively interest in our inquiry expressed by ordinary Canadians, and the range of concerns they were able to bring to our attention through these forums.

In addition to organizing these meetings for gathering responses to our discussion paper, this Commission sent an invitation to the public at large, to submit written arguments and discussion based on *Challenges and Choices*. In response, we received a further 352 briefs.

The Research Program

While this Commission's consultation process was taking place, the most extensive research program in Canadian history was under way. Jointly directed by three prominent Canadian scholars, it involved more than 300 studies in 19 major policy areas. During its course, determined efforts were made to foster cross-disciplinary thinking so that the unique perspective of a political scientist, an economist and a legal scholar might all be brought to bear on the same issue: productivity, for example, or trade. (A complete list of published research papers in 72 volumes is presented in Appendix D.) As with other Royal Commissions, our research has been important, not only in its primary function of providing direct assistance to the conduct of our inquiry, but also as a means of enhancing, for many years to come, the understanding of contemporary scholars, students, other interested readers, and policy makers generally.

The Report

This, then, was the basis on which we have produced our Report: extensive public consultation and solicitation of expert opinion; formal hearings in all parts of Canada; discussion papers and newsletters to keep Canadians informed of our activities; national debates of invited guests to focus on the major challenges of our time and place; and a research program based on excellence and interdisciplinary thinking to gather the best intelligence and analysis in Canada and abroad.

Commissioners began the process of producing this Report immediately after the second round of hearings, in June 1984. We established a unique and decentralized process that would respect and integrate information from the wealth of material obtained from our public hearings and our research program. Initial working drafts were written by eight teams co-ordinated by policy specialists and comprising senior researchers from economics, politics and law, and secretariat analysts, who condensed and summarized the material from the hearings. Individually and collectively, Commissioners reviewed and reworked, tore down and integrated drafts over almost a full year of intensive Commission deliberations.

Our discussions ranged from the role of state in modern society to soil degradation, from the paralysis of Cabinet government to the challenge of international competitiveness. Our overall concept has been to view state and the economy as integrated parts of the way society achieves its goals. We have looked to the future, viewed Canada in a global context and wrestled with those central issues concerning which we believe Canadians will have to make choices. In the end, we have formed a view of this country, how it works and what its potential can be. It is not "neat and tidy", but neither is life; it is an optimistic view, but one filled with major challenge for Canadians and their governments.

While Commissioners propose no single ideology to encompass answers to the many questions on our agenda, we nevertheless insist on the need to address the larger, interdependent contexts in which we live. It is essential to emphasize that the economic, social and political aspects of our Canadian experience interact with one another and, more broadly, with the international environment. We may not be able to describe that interdependence with precision. By trying to understand it, however, and, in particular, its consequences for our institutional arrangements, we contribute a minimum intellectual coherence to the particulars of our public life. This is a central objective of much of our Report.

A century ago all governments were small; today all governments are big. We cannot return to simpler times. The size of contemporary government in Canada, as elsewhere, is not the result of intellectual error, idiosyncratic factors or the personal goals of particular politicians. Instead, much of past legislation has been an experiment with the future. Learning from those past experiments, however, is not easy for political systems. Government is a pressure cooker, not a scientific laboratory; time to think is a scarce political commodity. The contribution of a Royal Commission, then, is largely an educational one that steps back from the political process, offers a different perspective and suggests broad principles to guide our future policy choices.

At times we were humbled by the enormity of the task. In the end what we have recommended is not a definitive blueprint but a series of linked proposals for Canada's future direction. The Commission has made these choices bearing in mind the institutional dilemmas we face and the individual dreams we hold. Canada is a tolerant, blessed and vital nation in an uncertain world of changing economic circumstances. Canadians will have to be ready to meet the challenge of that change.

Finally, Commissioners wish to record that the sizeable task set out before us would have been impossible to complete without the highly competent and dedicated staff we were fortunate to assemble. We wish to acknowledge and praise the high calibre of assistance we received from all of our staff including policy, research, secretariat, administrative, library, editorial, translation, secretarial and clerical personnel. Their names are listed in Appendix E, and our thanks extend to all of them.

While it is difficult to single out any particular contributions in the light of the extraordinary efforts of so many, we would like to record special gratitude to the senior officers most closely associated with the overall enterprise: J. Gerald Godsoe, the Executive Director and overall chief of staff; Alan Nymark, Director of Policy and project manager for the Report; Michel Rochon, Secretary, responsible for the hearings process; Ivan Bernier, Director of Research (Law and Constitutional Issues); Alan Cairns, Director of Research (Politics and Institutions of Government); David C. Smith, Director of Research (Economics) whose responsibilities were shared by co-directors Kenneth Norrie and John Sargent in the latter part of the Commission's work; and Harry Stewart who, as senior adviser on administration, ran a very tight ship.

PART I

A NEW PERSPECTIVE

PART I

Contents

Chapter 1 Canada: State, Society and Economy *3*
Chapter 2 Global Outlook *73*

Conclusions and Recommendations 208

CHAPTER 1

Canada: *State, Society and Economy*

Introduction *5*

The Canadian People *7*
Notes *13*

Canada's Constitutional System *14*
Notes *23*

The Task of Governing *24*
Notes *40*

State and Economy: The Domestic Role *41*
Note *57*

State and Economy: The International Role *58*

Conclusions *63*

CHAPTER 1

Canada:
State, Society and Economy

Introduction

The Royal Commission on the Economic Union and Development Prospects for Canada came into being on November 5, 1982. Commissioners' response to the almost boundless mandate fluctuated between excitement that almost nothing was beyond the legitimate scope of our inquiry and private moments of fear and insecurity. Our time frame was short for the task to be performed. Our freedom had to be controlled. We needed organizing criteria. We had to find patterns as we explored the seemingly infinite nooks and crannies of our nation's collective existence. We needed to bring together theories from the various social and legal sciences, and to blend them with what Canadians had told us in our hearings. Somehow, we had to bring order to our efforts.

We proceeded, somewhat paradoxically, in light of all these concerns, by heading off in many directions at once, with two complete rounds of hearings, a large and ambitious research program, and lengthy discussions. As we undertook our separate explorations, came together again, and parted once more in a frequently repeated cycle, we must all have harboured, in our quiet moments, the secret hope that our task was essentially like that of the sculptor who knows that there is a single perfect statue waiting to be released from the imprisoning marble, or of the true scientist seeking to identify those patterns in the universe which await the discoverer who will dignify their existence with a single pristine theory.

Reality resisted our efforts. We have not discovered a single, simple and compelling message. The patterns we have found, and to which we have responded, are daunting in their complexity. Canadians pursue multiple objectives in the domestic and international arenas. We Commissioners have had, accordingly, to provide many answers to the many questions implicit in our mandate.

We hope that our analysis will inform the diverse debates to which our mandate directs us, and which virtually encompass the entire agenda of governments in contemporary Canada. Although we concluded, for example, that the arms race and the prevention of global war were policy concerns outside our terms of reference, we have included aspects of foreign policy, aid to the less-developed countries, and global ecological concerns, along with our role in the international economy, which is central to our mandate.

If our contribution has any unique virtue, that virtue must reside in the scope of our Report, for which we have had to explore interdependencies often overlooked in the day-to-day process of governing which inevitably works against a comprehensive approach. Governing is also subject to the pressures of the moment, and these are hostile to a future-oriented perspective. As a Royal Commission, we have tried to be both comprehensive and forward looking. We have included future generations in our policy calculations. Further, we have not restricted ourselves to the pursuit of a narrow Canadian self-interest. In the world of the future, that would be unacceptably parochial and would deny our obligations to the humanity beyond our borders, with whom we share this planet.

Commissioners are convinced that in fulfilling our mandate, we have made considerable progress in addressing our country's future. We also have ample evidence that Canadians are a democratic people engaged in the never-ending task of collective self-education. This Report is our contribution to that ongoing dialogue. With the assistance of the many Canadians who participated in our hearings, we have tried to raise large issues, fundamental concerns and broad principles, in the course of making recommendations which we hope will contribute to the greater well-being of Canadians.

The Canadian People

We Commissioners did not approach our task from a clinical detached perspective; we constructed our analysis to serve a people who have much to be proud of, and who have made a relative success of evolving a civilized, humane, prosperous and democratic society in an imperfect world.

We soon became aware that the people of Canada, like other nations, are caught up in concerns which show little regard for state frontiers. Those concerns, be they ecological, economic or peace-directed, can be realistically addressed only by the interdependent international system of sovereign states and the network of norms and institutions which those states have constructed. While it is not difficult to detect an embryonic sense of our common humanity deriving from our co-existence on a fragile planet, the overwhelming political fact remains that the world is balkanized into states. There is no decision-making authority for humankind as such.

Canadians must work with and through the nation-state system which politically divides humanity, in our efforts to manage the innumerable interdependencies which stretch across frontiers, and which generate overlapping communities of shared fate with our fellow global citizens. The national self-interest of individual states which accords an almost automatic primacy to the needs of domestic populations must be tempered by an outward-looking sense of obligation based on concern for our collective future.

As we Commissioners looked out at the world beyond our borders, we were forcibly reminded that in comparative terms, Canadians are not newcomers on the global stage. Indeed, Canadians belong to one of that small number of contemporary states with an uninterrupted constitutional evolution of more than a century. In part, this achievement reflects our success in managing our domestic affairs; in part, the good luck of our geography. In any event, our self-image of a young new country is simply misguided. In the world of real comparisons, we are successful survivors. We are a tried and tested people, now well into our second century.

To look out at the more than 150 member states of the United Nations should also halt any expression Canadians might give to the platitude that Canada is a difficult country to govern. Governing is a difficult task everywhere, and we experience our own Canadian version of that universal problem. We should cease, however, to strain the credulity of the governors and the governed of most of the rest of the world's nations by implying that our governing task is especially arduous. The reverse is true. We have been favourably endowed by geography and history, with a modern economy, a skilled work-force, and democratic political arrangements. We are a tolerant people, skilled at compromise, and we have inherited a relatively peaceful society.

It is time, therefore, for Canadians to live comfortably with the fact that we are a fortunate mature people, who have travelled far together. The pilgrimage from colony to nation, which began in 1867, is over. The Constitution Act, 1982, by which we completed that incremental evolution marked off by such decisive milestones as the Balfour declaration of 1926, belatedly symbolizes a maturity we had long attained, but not yet formalized. It domesticates a comprehensive amending procedure for the Canadian Constitution and ends the anachronism which compelled Canada to resort to the British Parliament for amendments dealing with the federal division of powers and other matters.

We are now on our own. The United Kingdom has receded in importance for Canadians, both practically and psychologically. Today's world map does not display the reassuring red patches of half a century ago, from which Canadians of British background could gain a vicarious sense of pride and achievement. We continue to possess a valuable window on the world in the contemporary Commonwealth, and for many Canadians, an extra warmth and affinity for the United Kingdom remains. We retain monarchical forms and our link with the Crown, and we govern ourselves through parliamentary institutions derived from our British inheritance. These belong to us, however, as an independent nation.

France also is a country *pas comme les autres*. It has a special political and emotional significance for francophones, which is reflected in a strong representation of both the Quebec and the Canadian government in France. Our historic connection with French civilization now contributes to close links with *la francophonie* in Africa and elsewhere.

These connections with Britain and France are of special significance for many Canadians. They reflect our country's history and its roots in the French and English settlement of North America centuries ago, as well as the continuing prominence and benefits of our linguistic dualism and the cultural enrichment to which it contributes. Our strong contemporary links with France and with the United Kingdom, however, are not those of pupils to teachers or of children to parents. They are relations between equals.

Furthermore, English-speaking Canada is now multicultural, defined by language rather than by a shared British past. The metropolitan centres of anglophone Canada are home to a diverse population of many cultural backgrounds and various countries of origin. French Canada, too, is now multicultural. Because of the Quebec government's recent language policies, it is no longer possible automatically to equate French-speakers with the descendants of the approximately 65 000 *habitants* who remained after the retreat of the French Empire from North America more than two centuries ago. In little more than two decades, the concept of French-speaking Québécois has expanded to encompass a multicultural population, including immigrants from Haiti and refugees from Vietnam. In relative terms, therefore, the growing tendency is to define French-speaking Quebec by language rather than by a common past.

In Quebec and in our other nine provinces, each official linguistic majority shares provincial space with a linguistic minority of the other official language community. Relations between linguistic majorities and minorities in each province are now influenced by the language rights of the Canadian Charter of Rights and Freedoms. However, the noble purposes behind the Charter are still far from achieved. As the 1984 Annual Report of the Commissioner of Official Languages indicated, "progressive polarization threatens the probable extinction of most French-speaking minorities outside Quebec and, by ricochet, drastic reduction of English freedoms within that province." The Commissioner describes as a "national embarrassment . . . the number of English-speaking provinces that neither provide adequate 'minority-language education facilities' nor show much sign of doing so."[1] Clearly, in spite of the progress made since the passage of the Official Languages Act in 1969, much remains to be done if our performance is to catch up to our ideals.

We Canadians are also a multi-racial society, partly because of the liberalization of our immigration requirements in the 1960s. This change, in turn, reflected the increasingly multi-racial character of the international state system consequent on the decline of European empires and the simultaneous emergence of the United Nations as a forum for promoting racial equality. Our population is now much more a microcosm of the ethnic and racial diversity outside our borders than it was half a century ago. Our relatively generous refugee policy has made a particular contribution to our cosmopolitan composition.

These developments have made us a different people from our grandparents. We now have to forge a common Canadianism, not only out of our two founding peoples, but also from the growing ethnic, racial and cultural diversity of our population. This nation-building task is one we must pursue in the context of a global revival of ethnicity which has surprised social scientists and governments alike.

That ethnic awareness is evident in the contemporary self-confidence and assertiveness of Canada's aboriginal peoples, who have exchanged their former political obscurity for a high visibility sustained by various political organizations. Non-status Indians and Métis share in this general awakening of ethnic pride and identity. Since the boundaries and membership of these two groups are fluid and partly a product of choice, their numbers grow as ethnic self-consciousness spreads and special treatment and recognition by government appears increasingly likely.

Many of the Indian First Nations, to use the terminology of a recent House of Commons' report,[2] will evolve to various forms of self-government in the future. This politically and symbolically decisive modification of the ethnic order within Canada may also be reinforced in the next few years by the creation of Nunavut, following the possible division of the Northwest Territories. The new political jurisdiction with an Inuit majority would consist of a total population of about 15 000 persons in political control of almost one quarter of Canadian territory.

The ethnic and linguistic clauses of the Canadian Charter of Rights and Freedoms and the Constitution Act, 1982 reveal not only the growing ethnic diversity of the Canadian people, but also our more overt recognition and positive appreciation of that diversity. The English and French linguistic dualism of Canada receives special attention. Sections 16 to 23 of the Charter provide guarantees for our two official languages, including minority-language/education rights. Section 27 instructs the courts to interpret the Charter "in a manner consistent with the preservation and enhancement of the multicultural heritage of Canadians." Section 25 protects "aboriginal, treaty or other rights or freedoms that pertain to the aboriginal peoples of Canada." Section 35 of the Constitution Act recognizes and affirms "the existing aboriginal and treaty rights of the aboriginal peoples of Canada" and defines the latter to include "the Indian, Inuit and Métis peoples of Canada", thus giving the Métis a constitutional recognition they previously lacked. Section 15(1) of the Charter provides equality rights "without discrimination based on race, national or ethnic origin, [and] colour", as well as on other characteristics, while section 15(2) allows affirmative action programs for the amelioration of conditions of disadvantaged individuals or groups falling within the preceding categories.

This abbreviated and all-too-cryptic indication of the interaction of our developing ethnic diversity with selected aspects of our political and constitutional evolution is not meant to be a detour on the way to the basic issues of economic management and of the appropriate division of labour between state and market. We Canadians must first have a clear understanding of what we have become and what we might be in the future, sharing, as we do, a common country.

Since Confederation, Canadians have not possessed – and never will possess – a coincidence between the boundaries of our country and the boundaries of a single ethnic unilingual community. In Canada, as in most states of the world, the ideal of President Woodrow Wilson, that each historically defined ethnic nation should possess its own government, does not apply. Our collective identity as a single people must be fostered and sustained by a common Canadian citizenship into which are blended the varied forms of distinctiveness derived from our different pasts and our multiple ethnic origins. We have continuously to foster a moral coherence and a social solidarity out of the diversities which we bring to the national and provincial communities that must encompass us all. We bring to this task a collective identity which has already evolved as a result of our history, of enterprises we have undertaken in common, including our many achievements. We are involved in an ongoing enterprise to which we make our own contribution in the light of ever-changing requirements, such as our more complex ethnic and racial fabric, and this distinguishes our task from that of former Canadians who were citizens of a much younger country. Our evolving understanding of our own identity affects, at every turn, the policy decisions about our future course of action.

This social management task of government is as difficult and important as the task of economic management. To think otherwise is to have been asleep for the last quarter of a century in this country, and to be oblivious to developments elsewhere in the world. A lengthy list of recent events and controversies testifies to the powerful emotions tapped by issues of language, race, and culture: language policies in Quebec and in the rest of Canada; the controversy about bilingualism in air-traffic control; the threat to our survival as a united country, which was posed by an independence-oriented nationalism in Quebec; the policy of multiculturalism; House of Commons' committees dealing with visible minorities and with aboriginal self-government; and recent research by the Urban Alliance on Race Relations and the Social Planning Council of Metropolitan Toronto, indicating extensive job discrimination against racial minorities. Such issues involve our passions and our identities, and they challenge our capacity to treat each other equitably. Government's contribution to that capacity is not going to diminish, for it deals with the essential question, to which there is no permanent answer, of our identity as a people.

Every increase in the role of the state enhances the need and compounds the difficulty of working out an acceptable answer. The limited distant state could survive with a minimal answer to the question of the identity of a people its policies rarely touch. The positive big state of the contemporary era cannot. It affects our lives at every turn, and it needs our compliance and support if it is to govern effectively. A state which routinely places heavy burdens of responsibility on its citizens must be based on a strong sense of shared civic identity if its policies are to succeed. From the citizens' perspective, the seriousness of exclusion from the operational definition of the community is proportional to the role of the state in presiding over the distribution of the advantages and disadvantages of our common existence. It is not accidental that the enhanced state power of recent decades coincided with serious pressures on our national and provincial identities, nor that the Charter of Rights and Freedoms arrived on the scene when it did. The Charter simultaneously protects us from the state and, by stressing our citizenship, links us to it.

Like other democratic capitalist societies, Canada has recently witnessed a veritable explosion of self-conscious groups and social movements which extend beyond ethnicity, language and race: the women's movement seeking gender equality; the environmental movement drawing our attention to the fragility of the ecosystem of planet Earth; lifestyle groups which challenge traditional definitions of the family and of relations between the sexes; and the handicapped, who are no longer willing to accept that social and economic privation should be added to the unfair fate of physical or mental disabilities. These and other social movements and group demands co-exist and interact with more traditional cleavages based on class and region. In relative terms, along with language, race and ethnicity, they have grown in political significance.

Our national self-image is thus an evolutionary creation linked to former definitions and incorporating historic identities, but changing in response to the multiple domestic and international factors – linguistic, ethnic, racial, economic, religious, sexual and others – which impinge on the way we define ourselves. The state is the key actor in channelling this evolution toward a coherence which is necessary for its own efficient functioning and for social stability.

The state presides over a social arena in which various groups constantly vie for status and recognition. These groups seek to use the state to advance their own claims, and the state responds within the parameters set by the need for social cohesion and in terms of evolving citizenship criteria. In the last quarter of a century, the governments of Canada and of the province of

Quebec, in particular, have devoted remarkable attention to refashioning the collective images of their respective people. Other provincial governments have engaged in similar efforts, although they were not always driven by the same urgency. The instruments have been flags, language policies, bills of rights and charters, authoritative public statements, Royal Commissions, legislative committees, a referendum, and shifting criteria of appointment to highly visible offices such as those of Governor General, lieutenant-governor, and the Supreme Court.

The significance of this kind of activity is often misunderstood and underestimated in societies which assume the primacy of material and utilitarian concerns. However, as one analyst observes:

> *The formation of societies consists, at one level, in the construction of a symbolic order [which] entails, first, the definition of a collective identity which . . . becomes articulated in a system of ideas as to who we are as a people. This identity is represented in the multiplicity of symbols surrounding the rituals of public life, the functioning of institutions, and the public celebration of events, groups and individuals . . . individuals expect to recognize themselves in public institutions. They expect some consistency between their private identities and the symbolic contents upheld by public authorities, embedded in the societal institutions, and celebrated in public events. Otherwise, individuals feel like social strangers; they feel that the society is not* their *society.*[3]

Governments must provide meaning and recognition for the citizenry. This symbolic role for the state shades off into a social role in which governments intervene directly to modify the distribution of individuals and groups in preferred social positions. The policies they devise for these purposes are not without cost. They consume time, administrative resources and funds. In the case of language policies, hundreds of millions of dollars have been deployed in the effort to shape language use in the schools, in government bureaucracies and, especially in Quebec, in the economy.

While these policies often derive their primary impetus from non-economic categories such as race, ethnicity, language and gender, they can also have major consequences for the functioning of markets. They seek to modify, for example, the gender division of labour, the use of official languages in the public service, the ethnic composition of the work force, and the occupational distribution of the physically and mentally handicapped. The affirmative action provisions of the Charter, which have just come into effect, almost guarantee a major enhancement of the future role of government in improving the conditions of disadvantaged individuals and groups.

The social and symbolic roles of the state reviewed above are unlikely to diminish in the years to come. In relative terms, they will wax and wane, but they will not follow the business cycle, waxing when economic times are good and waning when they are poor, because the pressures that motivate them lie elsewhere. Governments manage society as well as the economy. In managing the former, they have major effects on the functioning of the latter.

Notes

1. Commissioner of Official Languages, *Annual Report 1984 in Brief* (Ottawa, 1985), pp. 1–2.
2. Canada, House of Commons, Special Committee on Indian Self-Government, *Indian Self-Government in Canada: Report of the Special Committee* (Ottawa: Queen's Printer, 1983).
3. Raymond Breton, "The Production and Allocation of Symbolic Resources: An Analysis of the Linguistic and Ethnocultural Fields in Canada", *Canadian Review of Sociology and Anthropology* 21 (May 1984), p. 125 (emphasis in original).

Canada's Constitutional System

More than a century ago, our predecessors founded a new country and set out to create a new nation for whom they provided a particular version of constitutional government. The institutions they put in place, especially parliamentary government and federalism, were derived from a mixture of history and choice. The result, in Canada today, is one of the oldest enduring systems of constitutional government in the contemporary world.

To a large extent, we Canadians not only carry out our public business through our constitutional arrangements, but we are also shaped and defined by them. Our sense of ourselves as a political community is a product of institutions derived from the past. Our overall governing arrangements are repositories of our evolving values; they define us as a particular citizenry with a history and a future. We are not merely consumers and producers who happen to share a common space. We are not a crowd of isolated individuals temporarily and accidentally assembled in a railway station, impatiently waiting for trains to take us to our separate real destinations. We have already arrived. Canada is our ancestral home, and Canadians have worked at improving it for more than a century. We are, although we seldom realize it, a historic people, including those recently arrived on our shores, who have added to our diversities and multiplied our cosmopolitan links to the larger world beyond.

The institutions bequeathed to us by history, therefore, are not a burden to be borne, but a heritage to be improved. Clearly, much of the endurance of our governing arrangements is the result of inertia, of the difficulty of achieving major change, of the self-interest of those who benefit from their location in the obscure niches of a complex system, and of our collective lack of imagination. In addition, however, our fidelity owes much to the fact that we feel comfortable with our system of government. We know how to work it. We recognize ourselves in the way it performs. We have adapted to one another.

This is not a recipe for blind allegiance, for ancestor worship in a country where custom is king. Our institutions are part of a living Constitution which evolves, and which we continuously reshape. At any given time, the particulars of our governing arrangements have been, will be and should be challenged for their biases, their insensitivities and their inefficiencies. The responses have been, and will be, human, and hence imperfect. The overall effect of those responses during more than a century has been a profound transformation of our institutions of government, albeit within a recognizable line of development. If Georges-Étienne Cartier and John A. Macdonald were to return today, they would experience both a reassuring sense of familiarity and a certain degree of disorientation in response to the consequences of incremental change.

The major institutional arrangements of federalism and parliamentary government were brought together in 1867, when the United Province of Canada, and Nova Scotia and New Brunswick came together to form the Dominion of Canada. Parliamentary government and federalism continue to structure our political life. The latter divides the jurisdictional capacity to act between provincial governments and the national government. The former, variously called "responsible government", "parliamentary government" or "cabinet government", structures the relationships between the executive and legislative branches of government.

On the whole, the marriage of parliamentary government and federalism has been a happy one. Federalism, with its division of jurisdictional authority between two orders of government, has facilitated the political management of spatially separated social, economic, ethnic, and linguistic diversities. Federalism is neither a luxury nor a shrivelled institutional survivor devoid of contemporary utility or moral significance. In terms of the most stringent functional criteria, federalism is an asset: it reduces the burden on any single government. The existence of provincial governments facilitates a more sensitive response to regional diversities than would be possible in a Canadian unitary state. By allowing provincial majorities to go their own way in matters under provincial jurisdiction, federalism also has democratic virtues. It eases the task of devising sensitive national policy by allocating jurisdiction for various regionally divisive issues to provincial governments. It contributes to the overall stability of the political system by increasing the likelihood that citizens will find one government attuned to their party preferences and policy goals.

In its own sphere, each government is sovereign. Each wields authority from the base of a division of powers which has undergone limited formal change since 1867. Each has its own bureaucracy, its own party system, and its own pyramid of political accountability from electorate to legislature to cabinet. Each has spawned a host of Crown corporations and regulatory agencies removed from the day-to-day control of legislatures and ministers. Each has its own monarchical representative in the form of a lieutenant-governor or the Governor General. Each responds to the particular society, economy and language groups within its territory, and each has visions and plans for its people. All are subject to the Constitution and to a judicial system capped by a Supreme Court which umpires the federal system.

Federalism derives a special justification from its contribution to harmonious relations between the French- and English-speaking communities of Canada. Over 80 per cent of the former live in Quebec, where they control a provincial government possessed of significant lawmaking authority in areas central to their language and culture. While the creation of provinces in 1867 was a response to the existence of separate colonies in the Maritimes, possessed of distinctive traditions and their own governing structures, and also to the English-speaking community of what became the Province of Ontario, it is unquestionable that the francophone community of Quebec was federalism's most ardent advocate and defender. This remains true more than a century later.

Francophone Quebecers seek survival and cultural continuity as a linguistic minority in a country with an English-speaking majority, which shares a continent with the dynamic English-speaking society of the United States. The strategies for survival have varied over the past century. In recent decades, the Quebec government has come to play a more prominent role in fashioning the response by which francophone Quebecers can simultaneously remain faithful to their historic traditions as a distinctive society and yet participate in the Canadian, North American and global community as a modern people. The modernizing Quiet Revolution of the 1960s was followed by the independence movement, culminating in the 1976 election victory of the Parti québécois, committed to sovereignty-association. The years from 1976 to 1980, and the referendum of the latter year are fresh in our memories and should not be forgotten. The victory of the "No" side was a victory for Canada and for a renewed federalism.

Clearly, at the time, there was considerable dissatisfaction with existing federal arrangements, even if the 40 per cent "Yes" vote to give the government of Quebec a mandate to negotiate the terms of a sovereignty-association agreement with the rest of Canada contained many strategic voters, as well as others fully committed to sovereignty association. Nevertheless, the essential message was clearly one of support for a Canada which was federal, a Canada in which the provinces, particularly Quebec, would play a prominent role, and in which French-speaking Canadians would participate vigorously and in proportion to their numbers in the national government.

We remind all Canadians of these events, not because those who forget the past are condemned to repeat it, but because the harmonious co-existence of French- and English-speaking Canadians within a common Canadianism requires constant nurturing, including institutional and constitutional recognition. That nurturing must occur at three levels:

- There must be full recognition of the essential role played by the government of Quebec to promote the flourishing of its French-speaking majority population which makes up more than four-fifths of all French-speaking Canadians.
- The national government must reflect our linguistic duality in its overall functioning and in the composition of its administration in order to meet the three goals of "actively providing service to the public, increasing equitable participation in the public service, and providing a genuine choice of language of work".[1]
- Canada as a whole, in both its national and provincial dimensions, must be responsive to, and supportive of, the official language minorities, francophone outside Quebec and anglophone within Quebec. The Charter, especially in its language provisions, is a prominent and functional constitutional instrument for these latter tasks.

No one who has lived through the last two decades will be tempted to believe that support for a strong provincial role in Canadian federalism is confined to Quebec, or that the national government's task of reconciling national and provincial concerns in areas of federal jurisdiction does not extend to all ten provinces. Elsewhere in this Report, Commissioners suggest reforms to the institutions of the central government to enhance its sensitivity and responsiveness to the provincial dimensions of our national existence, particularly to the less populous provinces. The Western and Atlantic provincial governments and their peoples have not always been satisfied that their concerns received adequate consideration in a national government numerically dependent on the two central provinces. No matter what reforms we adopt, such regional frustrations will never be entirely absent. The federalism manifested in the provincial order of governments contributes immensely to our capacity to live together co-operatively and fruitfully as one people. It does not, however, keep our provincial differences out of the national arena, where they must be reconciled and integrated with the goals we pursue in common as Canadians. We can do better, but we neither seek nor expect to eliminate inter-regional conflict.

From this general task of conciliation and leadership, Commissioners may have singled out the French/English, Quebec/federal-government dimension for somewhat greater attention than that given either to relations between the other provincial governments and communities and the national government or to the multicultural dimension within both English- and French-speaking Canada. If we have done so, it is not because we wish to downgrade the importance of the latter. These issues, too, are what Canada is about, and we discuss them at length elsewhere in this Report. Our position as Commissioners is simply that we do not bring to the assessment of the provincial, linguistic and ethnic facts of our Canadian existence a democratic presumption that all facts are equal. Such an approach would be naïve and paralyzing in its consequences. Our pre-Confederation history, the Constitution Act of 1867, the passions which attend language issues, and the Quebec/Ottawa, French/English tensions of recent decades make it clear to Commissioners that the positive reconciliation of our nation's French/English dualism, the challenge of which has impressed every foreigner who has studied our society, must always be one of the central tasks of statecraft in Canada.

Federalism in Canada, however, is not only about our provincial diversities. The Constitution Act, 1867 was designed to create a national community which controlled a national government to be employed by Canadians in the pursuit of Canadian goals. It was not expected that Canadians would shed their provincial identities and concerns in national politics; nor has that happened. Neither was it expected that in national affairs, Canadians would bring only their provincial selves to the bargaining table. In national affairs, Canadians were expected to be, and have been, more than the sum of their provincial differences. Conversely, British Columbians, Nova Scotians and Quebecers bring a Canadian dimension to their provincial civic roles. As Canadians we have developed a complex system of equalization payments designed to ensure that the residents of the "have not" provinces, in spite of their more limited fiscal capacity, receive an average level of provincial government services without subjection to above-average levels of provincial taxation. The Charter of Rights in the Constitution Act, 1982, even with its override provisions,[2] gives further evidence of a common Canadianism by establishing a minimum floor of judicially protected rights enforceable against both national and provincial governments; consequently, it sets limits to provincial divergences in the treatment of Canadian citizens.

The political process of federalism, accordingly, does not establish hermetically sealed boundaries between our national and provincial selves or between the national and provincial governments which, in specified areas, such as trade and commerce or property and civil rights, derive authority from the division of powers. In addition, with the growth of activist government within both national and provincial jurisdictions, the management of intergovernmental interdependence has become a practical concern for policy makers. Classical federalism, with autonomous governments operating within clearly demarcated jurisdictions, presupposes limited roles for government to which we are unlikely to return. Commissioners do not, however, believe that the division of powers is thereby irrelevant or obsolete: only that governments can no longer be indifferent to one another as they pursue their goals. We seek, and make recommendations for, a more fruitful collaboration between national and provincial governments than has sometimes characterized our country's recent past.

Commissioners' interpretation of the spirit of Canadian federalism, including the evolving relationship between the national and provincial governments and the national and provincial communities of Canada is complex, as befits a complex subject. Our basic position, which is presented in detail later in our Report, is that federalism as such will be no less necessary and appropriate to our future than it has been to our past. We also believe, given the co-existence of strong provincial and national governments, that some elaboration of intergovernmental machinery is necessary to improve policy performance in areas of overlapping responsibility. It is not only necessary to supplement existing arrangements in the intergovernmental arena, but also to link the national government more securely and directly to Canada's regional diversities by means of an elected Senate. This constitutional change will increase the power of the smaller provincial populations in national affairs and enhance the regional responsiveness of the national government. That government must not leave the representation of provincial interests exclusively to provincial governments. One of the weaknesses of a number of our national governments since the Second World War has been their inability, for various reasons, to speak for and to the provincial dimensions of our Canadian life.

The national government has an additional responsibility to play a leading role in the federal system on behalf of the national community which has emerged in more than a century of our history. This role involves federal leadership in fostering a developing pattern of national standards and common treatment for Canadian citizens in matters within provincial, as well as within federal, jurisdiction. The role is not new. It is delicate. It can be mishandled. It is also crucial. Had it not been properly played in the past, it is clear that our tax system, our social programs, and our rights would be much more fragmented than they are.

If we Canadians govern ourselves through federalism, which divides the capacity to act between the two orders of government, we govern ourselves within jurisdictions by a system of responsible government. This system brings together the executive and legislative branches of each government in a manner designed to ensure both decisive leadership and democratic responsiveness through the requirement that the political executive remain in office only as long as it retains the majority support of the elected members of the legislature. These members derive their authority from democratic electoral competition in which the citizens vote in individual constituencies for candidates belonging to rival partisan teams which seek the power to rule.

It is easy to draw attention to the various ways in which parliamentary responsible government falls short of idealized textbook descriptions: the continuing influence of money in political life; the unrepresentative nature of legislative bodies; the increasing number of interest groups which interact directly with the bureaucracy and the Cabinet; the excesses of partisan debate; the imbalance in access to expertise between cabinets and legislatures; the manipulative capacity which modern media and sophisticated polling techniques give to governing authorities; the extent to which the administrative state escapes the effective scrutiny and control of elected officials; the difficulties facing legislatures responding to the complexity and sheer volume of policy decisions in contemporary society, in which government assumes major responsibilities; and many others. Our response as citizens to these and other shortcomings, however, has not been and is not to give up the constant effort to renew and strengthen our traditional arrangements for governing ourselves. Our performance is always in tension with an idealized version of how we should govern ourselves within parliamentary frameworks and contributes to recurrent efforts to keep the system relevant to new conditions. In fact, given the transformation in the role of government since the theory of the functioning of responsible government developed in the nineteenth century, what is remarkable is the continuing relevance of the adapted system. We Commissioners, by our recommendations, seek to contribute to that relevance by proposing appropriate changes.

The extent of Canadians' recurrent efforts to minimize the gap between performance and ideal is impressive. On the one hand, we seek to be more open and democratic: hence the development of equitable criteria for constituency redistribution administered by impartial commissions, the steady extension of the franchise from its limited base of more than a century ago, and the control of election expenses. On the other hand, we also seek more efficiency by streamlining parliamentary procedures and by recurrent reorganizations of the executive branch to enhance the co-ordinating capacity of cabinets, as well as to ensure that the administrative branch of government is subject to political control.

However, the details of these efforts to revise and update our parliamentary democracy, in order to keep its performance from clashing with our ideals, are not the concern of this chapter. The relevant point is that we Canadians do not give up the battle. Responsible parliamentary government is the way in which we practise democracy. We constantly seek its improvement. We rarely consider its replacement. We do not view it simply as machinery instrumental to our ends, as part of the "throw-away" society. Parliamentary government is the embodiment of central, historic, political values which define Canadians as a particular political people. Parliamentary government is the major vehicle by which we seek to control the awesome power of the contemporary state and keep it responsive to our wishes.

Parliamentary government and federalism are thus interdependent givens of our existence. Neither should be viewed in isolation from the other. They are the arrangements through which we seek to combine leadership and democracy within two orders of government that divide authority over the same people. We have 11 co-existing systems of responsible democratic government, ultimately controlled by 11 electorates, which collectively govern us as a federal people. Federalism divides the authority to act. Responsible government controls the manner of its exercise. Jointly they determine who has governing authority over whom for what purpose, and ensure that such authority will be won, employed and controlled according to historic conventions and understandings.

Parliamentary government and federalism are subject to constant challenge and are capable of constant improvement. They are not, however, to be approached as if we had a clean slate on which we can write as we wish. We cannot rerun our history.

Federalism and responsible government no longer stand alone as the central pillars of the Canadian constitutional order. The 1982 Canadian Charter of Rights and Freedoms adds a third pillar which, as it is incorporated into our "living constitution", will modify the workings of both federalism and parliamentary government.

Like many profound constitutional changes, the Charter is the culmination of domestic and international developments over many decades. A central thread was the growing recognition that the state could be a cruel tyrant as well as a servant of the people. Buchenwald, Belsen and the Gulag Archipelago, which stand for mass crimes against humanity committed in our own lifetime, confirmed the accuracy of Lord Acton's dictum that "Power tends to corrupt, and absolute power corrupts absolutely."

The excesses of democratic governments have been mild in contrast to those of Nazi Germany under Hitler or the Soviet Union under Stalin. Democracy is clearly the first and central defence against the abuse of power. Nevertheless, various events in Canada such as the wartime treatment of Japanese Canadians, the Gouzenko affair and the secret spy trials of 1945–46, the vesting of quasi-judicial powers in various agencies of the administrative state, and the civil liberties cases of the 1950s from Quebec convinced growing numbers of Canadians that parliamentary supremacy should be checked by an independent judiciary protecting constitutionally entrenched citizens' rights. These domestic intellectual currents were supplemented by an international rights consciousness stimulated by the United Nations and reinforced by the ending of colonialism in Africa and Asia.

The relative decline of support for parliamentary supremacy which accompanied advocacy of entrenched rights also reflected the weakening appeal of the British model of government as Canada acquired increasing autonomy as a middle power in the post-war years. The ending of civil appeals to the Judicial Committee of the Privy Council in 1949, and the vesting of final appellate authority in the Canadian Supreme Court created the conditions for an indigenous Canadian jurisprudence which was a prerequisite for the implementation of a charter responsive to Canadian conditions.

The developing ethnic diversity of the Canadian population was an additional stimulus, for it increased the likelihood of discrimination and enhanced the utility of a charter as a tool to educate Canadians in the virtues and necessity of tolerance. More generally, the anticipated nation-building contribution of a charter defining Canadians as equal possessors of rights, and thus helping to cement a common citizenship, became more obvious in direct proportion to the increased ethnic diversity it was to encompass.

The erosion of support for parliamentary supremacy and the advocacy of entrenched rights developed steadily, if discontinuously, from the Second World War. The first major response was the 1960 Diefenbaker Bill of Rights, which related only to federal jurisdiction, was not entrenched, and was only weakly applied by the courts in the two decades which preceded its 1982 successor. Nevertheless, the 1960 Bill of Rights focused discussion on the idea of a charter and, by its very weaknesses fostered recognition of the need for a stronger instrument in the next stage of development of rights protection. The move from the 1960 Bill to the 1982 Charter revealed the incrementalism of democratic politics so characteristic of policy development in Canada.

The 1982 Charter derives, in part, from the same civil liberties' roots as the 1960 Bill, but the purposes it was to serve were broadened by political developments in the intervening years. Quebec nationalism, especially the independence movement culminating in the 1976 election victory of the Parti québécois, threatened the political integrity of the Canadian nation. The federal Prime Minister and his colleagues feared, with good reason, that unless French-speaking Quebecers could be induced to retain an identification with, and allegiance to, the federal government and a Canada-wide community, the country might not survive. The Official Languages Act of 1969, deriving from the Report of the Royal Commission on Bilingualism and Biculturalism, was a statutory response within federal jurisdiction. A charter with language protections and educational rights was viewed as an additional instrument to sustain francophone communities outside Quebec and thus the idea of a French Canada not confined to that province, as well as a means to support the English-speaking minority in Quebec. The overriding objective was to prevent the coincidence of linguistic boundaries with territorial boundaries, a possibility which the Liberal governments from 1968 onwards saw as leading to the break-up of Canada. In addition, the more general category of rights in a charter would strengthen the citizen base of the national community at a time when an aggressive provincialism, as enunciated by governments in several provinces, tended to define Canada as an aggregation of provincial communities.

Throughout this period of political tension, a growing civil rights constituency saw a charter as a vehicle to advance its objectives with the support of a constitutionally entrenched document. This was particularly true of the women's movement, aboriginals, the handicapped, and various ethnic and racial minorities: a charter could enhance their status in society and their position in the economy. The support of these groups was useful to the federal government, which encouraged their demands. The idea of a charter thus acquired politically significant backing from new political forces, organized on a group basis, whose political emergence was part of broader changes in Canadian society; these changes were paralleled in other advanced capitalist democracies.

The complex political process out of which the 1982 Charter emerged and its specific contents are elaborated elsewhere in this Report. Its general significance for constitutional government in Canada, however, merits a brief examination here.

The Charter confronts the federal/provincial discourse and dialectic of governments, to which our federalism has historically accorded a special prominence, with a competing citizen/state discourse. As a corollary of this change, it supplements the constitutional role of the Supreme Court as umpire of the federal system with an expanded role in the adjudication of citizen/state relations. This change in role transforms the image of the Court, makes it a more visible and significant institution, and influences the criteria relevant to its future composition as a judicial body with enhanced functions and elevated constitutional importance.

Supreme Court judges of the future will need to be cognizant not only of the constitutional parameters of federalism, but also of the evolving criteria required by a more philosophic rights-centred jurisprudence. In performing the judicial task imposed on them by the Charter, the Court has no long-term alternative but to articulate a philosophy of democracy, citizenship and community appropriate to the multiple cleavages of Canadian society and to the enhanced role of federal and provincial governments in our lives.

The Charter, even given the override provisions of section 33, which allow governments to bypass some of its provisions by permitted procedures, clearly encroaches significantly on parliamentary supremacy. Conversely, it elevates the status of the citizenry relative to that of government and provides powerful support to the idea of rights residing in the people. For individuals and groups, it provides an alternative process to that of Parliament and legislatures for the pursuit of particular public policy goals.

Thus the Charter, even with its *non obstante* clause as a concession to parliamentary supremacy, is a fundamental addition to the instruments which govern citizen/state relations. It not only elevates the status of the citizenry, both symbolically and practically, by carving out a sphere of citizens' rights beyond the reach of the state, but it also imposes positive obligations on the state with respect to language rights. Finally, in section 15(2), which came into effect in April 1985, it provides constitutional sanction for the state – indeed, it positively invites its affirmative action – to better the conditions of disadvantaged individuals or groups. That invitation will be taken up, and it will involve governments at both levels in micro-social engineering as they seek to readjust the status order produced by history: in the public sector, in education, and probably, by contract compliance, in the private sector.

While the Charter is the outcome of nearly half a century of thought and experience, its complete incorporation into our constitutional system will be the work of future decades.[3]

Notes

1. Commissioner of Official Languages, *Annual Report 1984 in Brief*, Preface.
2. Section 33 of the Charter authorizes Parliament or the legislature of a province to declare in an act that the Act in whole or in part shall operate notwithstanding Charter provisions pertaining to fundamental freedoms (s.2), legal rights (ss.7–14) and equality rights (s.15). Such a declaration has effect for a maximum of five years and may be re-enacted for additional five-year periods.
3. For a discussion, see R. Rainer Knopff and F.L. Morton, "Nation-Building and the Charter", in *Constitutionalism, Citizenship and Society in Canada*, vol. 33, prepared for the Royal Commission on the Economic Union and Development Prospects for Canada (Toronto: University of Toronto Press, 1985).

The Task of Governing

The scope and complexity of contemporary big government in Canada has transformed the relations between government and society, challenged our practices of responsible government, and greatly complicated the working of Canadian federalism. In the last half century, there has been a marked expansion of the domestic role of the national and provincial governments and a greatly increased importance of the international arena for the attainment of our goals. If we Canadians are to manage our collective affairs efficiently and democratically in the future, we must understand the extent of the expansion of government activity, the multiple roles of government, the various arenas in which those roles are played out, the proliferation of institutions which has accompanied that expansion, and the challenges thus posed to our traditional assumption that government is the servant of the people.

Much of our Report addresses these developments, and many of our recommendations are directed to a redefinition of the links between government and society, to improving the quality of our performance in selected policy areas, and to reforms of those central institutions of Parliament and federalism in which reside our capacity to manage our collective affairs in national and provincial politics as a democratic people.

In the nineteenth century, all governments were small. Now all governments are big. We cannot return to simpler times. The size of contemporary government in Canada, as elsewhere, is not the result of intellectual error, of idiosyncratic factors, or of the personal goals of particular politicians. The basic similarity of trends in democratic capitalist nations clearly indicates that in general, Canadians are dealing with broad systemic factors within which limited national variations are played out.

Commissioners agree with a recent author who argues that "In a very real sense, many issues of government are incapable of a final solution; they are conditions of existence."[1] While our room for manœuvrability is limited, it is not unimportant. Given the impact of government on our lives, the cumulative effect of a series of marginal moves in the right direction is qualitatively significant. The contemporary links between the governments and peoples of Canada reflect hundreds of incremental past decisions taken in response to particular pressures and not always in cognizance of their long-run consequences.

All legislation is an experiment with the future. To learn from past experiments, however, is not easy for political systems. Government is a pressure cooker, not a scientific laboratory. Time to think is a scarce political commodity. Moreover, ongoing programs acquire defenders who benefit from, or at least are habituated to, their operation. In addition, widespread agreement on relevant criteria of evaluation is often lacking. In these circumstances, the contribution of a Royal Commission is largely educational: to step back from the political process and take a long view which can contribute a different perspective, general criteria, and broad principles to guide our future policy choices. Such, in any event, is the perspective adopted by this Commission.

Elsewhere in this Report, Commissioners provide a detailed analysis of the growth of government and assess its consequences in particular policy areas. This material will not be duplicated in this opening chapter. Some observations about the growth of government in Canada are, however, necessary at this point to set the stage for the thematic discussions of subsequent sections. As stated above, big government is here to stay. We Canadians have to learn to live with it and to work out a *rapprochement* between its imperatives and our overall constitutional order of parliamentary government and federalism, to which a Charter of Rights has recently been added. Such a *rapprochement* requires a preliminary understanding of the complexities behind the phrase "big government".

By most measures, government in Canada is a much more prominent actor than it was half a century ago. Nevertheless, in comparative terms, total government expenditure in Canada, amounting to 45.8 per cent of gross national product in 1982, is in the middle of the range by the standards of the Organisation for Economic Co-operation and Development. Expenditure growth has been most extensive at the provincial and municipal levels. After intergovernmental transfers, the federal government's share of total government spending declined from 51.9 per cent in 1950 to 38.8 per cent in 1980, while the provincial/local share increased from 48.1 per cent to 59.1 per cent. Canada Pension Plan/Quebec Pension Plan accounted for 2.1 per cent in 1980.

These, however, are only crude measures of government activity, which must be supplemented by other indicators, such as public employment, regulation, loans and guarantees, equity interests, and Crown corporations, if we are to understand the significance of the state in Canadian economy and society. As two authors recently pointed out, these various measures "cannot be 'added up' as they are incommensurable."[2]

The difficulty of a comprehensive assessment is further compounded because the multiple interdependencies linking the governments of Canada and Canadian society and economy modify the behaviour of private actors in immeasurable ways. The behaviour of the latter is more and more subject to political calculations. They pursue their goals in a complex environment of incentives and disincentives which, in contrast to the world of our great-grandparents, are increasingly the product of government policies and programs.

Some suggestive indicators of government growth, and hence of links with our society and economy, are useful, however, to reveal its current pervasiveness. For example, government transfer payments to persons as a percentage of total personal income have increased from 7.2 per cent in 1950 to 12.5 per cent in 1980; government wages and salaries, including those of the military, have increased, as a percentage of total wages and salaries, from 12 per cent in 1950 to 24.4 per cent in 1980.

There has been a conspicuous increase in Crown corporations in recent decades, although aggregate data on their numbers are not entirely clear. Two authors recently identified 454 federal public corporations, as of May 1980, but added that a "large number [remain] unidentified." Another study identified 233 provincial Crown corporations in 1980, 75 per cent of which had been created since 1960, and 48 per cent since 1970, although the percentage of total assets created (33 per cent in 1960–80; 13 per cent in 1970–80) was much less. In the aggregate, Crown corporations have more diversified mandates than previously, and increasingly play entrepreneurial roles in resource sectors. Federal and provincial Crown corporations "may" produce about one-tenth of the gross national product.[3]

Crown corporations have recently been supplemented as tools of intervention by the practice of some provincial and federal agencies of acquiring equity interests in the private sector. According to a recent estimate, in 1983 there were over 300 mixed enterprises in Canada. In 1982, the *Caisse de dépôt et placement du Québec* had equity holdings in 183 companies; a year later, it had an equity portfolio of over three billion dollars.[4] The Alberta Heritage Fund, which has just begun to buy equities, clearly has the potential, given its assets, to acquire significant influence in the economy.

The regulatory activity of the state, too, has grown. Many regulatory agencies are governments in miniature, whose functions have evolved from policing to promoting and planning in sensitive spheres of socio-economic and cultural activity.[5] Between 1970 and 1979, more new regulatory statutes were passed by the federal government than in the previous three decades. Almost one-third of provincial regulatory statutes in place in 1978 had been enacted since 1960, and an estimate for 1978, before the National Energy Program (NEP), concluded that 29 per cent of gross domestic product at factor cost was subject to direct regulation.[6]

The welfare state, of which we had only episodic evidence prior to the Second World War, has become a complex and comprehensive set of programs which offers collective provision against the normal hazards of life, such as sickness and old age, as well as against the particular risks, such as unemployment, which attend economic fluctuations. Private economic actors are linked to the state in a maze of incentives and disincentives, opportunities and obligations. Countless subsidies, guaranteed loans, quotas, tax provisions, technical and research assistance, environmental regulations, and other instruments and policies too numerous to mention affect decision making in the economy.

As we have already noted, the state has an extensive social role as it responds to ever more-encompassing notions of equality. It readjusts relations between the sexes in labour markets and marriages; imposes a pattern of French- and English-language use in selected areas, which would not occur in the absence of state policies; seeks to raise the status and income of the physically and mentally handicapped; redefines the relations among, and relative status of, ethnic groups; and recognizes and enforces citizens' rights by means of bills, charters and fair-employment bureaus. In performing these social roles, the state both deliberately and inadvertently modifies our self-conceptions, and informs us which groups are rising and which falling, and which have been unfairly treated and need official support to redress their position. The state not only seeks particular objectives of an instrumental nature, such as the provision of wheelchair ramps for the disabled and improving the access of various groups to valued jobs by affirmative action, but in doing so it also contributes to an evolutionary unfolding of official conceptions of social justice which emerge out of controversy and struggle.

These multiplying roles for the state have been accompanied by an enhanced sophistication in the instruments available for their performance. The development of new instruments and administrative technologies transforms the context of citizen/state relations. Such instruments are never neutral, and contemporary government, powered by intelligence and purpose, contributes to their proliferation. We forget that payroll deductions of tax at source are a comparatively modern phenomenon, first used in 1942. The development of this powerful administrative capacity not only employs private businesses as unofficial state tax collectors, but greatly increases the ability of governments to extract resources from society. Our earlier fiscal dependence on the tariff at the national level, especially in the nineteenth century, was partly the result of the ease of its administration at the border and the relative absence of alternative instruments for collecting revenue.

The use and policy significance of instruments is closely tied to the development of theories by which we seek to understand their effect on economy and society. The budget was a more prosaic instrument before Lord Keynes revolutionized our understanding of its use as an instrument of economic policy. Keynesian theory, in the context of the successful management of the wartime economy from 1939 to 1945, which contrasted with the mass unemployment of the Depression, redefined the post-war role of the state for mass publics possessed of the franchise. The point is of general application and significance. The future role of the state, the choice of particular instruments of intervention, and the relative importance of institutions within government will partially reflect the findings of some academic scribbler puzzling over a recalcitrant theorem. Effective government combines knowledge and will. Without the former, the latter is a threat, not a hope.

New or refurbished theories, values and concepts change the lenses through which we view government and its responsibilities. An expanded understanding of the scope of equality is now widely held in the electorate, and provides a rationale for new government programs. The 1982 Charter will diffuse throughout Canadian society the idea of citizens as rights bearers, and will modify the relations between citizens and governments, as well as elevating the role and visibility of the Supreme Court. The specific label of "affirmative action", seldom used in our past, but now given a special legitimacy by its association with the Charter, not only provides governments with a new language to justify fine-tuned intervention in labour markets, but constitutes a political resource and an organizing theme for groups which can benefit from its employment.

A political system, therefore, nests in a bed of values and ideas, and is subject to their ongoing evolution in its environment. The democratic political process is not only open to such shifts in values and ideas, but encourages their emergence. This stimulus to experiment and innovation, however, operates at the margin. It is countered by the massive inertia of big government. Yesterday's ideas and values are already bureaucratized and embedded in programs that are resistant to change. Most of what governments do represents the continuation of earlier programs. New programs always form only a small proportion of total government activity. Established governments are thus unavoidably instruments of conservatism, more responsive to habit than to innovation. Further, given the extensive existing program links between government and society, nearly all new programs affect activities that are already subject to various policies.

The institutions and policies of Canadian governments do not relate only to our domestic concerns. The geographically fixed nation state exists in a global environment of cultural, economic, political, military and ecological influences that either play on its citizens and then are transformed into demands for state action, or generate international managerial responsibilities for the state, or both. A diminished proportion of the agenda of contemporary Canadian governments has its origin in purely domestic affairs. Indeed, so overpowering did external forces appear to be, particularly the multi-national corporation and footloose capital, that many scholars in the 1960s predicted the demise of the state. That prediction was premature. The state controls territory, possesses sovereignty, commands loyalty and has a far greater range of capabilities than any other international organization, governmental or private, including the multi-national corporation. The state as the dominant form of political organization has great survival capacity, not least because of the absence of a feasible alternative. The survival of the state attests to a phenomenon too often ignored: those who seek to establish new institutions must often employ as a means the very institutions they seek to displace. Those who control such institutions have a well-developed tendency and capacity to bend reform in their own interests.

We may expect the Canadian state, therefore, to survive and to constitute the future locus of political authority for our descendants into any middle-range future that need concern us. Compared to existing international institutions including the United Nations, the state, at least in its Canadian version, has much to recommend it. While it faces challenges, in Canada and elsewhere, from multiple international pressures, it is the most effective source for mobilizing authority and consensus that humanity possesses. We have learned to live with it. There is no alternative base for an equally powerful sense of loyalty and community transcending the state on which we could, if we desired, construct more encompassing political authorities. The state will remain the central institution for the governing of humanity for the foreseeable future.

Global interdependence does not produce homogenization, nor the disappearance of national identities. These tendencies are resisted, as one author reminds us, by:

> *. . . the distinctive cultural traditions which different national populations bring to the contemporary situation, and in the array of historically determined institutional arrangements with which they enter the contemporary era. These traditions and forms seem remarkably adaptable, and a high degree of*

variability in economic and political arrangements seems compatible with the management of a modern industrial society.[7]

Nevertheless, the state itself clearly exists in a more open international environment than it did even half a century ago, and it must contend with a greater range and intensity of international forces than its predecessors. This is particularly so to the extent that a state, like Canada, is liberal and democratic, depends heavily on international trade as we do, employs, like ourselves, a world language (or two), and is wealthy so that its citizens have extensive access to the electronic media which cross borders with facility. In addition, modern affluent societies such as ours contain numerous sub-cultures: scientific, academic, professional, youth, sports, and so on, which are linked with their counterparts in other countries, and among which goods, values, ideas and styles diffuse quickly with little concern for national boundaries. On all these measures, Canada tends toward the open end of the spectrum, a conclusion given further support by our co-existence with a dynamic capitalist neighbour whose technological skills are allied with the most highly developed mass culture of consumerism in the world. Furthermore, as a nation of immigrants, we have always been intimately linked to foreign lands, from which we have brought values, political ideologies, and varying versions of the purpose of life. The more diversified immigrant flow of recent decades has only added to this tendency and multiplied our links with other cultures.

It is instructive to note the international sources or external supports for various social movements which feed new ideas and values into domestic politics. The Canadian women's movement, for example, is the domestic expression of an international drive in the Western developed world to change the gender division of labour and, more broadly, the gender division of society. Its literature and its leaders speak to the common condition of women which, subject to significant national variations, is characterized by a second-class status that is no longer acceptable.

Canadian aboriginals, too, are linked in international forums, conferences, and associations with indigenous counterparts elsewhere who share similar aspirations for enhanced status, and who also experience a revived sense of their ethnic identity. The politics of Canadian aboriginals is truly international and has involved such actions as lobbying in the United Kingdom and appeals to the United Nations and its specialized agencies. The Inuit are joined with their ethnic kin in the Circumpolar Conference, which brings together Inuit from Greenland, Alaska and Canada. The articulate expression of rights and the demands for their protection are sustained and fostered by the United Nations Universal Declaration of Human Rights and by numerous special covenants and articles which are quickly transformed into resources in domestic politics. Political aspirations, alternative identities, competing values and new definitions of the appropriate relations between men and women, young and old, parents and children, and citizens and states sweep across national borders.

Political boundaries have always been permeated by the movement of values and ideas, but there is little doubt that this tendency has greatly accelerated, has moved into new social arenas, and now vitalizes the demands for social change which are made on particular national governments. In sum, the internationalization of social movements and political life is integral to the emergence of new issues and new interests in democratic politics that complicate the role of contemporary governments.

The international sources of domestic politics also inform the economic sphere. They derive from the new international political economy, created after the Second World War, with its deliberate bias toward interdependence among nations, its manifestations including the General Agreement on Tariffs and Trade (GATT), the International Monetary Fund (IMF), and the World Bank. The contemporary expression of that new international political economy is seen in numerous regional groupings of countries, particularly the European Community (EC), in the economic strength of Japan, in the diffusion of modern industrial methods and technological skills to growing numbers of newly industrializing countries (NICs), in the growth of non-tariff barriers as tariffs decline, in the apparent increased sensitivity of financial conditions in Canada to world financial developments, and in the relative redistribution of the power of individual states within the international economy in response to the preceding phenomena. These developments all occur in a context wherein the economies of the participating nations have become increasingly interdependent. That interdependence is now accompanied by a much greater dispersal of state power and economic strength than was true of the early post-war years. The gamble, which worked, was to purchase growth at the cost of economic interdependence based on an increasing international division of labour, and thus to accept reduced domestic control of economies less insulated than formerly. The costs, as well as the benefits, are most significant for countries, like Canada, which have a high degree of trade dependence.

Interdependence intensifies the links among national economies and makes each of them subject to the varied economic forces of the international economic system. In this international political economy, which is supported because of its contribution to growth, governments have to learn to concert their actions internationally in order to assert a collective political control over the international economy, have to refrain from exporting their problems which can lead to accelerating cycles of retaliation, have to support adaptive forces in their domestic economies, and have to cushion their domestic populations from an inequitable internal distribution of the costs of an economic interdependence from which all benefit. The need for internal adjustments varies directly with the degree of integration in the world economy. The attainment of a necessary economic adaptability is hindered by domestic political forces and economic interests which resist changes demanded by increasing foreign competition.

The international economic order is a political order with multiple managers. It is maintained and manipulated by individual states whose impact on its overall functioning is closely related to their economic strength, the extent of their trade dependence, and their domestic political arrangements. Although the international economic order is a regime of rules designed to constrain state policies damaging to the shared objective of economic growth, it is not thereby a system in which governments have retired from the game. Governments do not serenely observe the operation of international market forces without concern for their impact on their society, economy and people, and indirectly, therefore, on the status and power of individual states in the international system.

States constantly seek to reposition themselves in the international economy by adopting domestic policies to increase their ability to compete, by seeking changes in the rules governing economic transactions across frontiers, by forming free-trade associations or economic unions permitted by the rules, and by finding new instruments to pursue objectives which can no longer be pursued by means of traditional instruments, such as the tariff, the utility of which has been reduced by the GATT agreements. It is misleading, therefore, to view the post-war liberal international economic order as a market order. It is a political order within which national governments are prime actors in a system where they have allowed market forces considerable freedom to operate. States, like individuals, do not live by bread alone. Their international objectives are multiple. Economic goals are traded off for other goals as states juggle competing priorities in the international political economy, where political power and economic forces interact.

Market forces are constrained, not only by remaining impediments to trade, but also by considerations of high politics, linked to the political, ideological divisions of the world, between North and South and between the Soviet bloc and the Western alliance. GATT itself, and American policy toward it, came to be closely linked in the early post-war decades with the Marshall Plan and its objective of rebuilding the war-damaged economies of Western Europe to align former enemies and weakened allies within a liberal order of Western capitalism under American leadership. Nevertheless, the contemporary international regime of freer trade under GATT rules does include as full members several of the centrally planned economies of Eastern Europe.

Canada has been an important player in the post-war international order. For a period after the Second World War, we enjoyed a special prominence while Europe was engaged in reconstruction, her empires were dissolving, and numerous new developing states were emerging from colonialism. We were active in the North Atlantic Treaty Organization (NATO) and the United Nations, and prominent in peacekeeping operations; we played innovative roles in the ongoing transformation of the British Empire into the multi-racial Commonwealth, and built supportive relations with newly developing countries.

The conditions in which Canada played the preceding roles have changed. The Second World War is now four decades behind us. The international system is more complex, and there are many more players. The relative status of the superpowers has declined; there are numerous states whose population or economic power clearly makes them influential actors on the world scene; and there is an even larger category of small, weak states, many of which are desperately poor, and the governments of which are subject to recurrent threats from their own military forces or from disaffected subjects.

The interpretation of the contemporary international system and of Canada's place in it is a subject of debate among scholars. Here, as elsewhere, the theories, implicit or explicit, which inform behaviour are critical. We Commissioners are impressed with a recent analysis by two Canadian scholars who define Canada as a "principal power". They undertake their analysis from the premise:

> *That America's decline and the consequent diffusion of power in the international system have propelled Canada into the position of a principal power in the globe. Principal powers, like the great powers of old, stand in the top tier of the global hierarchy of power and act autonomously in pursuit of their own interests, rather than as mediators among others or agents for them. Yet this small set of states, unlike former great powers, have the additional task of creating — in concert and on the basis of their own distinctive values — a global order in an age when no single state or set of universal principles can perform the task.*[8]

Canadians do not always see themselves in these terms. This partly reflects our basic diffidence as a people, and the fact that our North American co-existence with the United States provides us with an inappropriate comparison from which to judge our international status. However, if we broaden our perspective to encompass the more than 150 states which now populate the international system, our relative status appears very different and unquestionably prominent. From this global perspective we are clearly in a small select group of states at the top of any overall system of ranking. This obviously does not mean that we can mould the international environment in our own image. Even superpowers cannot do that. It does mean that we need not avoid unilateral initiatives, and that we can pursue our international objectives by bilateral, as well as multilateral, means.

We bring distinctive assets to the international system. We have not been an imperial power with a history that gets in the way of our relations with a multi-racial world. Our proximity to the United States, along with our multiple political, economic and cultural links, gives us a unique relationship to the most powerful military state in the world. We have the relative freedom which comes from not being a superpower, without the impotence that characterizes the smaller and weaker states in the international system. We have a positive international reputation, and our two languages and cultural mosaic multiply our contacts in the international arena. The conduct of our foreign policy must not only be guided by the search for specific benefits, but also directed to the general impression that our international posture makes on other governments and nations. A positive image is important, as it enhances our capacity to achieve our international objectives.

As a democratic people, we seek to project into the global system the values of civility, tolerance and the peaceful resolution of international tensions. Some of our positive national identity comes from our international roles. In an increasingly interdependent world, composed of a proliferating array of states with diverse capacities and ambitions, there is much for Canada to do. As one of our research papers cogently argued, Canada, one of the world's great coastal states, should play a prominent leadership role in world ocean development and management.[9] This is one of the growth areas of international law in response to developments in ocean technology. The new Law of the Sea represents an expansion of state authority and public administration into extensive and fairly distant areas of the ocean. We also recommend continuing attention to the developing world. Strong links of aid and trade established now will pay dividends to future generations of Canadians by contributing to a more stable world environment and by nurturing future trading partners.

In performing these and other international roles, we should not, and cannot, neglect self-interest. Purely Samaritan roles and re-election are incompatible for democratic governments. However, peace is obviously in our interest. Improved economic performance in the developing world is of long-term benefit to us as a trading nation. Multiple contacts outside North America help to differentiate us politically from our American neighbours, with whom we are economically linked. National self-interest is a supple concept.

As we shall note later, recent changes in the international political economy suggest to this Commission the need for a reassessment of Canada's position within it. Our nation has a shared responsibility for the general maintenance of that liberal international economic order from which we benefit, and to the creation and development of which we have positively contributed. Our government also has a responsibility to the Canadian people to do what every government does, to manœuvre within its framework so as to maximize the ratio of advantages to disadvantages which we derive from our participation.

If we consider the growth of the role of the state in our domestic society and economy in conjunction with its growing international role, several salient features quickly emerge. In both the domestic and the international arena there is an increasing cast of actors. To take a simple illustration: in 1945, the combined Cabinets of the nine provinces and the national government contained only 118 ministers. Forty years later with ten provinces, there are 269. Further, there has been a noticeable growth of Crown corporations and regulatory agencies removed in various degrees from the effective political control of cabinets and legislatures. Within each jurisdiction, but especially the larger ones, the search for co-ordinating mechanisms and central agencies to control fragmenting tendencies is never-ending. The contrast is striking between the present situation and the period before the Second World War, when Cabinet policy decisions were not even recorded.[10]

The international arena has similarly grown from relative simplicity to greater complexity. There are more actors pursuing more objectives in more arenas than ever before. The United Nations has grown from its original 51 charter members of 1945 to over 150 members. The GATT has grown from its original 23 members of 1947 to 89 member states, while 30 other countries maintain a *de facto* application of GATT rules. A growing network of international organizations, institutions and alliances has developed to manage relations among states in the pursuit of military, economic, cultural, ecological, scientific, humanitarian and other objectives. Growth has been so dramatic that some scholars question the capacity of national governments to monitor and control the multiplicity of international actors they have created.[11] The number of international intergovernmental organizations has nearly doubled in every decade since the turn of the century and is now in the neighbourhood of 300.[12] International non-governmental organizations have multiplied from 134 in 1905 to 2600 by 1980.[13] These figures do not include multi-national corporations, which have proliferated since the Second World War; the larger of these rival smaller and weaker states in their capacity, in selected areas, to influence the international system.

This explosive growth, which still continues, testifies to the interdependence among states and peoples, and to the efforts to subject that interdependence to rules. Although there is a division of labour in the world of international organizations, and many of these organizations are directed to distinct subject matters, humanity faces a task, unique in human history, of international public administration and regulation external to the conventional limits of state sovereignty.

Perhaps the most dramatic example of the complexities of contemporary international diplomacy was the third United Nations Conference on the Law of the Sea (UNCLOS III) which lasted fourteen and a half years, from the summer of 1968 to December 1982. The sessions of the conference, which followed two earlier and smaller conferences, UNCLOS I and UNCLOS II, held in 1958 and 1960 respectively, attracted between 2000 and 3000 delegates. Over 150 delegations attended. The immense treaty which emerged, consisting of 320 articles and nine annexes, has been signed by 134 states. Almost a dozen states have ratified it, and it is expected that by the end of the 1980s, a majority of nations, including Canada, will have become bound by it, as parties, under law of treaties. It is in fact a "constitution of the oceans", the indispensable legal framework for virtually all future activities at sea.[14]

Domestic and international institutional complexities reinforce one another. Both orders of government in Canada are active in the international field as the internal divisions of Canadian federalism develop external manifestations. Since the tariff, which is under the exclusive control of the national government, is now supplemented by non-tariff barriers (NTBs) on the agenda of foreign economic policy, the division of powers in Canadian federalism acquires foreign-policy significance, because numerous NTBs are under provincial jurisdiction. The growth of NTBs reflects the declining utility of the tariff under GATT arrangements and the efforts of domestic sectors of the economy to protect themselves against the liberalization of trade which their own governments have helped to engineer.

Scholars write of the growing international dimensions of domestic politics and equally of the domestic sources of international politics. The traditional concerns of "high politics" – peace and security and the geopolitical objectives of states, pursued by diplomacy, with generals waiting in the wings – are supplemented and sometimes surpassed in importance by "low politics", which are concerned with trade, investment and the international financial system. A research study for this Commission analysed a succession of efforts by Western states to reorganize their departments of external affairs to co-ordinate more effectively their external policies.[15] Another study focusing on Canada revealed the multiplicity of government departments engaged in foreign economic policy, the rivalries among them, and the extreme difficulty of devising and implementing coherent policy.[16]

The varied roles of government previously described and the factors lying behind government growth, do not leave untouched our institutional legacy of parliamentary government and federalism. Many of the tensions and difficulties facing the institutions of the Canadian political system are products of that growth. The basic institutions of our constitutional system, excluding the Charter, emerged in simpler times, and clearly their performance and the values they embody would be less seriously threatened if we could "roll back" the state. In fact, Commissioners believe that in selected areas, some disentanglement and simplification of the role of government in society and economy is desirable and feasible. However, we do not visualize a massive disengagement, given the diversity of the roles played by governments. We must, therefore, directly address the impact of big and powerful governments on federalism and parliamentary democracy.

The growth of government has been accompanied by enhanced efforts within individual governments in Canada, between the two orders of government in Canadian federalism, and among states in the international arena to co-ordinate their policies. The reality, however, is a wider dispersal of political and bureaucratic power among increasing numbers of official actors with varying degrees of autonomy. As all politicians and bureaucrats know, and as various of our research studies have clearly demonstrated, no single government is a monolithic unitary actor. On the contrary, contemporary government in Canada, as elsewhere, is comprised of a host of competing and co-operating departments, bureaus, and agencies, in each of which selective visions of the public good interact with bureaucratic ambitions to produce policies which are not always exclusively concerned with the problem allegedly on the table. We recognize these facts because, like our response to the law of gravity, non-recognition is ridiculous. Bureaucracies, public and private, would not be the focus of competing schools of academic analysis if they were machines impervious to considerations of "turf", career advancement and security.

Superimposed on the competing and co-operating subdivisions of the federal state, those possessed of highest state authority, prime ministers, premiers, cabinet ministers and senior public servants, have their own views of the appropriate role of the state in society and economy, and of the relative roles of federal and provincial governments. Their visions of the future do not exclude a concern to maintain and, in certain circumstances, enhance the status and power of their government *vis-à-vis* other governments or, in other circumstances, *vis-à-vis* society. Like rectors of ancient universities and prelates of ecclesiastical organizations with long histories, the political and bureaucratic élites atop the pyramids of government power at national and provincial levels are servants of continuity and survival. In pursuing these and other objectives, they are inevitably constrained by the democratic process, but to deny that they possess a measure of autonomy which they employ in the pursuit of their version of the public good is to be impervious to the facts of power. The democratic state is more than a mirror of society, and more than a cash register mechanically ringing up the shifting balance of power among the contending interests in the society and economy of the country. These inescapable facts of the democratic process and of state power constitute essentials of the institutional environment within which we Commissioners seek to promote democratic values and the positive contribution of government to economic performance.

In 1945, Canada's national government was, by contemporary standards, small and compact, and an informal mandarinate supplied cohesion. Within the federal system, the provinces were still weak from the combined effects of Depression and war. Canada, in 1945, was a significant middle power among the handful of states not devastated by war which, under American leadership, reconstructed the post-war world on the Western side. Since then, there has been a multiplication of state actors on the international scene and a relative decline in American hegemony, along with the growth of centrifugal trends in Canadian federalism as the provincial governments expanded their capacities and ambitions; there has also been a diffusion and fragmentation of power within individual governments in Canada and elsewhere.

The multiplication of separate focuses of power within each government in Canada and in the international arena means that the pursuit of domestic or international objectives typically requires the bringing together of shifting groups of discrete actors with different constituencies, competing goals, varying skills, differences in power, and with attitudes ranging from suspicion to trust. For any single actor, the pursuit of goals involves the creation, modification and management of institutions and the relations among them. In the international political economy, this complexity interacts with the concentrations of economic power in the multi-national corporation and in international finance.

In contrast to the late 1940s, the domestic and international world of power and authority is much more diffuse, with more centres of action and with more diversified agenda. This is a world in which the tasks of management multiply the contacts between political executives, both domestically and internationally. If Canadian federalism is, from one perspective, appropriately called "executive federalism", the international system can be labelled "executive internationalism". This trend to executive dominance is inherent in the domestic and international demands placed on modern governments. More generally, much of the time of public officials is devoted to dealing with public officials in other bureaus of the same government, and with administrators of other governments. Government organizations are interdependent. They rely on one another to implement programs. This gives rise to interorganizational politics in domestic and international arenas in which complex patterns of co-operation and competition are played out. While competition between a multiplicity of actors means that we are far different from an élite cartel, it is not easy to be confident that overall, these variegated networks of institutions are functionally adequate for the tasks placed on them, or that the practices of democracy devised for a less complex world can keep such machinery accountable in domestic and international arenas. It is for this latter reason that Commissioners seek an enhancement of accountability mechanisms and democratizing tendencies.

The growth of government in Canada alters the distribution of power between administrators and politicians, and between cabinets and legislatures, as well as between the public and private sectors. Power moves upward to cabinets, downward to senior public servants, and horizontally to the public sector of Crown corporations and regulatory agencies which escape the ongoing supervision of elected representatives of the people. Power flows in the direction of expertise and to those who control information. Enhanced roles for government tend to increase the indispensability, power and autonomy of the public service. The ongoing administration of the details of policy instituted years ago inevitably escapes political scrutiny in normal circumstances. The sheer magnitude of what governments do congests legislative timetables and, combined with the imbalance in access to resources between cabinets and legislative bodies, is in conflict with a parliamentary regime of informed discussion. In such circumstances, the chain of accountability from cabinets to elected members to voters is weakened.

A further weakening of accountability derives from the proliferation of interest groups which often bypass both Parliament and the parties, and interact directly with the dispersed administrative bureaus of the contemporary state. Commissioners are disturbed by these developments, although we recognize their partial inevitability. Nevertheless, in subsequent sections of our Report, we make recommendations designed to control their excesses within a strengthened parliamentary system responsible to the electorate.

Federalism is also affected by the co-existence of two orders of government, each endowed with impressive arsenals of resources, and each intervening from divergent perspectives in the society and economy of the country. Federal and provincial governments have never been able entirely to ignore the operations of the other. Indeed, the Confederation Act, 1867 contained various clauses which presupposed their partial interdependence. They shared the concurrent fields of agriculture and immigration, subject to federal primacy in case of conflict. The federal government made obligatory financial payments to the provincial governments to cover the shortfall between their revenue-raising capacities and their anticipated expenditure requirements. The federal government had a general power to disallow provincial legislation within one year of its passage and appointed the lieutenant-governors who could reserve provincial legislation. Finally, the declaratory power gave the Parliament of Canada the power to declare a work, even if wholly situated within a province, to be for the general advantage of Canada or of two or more provinces, and hence subject to national jurisdiction. In spite of these exceptions, at least relative to the contemporary situation, the national and provincial governments operated with a high degree of autonomy and independence of the other.

From the Second World War to the present, a complex network of agreements and committees, built on earlier precedents and capped by the First Ministers' Conference, led to an extensive pooling of fiscal resources and jurisdictional capacities among governments and across the division of powers in selected areas. The federal spending power allowed the national government to influence provincial priorities by making funds available under conditional-grant programs for specific purposes. The welfare state was largely constructed by joint federal and provincial action. Federal/provincial fiscal arrangements and equalization payments sought to harmonize taxation efforts and to supplement the revenues of the poorer provinces in the interest of equity. Networks of professionals with common expertise worked collaboratively from their separate positions in distinctive governments to advance common programs. Regional development policy, especially under Department of Regional and Economic Expansion (DREE) General Development Agreements instituted in 1973, brought federal officials into intimate collaborative arrangements with provincial governments. Bureaus and agencies of intergovernmental affairs came into being, especially in the 1970s, to manage the interdependence of governments in the federal system. Several provincial governments opened offices in Ottawa to monitor developments of special relevance to their interests.

Concurrent with these developments, there were major conflicts which proved difficult to resolve, especially those dealing with energy, resources and foreign economic policy. In area after area, the two orders of governments, deriving their authority from a division of powers which had undergone little formal change since 1867, found themselves acting in overlapping policy areas. In particular cases, contradictory policies, simultaneously pursued, frustrated the efforts of both governments. There was also extensive interprovincial competition, especially to attract investment and with respect to procurement policies which favoured local producers, and negligible interprovincial machinery to regulate it.

Federal/provincial competition is not just an affair of governments which leaves the society and economy of our country untouched. In a unitary state, the decline of the market results in a simple displacement of private by public decision making. In a federal system characterized by competitive interventions from both orders of government, matters formerly handled privately in markets and by other non-political decision makers, for whom the federal division of powers was, in practical terms, irrelevant, are caught up in federal/provincial competition. The sphere of activity outside the political, and therefore effectively outside the federal, system constantly shrinks as federal and provincial jurisdictional differences penetrate ever more deeply into formerly private realms of economic and social behaviour.

Much of this Report attempts to assess the consequences of this situation, which was not foreseen at Confederation, and to suggest reforms where appropriate. Our reforms, however, must be compatible with our primary concern to preserve the pattern of accountability which resides in responsible government. The striking of bargains, often in private, in the intergovernmental arena, weakens the capacity of legislatures to control cabinets. Commissioners do not wish to see that capacity weakened by an undue proliferation of intergovernmental mechanisms which further remove executive authority from public scrutiny and parliamentary control. Thus, while we recognize the need for stronger intergovernmental machinery and for privacy in negotiations, we also suggest reforms to facilitate legislative scrutiny of the intergovernmental dimension, and to facilitate citizens' input into the institutions we are proposing to strengthen the economic union.

We appreciate that among the traditional virtues of federalism are its openness to experimentation and the diffusion of successful experiments to other jurisdictions. Indeed, one of the ways in which federalism responds to new demands derives from the entrepreneurial efforts of competing politicians from different jurisdictions to gain support and allegiance. Thus the adversarial process within federalism serves the same function as that within parliamentary systems, in keeping governments responsive and sensitive. From this perspective, even the acrimonious confrontations between Quebec and the national government leading up to the 1980 referendum, followed by the divisive process which led to the Constitution Act, 1982, may be positively cited for their long-term contribution to a more harmonious partnership between French and English within Canadian federalism.

We Commissioners believe, accordingly, that it is easy to exaggerate the negative effects and to undervalue the positive functions of what superficially appear to be unseemly confrontations between rival governments of a common people. We also believe, however, that in the same way that states regulate competition among themselves in the international system, and that competition in the market is constrained by rules, so some elaboration of institutional arrangements in the intergovernmental arena is essential. We make appropriate proposals to this effect in a subsequent chapter, always with the full recognition of the primacy of the values associated with parliamentary democracy within each jurisdiction.

Our democratic assumptions lead us to believe that the growth of the state is a direct response to citizen demands, and that the nature of the response is functionally appropriate for their satisfaction. Neither assumption is automatically valid. Much of the policy output of the state is driven by internal government dynamics and is coloured by political and bureaucratic purposes which the citizens may not share. Its appropriateness to the problems it addresses is affected, sometimes negatively, by the internal structure of the state. Unanticipated effects of government policy also derive from the relative ignorance which often attends the design and implementation of complex programs that interact unpredictably with the multiple private goals of the affected interests.

None of the above analysis is intended to deny that there is, or should be, a division of labour between citizens and the political and administrative élites in charge of governments. Ours is a representative, not a direct, democracy. This Commission suggests only that it is always necessary to keep under scrutiny our constitutional and institutional arrangements, as well as the substance of particular policies. Deficiencies in the latter may derive from shortcomings in the former.

Each generation of Canadians has had to rework parliamentary government and federalism in light of new circumstances. We are not immune from that obligation, to which has been added the necessity of adapting both sets of institutions to the Charter newly added to our constitutional system.

Notes

1. Richard Rose, *Understanding Big Government: The Programme Approach* (London: Sage, 1984), p. iii.
2. John L. Howard and W.T. Stanbury, "Measuring Leviathan: The Size, Scope and Growth of Governments in Canada" in *Probing Leviathan: An Investigation of Government in the Economy*, edited by George Lermer (Vancouver: Fraser Institute, 1984), p. 91.
3. *Ibid.*, pp. 92 and 164–65.
4. *Ibid.*, pp. 93 and 181.
5. Richard Schultz and Alan Alexandroff, *Economic Regulation and the Federal System*, vol. 42, prepared for the Royal Commission on the Economic Union and Development Prospects for Canada (Toronto: University of Toronto Press, 1985).
6. Howard and Stanbury, "Measuring Leviathan", pp. 92 and 155.
7. Alex Inkeles, "The Emerging Social Structure of the World", *World Politics* 27 (July 1975), p. 495.
8. David B. Dewitt and John J. Kirton, *Canada as a Principal Power: A Study in Foreign Policy and International Relations* (Toronto: Wiley, 1983), p. 4.
9. Douglas M. Johnston, *Canada and the New International Law of the Sea*, vol. 54, prepared for the Royal Commission on the Economic Union and Development Prospects for Canada (Toronto: University of Toronto Press, 1985).
10. A.D.P. Heeney, "Cabinet Government in Canada: Some Recent Developments in the Machinery of the Central Executive", Canadian Journal of Economics and Political Science (Spring 1946), p. 285.
11. Andrew M. Scott, *The Dynamics of Interdependence* (Chapel Hill; N.C.: University of North Carolina Press, 1982), p. 195.
12. *Ibid.*, p. 152.
13. Bruce Russett and Harvey Starr, *World Politics: The Menu for Choice* (San Francisco: W.H. Freeman, 1981), p. 55.
14. Johnston, *Canada and the New International Law of the Sea.*
15. Robert Boardman, "The Foreign Service and the Organization of the Foreign Policy Community: Views from Canada and Abroad", in *Selected Problems in Formulating Foreign Economic Policy*, vol. 30, prepared for the Royal Commission on the Economic Union and Development Prospects for Canada (Toronto: University of Toronto Press, 1985).
16. Gerald Wright, "Bureaucratic Politics and Canada's Foreign Economic Policy", in *Selected Problems in Formulating Foreign Economic Policy*, vol. 30, prepared for the Royal Commission on the Economic Union and Development Prospects for Canada (Toronto: University of Toronto Press, 1985).

State and Economy: The Domestic Role

The relationship between states and markets, each subject to their own organizing criteria, is once again on the agenda of democratic governments in Canada and elsewhere. One of the central issues for this Commission is that of the appropriate division of labour between the state and the economy. Our goal is to clarify that debate, disentangle the complex issues involved, and suggest criteria to govern the future unfolding of the relationship between these two powerful systems which interact, which need each other, and within which we act as citizens, as consumers and as producers.

In states, we are citizens, governors and governed, the bearers of rights and the carriers of obligations. In markets, we are consumers and producers, workers and managers, lenders and borrowers. In the former, we govern ourselves, impose order on threatening anarchy, and decide how we shall share the burdens and benefits of our collective existence as Canadians and as provincial residents. In our civic capacities, we also reach out through the state to the international system in which Canada participates with other states in the pursuit of national and international objectives. That world system has no other source of political order than the network of agreements constructed by governments and the shared norms to which they subscribe out of prudence, fear and respect for their content. We are also connected to the international system through markets which facilitate mutually beneficial economic transactions across borders. These same markets sometimes transmit influences, such as inflation and commodity-price fluctuations, that are less welcome.

In the Western world, over the past several centuries, markets have been organized by the price system, which transmits cues to the buyers and sellers of goods, services, labour and capital. In the contemporary mixed economies and welfare states of Western industrial democracies, most economic decisions – to buy and sell, to invest, to offer one's labour or hire the labour of another – are made by private actors in market situations. The market allocates resources impersonally to their most profitable use in a context of consumer sovereignty.

Markets do not exist in a vacuum. They function more efficiently in some settings than in others. Yet they have a spontaneous capacity to emerge in the most unpropitious circumstances. Black markets, or the underground economy, flourish in collectivist economies, lubricating the clumsiness of state directives and often adding to efficiency as a by-product of mutually beneficial illegal exchange transactions. In democratic societies with extensive market freedom, there is always a category of proscribed exchanges pertaining to drugs, gambling, prostitution and other activities which society often prefers not to sanction. However, markets flourish here as well, often at heavy cost, in sordid conditions, and in a context of crime. Markets are ineradicable.

Markets and states have different organizing principles. States are concentrations of coercive authority backed by force which govern particular citizenries within fixed boundaries. States are historical products. They have remarkable survival capacity. They provide, by maintaining law and order, the minimum framework of security for the pursuit of private goals in society and economy. They are the vehicles through which the passions of nationalism find constructive and destructive outlets.

Democratic constitutional states, of which Canada is one, are constrained by the elevated purposes they serve. They seek to civilize power, to subject government to the rule of law, and to make their people into a citizenry with rights against government and with a capacity not only to influence the direction of public policy by the arrangements and practices of representative democracy, but periodically to change the composition of the ruling political class. In liberal constitutional orders, such as that of Canada, the wielders of power step down when the electorate signals its preference for another set of rulers. Political systems with built in mechanisms for the orderly transfer of power in response to the wishes of the electorate are not the norm in the contemporary world. In Canada, we take for granted this rare human achievement, the equivalent in politics of the Marquis of Queensberry rules in boxing. We should not. The concept of a loyal opposition treated with respect while openly campaigning to replace the government of the day is a social invention virtually without equal for its contribution to human dignity, civility and freedom.

The market economy, characterized by decentralization, and sensitive to the shifting cues of the price system is also a significant social invention. It is highly flexible and responsive, and it co-ordinates innumerable private economic decisions without resort to coercion. It was not Henry Ford, but Karl Marx, who asserted of the bourgeoisie in the Communist Manifesto:

> *It has been the first to show what man's activity can bring about. It has accomplished wonders far surpassing Egyptian pyramids, Roman aqueducts and Gothic cathedrals; it has conducted expeditions that put in the shade all former Exoduses of nations and crusades . . .*
>
> *The bourgeoisie during its rule of scarce one hundred years has created more massive and more colossal productive forces than have all preceding generations together. Subjection of nature's forces to man, machinery, application of chemistry to industry and agriculture, steam navigation, railways, electric telegraphs, clearing of whole continents for cultivation, canalization of rivers, whole populations conjured out of the ground – what earlier century had even a presentiment that such productive forces slumbered in the lap of social labor?*[1]

In contrast to states, which are geographically fixed and historically rooted, the market economy is hostile to national boundaries, constantly generates new products, and is forward looking. Its natural tendency is to organize and distribute economic activity according to non-spatial criteria, a tendency in conflict with the immobility of states and their concern for the social stability of their citizens.

Free markets, like democratic states, are crucial institutional arrangements, not only for the achievement of economic goals, but also for their contribution to human freedom and dignity. Both logic and history confirm that political democracy and individual freedoms are sustained by a significant degree of autonomy in a private economic sector, and that they are incompatible with an economy in which such autonomy is non-existent.

Democratic states and free markets need one another. The market performs valuable political functions, in addition to economic functions, for society, and thus greatly reduces the demands on the state. The primary political contribution of markets is that they locate essential decision-making processes concerning production and consumption in private hands, within a framework which, in general, provides a broad "accountability", or responsiveness to the consumer. Accordingly, markets reduce the knowledge requirements and managerial obligations of government. Secondly, markets generate the economic product from which the state can extract resources for the pursuit of its varied objectives. Thirdly, markets contribute to political freedom by providing a realm of autonomy, outside the detailed reach of the state, to which individuals can retreat when they are out of favour with political authorities. Market economies decentralize and diffuse power. Opposition parties and free markets are integrally linked, one to another, in democratic societies. The relative autonomy of markets reduces the sanctions available to the state and sustains the capacity of citizens to criticize state policies by providing the social and economic supports for political freedom. This issue is not idle theorizing, nor is it applicable only to non-democratic societies. There were occasions in Commissioners' hearings when powerful private economic actors whose fortunes closely depended on government discretion, were afraid to voice in public their opinions of government policies for fear of the consequences.

Markets also need states. Markets require order, the rule of law, respect for property rights, the enforcement of contracts, reliable weights and measures, a system of currency, and an infrastructure of transportation and other facilities which markets provide only with difficulty. The human skills required to function successfully in market processes result from state action in education and training, supplementing the basic education in social skills provided by the family.

Markets and states are deeply intertwined in the modern world. The state plays many roles, some of which have a significant impact on the economy even when their purpose is not explicitly directed to modifying economic performance. Further, the relation of states to markets has an international, as well as a domestic, dimension, as we consider below.

State/market relations raise central questions of democratic politics and economic policy. Canadians had one version of the state role at Confederation. The central economic goals of Confederation were to enlarge the domestic market by political union, which would remove tariff barriers between the colonies, extend the new Dominion to the Pacific, populate the Prairies with immigrants, provide the transportation infrastructure which the new technology of railways facilitated, and enhance Canadian credit rating on London markets. The national government was given the major economic powers, according to the understanding of the Fathers of Confederation.

Railways and immigration were supplemented as instruments of economic direction by the National Tariff Policy of 1879. This policy sought to foster domestic industry in the context of East-West economic integration, within which the principle of comparative economic advantage would dictate the spatial distribution and nature of economic activity in Canada.

The subsequent economic history of Canada within the National Policy framework is an oft-told story which is outlined elsewhere in this Report, and need not be elaborated here. It is to be noted, however, that the National Policy was regionally divisive and was criticized by the Maritime and Western provinces as exploitation in the interest of the manufacturing heartland in Ontario and Quebec. Protest was especially articulate in the three Prairie provinces and evoked a succession of regional parties hostile to the power of Ontario and Quebec in national politics, power which derived both from their numerical strength and from the system of party discipline behind which regional minorities could be out-voted in the privacy of national party caucuses. Perceptions of exploitation and colonial status were aggravated by the fact that the national government retained control of the land and resources of the three Prairie provinces, "for the purposes of the Dominion", until 1930. Western farmers and their provincial governments correctly perceived that they existed in a political economy within which market forces operated under political constraints that reflected the distribution of political power among regions and the jurisdictional division of powers between the two orders of government.

The Great Depression of the 1930s, which led to the downfall of the Weimar Republic in Germany and threats to democracy in other countries, was perceived in Canada both as a crisis of federalism and as a crisis of capitalism. The former constituted the agenda of the Royal Commission on Dominion-Provincial Relations (the Rowell-Sirois Commission), established in 1937, which reported in 1940. Inevitably, many observers viewed the crisis of capitalism as a crisis of federalism, because it was the alleged incapacities of the latter, with its divided power structure, which prevented an effective governmental response to the former.

In the 1930s, the debate over the economic role of the state was conducted with a passion unique in our history. Conservative Prime Minister R.B. Bennett informed Canadians, in his famous "New Deal" broadcasts of 1935, that capitalism was crumbling and could be saved only by state intervention. The newly formed Co-operative Commonwealth Federation (CCF) proposed an extensive increase in state involvement by means of planning commissions and nationalization. Social Credit, inspired by the monetary theories of the Scottish engineer, Major C.H. Douglas, defined the problem in terms of an inherent demand deficiency, a fatal flaw in the financial system which could be rectified by the distribution of additional purchasing power. In British Columbia, Premier Duff Pattullo instituted a provincial version of Franklin D. Roosevelt's "New Deal" under the slogan "Work and Wages". A poignant indication of the relation between the economy and political democracy emerged in Newfoundland, then a self-governing Dominion. Faced with bankruptcy, its people were compelled to give up self-government, after the 1933 Newfoundland Royal Commission Report (the Amulree Report) examined the presumed incompatibility between fiscal insolvency and democracy. For 15 years, from February 1934 until it joined Canada in 1949, Newfoundland was ruled by Commission of Government and reverted to the status of a non-self-governing colony under the direction of Whitehall.

The intellectual ferment of the Depression was partly left behind with the Second World War, out of which the modern role of government in Canada emerged. Under national government management of the war effort, which was facilitated by the centralization of taxing authority in 1941, full employment was restored, massive resources were devoted to the war, manufacturing was stimulated by war contracts, and the standard of living rose. Concurrently with these developments, which appeared to indicate the efficacy of an economic management role for the central government, especially when contrasted with the grim Depression experience of the 1930s, the ideas of Lord Keynes and Lord Beveridge were digested by policy makers. Keynes, whose theories were written with a unitary-state model in mind, dealt primarily with the theory of a closed economy which neither traded nor engaged in capital-market transactions with the outside world; it indicated, to oversimplify, that contra-cyclical budgeting could level out aggregate demand and maintain full employment. Beveridge contributed the intellectual underpinnings of the modern welfare state by justifying an extensive social security system as a defence against the evils of unemployment, ill health, and the hardship of old age.

In conjunction with other currents of thought, these ideas set the intellectual framework for a post-war economic leadership role for the federal government, and for the construction of a comprehensive welfare state. These domestic policies were related to the move to a liberal, international, economic order, outside the Soviet bloc and the developing world, organized under the framework of the IMF and the GATT, within which barriers to the international mobility of goods and capital were to be progressively reduced. A widely held belief among the architects of post-war economic policy was that openness to the international economy was compatible with domestic economic management.

Capitalist markets are not only efficient instruments for the performance of economic activities, but they are also systems of power. This is so not only in the relations among managers, owners and workers, but also in terms of the market-generated distribution of income among individuals and social classes. Income in societies, especially where there are limited subsistence possibilities, is a major instrument of power, for it determines our ability to command resources for our personal use and hence our capacity to live with dignity.

Political democracy has profound effects on the market system. Those who are brought together in markets as workers and managers, consumers and producers, or buyers and sellers are also democratic citizens with political rights. In that latter capacity, and employing democratic political processes, citizens challenge the market distribution of power and income; they use the state to impose criteria of equity which modify market outcomes. The result is the welfare state, an embodiment of concepts of sharing which subordinates market results and our status as actors in the economy, to citizenship concerns and community values. Millions of Canadians depend on the income-security provisions of the welfare state for their standard of living and their general well-being. In 1982, government transfer payments to individuals accounted for nearly 11 per cent of average income. They contributed more than 60 per cent of the income of the lowest fifth of the population.

Thus the distributional consequences of capitalist markets are deliberately altered by transfer payments and also by the collective provision of goods distributed outside the market system and often provided without charge to the citizens. The vertical power of management within firms and industries is balanced by unions, is subject to legislation affecting safety in the work-place, and is generally constrained by an emerging category of worker rights which controls the exercise of employer discretion. Contemporary employer self-interest acts as an important internal constraint on management power. Higher productivity requires a harmonious relationship in the work-place, creating a tendency to share power between management and the workers. With higher-skilled employees, motivation in the work-place becomes more important as jobs are seen to require creativity, innovation and increasing skills. Adversarial relationships come to be viewed as counterproductive, given the growing realization of the substantial interdependence of capital and labour.

At the most general level, capitalist economies and democratic politics are rendered compatible by the welfare role of the state. There are debates at the margin. The particulars of how the state-welfare role should be handled in the interest of values pertaining to economic efficiency, to human dignity, and to evolving conceptions of equity, including the relationship among risk, innovation and reward, are always controversial. We seek to learn from experience. A mature democratic polity is always engaged in learning, profiting from its past experiments, and tentatively launching new policy initiatives into a partially unknown future. However, the welfare state in general, with its central core of common citizenship, and that concern for one another which flows from our collective existence, is debatable only at the margin. It is a necessary response to social problems and conflicts which are inherent in large-scale industrial society, which are beyond the scope of philanthropy to handle, and which are sufficiently serious that neither social stability nor social integration would be possible in its absence. Without the stabilizing integrating contribution of the welfare state, support for the relative autonomy of capitalist markets would crumble.

The welfare state, however, is a complex arrangement of social policies and values which must be reduced to its central features if we are to assess its performance. Commissioners have concluded that our social policies should serve four values:

- Equity in the distribution of rewards based on evolving concepts of social justice which lead us to prefer outcomes different from those that market mechanisms generate
- Security that provides a degree of protection against such risks as illness or the dislocations of a dynamic economy
- Opportunity to participate in the economy in order to improve our position and to sustain our self-identity which, in the modern world, is closely tied to work

• Sharing, the moral expression of our feelings of community, from which derive our sense of equity and our willingness to provide reasonable security for one another and to distribute employment opportunities fairly.

How we Canadians serve these values is not a matter of indifference, for they consume resources. We properly, therefore, apply efficiency criteria to our social policy instruments and, other things being equal, prefer instruments which impose minimum constraints on market mechanisms and thus minimum constraints on efficiency.

It follows that the welfare-state debate in liberal capitalist democracies such as Canada is not open-ended. It focuses on means, not purposes. Capitalism is, of course, compatible with authoritarian regimes within which trade-union rights are suppressed, massive inequities in the distribution of income and privileges are tolerated, and the coercive capacity of the state is ubiquitous. Canadians have not chosen that route. Our division of labour between state and market is responsive to criteria filtered through democratic processes and, so, responsive to the concerns of citizens. Neither have we chosen the route of a dirigiste economy, which subjects the market to comprehensive state control. The "positive state" tradition in our history, which has supported an influential role for governments in the economy, has nevertheless always assumed that most economic decision making will be in private hands.

Thus, controversy over the state role in Canada focuses on the middle ground between extremes. Much of this Report is addressed to that controversy, but Commissioners do not forget the general consensus in favour of the welfare state and a mixed economy which is not caught up in the fray of battle. Neither do we deny the significance of changes of policy, of instrument choice, and of target in the contested middle ground. On the contrary, we believe that in several areas, the present division of labour between state and market, the product of decades of incrementalism, contributes neither to our economic nor to our political objectives.

With respect to several of the basic provisions of the welfare state, for example, we Commissioners have concluded that fundamental reform in several areas is both possible and desirable. The welfare state, like other complex interrelated programs, particularly those which involve both orders of government, and which have evolved incrementally over long periods of time is, not surprisingly, characterized by some contradictions and unanticipated negative consequences.

The area of income security, one of the vital components of our welfare state, is one of several major policy areas where Commissioners think it necessary to take a comprehensive approach leading to significant restructuring. Commissioners' goal is not to dismantle this aspect of the welfare state, but to generate a closer fit between the instruments governments employ and the goals Canadians seek. We have identified the basic goals of the welfare state on a previous page, and our analysis and proposals are presented in detail in Part V of this Report, which deals with Human Resources and Social Support.

Our proposed changes to income-security provisions are radical, not cosmetic, and wholesale rather than tinkering at the margin. The sweeping nature of our proposals is contained in our proposed new Universal Income Security Program (UISP). This Commission believes that the implementation of a UISP with a universally available income guarantee, subject to reduction at a relatively low "tax back" rate for earned income, constitutes the most appropriate foundation for Canada's income-security programs. The appropriate UISP benefit levels will change over time.

The replacement of most of our current income-security programs and several of our tax exemptions and deductions would allow the Government of Canada to make available, in 1985, a basic income guarantee of $2750 per adult (and for the first child in a single-parent family) and $750 per child; benefits would be reduced at a rate of $20 for each $100 of other income. The elderly would receive an enriched option. We consider these levels to be generally appropriate in 1985 for a federal income-supplementation program.

UISP would greatly simplify our income-security system. It should replace the following existing programs: Guaranteed Income Supplement, Family Allowance, Child Tax Credits, Married Exemptions, Child Exemptions, the federal share of Canada Assistance Plan social assistance and, eventually, Federal Social Housing Programs. If the personal income tax exemption were also eliminated, the income guarantee could be raised to $3825 per adult per annum and $765 per child. Like most other complex policy areas, our income-security proposals involve federal/provincial relations. Some of the tax changes which would accompany the introduction of UISP would generate substantial increases in provincial tax revenues. Commissioners believe that these provincial revenue gains should continue to be devoted to the income-security area, partly because our UISP proposals are not intended to provide fully adequate benefits for all individuals who have no other earnings or income.

We have assumed, in our overall calculations, that the "windfall" gains accruing to provincial governments as a result of the federal changes will also be applied to the provision of income supplementation. We acknowledge, however, that complicated federal/provincial bargaining will be necessary to ensure this end. We also recognize that for some families with no other income, the UISP guarantees will not be fully sufficient. Since the provincial share of Canada Assistance Plan social assistance payments will remain in the hands of provincial governments, we assume that provinces will continue to provide special needs-tested top-ups for such people. If they did so, provincial payments would add, on average, approximately $3500 to $4500 to the basic levels, making $12 500 to $13 500 available to Canada's poorest families under Commissioners' preferred option. Readers are referred to Part V "Human Resources and Social Support" for a more detailed discussion.

We Commissioners do not underestimate the radical nature of these proposals, the probability that they will have to be phased in along with other of our proposals, and the important federal/provincial considerations which are involved. We are convinced, however, that the package of programs making up our existing income-security system is ineffective, far too complex, creates work disincentives, and is inequitable. Some observers have even questioned its sustainability. These are large claims which are substantiated in Part V of this Report. Further, our total income-security program which, of course, goes beyond the programs which UISP would replace, carries an estimated cost for federal and provincial governments for 1984–85 of $61.6 billion, the equivalent of over 13 per cent of Canada's gross national product. Such expenditures have critical effects for our economy and, at a more personal level, for millions of Canadians. The citizens and governments of Canada cannot allow expenditures of this magnitude to be poorly tailored to achieve their objectives. A Royal Commission would be derelict in its responsibilities if it did not seek to enlighten Canadians on the issues involved, and to make proposals which can lead us all to a better future.

The relations between state, economy and society are so complex, so intimate, and so profound in their consequences for the way we live that they must be subject to periodic comprehensive review. The *ad hoc* approach to policy making has its place in democratic politics, not least because incremental policy change minimizes the disruption of prevailing social patterns, and also facilitates social learning. The latter, however, requires retrospective evaluation of the extent to which past policies have achieved their objectives, particularly when they are juxtaposed with other related policies introduced at different times and often with insufficient attention to their fit with what has gone before.

Commissioners believe that our overall income-security system has grown so complex and become so intricately intertwined that further incrementalism is likely to be both difficult to achieve and counterproductive. The system is now so interdependent that to deal with isolated parts of it not only generates the resistance of particular beneficiaries, but produces adverse consequences elsewhere in the system. Further, it is impossible to make coherent moral sense of the present incoherent system by more *ad hoc* intervention. What is required is political leadership, appealing to a broad public interest, which will seek to simplify and rationalize the existing aggregation of programs, in the interest of the general income-security goals which Commissioners believe Canadians wish to have served in this social policy area.

The world of governments and politics has a much greater capacity to launch experiments than to learn from them. Commissioners have attempted to remedy that deficiency in the income-security area and elsewhere.

The three decades between the end of the Second World War and the 1970s, witnessed a remarkable growth in Canadian prosperity, as well as low unemployment and inflation rates, at least by contemporary standards. The welfare state was rounded out by the late 1960s. Regional economic development became a significant policy concern from the Diefenbaker period to the present. The provinces came to play more significant roles in promoting economic development and disposed of an increasingly larger share of total government expenditures. They were no longer willing to allow their economic futures to be solely determined either by the market or by federal policies. Accordingly, those economic policies which presupposed a centralized, national government-dominated, federal system, suffered a relative decline in feasibility.

The disruptive decade from the first oil shock of 1973 to the present constitutes the backdrop to this Commission. In terms of the various conventional criteria by which we judge economic performance, the last decade has witnessed significant shortfalls from our achievement over most of the quarter century following the Second World War. A poor productivity performance combined with rapid inflation left many Canadians wondering what had happened to the sense of unlimited opportunity so prevalent during the Centennial celebrations of 1967. The 1981–82 recession has left an even more bitter legacy of unemployment, and the prognosis is that it will take many years to create sufficient jobs to employ thousands of presently unemployed Canadians.

Along with other capitalist economies, we have had an unemployment rate which fluctuated sharply upward above previously accepted levels; a marked slowing in productivity improvement; the co-existence over an extended period of high unemployment and extreme inflation, large and protracted government-budget deficits; unprecedentedly high interest rates and widespread business failures; financial instability and exchange-rate disturbances; and severely depressed economic sectors and regions. Many of these very serious problems in Canada appear to have reflected significant structural shifts and the cumulative effect of underlying changes in the economy and society, rather than simply the consequences of a severe cyclical dislocation from which we might recover with the relative ease of earlier experience. Their worst feature has been the ratchetting up of unemployment. Despite an impressive longer-term increase in the total number of jobs, there is a widespread assessment that unemployment – whether stemming from a deficiency of total demand in the economy or from basic structural factors – is likely to persist at unacceptably high levels into the next decade.

Much of this Commission's Report, particularly in Parts III and V, seeks to explain these developments, to suggest appropriate policy responses and, in general, to reassess the relations between state and market, both domestically and internationally. Our long-run concern must be to restore higher rates of growth in both production and employment. To that end, we advocate an increased openness to international competition and, in particular, the conclusion of a free-trade arrangement, encompassing non-tariff barriers (NTBs), with the United States. The explicit premise behind our free-trade proposals is that the Canadian economy must be made more competitive, and that domestic adjustment-retarding policies must be replaced with adjustment-facilitating strategies. Our basic international stance complements our domestic stance. We must seek an end to those patterns of government involvement in the economy which may generate disincentives, retard flexibility, and work against the desired allocation of resources.

The disappointing economic performance of the past decade, together with the toughened international climate, has drawn particular attention to the role of government in strengthening growth and employment prospects. Energy price "shocks", crises in financial markets, a resort to protectionism, and the success of Japan and newly industrializing countries in challenging the production supremacy of Western European and North American industries has called into question the development policies and programs of governments. In addition, the technological race has raised anew century-old fears of worker redundancy in the march for improved productivity. Increasingly, debate has focused on the appropriate industrial policy or strategy a country should follow.

This Commission received a great many submissions on this issue, reflecting a wide dichotomy of thought ranging from a government "hands-off" approach to a much more interventionist, targeted approach. In essence, intervenors before this Commission expressed their view of the role of the state in marshalling and directing the human, capital and natural resources that define our productive capacity. The views embraced both technical judgements about what will make our economy perform better, and value judgements about the ranking of goals in our society. In a small open economy such as Canada's, to speak of industrial policy is to address the very fabric of our nation. Trade policy, regional policy, education and training, labour-management relations, the regulatory framework, the taxation system, treatment of foreign investment: these and many other factors are components of industrial policy.

Given the complexity of the subject matter, it should surprise no one that a national consensus on industrial policy is so elusive. Our major trade partners have encountered the same diversity of thought, and each has experimented with various approaches in an effort to strengthen its competitiveness. None has demonstrated a consistent pattern that suggests a prescription for success. Canada must forge its own industrial approaches that best suit its federal form of government, its heavy reliance on natural resource-based exports, and its geographically dispersed industry and markets.

Most Canadians are naturally inclined to believe that our federal and provincial governments ought to be able to co-ordinate their activities so as to give our industries the competitive edge they need to compete effectively both in domestic and in international markets. That degree of co-ordination might take place in a rational world, but, in its extreme form, it would also constitute a basic denial of the genius of the market economy. To select those areas in which we presume ourselves to have a comparative advantage over other countries is to assume that governments are as able as markets, if not more so, to judge the rapid changes taking place globally in consumer demands and production processes. This is an assumption that belies experience and defies the flexibility and adaptability so evidently required to compete effectively.

Nevertheless, to risk rousing suspicion that it supports an interventionist, targeted industrial policy does not invalidate an influential role for the state. Indeed, the issue is not whether to form an industrial policy, for implicitly or explicitly, an industrial policy follows from the decisions governments make regarding tax policy, trade policy and the many factors that bear upon the efficient allocation of human, capital and natural resources. As in the case of social policy, Canadian governments, in designing their economic development policies, have proceeded, over the post-war years, in an incremental, *ad hoc* manner. While they have introduced such policies with the intent of supporting a particular set of industries, they have too often overlooked the obvious: support demands tax and other resources, at the expense of other

Canadians. Moreover, the unpalatable consequences of a dynamic economy, such as inefficient and faltering firms, have too often been cushioned to the detriment of more productive and better-paid employment opportunities. Industries in decline have been shored-up, rather than encouraged to adjust to new realities. Intensified international competition requires that Canada's industrial policies be more attentive to enhancing the productivity and competitiveness of our economy. Industrial policies, in short, must be made more harmonious with market forces than past practice has made them. The implications of this conclusion suggest a fundamental realignment of industrial policy, both at the federal and at provincial levels. Commissioners also suggest that such realignment must take place in an economic context within which natural resources will play a diminished role, in a relative sense, in our economic future.

The natural resource sector's contribution to Canada's economic well-being, cultural life, and political traditions and institutions has been immense. It has become clear in recent years, however – if it was not clear before – that Canada's natural resource endowment is not unlimited, that our foreign markets are not secure, that growth in demand is unlikely to match the post-war record, and that substitute materials are becoming even more important.

These problems do not herald the disappearance of our basic resource industries. Relative to other nations, Canada remains well endowed with natural resources. The outlook for oil and gas, a few minerals, hydro-electricity and Western grains is favourable, and the dollar value of production in the resource sector will continue to grow. Nevertheless, the share of output in this sector will decline, relative to the share of output in other sectors of our economy. This pattern of relative decline will mean that in general, Canadians can expect no net gain, in the future, in resource-sector employment: instead a growing proportion of Canadians will find their jobs in factories or offices.

However, the prospect of a decline in the relative importance of the resource sector in relation to our national economy is no reason to neglect its problems or its claims. Resource industries are still essential to the economic life of many regions of Canada. Moreover, we have an obligation to pass on to future generations a variety of viable resource industries founded on a natural endowment that is as secure and as healthy as we can make it. Canada's success in resource production owes as much to human ingenuity as it does to the resource endowment itself, and many of the problems of the sector can be overcome, or at least diminished, by appropriate applications of that ingenuity.

We Commissioners are conscious of the fact that we have taken a long-term perspective. Our major task is to improve the growth performance of the Canadian economy into the twenty-first century. Our long-run strategy, however, addresses three major concerns which are not at all easy to disentangle in the medium or longer term:

- Enhance economic growth by policies designed to increase efficiency and productivity and thus generate a more competitive economy

- Reduce the rate of unemployment to the lowest levels at which an acceptable rate of inflation can be held more or less stable, and lower the rate at which this takes place
- Minimize the fluctuations in the business cycle, so as to provide a more stable framework for growth and employment opportunity.

These interrelated concerns were spoken to and elaborated at length in our hearings, and much of our research program has been devoted to their analysis. As already noted, our Parts III and V, in particular, explore these issues, seek to clarify their nature, and recommend policy responses. Apart from the structural problems of productivity, efficiency and competitiveness in the face of a generally slower world economy, over most of the past decade the conundrum of combined high unemployment and rampant inflation proved especially difficult. It remains as a continuing challenge, even though the rate of inflation has now receded to more livable levels.

It is important, therefore, to focus on this issue. For the sake of precision, current economic literature has coined the awkward term, "the NAIRU", as representing the non-accelerating inflation rate of unemployment. The term indicates that rate of unemployment in a free-market economy, below which the underlying rate of inflation in the price level is likely to spiral upward. For much of the post-war period, this rate of unemployment in Canada was assessed in the range of 3 to 5 per cent, but because of the accumulation of structural, institutional, demographic, and social changes in the labour market and in the economy generally, it is now broadly argued that this rate of unemployment, the NAIRU, has moved up to a range of 6.5 to 8 per cent. Commissioners find this unacceptable and recommend a variety of measures to reduce both structural and frictional unemployment. Expansionary demand policy is considered inappropriate and counter-productive when unemployment is below this range. If demand were expanded in such circumstances, it would probably result in an increase and acceleration of the rate of inflation and achieve no lasting gain in the reduction of unemployment. However, our unemployment rate of 11.2 per cent, as of mid-March 1985, is significantly above the aforementioned estimate of the NAIRU.

Our Report also seeks to diagnose and clarify the now widely accepted limitations of fiscal and monetary policies at the macro-economic level to manage the level of demand in such a way as effectively to level out short-term fluctuations in both employment and the price level. More generally, particularly given experience since the end of the 1960s, there is greater doubt about the capacity of the government to "fine-tune" the domestic Canadian economy through discretionary monetary, fiscal and exchange-rate policy. This declining effectiveness of short-term macro-economic policy partly reflects the much more tightly integrated structure of the Canadian economy with the world economy and, particularly, the close interrelationships of the international capital markets. There are also significant complexities on the domestic front. Not the least of these, in addition to the older, well-known lags in information availability, problem recognition, policy implementation and response in the market, are growing institutional rigidities and attitudes, administered prices and market power, a more diverse and intricate financial system, and the elusive subtleties of psychology, confidence and expectations, rational or otherwise. We explore these questions at some length in Part III and conclude, with respect to cyclical stabilization policy, that beyond the need to restore overall financial and economic confidence, the operation of labour markets is a crucial determinant of the average levels of unemployment that we can reach. We also conclude that to reduce the rate of unemployment, even to the current estimate of NAIRU, will require that traditional instruments of policy will need to be supplemented by new mechanisms to help smooth out the cycle.

As regards the question of the longer-run average trend of unemployment, we Canadians must pay special attention to the operation of labour markets and their institutional characteristics. The recognition of the relative decline in effectiveness of short-term macro-economic policy was accompanied by a shift of focus on the part of some economists to the structural characteristics of the economy. Their research has uncovered rigidities in the labour market which reduce the adaptability of the economy at the cost of higher unemployment and lower growth in recession periods than would prevail in their absence. Various features of our Unemployment Insurance system, for example, which are discussed at length below, seriously inhibit labour-market adjustments and contribute to high unemployment rates.

To respond to the serious shortcomings of the Unemployment Insurance (UI) program, Commissioners recommend a major overhaul of the system in conjunction with implementation of our proposals on income security. We seek to align the UI system more closely with insurance principles. This reform will encourage the adjustment necessary for our economic future, adjustment which the existing system now sometimes discourages. Our proposals include changes in the structure of benefits and the implementation of experience rating in the establishment of UI premium rates; the premiums would be proportional to the risk of unemployment calculated on a firm-by-firm basis. These changes would result in a major cost reduction in benefit payments of at least $4 billion at March 1985 rates of unemployment. It is important to emphasize that the combination of UI changes and our proposed UISP will provide more adequate incomes for those low-income Canadians who are attached to the labour force. The poorest Canadians, those without any labour-force attachment, would also see their incomes increase.

Commissioners believe that the reduction of impediments to adjustment processes must be supplemented by positive support for labour mobility. Our Transitional Adjustment Assistance Program (TAAP), financed, in part, by the savings on UI, will offer adjustment assistance for Canadians, provided that they are willing to move or to undertake retraining to improve their employment prospects. Entitlement to use TAAP must be based on willingness to undertake adaptive behaviour.

The TAAP program would provide greatly expanded support for portable wage-subsidy programs, mobility grants, training programs, and early retirement. It could also be used to provide compensation for losses in assets, such as housing, resulting from the decline of communities. While the individual components of the program are not new, the financial extent of the adjustment program we propose is significantly larger than current government expenditures. We visualize an annual TAAP pool of about $4 billion in the context of a coherent integrated approach to training and mobility. This is one of our major proposals to reduce the NAIRU and thus to improve the efficiency of the economy and the earnings of individuals, as well as to lower the rate of unemployment.

Here, as elsewhere in our Report, our objectives are not only to get Canadians to understand the particulars of the policy reforms we propose but, equally, if not more important, to have Canadians understand the theory and philosophy which are behind them. Attempts to lower the NAIRU by TAAP, UI reform and other measures require major changes in social and industrial policy and direction, involving two orders of government and the private sector. Such changes will not be achieved overnight, and their effects will not be felt immediately.

Why should we Commissioners make such proposals? And why should Canadians listen to them? Essentially, our position is the reverse of that attributed to an American Senator who, when asked what he had done for posterity replied: "Nothing! What has posterity done for me?" We disagree. We are concerned with the next generation of workers as well as this generation, and we are particularly concerned about contemporary youth unemployment. Commissioners believe that citizenship in a country which has given us so much, partly as a result of the labours of those who have gone before, carries with it an obligation to be concerned for those who are now entering our labour force, those who are already in it, and for future generations.

The various rigidities in our labour markets and in industrial structure are not inherent in modern economies, and some of them are peculiar to, or more prevalent in, Canada than in other industrialized countries. The rigidities are found in government legislation or policies and in private practices sanctioned by governments. Various policy changes, including our UI and TAAP proposals, as well as our proposal to encourage gains-sharing arrangements which would probably lower the NAIRU, are detailed in later chapters.

Although the modification of particular practices might result in very significant benefits to society as a whole, this is not always true for the individual participants. In the short run, the latter are often caught in patterns of behaviour dispersed in thousands of decentralized decision-making arenas. Individual actors cannot change the system, and co-ordinated private action is difficult. Government leadership, accordingly, is essential. In Canada, that leadership is itself sometimes rendered difficult because the authority to act is spread over 11 governments.

Policies to lower the NAIRU and policies to enhance our growth performance both drive us in the same direction: toward a greater reliance on the flexibility of markets and policies which facilitate competition and adjustment, an approach in striking contrast to some existing policies. On occasion, for example, aid to declining industries has been extremely costly per job saved. In 1979, the cost to the economy per job saved by tariffs and quotas for the Canadian textile and clothing industry was $34 500, at a time when the average annual income of textile workers was $10 000. Rather than subsidizing clearly uneconomical enterprises and retarding adjustments, this Commission recommends making payments directly to workers, in conjunction with the use of programs to facilitate training and mobility.

Modern economic life is characterized by pervasive change. The ratio of flexibility/rigidity in the economy has an independent effect on the success/failure of the economy's response to change. We are convinced by our analysis that a number of existing policies hamper the adjustment process and contribute to an unnecessarily high NAIRU. Such policies are counterproductive if our goal is economic growth; they are also inequitable because they increase unemployment and reduce human dignity by the maldistribution of work opportunities and of income, to which they contribute. The existing system of social assistance, for example, in which benefits fall dramatically if the recipient earns income, discourages a return to the workforce, to the detriment both of the individual and of society, although the disincentive is probably less serious when the unemployment rate is very high.

The increase in the NAIRU rate and our policy proposals to reduce it must be put in a broader context which relates, essentially, to our interpretation of the overall political process in democratic systems characterized by an extensive role for government. To focus on the labour market can subtly lead us to believe that we are examining the workings of the economy, which can therefore be explained by economic analysis alone. We agree that economic analysis is a powerful tool to explain the costs of impediments in labour markets and to suggest appropriate directions for reform. It is Commissioners' belief, however, that an explanation of how those rigidities developed and how they can be overcome requires an expanded perspective which locates developments in labour markets in the context of the socio-political process, out of which they emerged and through which they can be modified.

To refer to the central significance of the political process as we seek to understand the NAIRU, and the labour-market phenomena to which it is intimately linked, is to direct attention to three phenomena. First, there is the *ad hoc* nature of policy-making by government. Complex batteries of programs often develop from tentative initial steps by governments which had no idea of the evolutionary policy process they were setting in place. The present UI program, for example, is vastly expanded in scope and purpose from the rather modest beginnings of the 1940 legislation passed following a constitutional amendment of the same year, giving constitutional jurisdiction in the area to the federal government. In addition, much legislation occurs at the margin of existing programs, supplementing and patching up where visible deficiencies appear, to which a response cannot be delayed.

Secondly, the cumulative effects of dozens of policy initiatives of previous decades, each of which has probably been subject to ongoing modifications in response to various pressures, produces consequences which no one intended. The result often is internal contradiction in the policy field, broadly defined. This complexity baffles some of those on the receiving end and provides opportunities for others, more resourceful or with more resources, to exploit the maze of programs they manipulate in ways unintended and unforeseen by those who devised the programs in earlier years.

Thirdly, the relative freedom which may attend choice of programs at their inception, especially if the state is playing a leadership role, is greatly diminished once programs are in place, for their beneficiaries will resist changes to programs to which they have become habituated, and which they interpret as entitlements. To change policy direction, in other words, is to disturb complex arrangements sustained by the conservatism of clientele groups.

From these perspectives, it is evident that the socio-political processes behind the network of programs which links citizens and governments tends to generate rigidities which are not easily overcome even when the advantages of new policy direction are clear, and the resultant contribution to the public interest may be self-evident to detached observers. Commissioners believe that these socio-political tendencies – *ad hoc* policy development, unintended cumulative consequences of multiple separate initiatives over time, and resultant rigidity – characterize many policy areas. Various clientele groups and beneficiaries resist significant changes of policy direction when new understandings develop, or when there is a shift in the environment or in the goals that should be pursued. In such circumstances, as for example when policies contribute to an unacceptably high NAIRU, the obligation imposed on government is clear.

Scholars are now increasingly aware that national economies have different institutional characteristics which lead to differential performance in terms of output and employment. The NAIRU level is influenced by various institutional arrangements and policies incrementally developed in past decades. Their contribution to raising unemployment was typically unintended and, in most cases, unknown when they were instituted. A failure to reduce the NAIRU in the period ahead, however, must be seen as a deliberate policy choice, a failure of will, or an inability to overcome the resistance of the beneficiaries of generally inequitable arrangements. Our approach to this issue is in broad sympathy with our general advocacy of enhancing market forces and the competitive capacity of the Canadian economy by various measures, including Canada-U.S. free-trade, a proposal which we review in a preliminary way in the immediately following pages.

Note

1. Karl Marx, *Birth of the Communist Manifesto*, edited and annotated, with an introduction by Dirk J. Struik (New York: International, 1971), pp. 92, 94.

State and Economy: The International Role

The relation between the state and the market, between the polity and the economy, has an international, as well as a domestic, dimension. For a nation as heavily dependent on international trade as Canada, that dimension is of special importance. Changes in the global economy, now as on previous occasions in our history, challenge Canadians to respond positively to a new international environment if we are to have acceptable future growth performances. The necessary response will require significant adaptation in our economy to meet international competition; the adjustment of social and industrial policies to support that adaptation; a vigorous bilateral pursuit of more secure access to the U.S. market, combined with continuing multilateral approaches; institutional changes in Canadian federalism to increase our efficacy in the negotiation and implementation of trade agreements; and countermeasures to preserve an effective political autonomy as we further open ourselves to competitive forces from abroad. It is a great challenge Commissioners set out for Canadians, yet it is a challenge we have no alternative but to meet.

Canada has made extensive contributions to the creation of a liberal international order governed by multilateral institutions whose acronyms, such as GATT, IMF and UNCTAD, daily remind us of the international institutional network designed to control the excesses of economic nationalism. At the same time, we have steadily, albeit with some fluctuations, been drawn into a more closely integrated trading interdependence with the American market. The percentage of our merchandise exports going to the United States increased from 59.8 to 76.3 per cent from 1954 to 1984, while the percentage of our merchandise imports from the United States remained level at 72 per cent. For Canada, the post-war opening up of the international economic order has not been accompanied by a diversification of our trading partners. The reverse has happened: our post-war participation in the global economy has led to an increasingly continental economic integration of our trade patterns.

This trade interdependence with the United States has resulted, in part, from particular Canada/U.S. arrangements: the Defence Production Sharing Agreement of 1959, and especially the Auto Pact of 1965. It also reflects earlier, bilateral, mutual tariff reductions in the 1930s, and subsequently. Yet we Canadians have also sought to reduce our dependence on the American market, most notably during the Conservative governments of John Diefenbaker from 1957 to 1963, when we tried unsuccessfully to divert 15 per cent of Canadian trade from the United States to the United Kingdom, and later by the "Third Option" policy of the Liberal government in the early 1970s, with its trade-diversification objectives which led to our contractual link with the European Community in the mid-1970s. This, however, had little effect on our trade patterns. We have extensively used federal and provincial trade missions to gain access to promising markets. Our tendency to tie our foreign aid to Canadian procurement, a practice to which we resort more than most countries that belong to the Organisation for Economic Co-operation and Development (OECD), has presumably had a marginal effect in increasing our exports to developing countries. We have been good citizens of the multilateral trade regime produced under the auspices of the General Agreement on Tariff and Trade (GATT), and we have participated vigorously in the various GATT rounds which, since the Second World War, have dramatically reduced tariff barriers on a most-favoured-nation basis. In spite of this record, the overall trend toward increasing trade integration with the United States has continued.

The unique aspect of our situation is not the extent of trade dependence of our gross national product (GNP), as several of the smaller OECD countries have considerably higher percentages, although we are above the the overall OECD average: 28.2 per cent in 1981 when the OECD average was 19.8 per cent. Our real uniqueness resides in our marked dependence on one country. Of the OECD countries which export more than 20 per cent of their GNP, not one is as dependent on a single national market as is Canada.

It is this combination of our relatively high trade dependence, in general, with its very high concentration in one national market, which singles us out. The problem raised by this dependency is the insecurity of our access. The issue is not primarily tariffs, which are already low in each country on the products of the other – although more so on the U.S. side – and which will be even lower by 1987, when the last round of GATT tariff cuts will be complete. The problem resides in the increasing U.S. resort to non-tariff barriers (NTBs), which threatens to disrupt our access for particular commodities. The uncertainties thus created thwart the rationalization of production in Canada, which secure access would foster, and also encourage Canadian investment in the United States to avoid the imposition of non-tariff barriers. We suffer from interdependence without security in a context wherein our dependence on the U.S. market is not reciprocated by an equivalent American dependence on the Canadian market.

Although post-war trade liberalization had political purposes, as we have noted, partly based on the traditional nineteenth-century liberal, free-trade assumptions of Cobden and Bright that networks of economic interdependence transcending state boundaries contributed to peace between nations, its primary purpose was economic. The post-war trade liberalization contributed to perhaps the most dramatic period of prolonged and widespread economic growth in human history, based on the more efficient operation of international markets. At the most general level, free trade is designed to protect markets from efficiency-distorting state interventions which turn borders into barriers. The declining economic significance of borders is indicated by the almost doubling of the proportion of goods and services that crossed national boundaries between 1950 and 1980, from 11 per cent of world output to 21 per cent.

This Commission strongly supports continuing Canadian efforts in multilateral arenas. Our preferred outcome would be a successful GATT initiative leading to the further multilateral reduction of tariffs and, more important, non-tariff barriers. However, with 89 members and 30 other countries which maintain a *de facto* application of GATT rules, GATT has become an unwieldy decision-making forum. In addition, the non-tariff barriers which we seek to reduce are often difficult to disentangle from a variety of domestic policies of the GATT-member states. They are elusive prey for effective regulation, particularly given the limited administrative capacity of the GATT as an international institution. Thus, while Commissioners support continued efforts to work through the GATT, we are not sufficiently optimistic about the possibilities of major breakthroughs in the short term to advocate an exclusive preoccupation with the multilateral GATT system. Further, the major benefit for Canadians of a successful GATT reduction of non-tariff barriers would be increased security of access to the U.S. market. The United States will be our major market, whether or not there is another successful round of GATT negotiations. The fact is, therefore, that the multilateral route which we prefer has, as a primary objective, an increase in the security of our dominant trade relations with the United States.

Given the preceding analysis, this Commission recommends a concurrent negotiating focus, with the United States directly on our bilateral relationship. We support the pursuit and eventual implementation of a Canada-U.S./free-trade arrangement to encompass both tariff and non-tariff barriers. Canada-U.S. free trade pursued by direct negotiations between the two governments has a much greater likelihood of success than its indirect pursuit through multilateral negotiations. Moreover, we shall require significant exemptions and safeguards from the free-trade arrangement we seek, and those safeguards are much more likely to be obtained in a bilateral arrangement than in a multilateral forum where each government will bring its own preferred safeguards to the bargaining table. Finally, there are disturbing tendencies in the GATT system and in the global economy: the increase in managed trade, developing protectionist pressures in the United States, and the general possibility of a growing resort to retaliatory trade measures by the major powers if the global trading system should begin to fragment. In these circumstances, we Canadians must supplement our general reliance on the multilateral GATT route by carving out secure access to the American market, using bilateral approaches.

On the basis of our own research and numerous prior studies, this Commission is convinced that Canada-U.S. free trade will produce significant net economic gains for Canada. The increase of Canadian gross national product consequent on free trade with the United States, involving, as it does, the mutual elimination of most tariff and non-tariff barriers, is expected to be in the neighbourhood of 3 to 8 per cent, and those figures do not include the substantial gains from securing that access. The short-term costs of trade liberalization are real, but they are small, by comparison, and manageable, with appropriate adjustment measures. Although the precise figures are disputable, an extensive body of research extending over several decades holds unanimously that free trade with the United States will bring Canada significant gains which will be widely spread throughout our country.

Free trade is the main instrument in this Commission's approach to industrial policy. It is based on the same intellectual thrust which governs Commissioners' approach to domestic economic policy: that the role of governments is not to retard competitive market forces, but to complement them by positive adjustment measures.

Canadian history makes it clear, however, that free trade with the United States is a political issue. It raises a variety of concerns related to Canadian autonomy and the preservation of distinctive Canadian values. At the most general level, the concern of Canadians will be the compatibility of tighter and more secure trade integration with the survival of a meaningfully independent Canadian future.

Commissioners recommend a free-trade area rather than a customs union or a common market because the former preserves our autonomy in commercial policy toward third countries and allows domestic controls on the movement of capital and labour across borders. Canada would doubtless seek modifications to the free-trade regime for agriculture, selected services and energy. Canadians would also require provisions which would allow for certain regional development policies and protection for basic cultural policies.

Throughout our history, Canadians have worked to create and preserve a distinctive Canadian society making politically autonomous choices in the shadow of a dynamic and powerful neighbour. Commissioners are fully aware of this achievement, and we share our fellow-Canadians' pride in it. We believe, nonetheless, that a secure trading arrangement will not reduce our distinctiveness or our autonomy in other spheres. We can preserve a distinctive Canadian society capable of making independent policy choices, including those relating to foreign policy, in order to transmit a freedom of manœuvre to our descendants not dissimilar to what we now enjoy. Such an outcome is not only a possibility, but a high probability if sustained by the various policy measures we recommend later in this Report. Not only do we advocate ongoing pursuit of our international economic objectives in the multilateral GATT arena to supplement our bilateral Canada-U.S./ free-trade initiative, but we also distinguish between the trade bilateralism of the latter and our vigorous pursuit of non-economic objectives in other multilateral forums and in other bilateral relationships outside the North American orbit.

We are supported in our general belief that our autonomy and identity will not be undermined as a result of such free trade by the fact that the process of economic integration within Canada has been accompanied by a strengthened role for provincial governments, based on continuing strong senses of community and identity at the provincial level. Further, we note that the superficially homogenizing aspects of modern life, reflecting the penetrative powers of the media and consumerism, have coincided with a new emphasis on identities based on gender and ethnicity. We do not therefore see increased trade integration as threatening the survival of a flourishing Canadian uniqueness. Trade interdependence, political autonomy and cultural distinctiveness are not incompatible.

The Canadian nation is not a weak and fragile plant doomed to disappearance merely because we trade more freely and securely with our American neighbour. Free trade will reduce regional divisions and enhance Canadian confidence. Canadian nationalism and our collective identity as a people are deeply rooted in more than a century of our evolutionary common existence. It is not unrealistic to assert that our distinctive sense of ourselves as Canadians will be fostered by the juxtaposition of more integrated trading patterns with a co-existing autonomous Canadian state system. Further, the increased gross national product which free trade will bring will provide us with more resources to devote to Canadian goals. Finally, we are convinced that in the modern era, one of the crucial components of a satisfying Canadian identity is to be found in our economic capacity to perform at a high level in a competitive world. A long-run decline in our relative growth performance, compared to that of other nations with which we habitually compare ourselves, is a recipe neither for a meaningful independence nor for a satisfying sense of self. Since free trade with the United States, encompassing mutual controls on non-tariff barriers, is one of the main levers available to raise Canadian growth prospects over the long term, this Commission views its absence as limiting our real independence.

Our task as Royal Commissioners is to clarify issues and to focus discussion. Canadians no longer exist comfortably in the North Atlantic triangle, in which our autonomy was based on a shrewd balance between our simultaneous extensive dependence on the United States and Great Britain. As our trade figures reveal, in this aspect of our existence, North American geography has triumphed over the British economic connections derived from our colonial origins in the British Empire. The National Policy of 1879, designed to integrate us on an East/West basis and supplemented by later imperial preference to link us with British markets, is now but a shadow of its former self. Our tariffs have declined dramatically in the last four decades, and further declines under GATT will take effect to the close of 1987. Britain, a much weaker power now than when we began our Canadian journey in 1867, has joined the European Community. Our trade with Britain is much reduced from earlier times: it represented 2.2 per cent of our merchandise exports and 2.5 per cent of our merchandise imports in 1984, well under half of our growing trade with Japan. The United States is now overwhelmingly dominant as our major trading partner. We can no longer judiciously balance ourselves in trade between the United States and Great Britain. We have tried to diversify our trading patterns without much success, although presumably, we would have been even more dependent on the American market in the absence of such efforts.

Central to Commissioners' policy recommendations is a rejection of protectionism and of a *dirigiste* industrial strategy behind tariff and other barriers. We doubt the capacity of governments in Canada to implement an explicit, detailed, industrial strategy, and to pick "winners". The stimulation of competition is the key to economic growth and productivity improvement. Our domestic market is too small for us to look inward for salvation and to reduce the ties of international economic interdependence which already exist.

Freedom begins with the recognition of necessity. There is no utility in policies based on illusions. Our choice of a future must be based on our present position, not on some other hypothetical starting point where we might now be, had history turned out differently. The fact that we Commissioners see no superior alternative to Canada-U.S. free trade does not, however, lead us to trivialize the significance of the policy we are suggesting. On the contrary, we recognize it as proposing a fundamental change in the relationship between states and markets in North America and, in the light of our history, a major symbolic change in Canadian/American relations. Each country is being asked to give up specified policies, tariff and other, tailored to its domestic economy in the interest of its proposed partner. Restrictions will apply to provincial and state governments, as well as to the central governments. Greater freedom to market forces transcending the border can be purchased only at the price of greater restrictions on selected domestic economic policies of governments.

The principle of comparative advantage must be the primary determinant of our position in the international division of labour. Commissioners advocate a greater reliance on international market forces to determine the evolution of the economy in the future than has been true in the past. We Canadians are at a turning point in our history. The National Policy of 1879 has played itself out. This Commission is convinced of the general superiority of competitive market forces to the attempts of governments in Canada to pick "winners" and "losers". Protectionism is counterproductive and self-defeating. In a world of growing regional trading blocs, Canada is one of the few industrial countries lacking secure access to a market of over 100 million people.

This Commission asks the governments and people of Canada to debate openly and vigorously the desirability of formally recognizing that we Canadians must come to terms with our trade relationship with the United States. The issue is not one to be confused or obscured by portraying the change as only incremental. We have recently gone through a traumatic experience in which the break-up of our country was a distinct possibility, as the people of Quebec openly debated their future in a referendum campaign. That debate is a striking example of how a free and democratic people should confront its future. A mature people concerned for its own honour and for the integrity of the democratic process has both the capacity and the obligation to make major choices in the context of public discussion. If we compromise the democratic virtues before we go to the bargaining table, we shall confirm the fears of those who assert that a free-trade arrangement will reduce our autonomy and erode our political integrity.

Conclusions

To look back on the past half century of relations between the state and the market, and the state and society in Canada is to observe the Canadian version of a process of expansion of government activity typical of the OECD nations. Although it is tempting to concentrate on the domestic sources of that expansion, to do so would provide us with only limited insights.

Clearly there were common factors among the OECD nations behind that state expansion, factors deriving from similarities in socio-economic conditions and the political demands for government action to which they led. Governments enjoyed an enhanced bureaucratic capacity that was part of the long-term political response to the Depression of the 1930s, which had undermined the moral legitimacy of a relatively self-regulating capitalism. The relative status of markets and states shifted to the advantage of the latter and contributed to a general drift of power to governments. This shift received an extra boost from the remarkable post-war economic expansion of the years up to the early 1970s. Affluence and more sophisticated bureaucracies greatly increased the capacities of governments to extract resources from society for state purposes. In relative terms, governments and electorates could avoid hard choices, as it seemed possible to have their cake and eat it, too.

Inevitably, as political allocations changed market outcomes, citizens and private economic actors increasingly saw the political arena as an alternative means for the attainment of goals hitherto pursued more exclusively in the private economy and society. In times of economic insecurity, individuals formerly sought assistance from kin, the church or private charity. Now they turned to the state. For particular corporations, access to governments became the means to profitability. Government-relations staffs within corporations and private consultants who knew how to work the system emerged to exploit the new possibilities. Human behaviour had not changed, but it operated within a new distribution of state and non-state incentives and disincentives. Political changes in the rules of the game induced individuals and organizations to rearrange their affairs to maximize the benefits of their interactions with governments.

The political process developed a momentum behind the enhanced role of government in the determination of social and economic outcomes. Contemporary mass democracies, such as Canada, have experienced a dramatic expansion of the politically relevant public, accompanied by a more open and responsive political system. The suffrage is now universal and is supplemented by a multiplication of interest groups making demands on the state. These pressures are reinforced by the contemporary media, especially television, which reduce the distance between the governors and the governed and contribute to the mobilization of demands. The contrast between the relative obscurity of aboriginals before 1960, when status Indians lacked the vote, and the visibility their demands now enjoy is illustrative. We cannot turn the clock back, and as the case of aboriginals testifies, it would be immoral to try to do so.

A further factor was at work. State élites and private citizens did not derive their expectations from insulated national perspectives indifferent to the policies of other governments and nations. The mass media, extensive foreign travel, and international organizations such as the OECD engender constant comparisons with the policies of other countries. There was a reinforcing "contagion" effect at work which cumulatively led each political process in the same direction, albeit at slightly different rates and with varying emphases. In the same way that anti-imperial sentiments in the post-war world swept across colonial boundaries and toppled European imperial regimes in Africa and Asia, new understandings of the role of the state swept across the developed world and toppled concepts of a more limited role for governments.

While the political process which produced the contemporary role of the state in the society and economy of Canada was guided by a broad assumption of an appropriate state role, the particular policies which were put in place in half a century of experimentation were *ad hoc* and piecemeal. The welfare state, our tax system, and our industrial policies, among other examples, are classic illustrations of incrementalism, the piecemeal accretion of policies over decades to produce overall results which no one willed or intended and which often lack coherence. The state is not a single actor guided by a far-seeing comprehensive intelligence fully conscious of the long-term effect of incrementalism. The aggregate role of the contemporary state in Canada is the unintended cumulative consequence of thousands of particular decisions and policies scattered across half a century.

From the vantage point of the mid-1980s, at a time when there has been a pause in the acceptance of the taken-for-granteds of yesterday, we must ask the no-longer-taboo question of whether we can continue on the path where incrementalism has placed us. The raising of that question derives from the emergent realities of global competition which confront states and peoples in the closing years of the twentieth century, and which are the subject matter of much of this Report. This is a time for reassessment, for the search for new directions, for the application of analysis unencumbered by an automatic acceptance of yesterday's assumptions.

Such a reassessment is not easy. It requires both an understanding of how we reached our present situation and a realistic recognition of the limits of our manœuvrability. The momentum behind the existing links between the state and society in Canada, as elsewhere, is akin to the momentum behind a huge, loaded, oil tanker steaming full-speed ahead. A significant change of direction takes time. We should not forget the more than two million Canadians, including education and hospital employees, who work for the 11 senior governments of Canadian federalism and for local governments. They and their families are not indifferent to the fate of the programs around which their careers have been built. Existing state/society and state/economy relations are embedded in thousands of discrete pockets of self-interest and well-established expectations among both the providers and the immediate beneficiaries of particular policies. The state, for all its theoretical power, is deeply embedded in society and economy as a result of the innumerable past policies which tie it down. Big governments have multiple constituencies habituated to the benefits and protections they receive from the state. Economy and society are caught up in a multitude of linkages with the state, which have come to be viewed as habitual and, if positive, as entitlements or social rights.

A change of direction will be achieved neither by administrative fiat nor by lucid analysis alone. The latter confronts the power and desire of special interests to obfuscate and to equate with the public good the particulars of their privileged treatment which, from society's viewpoint, may be counter-productive.

The political process is not an academic seminar in which the participants share a commitment to truth, but a process in which ideas confront bureaucratic and political power, self-interest, parochialism, propaganda and slogans. We do not despair. This is the human condition and there is no more point in dissipating energy by railing against it than there is in resisting the endless cycle of the seasons.

Commissioners' assessment of the future role of government in Canada is scattered across the close to 2000 pages of the Report which follow. Our proposals fall into two categories. The most obvious are the recommended changes in particular policies; of equal importance are reforms directed to improving the political process out of which future policies will emerge.

In the first category, Commissioners believe that in some important areas we Canadians must significantly increase our reliance on market forces. Our proposals to increase our openness to the international economy and, specifically, to enter into a free-trade arrangement with the United States reflect our general preference for market forces over state intervention as the appropriate means through which to generate incentives in the economy, from which growth will follow. Domestically, we have identified a number of market-distorting, growth-suppressing policies which redistribute income to protected and privileged enclaves in the economy, reduce economic efficiency, and inhibit flexibility. We recommend that in contrast to these policies from which Canadians suffer in the aggregate, the interventionist policies of the state should facilitate adjustment to those market processes which are growth creating. We must enhance the essential inputs to the productive process – labour, capital, research and development and management – and create more positive incentives to efficient allocation of resources, through industrial policies geared to productivity and competitiveness, whether in manufacturing or resources or the service sector. Too many of our existing policies result in rigidities in labour markets, extensive protection for declining economic sectors lasting far beyond appropriate transitional measures, and price-raising marketing regimes which increase costs to consumers.

In general, we seek, in the interest of efficiency, to modify the network of policy links connecting the state and the economy and society of Canada. This requires governments to reduce the disincentives which their own policies have placed in the way of behaviour that fosters an adaptive economy and society contributing to the highest-possible living standards compatible with individual liberty and an equitable distribution of well-being.

In addition to the suggested changes in particular policies, we have concluded that the political system itself requires the attention of policy makers. Canadians face major challenges in the coming decades. Although there may be some relative enhancement of market forces in the future, governments will continue to be central players in determining the quality of our response.

The political process of fragmented incrementalism was tolerable, and perhaps inevitable, in a period of economic growth. It is less appropriate for a future which may challenge Canadians' capacity to determine and implement the appropriate trade-offs between equity and efficiency. Governments of the future will have continuing, and probably enhanced, requirements for legitimacy and support. While the latter derive from many sources, in the long run they are strengthened by the visibility of trade-offs, by the openness of public discussion, and by the appearance and reality of a participant democratic citizenry interacting with elected politicians in parliamentary forums.

A revitalization of parliamentary government and major refinements in our federal system are prominently featured on this Commission's reform agenda. More generally, we wish to remind Canadians that a "living Constitution" requires constant attention if it is to respond to new pressures while remaining sensitive to its basic values. Such responsiveness is not automatic. It is always, in some part, the result of conscious efforts by leaders and analysts mediating between historic institutions and a changed environment.

This Commission, like many others, has had to develop an approach to federalism. Since 1867, federalism and parliamentary government have been the central features of our constitutional system. Both institutional arrangements appear repeatedly in this Report, as does the Canadian Charter of Rights and Freedoms, which our nation has recently added to its basic constitutional arrangements.

In different chapters of this Report, depending on the context, federalism is described, and implicitly defined, in different ways. This is not surprising, for our federalism is complex, and different issues single out different aspects for attention. Furthermore, federalism is a system of political competition, and the competing governments seek to bend its definition in light of their own goals and purposes. Federalism, in other words, is a contested concept, and the future politics of federalism ensure that no definition of federalism proposed by a Royal Commission will put an end to controversy over its "real" meaning.

Nevertheless, these varying definitions are not without significance simply because no single definition can permanently vanquish its rivals. Definitions help to structure the world of political action and thus have policy consequences. This Commission, with its broad-ranging mandate, has immersed itself in the theory and practice of federalism, in the light of our history and of the demands we anticipate from the challenging future which Canadians face. Commissioners wish, accordingly, to communicate as clearly as possible our view of federalism.

The phrase "executive federalism", which has entered our vocabulary, draws our attention to the interdependence between the two orders of government and to the intergovernmental machinery which has evolved in response to that interdependence. We Commissioners recognize that interdependence and, especially in the context of the economic union, we appreciate the necessity of rules and institutions to maximize its benefits. We do not, however, view interdependence as the essence of federalism. Rather, we see it as a by-product of the co-existence of activist governments, responsible to their own electorates, which unavoidably are often involved in overlapping policy areas, albeit from the base of distinctive jurisdictional authority.

In the 1960s the phrase "co-operative federalism" acquired popularity. It was an attempt to define executive federalism in terms of a particular norm: that of co-operation. The phrase clearly drew its strength from important developments, specifically the development of the welfare state. This brought together federal funds and provincial jurisdiction in a number of areas, to protect Canadians against various risks which attend modern industrial society, along with the universal problems of illness and those which often accompany old age. Co-operative federalism was also a useful label to apply to the fiscal arrangements which developed in stages from the Second World War. These arrangements produced significant simplification of the exercise of taxing powers and expenditure responsibilities by the two orders of government and also to increased revenues for the poorer provinces by means of equalization payments.

Commissioners share the general Canadian support for these positive intergovernmental arrangements which, along with other intergovernmental agreements, constitute the policy substance of co-operative federalism. On the other hand, we resist the intellectual tendency, to which an uncritical use of the phrase "co-operative federalism" can lead: to assume that an absence of co-operation in particular areas is a sign of failure deserving condemnation. To appear to oppose co-operation, or to question its utility, is to risk being misunderstood. Commissioners are not against co-operation, but we oppose the argument that it is the supreme value to which all other values are subordinate.

Co-operation between the two orders of governments cannot be the essence of federalism or the dominant criterion which should inform our evaluation of federalism's performance: carried to such extremes, the stress on co-operation destroys federalism. Governments cannot simultaneously be responsive to their own electorates and judged according to the single criterion of whether they co-operate and harmonize their policies in all areas where these policies affect those of other governments. The major responsibility of the eleven governments of our federal system, as well as those of Yukon and the Northwest Territories, is to their own electorates. From Commissioners' perspective, federalism is most appropriately viewed as a system of separate responsible governments, based on a division of powers which still has meaning. Such governments are accountable to the legislatures and electorates of their own jurisdiction. To deny this is to deny the compatibility of democracy and federalism.

This view necessarily means that there will be competition between governments, that each government has an autonomous capacity to act, and that the exercise of such autonomy is not only proper, but a necessary consequence of federalism. To oppose such competition is implicit advocacy of a unitary state, which is neither possible nor desirable for Canada.

In the final analysis, the degree of intergovernmental co-operation that prevails is a matter for electorates to determine as they make their decisions to reward or punish incumbent governments for their actions. Accordingly, the most appropriate ratio of competition to co-operation in Canadian federalism will emerge to the extent that the federal and provincial political systems are internally democratic. It is for this reason, among others, that the major reform thrust that this Commission has directed to our constitutional system is to strengthen democratic responsible government. We believe – although ultimately it is for electorates to decide – that competition, as a by-product of the autonomy of governments, is a desirable feature of federalism and will continue to energize our politics in future decades. In fact, we go further and assert that intergovernmental co-operation is an outcome of competition policed by separate electorates. Governments which provide electorates with either too much or too little competition will ultimately find themselves on the opposition benches. It is our belief that if co-operation becomes a requirement which must be met, rather than an outcome which emerges in particular situations, the result will be to paralyze the federal system, and the federal and provincial democracies of which that system should be the servant.

The central premise of our perspective on citizen/state relations is that big government requires more democracy, not less. In part, this reflects the classic fear of unchecked state power, to which Canada's recent adoption of a Charter of Rights and Freedoms is a partial response. More generally, however, it reflects Canadians' basic position on the appropriate form and practice of parliamentary democracy in the late twentieth century.

We do not view democracy as a cycle of infrequent elections between which citizens revert to apathy. Governing is an every-day activity, while elections occur only every three or four years. Consequently, the health of our democracy is contingent on the nature of the relation between cabinets and legislatures, and legislatures and the citizenry. The decline of legislatures has been a common theme for many decades. The reason for that recurring attention among students and practitioners of parliamentary government is that legislatures are central to our conceptions of how we should govern ourselves. The aggrandizement of government tends to strengthen executives at the expense of legislatures. Powerful cabinets headed by prime ministers who dominate the media need to be counterbalanced by legislative bodies with an enhanced capacity to scrutinize, monitor, debate and discuss what the government is doing. Legislatures are our primary instruments to ensure that governing is carried out in public.

Legislatures have been weakened by the general trend to executive dominance characteristic of big government, by the particular stimulus to that trend provided by executive federalism, within which deals are struck and presented to legislatures for approval and, probably most important, by the general fragmentation of the political process. This last phenomenon is evident in the tendency of interest groups to bypass parties and Parliament, and to deal directly with ministers and public servants. This tendency is an inevitable consequence of the mutual benefits to both parties which come from sharing information, and it contributes to various understandings among private and public actors who need one another.

On the other hand, the modern democratic state has needs that are threatened by a fragmented politics of interest-group accommodation. The scope of contemporary government provides multiple opportunities for special interests to exploit their privileged access to government at the expense of the larger public. These opportunities are enhanced to the extent that access is in private arenas which pay little attention to the trade-offs involved.

The need to make trade-offs more visible is not based only on a desire for better trade-offs as such, but also on the larger requirement of modern governments for citizens capable of self-restraint in the political arena. The multiple interest groups of contemporary Canadian democracy must be funnelled into the forum of Parliament in settings which emphasize the constrained nature of policy choice in the real world.

Contemporary government cannot achieve many of its most important goals without the positive support of the relevant public. It needs a richer sense of citizenship than did its less active predecessors. It needs a significant capacity to mobilize consent. It has a never-ending task in educating the citizenry in realities which cannot be avoided. As the international arena becomes increasingly consequential for domestic politics, that task must grow in importance if the government is to succeed in broadening the citizens' awareness about the country's position in the global economy and its international responsibilities. We Commissioners believe that the international political economy of the future will be tough and competitive, and that meeting that competition will be facilitated by a political process which puts illusion and narrow self-interest on the defensive.

The need for education is mutual. Governments do not have monopolies of insight. They need the ideas and information scattered across the society their policies affect. Governments are prone to secrecy and arrogance. Legislatures with committee procedures which incorporate the relevant expertise of the country can help to make governments better informed and more modest.

For these reasons, Commissioners conclude that parliamentary democracy must be strengthened, and legislatures must become more central arenas for public debate and education. The elected Senate we propose is designed to strengthen the voice of the less populous provinces in the national Parliament, and thus to render more visible those trade-offs between majority rule and the interests of provincial communities that are inherent in a parliamentary federalism.

We recommend a small number of new parliamentary committees focusing on comprehensive policy matters: economic policy, regulatory policy, Crown corporations, and federal/provincial relations, for example, before which interest groups, research bodies, and others would appear. It is our hope and expectation that such forums would educate special interests in the compromises involved in governing for the whole society.

The extension of democracy which is required by big government is not one of more fragmented participation, but one which addresses Canadians as citizens and seeks our involvement in common tasks. The Charter has recently strengthened the citizenry in its possession of rights and reminded governments that their power is not without check. Citizens, no less than the state, have obligations. A balanced political process is one in which rulers exercise self-restraint to respect the rights of the citizens, and the latter embed their practice of rights in broad understandings of obligation to the community.

The liberal political order of democratic capitalism did not develop with the contemporary scope of government in mind. It has adapted surprisingly well to the process of expanding government responsibilities. Nevertheless, the easy days of incremental government growth carved out of an expanding pie will not characterize our future. Our task will be to find ways to control the political market and the expectations and behaviour which accompanied its expansion in the last half century. The related task will be the ongoing revision of our policy responses to new circumstances.

Both of these tasks involve political education, for which legislatures are the obvious vehicles for instruction. That cabinets and prime ministers will be centrally involved in that task, Commissioners take for granted. Their contribution, however, needs to be supplemented by the creative tensions of the adversary politics of Parliament, and the probing contributions of investigative committees and broad-ranging comprehensive policy committees which can involve the elected representatives of the public, as well as citizen participation. This is the route to which the political theory of parliamentary government directs us.

Our policy recommendations in particular areas, as well as our suggestions for reform of our system of government, apply to the Canadian case, and Commissioners make no claim for their universal applicability. One characteristic of the contemporary international political economy is that the universe of comparative examples has greatly increased. There are new actors on the global stage of international economic competition. They employ structures and practices of government derived from particular histories. They bring different traditions to the relations between state and market, between management and workers, and between the private assumption of risk and the provision of social safety nets. Their existence and dynamic economic performance, particularly those of the newly industrializing countries (NICs), change the terms of international political and economic competition and lead to an introspective self-questioning of traditional practices among the more established actors.

It is necessary for Canadians to steer carefully between two temptations, a faddish pursuit of the different, and a mulish refusal to learn. This Commission has tried to steer between those two extremes.

Individual states in the world have different capacities to pursue particular economic policies. These differences reside partly in constitutional arrangements and the structure of the state itself, but they are also found in varying patterns of international economic interdependence and of the organizational structure of business and labour. Canadians are precluded from opting for tripartism, in which the state, business and labour collaborate across a broad range of economic policy domains, including the determination of wages, by the dispersal of power in the federal system and by the absence of centralized organizations of business and labour, as well as by the extent of non-union labour. The small size of our domestic market weakens whatever attractions might possibly reside in protectionist measures if we had five times our present population. While federalism does not entirely undermine, it certainly dilutes, our enthusiasm for a state-led, highly interventionist, industrial strategy. Our trade dependence on the American market, which has evolved, in spite of our efforts of diversification, over recent decades, has convinced this Commission that we must concentrate our efforts on obtaining secure access to the American market, on which continental economic forces have made us increasingly dependent. We cannot choose to cut back significantly our trading integration with the United States without risking severe economic dislocation, cessation of economic growth, and a resultant political instability. In the longer term, successful competition in a North American context will lead to a greater ability to compete abroad and diversify our markets.

More generally, our understanding of the nature of Canadian political society and the political theory embedded in our institutions drives us to "work with the grain" of our political tradition. We have more than a century of experience with parliamentary government and federalism. A rich domestic literature exists which explores their intricacies. Scattered throughout our society in legislatures, cabinets, courts, universities and elsewhere, there are many guardians of the Constitution, steeped in its lore and prompt to rush to its defence. So, in constitutional terms, our comparative advantage lies with federalism and parliamentary government. We are now in process of digesting a major addition to our constitutional system: the Canadian Charter of Rights and Freedoms. In its broad features, then, our basic institutional framework is a "given". We lack the option of deciding that we could face our future better as a unitary state or with a congressional system. We must work to improve what we have, rather than postulating options outside our tradition.

In other words, Commissioners' proposals apply to this country, with the constraints and opportunities provided by its system of government, the nature of its domestic economy, the pattern of its international economic interdependence, the existing organization of business and labour, its location next to the large American market with its advanced economy, and other features. Canada's policy choices are also conditioned by the constraints and opportunities in the international economy, and the interests and capacities of other states which bring their own concerns to the common bargaining tables where nations meet.

The preceding position is both obvious and all too often ignored. Commissioners have rejected various options in deference to the aphorism "You can't get there from here."

The policy options we have selected are feasible. We believe that they will lead to a better future for ourselves, our children and our grandchildren. We admit that when all our proposals are added up, some Canadians will describe us as idealist. We accept the label. We deny, however, that we are naïve idealists. We reject as naïve realists those who deny the capacity of Canadians to meet the challenge of the future. We have confidence in our fellow citizens.

CHAPTER 2

Global Outlook

Introduction *75*
Notes 77
The Human Environment: The Population Explosion *78*
Notes 83
The Global Natural Environment: Under Stress *84*
Food and Agriculture *84*
Energy *90*
Industrial Raw Materials *93*
Minerals 93
The Forest Resource 98
The Environment *100*
Water 102
Acid Rain 103
Degradation of Soil 104
Nuclear Wastes 105
Destruction of Tropical Forests 106
The Greenhouse Effect 107
Extinction of Species 109
Conclusions 110
Notes *110*
The Global Human and Physical Outlook: General Implications for Canada *113*
The Knowledge Environment: The Challenge of Change *115*
Can Technology Solve World Problems? *115*
Science and Technology in the Global Context *115*
The Significance of Technological Change *117*
Notes *126*
The Economic Environment: Structural Shifts and Long-Term Trends *127*
Interdependence at a Crossroads *127*
Economic Performance over the post-War Period *130*
Structural Shifts in Economic Activity *140*
Productivity, Living Standards and Competitiveness *150*
Emerging Trade Realities *156*
Job Security in a Rapidly Changing World *162*
The World Economic Outlook *166*
Notes *171*

The Global Political Environment *172*
The United States *172*
Structural Problems *173*
Growing Inequality *173*
Declining Relative Wealth *174*
Increasing World Interdependence *174*
The Political Foundations *175*
Looking Forward *176*
Western Europe and the European Community *178*
Japan *181*
The Soviet Union and China *183*
The Less-Developed World *185*
Conclusions *188*
Notes *190*
Global Options *191*
The Future as a Continuation of Past and Present Experience *193*
The Future Marked by Discontinuity *195*
Canada's Stake in the Alternative Outlooks *196*
Notes *198*
Implications for Canadian Foreign Policy *199*
Notes *207*
Conclusions and Recommendations *208*

CHAPTER 2

Global Outlook

Introduction

Commissioners have remarked the new, more dynamic attitude of Canadians displayed in our extensive hearings. At a time when Canada was only beginning to emerge from the worst recession since the 1930s, the spirit of Canadians was positive. We believe, however, that Canadians still are less in tune with the world and their future, and more concerned with our nation's present domestic problems than circumstances warrant.

Canada is one of the industrial nations most vulnerable to global forces of all kinds. Exports account for some 30 per cent of Canada's national output, yet our country's competitive position at home and abroad is vulnerable because we lack assured access to a market of 100 million people or more. Through far-reaching links of trade, aid and diplomacy, however, we have become closely involved in what the late Marshall McLuhan aptly termed the "global village".

While it is not part of Commissioners' mandate to delve deeply into the nature of developments abroad, we cannot consider Canada's future prospects in isolation from those of the rest of the world. Earth's nations have become increasingly interdependent since 1945 so that developments abroad often have particularly wide-ranging implications for the way in which we Canadians conduct our affairs. Rather, we must therefore identify the underlying forces at work around the globe, and consider the consequences of events abroad and their implications for this country.

The public's perception of the world was dramatically altered, in the 1970s, by the pessimistic views of "global modellers" who argued that major supply shortages inevitably limit growth. The sectoral experts, using more traditional techniques, countered in rebuttal, however, with relatively optimistic forecasts of continuing growth, noting that changes would lead to substitutions and to reduced demand for goods in short supply.

Over time, the debate has broadened significantly, and it has been reinforced from other sources, such as the Interfutures project of the Organisation for Economic Co-operation and Development (OECD), the report *Japan in the Year 2000*, commissioned by the Japanese government, and Tinbergen's report, *Reshaping the International Order*, undertaken for the Club of Rome.[1] In addition, there are a number of schools of thought on these matters, ranging from the "long-wave" business-cycle theorists to those who stress the "politics of entitlements" as inhibiting the normal adaptability of capitalistic society.[2]

Canadians must become more aware of the global context and the choices that lie ahead. For these reasons, Commissioners decided that it was important to include in our Report a survey and analysis of the major trends evolving in the world, in order that Canadians might better assess for themselves, in this global context, the opportunities and problems which are of greatest concern.

We have not taken account of certain fundamental themes, such as the arms race and the prospects of a nuclear holocaust. Concerning such grim subjects, we would note two points only. First, the political theory of deterrence, on which global security has been based for the last 40 years, is being seriously questioned, and the transition, if there is to be one, to a new strategic policy will be critical to collective security and to continued human existence. Like other Commissions before us, we must assume that our civilization has a future. Secondly, the economic value of the defence industry is so large that it dwarfs any other single sectoral activity. The Palme Commission[3] has stated that in 1982, total military spending exceeded U.S. $650 billion. That sum represented the spending of more than one million dollars a minute.[4] The world must find ways of transferring this vast wealth to more humanitarian ends.

We have focused on five particular aspects of global developments:

- The human environment, where there is every indication that between 1980 and 2025, the world's population will virtually double, rising from 4.4 billion to 8.3 billion persons. A doubling of population has implications, both national and international, for the demand for food and other resources, for economic relationships, and for political stability. In sum, these implications are so far-reaching that they defy full understanding.
- The natural environment, where the world faces serious problems arising from grossly uneven distribution of resources and the consequent risk of shortages in food and other industrial commodities in certain areas. More fundamental perhaps, in the long term, is the fact that we are on the threshold of selective, irreversible, environmental damage.
- The knowledge environment, where the advances generated by science and technology are transforming our society and confronting humankind with the basic challenge of change.
- The economic environment, where the world faces the problems of achieving a steady, non-inflationary, high-employment, growth path. In the future, these problems will give way to the even more critical and more extensive challenges of solving the problems of inequality between rich and poor nations.

- The global political environment, which reveals a general tendency in the major countries and regions to become self-absorbed but leaves open the possibility of positive developments as signs appear that economic forces are gaining credibility in non-democratic and traditionally non-capitalist states.

All these developments affect the values which we Canadians have acquired, as well as the political environment and public and private institutions shaped by those values.

Against this background, this part of our Report examines two possible scenarios. The first supposes that all nations – rich and poor, developed, newly industrializing and developing – will work together in a reasonably rational fashion to ease major world problems in ways that will best serve their common interest. The second assumes that the existing world order is unable to cope with the changes required to resolve major problems. In fact, the future, as always, remains shrouded in mystery. While this circumstance must not deter Canadians from seeking to prepare for the unfolding of events in the months and years ahead, we should not blindly extrapolate from past trends to make judgements about the future.

In the final section of this chapter, Commissioners review the Canadian "internationalist" tradition embodied in our foreign policy and assess whether or not this is the time to refashion and reinvigorate Canada's role on the world stage, in full recognition of the changing roster of global issues and of the evolution of world power. In the face of the new set of challenges outlined in the following pages, there would appear to be a need for Canadians and their governments to work harder at understanding our global environment, to respond wisely and quickly as circumstances warrant, and to take a stronger leadership role in shaping the forces of our future.

Notes

1. See Interfutures, *Facing the Future: Mastering the Probable and Managing the Unpredictable* (Paris: OECD, 1979); Japan, Long-Term Outlook Committee, Economic Council, Economic Planning Agency of Japan, *Japan in the Year 2000* (Tokyo: The Japan Times, 1983); and Jan Tinbergen, *Reshaping the International Order: A Report to the Club of Rome* (New York: Dutton, 1976).
2. See A.R. Dobell and B.R. Kennedy, "Global Futures and Canadian Prospects: A Review of the Global Modelling Literature", in *Economic Growth: Prospects and Determinants*, vol. 22, prepared for the Royal Commission on the Economic Union and Development Prospects for Canada (Toronto: University of Toronto Press, 1985).
3. The Independent Commission on Disarmament and Security Issues was launched in Vienna in 1980, under the chairmanship of Olof Palme, former Prime Minister of Sweden. It was a unique group of international statesmen and leaders bridging East and West, North and South. In 1982, the Commission released its final report, *Common Security* (London: Pan Books).
4. Notes for remarks by Ivan Head, President, International Development Research Centre (IDRC), to the National Defence College, Kingston, September 10, 1984.

The Human Environment: The Population Explosion

For millions of years, the species *homo sapiens* lived in balance with the natural environment, tapping the resources of the planet only to an extent that assured survival and reproduction. The total numbers of the human species, like those of all other species, were controlled through natural forces of birth, death and occasional catastrophe. By contrast, the second half of the twentieth century stands out for its remarkable population growth. Consider that in A.D. 1, the world supported about 300 million people. More than 1500 years passed before its population doubled. Only in the eighteenth century did the number of births start greatly to outpace the toll of deaths: between 1750 and 1900, the earth's population rose steadily to 1.7 billion, that is, doubling again in one-tenth the time. From 1900 to 1950, the population-growth rate accelerated to a figure of 1 per cent a year. After 1950, the annual rate of growth increased once more to a remarkable 2 per cent. Over the short span of the past 30 years, as Figure 2-1 shows, world population has nearly doubled again, from 2.5 billion to 4.5 billion.

Until the mid-twentieth century, the rate of population growth was approximately the same in all regions of the world. By the 1970s, however, the number of births per woman (that is, the fertility rate) had fallen, in most developed countries, to a point near, or even below, the "replacement" level of fertility: the number of births per woman required to ensure that the parent generation is replaced. Europe currently has a sub-replacement fertility level, as have Eastern Europe and Canada. The Soviet Union's fertility rate stood at 2.3 in 1980; this very high rate reflects the influence of the Asian Soviet Republics.

By contrast, the post-Second World War experience of developing countries has been very different; it is, indeed, unprecedented. Fertility rates in those countries remained historically high, rather than declining as they did in the developed countries; moreover, life expectancy began to increase dramatically as a result of improvements in health conditions. In consequence of these two factors, the growth rate of developing-country populations began to soar, reaching an annual increase of 2.4 per cent in the 1960s. The current slow-down to 2 per cent annual growth simply reflects statistics that are heavily skewed by the experience of China, where birth-control programs have already reduced the average number of children per family to two. Moreover, since 1979, Chinese authorities have been enforcing an ambitious plan to limit offspring to one child per family, in order to prevent the present population figure of 1.04 billion from rising above 1.2 billion by 2000. In other developing countries, however, most families now have at least four or five children. In Africa and Central America, the rate of population growth is still rising.

Even when fertility drops to replacement level among women of child-bearing age, a country's population does not immediately cease to grow, since a younger generation has still to reach child-bearing age. The resulting growth is known as the "momentum effect". One-quarter of the population of the developing world is between the ages of five and fourteen. Consequently,

FIGURE 2-1 World Population, A.D. 1-2150

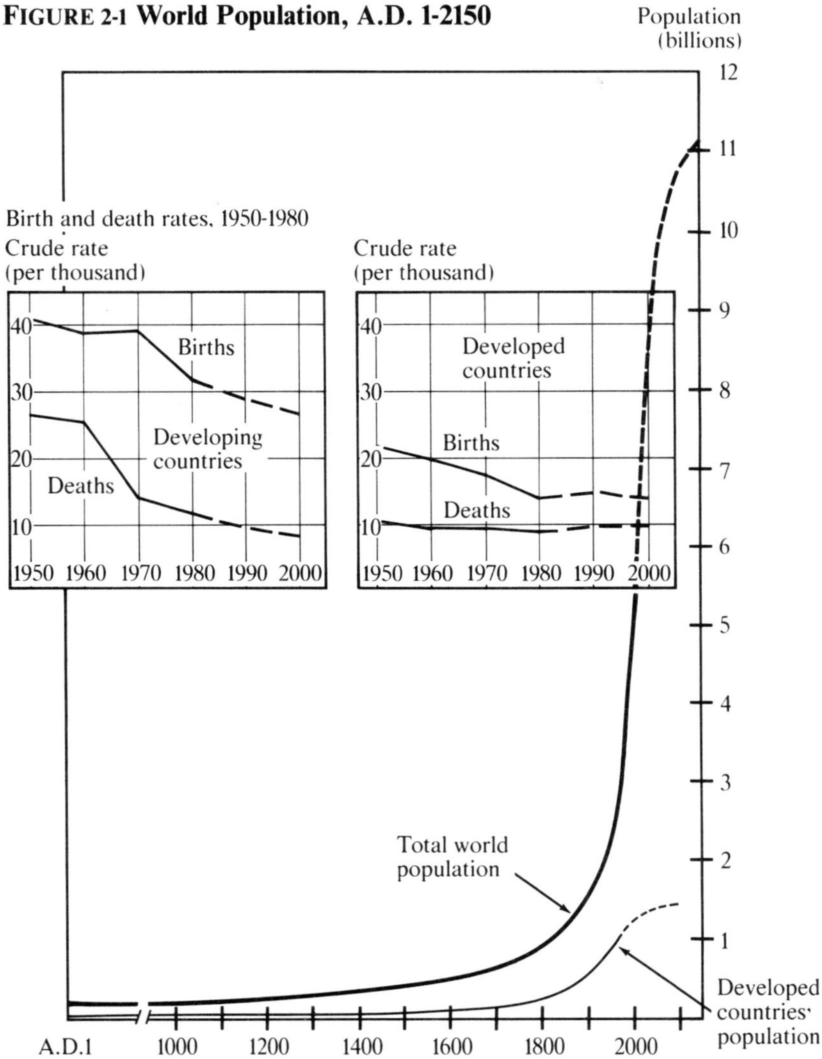

Source: The World Bank, *World Development Report 1984* (New York: Oxford University Press for The World Bank, 1984), p. 3.

population-growth rates will remain high for several decades, even in those developing countries which have achieved a slow-down in the fertility rate.

The population projected by the International Bank for Reconstruction and Development (World Bank) for various regions of the world, from 1980 to 2050, is presented in Table 2-1. Where fertility is still high, in Africa and parts of South Asia, for example, the World Bank assumes that the rate will start to decline before the end of this century and will continue to fall rapidly thereafter. These are bold assumptions. Their realization requires that the transition from current fertility rates to replacement-level rates, a process which took over 150 years in the United States, be completed within a dramatically shorter period in developing countries. Yet the societies expected to conform to these demanding requirements are largely, poor, rural and little-educated.

TABLE 2-1 Population Projections, 1980–2050

Selected Regions	1950	1980	2000	2025	2050	Total Fertility Rate 1984 (%)
	(population in millions)					
Africa	223	478	898	1 631	2 276	6.4
East/South-East Asia	587	1 533	1 968	2 415	2 600	2.6
South Asia	695	943	1 434	2 023	2 453	5.0
Latin America	165	356	535	731	854	4.0
Total for less-developed countries	1 670	3 297	4 882	6 939	8 398	4.0
Total for developed countries	834	1 138	1 263	1 358	1 380	2.0
Total world	2 504	4 435	6 145	8 297	9 778	3.5

Source: 1950: United Nations estimates. Other years: My T. Vu, *World Population Projections 1984: Short- and Long-Term Estimates by Age and Sex with Related Demographic Statistics* (Washington, D.C.: The World Bank, 1984).

Note: These data are not to be taken as predictions, but as projections of what could happen, given reasonable assumptions.

Despite the World Bank's possibly optimistic assumptions, the figures shown in Table 2-1 are sobering. In the year 2000, the global population will stand at an estimated 6.2 billion, an increase from 4.4 billion in 1980; by 2025, a date within the normal life span of Canadians now under 35 years of age, it is projected to be 8.3 billion, nearly double the 1980 level. The annual average increase in population expected to the end of this century is 87 million persons. Ninety-three per cent of this increase will occur in the world's six least-developed nations. The total population of all developing countries, standing at 3.3 billion in 1980, will rise to almost 5 billion by the turn of the century and will be 7 billion by 2025, more than doubling in those 45 years. Projections indicate that the developing world will account for 83.5 per cent of the world's population in 2025; its share was 74 per cent in 1980. Within the developing world, predictions indicate, 70 per cent of the population will be concentrated, by the turn of the century, in only eight countries: China, India, Indonesia, Brazil, Bangladesh, Pakistan, Nigeria and Mexico.

As if the divergence in population growth in the developing and developed worlds were not sufficiently marked, projections of the process of urbanization also have dramatic implications. The "Declaration on Population and

Development"[1] produced by the United Nations' International Population Conference, 1984, held in Mexico City, stated that 48 per cent of the developing world's population might live in cities by the year 2000, an increase of 35 per cent over the 1980 figure. Latin America and the Caribbean will be highly urbanized; in 1980, 65 per cent of their people already lived in cities, and that proportion will grow to 75 per cent by the turn of the century. In industrialized countries, urbanization is already advanced, with 77 per cent of the populations living in cities, but those cities will continue to grow, accounting for 84 per cent of the population totals by 2000. In 1950, six of the world's cities had a population of five million or more people. By 1980, that figure applied to 26 cities; by the year 2000, it is estimated, there will be approximately 60 cities (45 of them in the developing countries) with populations of over five million, and there will be 22 cities with over 10 million inhabitants. The United Nations projects that if historic trends continue, Mexico City will have 26 million residents by the year 2000 – the city's own estimate is 36 million – Calcutta will have 20 million, and Manila will have 13 million.[2] It goes without saying that rapid population growth and urbanization will put even more pressure than already exists today on sanitation facilities, water, food and medical supplies, shelter and employment opportunities. By 2000, less-developed countries (LDCs) may have to increase urban services by two-thirds just to maintain 1975 levels of service per capita.[3]

Difficult as urban conditions are and will continue to be, conditions are worse in rural areas of many parts of the world. The continuing deterioration of already-severe situations is increasing the rate of migration from the country to urban areas. In Africa, for instance, which has a population of more than 500 million people, the net result of this process was a steady drop in food production per person in the 1970s. In South Asia, there was zero growth in food production per capita.[4] High rates of population growth have also been a major factor in increasing the demand for firewood, the prime source of energy for the vast majority of inhabitants of the developing countries. This rising demand has led to widespread deforestation in the endless search for fuel, often followed by flood damage in regions downstream. In Tanzania, firewood has become so scarce that a member of each household spends 250 to 300 days per year simply gathering fuel wood.[5] The Food and Agriculture Organization of the United Nations (FAO) has predicted that by 2000, the countries of Latin America, tropical Africa and tropical Asia will all suffer an acute scarcity of fuel wood.

Over the past 30 years, many developing countries managed to raise average per capita income, even though their populations were growing rapidly.[6] No such progress was made in most countries of sub-Saharan Africa and South Asia. The aims of development, however, go beyond mere accommodation of more people, to further improvement in the quality of people's lives. Continuing, rapid, population growth is more than likely to impose a correspondingly low quality of life on millions of persons. Even if extraordinary campaigns are mounted to reduce the birth rate of developing countries where rapid population growth remains a problem, world population will rise to levels that will make it extremely difficult, if not impossible, for a large proportion of the world's people to achieve decent living standards. Moreover, for the foreseeable future, four-fifths of the world's output will continue to be produced and consumed by one-quarter of its population. Absolute disparities of income among countries are widening, not narrowing,[7] and an inhabitant of the developed world can still expect to live, on average, 16 years longer than a counterpart in the developing world.

While considerable controversy and prediction still surround the issues of population growth, there is a clear possibility that the further rapid increase projected may exceed human capacity to mobilize the resources required to meet and sustain humanity's future needs. Already, some 500 million people are seriously undernourished.

The United Nations' "Declaration on Population and Development" was supported by developing and developed countries alike. It stated that active policies and political commitment to reduce population growth are essential if the nations of the world are to avoid permanently foreclosing certain options for long-term development. It also underscored the need for government leadership in individual countries, as well as the necessity for international co-operation. Progress, however, will depend on the availability of large financial resources. Foreign aid now supports about 25 per cent of all family-planning costs in developing countries. The World Bank has estimated that $7.6 billion (in 1980 dollars) must be spent if the developing world is to achieve a rapid decline in fertility rates by 2000. This amount represents four times the money spent on population-control programs in 1980.[8]

Because Canadians face no problem of overpopulation, and because we enjoy a country where "wide open spaces" are legendary, it is sometimes difficult to comprehend the world-population problem. Canadian population projections conform to those of the developed world. At the peak of the post-war "baby boom", in 1959, the number of births per Canadian woman, or Canada's fertility rate, was 3.9 per cent. Astonishingly, by 1971, the fertility rate had fallen to replacement level, at 2.1 per cent, and by 1978, it had fallen further to 1.7 per cent, where it remains today. Even if the current sub-replacement fertility rate persists, however, the Canadian population will continue to grow, at least to the year 2000, because of population-growth momentum; by the turn of the century, Canadians will number about 26.5 million. Subsequently, the population could begin to decline, assuming sub-replacement fertility rates and zero net increase in immigration.[9] Another study, which assumed a medium fertility rate, a medium rate of mortality and medium net immigration, predicted that Canadian population figures would reach 32 million in 2006.[10]

If, however, as Commissioners believe, the global outlook is dominated by the massive projected growth of the world's population, how is Canada to respond to the population explosion in the developing world? If we set aside the perennial questions of aid and of support for birth-control programs, how will Canadians react to the pressures to accommodate a growing number of immigrants and political refugees from these over-populated countries? And since population influences world trade and development, how will the developed countries generally, and Canada, in particular, respond to the call to increase trade with less-developed countries? What will be the long-term reaction to the huge pool of inexpensive labour available in those countries? What greater pressures will be placed on Canadian resources of all kinds? Have we Canadians a moral responsibility to preserve our land and to adapt our agricultural output to meet the needs of the world at large? Is it realistic to expect Canada to increase enormously its food production?

Although there are no easy answers to these questions, Commissioners seek to provide some responses throughout this Report. It is certain, however, that the period of transition to a more stable world population will pose complex and difficult problems. Nevertheless, Commissioners believe that as a basic principle, Canadians should recognize a moral imperative to produce some constructive responses to the challenge, through active participation in international bodies which focus on population- and development-related activities. The fate of the developing countries is very much our concern and should evoke our compassion. Population issues should be a priority for all developed countries. By advocating their importance, Canada can make a significant contribution to human well-being.

Notes

1. United Nations, Department of Technical Co-operation for Development, *Report of the International Conference on Population*, 1984 (New York: United Nations, 1984), pp. 2–5.
2. See United Nations, *Report of the International Conference on Population.*
3. See United States, Council on Environmental Quality and the Department of State, *The Global 2000 Report to the President: Entering the Twenty-First Century* (Washington, D.C.: U.S. Government Printing Office, 1980), vol. 1, p. 12.
4. See Robert S. McNamara, "Time Bomb or Myth: The Population Problem", *Foreign Affairs* (Summer, 1984): 1107–31.
5. *Ibid.*, p. 1118.
6. *World Development Report 1984* (New York: Oxford University Press for The World Bank, 1984), p. 7.
7. *Ibid.*, pp. 6, 100.
8. *Ibid.*, p. 180.
9. See Statistics Canada, *Current Demographic Analysis: Fertility in Canada: From Baby-boom to Baby-bust*, by A. Romaniuc (Ottawa: Minister of Supply and Services Canada, 1984).
10. See Frank T. Denton, Christine H. Feaver, and Byron G. Spencer, *The Future Population and Labour Force of Canada: Projections to the Year 2001*, a study prepared for the Economic Council of Canada (Ottawa: Minister of Supply and Services Canada, 1980).

The Global Natural Environment: Under Stress

Food and Agriculture

Since the end of the Second World War, agricultural productivity in the developed countries of the world has risen to levels that would have seemed unbelievable a century earlier. For many countries and many products, the problem has been to prevent production from outstripping demand. Not all countries and people, however, have shared in the benefits from these impressive gains. Only one-third of the population of developing countries (excluding China) lives in lands which produce enough food to supply their people. In some countries, food production has increased at roughly the same pace as population; tragically, in others, the rate of population growth has far outstripped the increase of food supply.[1] Furthermore, the positive agricultural trade balances of some developing countries have been whittled down as their imports have increased much more rapidly than their exports. These developments have occurred in spite of the "Green Revolution" of the early 1970s, which was achieved through adoption of new high-yield crop varieties in such countries as India, Mexico, the Philippines, Pakistan and Turkey. Thus recent decades present a mixed picture in agriculture and food production: impressive gains have been made globally, but most of the benefits have accrued in countries already enjoying some advantage.

Africa provides the most striking example of the inadequacy of local food production; television has brought the stark reality of this human tragedy into Canadian livingrooms. While one cause of famine lies in substantial increases in demand for food as a result of rapid population growth, there also exist a number of factors, both natural and human, which limit the supply of foodstuffs. These factors include persistent drought; deterioration of the soil and the return to desert of once-arable land, through overuse and poor husbandry; the movement of populations from rural to urban areas; depressed agricultural prices as a result, for example, of government-imposed controls; and severe financial and organizational constraints on the adoption of technologies that would enable increased agricultural productivity.

The fundamental problem in feeding the world's population is not one of inadequate capacity for production, but of unequal distribution of that capacity in relation to population. No absolute food shortage on a global basis exists now or will exist in the foreseeable future. Current global grain production is more than enough to provide every man, woman and child in the world with a life-sustaining 3000 calories and 65 grams of protein per day. Nevertheless, it is also all-too-grimly evident that massive starvation is a fact of world society. The distributional problem means that a future increase in total food output will not, of itself, directly reduce the incidence of starvation. Among those who have studied the issue, there is widespread consensus that a comprehensive strategy for the development of poorer countries is required. Such a strategy would include measures, such as agricultural research and development (R&D), to promote the developing countries' ability to provide their own food.

The Food and Agriculture Organization of the United Nations (FAO) has recently forecast the world's food situation to the year 2000, on the assumption that present trends in technological improvements and population growth will continue.[2] The projection shows that world demand for food could increase by 50 per cent over the next 20 years and more than double again by 2050. The chief cause of the problem raised by this forecast is not the average annual growth in demand for food, but rather that by far the largest additional requirements will occur in poor countries whose combined population is projected to reach seven billion persons in 2025. Continuation of recent trends in demand and supply would, in fact, bring about a slight increase in average food production per capita for the developing countries as a whole. In some of the poorest countries, however, per capita food consumption will, at best, remain unchanged. No fewer than 34 countries, accounting for half the population of the 90 developing countries studied by the FAO, will suffer from inadequate per capita calorie supplies at the turn of the century.

Figure 2-2 shows that the number of the world's seriously undernourished people stood at some 434 million in the mid-1970s. The FAO expects the number to rise to 510 million by 1990 and increase further to 590 million by the year 2000. These data represent the daily physical deprivation of fellow human beings in numbers already 20 times the population of Canada. The FAO projection means that by the end of this century, at best, one person in six in the developing world, excluding China, will be forced to exist on a diet too poor to support a normal life. The countries of South Asia and Africa will remain the most adversely affected. Even for the much better-fed populations of Latin America and the Near East, there will be a considerable increase in the absolute number of seriously undernourished people. There is no doubt that the number suffering will be much higher if countries are unable to afford to import food.

Indeed, for the world as a whole, none of the basic resources required to expand food production – land, water, energy, fertilizer – can now be considered abundant or inexpensive. In developing countries, the agricultural concern requiring the greatest international efforts is the serious degeneration of very significant portions of arable land. Population pressures have caused grave over-exploitation of soils. Irrigation, overgrazing and denudation of huge forest areas to obtain a supply of wood for fuel and to clear land for farming have further reduced the soil's capacity to produce. The International Institute for Applied Systems Analysis (IIASA) and the FAO have conducted a joint study to estimate future food production in 117 developing countries. Findings showed that even if these countries utilize their current level of farming technology and all their arable land, 50 per cent of them lack the land resources they will require to meet their people's food needs in 2000.[3] It is estimated that 85 per cent of projected production increases will be conditional on increased productivity, and only 15 per cent will result from expansion of the cultivated land base.

The problem, therefore, cannot be solved through continuous expansion of agricultural land. The increase in food production needed in the developing world over the next decades will require political will, social and institutional changes, large investments and extended research and education. India provides an example: although it made great strides in agricultural output in

FIGURE 2-2 Undernourishment in the World

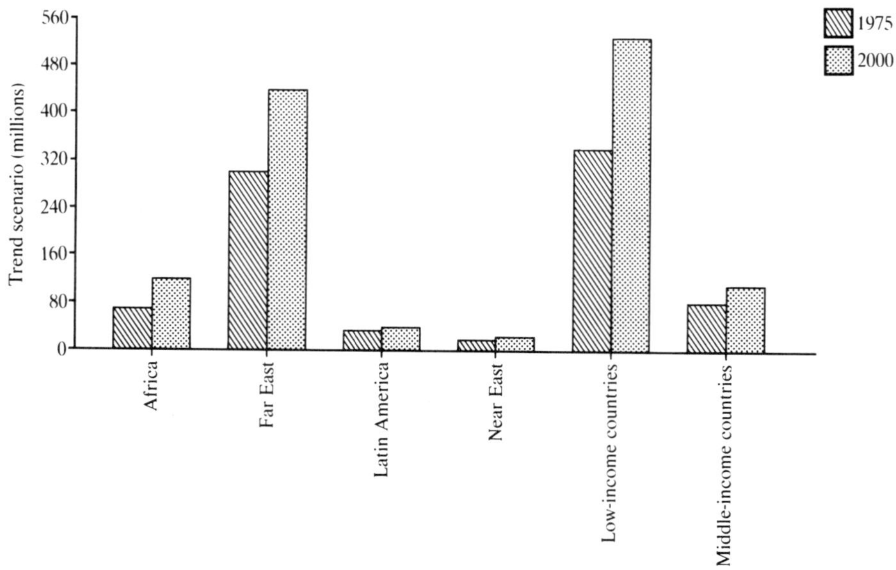

Source: Food and Agriculture Organization of the United Nations, *Agriculture: Toward 2000* (Rome: FAO, 1981), p. 21.

the late 1960s, it has been unable to co-ordinate the resources, policies and programs essential to continue its rapid development.

China, beyond doubt, offers a remarkable example of policy planning in agriculture. That nation, with 7 per cent of the world's farmland, feeds nearly one-quarter of the world's population. Its productivity growth has been particularly impressive since the late 1970s and has more than kept up with its population growth. There are, however, obvious physical constraints on further increases.[4]

Clearly, in the final quarter of this century, the global food economy is being radically transformed. Two developments are highly visible: first, fewer countries are now able to produce a comfortable margin of excess food; secondly, the world is depending more and more on North America, particularly the United States, for its supplies of cereals. Together, these two developments create new roles and responsibilities for Canada and the United States. Canada has not sought this responsibility any more than the Middle Eastern nations have planned their abundance of oil, but Canadians must reckon with it, nonetheless.

An estimate of world agricultural trade flows likely to occur in the year 2000, compared with those that did occur between 1978 and 1980, was prepared for the U.S. Department of Agriculture by the Resources for the Future Group; their projection is summarized in Table 2-2 and Figure 2-3. Both the table and the figure make it clear that for cereals and oil-seeds, the most important commodity group, North America will be by far the largest source of surplus supply. In fact, even by the end of the 1970s, those countries that remained significant grain exporters could be counted on the fingers of one hand; this represented a dramatic change that has occurred since the Second World War. Those few countries exporting grain today – and Canada stands high on that list – dominate world trade in grain.

Table 2-2 clearly shows the extent of the projected increases in imports of grains and oil-seeds – in line with FAO projections – in Africa, Asia, the Middle East and Eastern Europe, even though domestic production in those countries will have increased substantially as a result, primarily, of increased crop yields. These projections are complicated by the fact that the sub-Saharan African countries and some South Asian countries are unlikely to acquire enough foreign-exchange earnings to pay for major food imports, as has been tragically evident in the past few years. Grain imports by the Soviet Union are projected to stabilize at about 30 million tonnes annually.[5]

The world's fisheries constitute a major source of protein for the most heavily populated areas of the globe. Many estimates indicate that the world can expect only modest gains in yield from traditional fisheries; these sources could only increase total yield to 90 or 100 million tonnes per annum from the

TABLE 2-2 Estimates of World Trade in Major Commodities

(in millions of tonnes)

Region	Meat 1978–80	Meat 2000	Milk Products 1978–80	Milk Products 2000	Cereals 1978–80	Cereals 2000	Oil-seeds 1978–80	Oil-seeds 2000
North Africa/ Middle East	–0.7	–3.9	–6.3	–12.9	–24.1	–46.5	–1.4	–5.4
Sub-Saharan Africa	0	–0.1	–0.7	–1.3	–4.4	–29.3	2.2	–5.4
European Community	–0.4	1.0	8.0	14.8	–1.2	20.0	–30.4	–39.3
Other Western Europe	–0.2	–0.2	1.0	1.0	–9.7	–8.3	–5.1	–7.4
U.S.S.R.	–0.5	–0.5	–3.0	–2.0	–24.6	–29.8	0	1.1
Eastern Europe	0.6	1.0	–0.1	–0.1	–14.2	–19.7	–6.9	–8.2
South Asia	0	0	–0.5	–0.5	2.1	–13.8	2.7	2.1
East Asia	–0.8	–1.2	–1.7	–2.6	–29.8	–53.1	–5.9	–16.6
CPEs[a] of Asia	0.2	0.4	–0.2	–0.6	–15.0	–31.6	–1.1	1.8
Oceania	1.6	5.0	5.9	9.3	14.0	25.3	0.1	–1.2
Latin America	0.5	–1.6	–2.1	–3.9	–5.8	–9.8	15.2	19.7
North America	0	0.1	–1.1	–1.1	122.9	196.6	34.2	54.4

Source: Kenneth R. Farrell, Fred H. Sanderson, Trang T. Vo, and Michael F. Brewer, "Meeting Future Needs for United States Food, Fiber, and Forest Products", in Joint Council on Food and Agricultural Sciences, *Reference Document: Needs Assessment for Food and Agricultural Sciences* (Washington, D.C., 1984), p. 41.

Note: The symbol – stands for imports. Positive totals indicate exports.

a. Centrally planned economies: European and non-European Comecon countries, China, North Korea, Kampuchea, Yugoslavia, Albania.

FIGURE 2-3 Production and Consumption of Cereals in Specific Regions, 1978-1980 and Projected for 2000

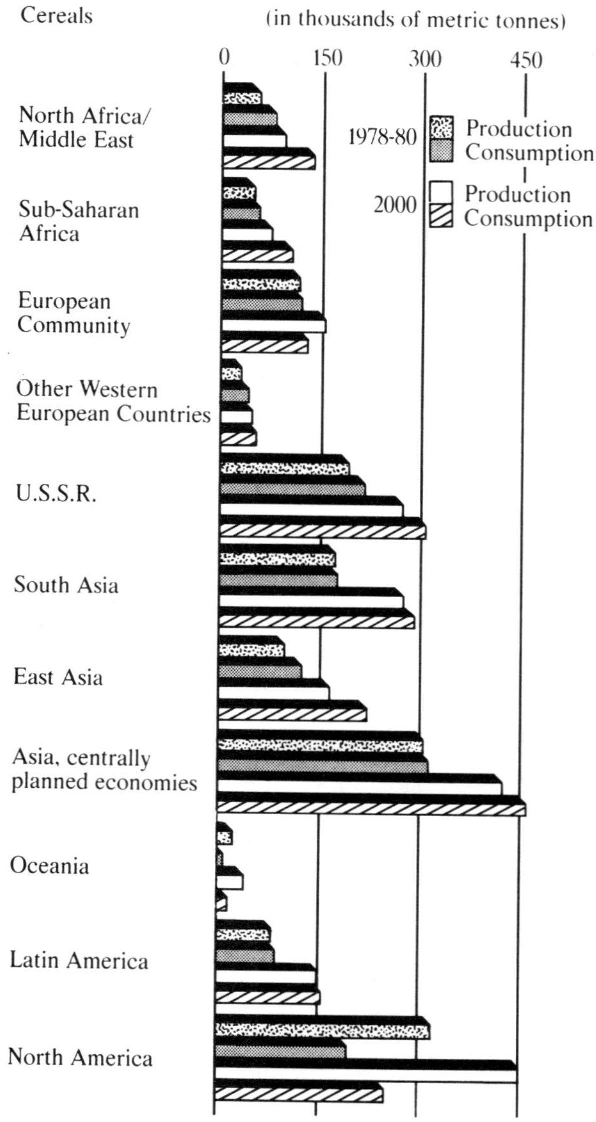

Source: "Feeding a Hungry World", *Resources* (Spring 1984), p. 9. Based on a report to the U.S. Department of Agriculture by Kenneth R. Farrell, Fred H. Sanderson and Trang T. Vo of Resources for the Future. (Study cites U.N. Food and Agriculture Organization for historic data.)

current 70 million tonnes, even if they tapped new species of fish and curbed waste. In face of these expectations, by the year 2000, demand for fish is projected to triple in developing countries[6] and to reach a total world figure of between 114 and 125 million tonnes. Although both sea-water and freshwater aquaculture might do much to meet regional shortfalls, additional efforts will have to be made if increases in harvest from a "Blue Revolution" are to be used by low-income countries.

On a more promising note, improved agricultural techniques have continued to defy predictions that population would exceed the world's ability to produce adequate food supplies. Recent developments in biotechnology raise the possibility of further dramatic increases in food production. We Commissioners were informed during our hearings that:

> *There is little doubt that the Biotechnical Revolution is in its infancy and that biotechnical industries will rapidly emerge as cornerstones of the economies of modern nations in the latter part of this century. Food production is a mainstay of our current economy and the provision of food to the poorer nations will surely remain as a major challenge for mankind for many decades. It is virtually inevitable that food will be synthesized in large-scale biotechnical plants and that the relative importance of conventional farming of the land will diminish. The implications for Canada are profound. Clearly we must establish a leadership position in all aspects of biotechnology and in all regions of Canada.* Len Bruton, Brief, September 2, 1983, p. 3.)

Evolution to high-technology agriculture will not take place overnight, however, and cannot be expected to solve the problems of very tenuous food balances or shortages in some countries that will escalate over the next few decades.

In light of the deteriorating world-food situation, what are the adjustments to be made in Canadian trade-and-aid policy and in Canadian agriculture? Clearly, the growth in demand for Canadian agricultural products will derive, primarily, from expansion of foreign demand. The food situation in the developing world suggests a moral imperative, as well as an economic opportunity, for Canadians to make further efforts both to increase the efficiency of our food-production system and to preserve our land base, conserve our soil, and divert some of our production capabilities to growing crops, such as high-yield, semi-dwarf wheats of the "Triple-M" type, suitable for export to those countries with huge import requirements. To make such a commitment to a global food strategy would require government participation and a change in the incentives offered our agricultural sector to participate in this reorientation. Moreover, important as these modifications in our food-production policies must undoubtedly be, there is no sense in Canadian farmers and fishers producing a surplus of foodstuffs if these cannot be distributed to needy nations, and if financial mechanisms are not in place to support a global co-operative effort to feed the world's disadvantaged people. To these ends, support for significant reform of international institutions involved in food distribution and the financing of projects that will promote the greater self-sufficiency of developing nations should be a priority for Canada. Clearly, however, no matter what radical changes we may make in our agricultural policy, Canada alone cannot solve the world's nutrition problems; the onus remains on the developing countries to make the required internal changes of a social, political and institutional character. In the end, the levels of world hunger can only be reduced on a sustained basis by raising economic growth, lowering the rate of population increase and reducing income inequalities.

Energy

World production of crude oil and natural gas multiplied five-fold between 1950 and 1973, and throughout the 1970s these hydrocarbons accounted for nearly 70 per cent of world commercial energy use. In 1980, the world's available oil reserves were judged to amount to approximately 640 billion barrels. To put these numbers into some perspective, Exxon has estimated that current reserves of oil will last 30 years; British Petroleum's estimate is 40 years. Estimates of ultimately recoverable resources have tended to settle on the figure of 2000 billion barrels, or approximately three times known reserves.

In its brief to this Commission, Shell Canada Limited noted that in spite of the dramatically higher oil prices of the past decade, global reserves over that period increased by less than 10 per cent, as compared with the doubling of oil reserves in the previous decade.[7] Shell concluded that the world supply of crude oil will not increase substantially until the 1990s. Exxon has also estimated that exploration during the years before 2000 will yield from 8 to 15 billion barrels annually, a decrease from the approximately 28 billion barrels discovered annually before 1970.[8] This means that the rate of oil discoveries would fail to match the rate of current production, thus reducing known reserves.

In 1982, the International Energy Agency (IEA) predicted that to the year 2000, oil production will rise only slightly in all producing countries. Oil output in North America, the North Sea and the Soviet Union is projected to level off or decline after the mid-1980s. According to the IEA, the Organization of Petroleum Exporting Countries' (OPEC) production could well be constrained by declining reserves in some countries and political decisions in others. Supply and demand figures and projections are shown in Table 2-3. During the 1960s, world consumption of oil expanded at an annual average rate of 6.0 per cent, whereas for the 1970s, because of OPEC increases in oil prices, the rate of expansion was only 3.1 per cent. During the remainder of this century and into the next, the rate of consumption is expected, again, to rise more slowly. Generally speaking, the more recent the projections, the lower the anticipated growth rates.

The IEA has predicted that there will be little if any, increase in demand for oil in countries belonging to the Organisation for Economic Co-operation and Development (OECD) to the year 2000. (See Table 2-3.) For the most part, this stability of demand is the result of the move to energy-saving equipment, insulation and other means of conservation, which began with the first "oil shock" in 1973 and now has developed a momentum of its own. On the other hand, IEA has predicted that demand for oil from the less-developed countries (LDCs) and from OPEC countries themselves will more than double by 2000 as a result of urbanization, economic development and industrialization. By 1990, this growth, combined with the minimal projected increase in

TABLE 2-3 World Oil Demand and Supply Projections

	(million barrels per day)			
	1980	**1985**	**1990**	**2000**
World demand				
OECD	38.7	35-36	34-37	33-43
OPEC	2.9	4	5-6	8-9
Non-OPEC LDCs	7.9	9-10	11-13	17-22
Total	49.5	48-50	50-56	58-74
World supply				
OECD[a]	14.8	15	14-13	15-13
OPEC	27.5	23-26	27-29	24-28
Non-OPEC LDCs	5.3	8-9	8-11	9-13
CPE[b] Net Exports (Imports)	1.3	1-(1)	0-(2)	0-(2)
Total	49.5	48-50	50-52	49-53
Excess demand	0	0	0-4	9-21

Source: International Energy Agency, *World Energy Outlook* (Paris: OECD, 1982), pp. 14, 23, 24.

Note: Where a range of figures is shown, these represent high/low-demand situations hypothesized by the IEA.

a. Includes Synfuels.

b. Centrally planned economies.

production, could cause world demand for oil to outrun supply. The resulting shortage would worsen to the year 2000. Submissions to this Commission generally support this view of the global situation.

The outlook for the international price of crude oil is highly uncertain, although the IEA suggests that if shortages become more serious in the 1990s, substantial price pressures will build up once more. Certainly, nothing is forever in the oil business, whether shortages or gluts, and the projections that do exist often do not accord enough weight to political forces. The twin oil shortfalls of the 1970s reflected politics, not geology, and a major political disruption – a revolution in a major producing country, for example – could tip the balance once again toward OPEC and higher prices. The difference now, however, is that the solidarity of the OPEC cartel has been weakened, primarily on account of shut-in capacity (that is, capability to provide more oil than demand warrants), and because non-members of OPEC have considerably increased their production of oil, and OPEC's customers have embraced energy efficiency.

Analyses made by the oil companies suggest that the real price of world crude oil will remain stable or will rise only slightly in the short term, barring any major escalation in Middle East conflict. After 1990, however, the world-wide scarcity of crude oil, coupled with the greater expense of developing new oil sources, will translate into higher real oil prices in the international market. Thus, real crude oil prices might rise between 2 and 4 per cent per annum after 1990; the lower rate would reflect slow economic growth.

Because prices for fossil fuels have risen relative to other commodities, and because supply disruptions are a constant possibility, countries importing oil will increasingly diversify their energy-supply sources and will find investment in renewable energy sources relatively more attractive. No one can predict exactly when the world's very heavy reliance on fossil fuels will be significantly altered, but there are signs that the beginning of the end of the age of oil is already in sight. Exxon has forecast that the proportion of oil in the energy mix of the non-communist world will fall from the present 46 per cent to 41 per cent by the year 2000.[9] The share of natural gas in the energy market of the non-communist world will also drop slightly. Nevertheless, as Table 2-4 shows, oil and gas will remain the major sources of energy for quite some time to come.

The production of coal and nuclear power, along with synthetic fuels such as oil extracted from the tar sands, is expected to increase rapidly after the turn of the century and to provide the major growth in energy sources until the year 2030. With the global decline in the use of oil since the 1970s, the use of coal began to increase because of its relative abundance and low cost. The coal share, after falling from 63 per cent of world commercial energy use in 1950 to 31 per cent in 1978, is now increasing. Nuclear power's overall contribution to the world's energy sources reached just 3 per cent in 1980. Although this figure may seem negligible, the International Energy Agency has forecast that nuclear power will account for 10 to 11 per cent of global energy use by 2000, primarily in the developed world. Exxon predicts a similar rise in the use of nuclear power in the non-communist world, but believes that nuclear energy will not be used as widely as it could be, because of widespread concern about its safety, particularly in the United States.[10]

TABLE 2-4 Energy Mix, 1984 and Projections for 2000

(non-communist world)

Energy Sources	% **Share of Energy Use 1984**	% **Share of Energy Use 2000**
Solar/Other	2	2
Hydro	8	9
Nuclear	5	8
Coal	20	21
Gas	19	18
Conventional oil	46	41
Synthetic oil	< 0.5	1
	100	100

Source: Information supplied to this Commission by Imperial Oil Limited and Exxon Corporation.

Advances in solar power, wind power, biomass, photovoltaics and other more traditional sources of electricity, may prove more attractive to some countries. There will be significant expansion of alternative energy sources to the year 2000, but their overall share of the world energy mix will remain insignificant, amounting, perhaps, to 2 per cent of energy use in the non-communist world.

The lesson to be learned in the energy field from the 1970s and early 1980s is that the price mechanism does work. Although Canada, and indeed the world, experienced considerable social, political and institutional strains, extensive adjustments took place. The designers of policies for the future would do well to build on this lesson.

Oil and gas will remain the major sources of energy in Canada until well into the next century. However, the major change expected before the year 2005 is a decline in the relative importance of oil and an increase in that of natural gas and primary electricity; this last form of energy will derive particularly from hydro and nuclear sources, although the use of coal-fired electricity is expected to expand as well. The National Energy Board has predicted that total Canadian primary-energy demand met by oil will fall from 32 per cent to 21 per cent, while the energy demand met by natural gas will rise from 18 per cent to 21 per cent and that met by hydro, from 28 to 31 per cent.[11]

For Canada, the significance of the world-energy outlook appears to be mixed. Canadians can take some comfort in the prospect of being able to maintain a reasonable degree of energy security for several years to come: indeed, our oil and gas industry is well situated to contribute to our economic development for a good part of the next century, particularly if rising prices make the exploitation of higher-cost reserves commercially practical. In an increasingly interdependent world, however, we must be concerned about the adverse consequences that could follow if by 1990, as the IEA suggests could happen, world demand for oil begins to outrun supply. This eventuality could create further disruptive price or supply shocks which could affect the prosperity of our major trading partners and, thus, the overall prospects for economic growth.

Industrial Raw Materials

Minerals

On a global basis, serious depletion is an unlikely possibility for most minerals, at least until well into the twenty-first century. If sea-bed deposits are taken into account, estimates of available global resources of such minerals as cobalt, nickel, molybdenum, vanadium and manganese are more than doubled. More important than the actual physical supplies, however, are circumstances that will determine the economic and political feasibility of mineral recovery in the years ahead. These include such varied factors as: the geographical distribution of reserves; the costs of extraction, including demands on energy and effects on the environment; the adequacy of returns to mining companies, which could be reduced by any periodic return to high real rates of interest; nationalization of mining operations; the political climate; and the critical item of prices. These elements establish the practical limits of supply.

Many of the countries that possess significant mineral reserves are not the major consumers. Since the beginning of the industrial revolution, the developed countries have been the predominant consumers of mineral resources. The developing countries, despite the fast growth in some of the newly industrializing countries (NICs), still account for less than 12 per cent of the market for the most-traded minerals.

The industrialized countries are considerably more concerned at present about maintaining assured access, on reasonable terms, to available raw materials than about the possibility of future global shortages of certain physical resources. Not only Western Europe and Japan, but most of the East European countries, as well, and about 70 per cent of all developing countries have very limited reserves of minerals. In the last century, Japan and Europe became net importers of minerals, as did the United States in the 1930s. The United Kingdom is totally dependent on imports for 22 of 27 minerals important to its economy; the European Community (EC) for 13; Japan for 14; and the United States for two.[12] The uneven distribution of global resources creates a potential threat to the consuming nations' security of supply, a security which could be disrupted by the imposition of politically motivated sanctions or by obstacles to the resources delivery. Strategic decisions have prompted the United States and other countries to search for new alloys to replace metals imported from politically sensitive countries. In the United States, for instance, nickel, aluminum and titanium are being combined in new ways to replace cobalt, tantalum and columbium.

In 1977, the OECD calculated, approximately as follows, the distribution pattern of reserves (that is, known economically recoverable resources) for the 20 most important minerals:

- Forty-four per cent of reserves were held by the Western industrialized countries, that is, members of the OECD plus South Africa; 23 per cent were held by Eastern countries and 33 per cent by the developing countries.
- Almost 90 per cent of the reserves held by the Western industrialized countries were located in the United States, Canada, Australia and South Africa.
- In the developing countries, too, many of the reserves were held by a few countries, such as Brazil, Mexico, Indonesia, Zaire and Peru.
- Russia possessed more than 80 per cent of the discovered reserves of the centrally-planned economies, but this proportion was subject to change, since exploration in China was still in its earliest stages.[13]

More recent figures show that 75 per cent of the reserves of each of 16 important minerals is held by a group of only five countries (as illustrated in Table 2-5), a group that varies from mineral to mineral. In no instance do the top five countries hold less than 60 per cent of world reserves of the 25 minerals cited in Table 2-5. Canada figures prominently among the top five reserve holders in 15 mineral groups.[14]

TABLE 2-5 World Mineral Reserves: Percentage Shares of Important Minerals Held by the Top Countries

(1981 estimates)

Mineral	Country or Area	Per Cent Share	Mineral	Country or Area	Per Cent Share
Asbestos	Canada	35.6	Gypsum	U.S.A.	14.9
	CPEs[a]	26.9		Canada	10.3
	South Africa	21.2		France	8.6
	Other MEs[b]	12.5		U.S.S.R.	8.3
	U.S.A.	3.8		Spain	7.8
Bismuth	Australia	18.9	Ilmenite	Canada	25.2
	Canada	15.8		Norway	21.2
	Bolivia	14.4		India	20.2
	Japan	13.5		South Africa	15.1
	U.S.A.	9.9		Australia	7.2
Chromium	South Africa	67.6	Iron Ore[d]	U.S.S.R.	28.7
	Zimbabwe	29.7		Brazil	20.0
	Finland	0.8		Australia	10.9
	CPEs	0.6		Canada	8.5
	Turkey	0.1		India	5.7
				U.S.A.	5.4
Cobalt	Zaire	38.2			
	CPEs	13.2	Lead	U.S.A.	26.7
	Zambia	11.8		CPEs	16.4
	U.S.A.	10.3		Australia	13.9
	Philippines	5.9		Canada	13.3
				Yugoslavia	3.6
Columbium[c]	Brazil	93.4			
	Canada	3.5	Manganese	U.S.S.R.	44.4
	Nigeria	1.8		South Africa	40.7
	Zaire	0.9		Australia	6.1
				Gabon	2.9
Copper	Chile	19.2		Brazil	1.6
	U.S.A.	17.8			
	U.S.S.R.	7.1	Mercury	Spain	32.7
	Zambia	6.7		U.S.S.R.	11.3
	Canada	6.3		Algeria	7.9
	Peru	6.3		U.S.A.	6.8
	Zaire	5.9		Mexico	5.6
Gold	South Africa	58.3	Molybdenum	U.S.A.	54.4
	Other MEs	17.5		Chile	24.9
	CPEs	15.8		CPEs	9.2
	U.S.A.	5.8		Canada	6.6
	Canada	2.5		Peru	2.3
Nickel	New Caledonia	25.1	Tin	Indonesia	15.5
	Canada	14.4		China	15.0
	Cuba	5.7		Malaysia	12.0
	Other MEs	36.8		Thailand	12.0
	Other CPEs	13.5		U.S.S.R.	10.0
				Bolivia	9.8

TABLE 2-5 (cont'd.)

(1981 estimates)					
Mineral	**Country or Area**	**Per Cent Share**	**Mineral**	**Country or Area**	**Per Cent Share**
Platinum	South Africa	81.2			
Group[e]	U.S.S.R.	16.7	Tungsten	China	46.9
	U.S.A.	1.4		Canada	14.8
	Canada	0.8		U.S.A.	8.6
				U.S.S.R.	7.3
Potash	Canada	68.7		Australia	3.8
	CPEs	24.8			
	West Germany	2.6	Vanadium	South Africa	42.2
	Israel-Jordan[f]	1.5		U.S.S.R.	39.2
	U.S.A.	1.5		China	12.7
				Australia	0.2
Silver	CPEs	23.7		Finland	0.07
	U.S.A.	21.6		U.S.A.	0.07
	Canada	19.0			
	Mexico	12.6	Zinc	Canada	26.8
	Peru	7.2		U.S.A.	20.0
				Australia	10.0
Sulphur	Canada	11.0		Peru	2.9
(elemental)	U.S.A.	7.7		Mexico	1.3
	Mexico	4.0			
	West Germany	1.3	Zirconium	Australia	29.2
	Spain	1.3		South Africa	25.0
				U.S.A.	16.7
Tantalum	Thailand	33.3		India	6.3
	Australia	20.8		CPEs	12.5
	Nigeria	14.6			
	Canada	8.3			
	Zaire	8.3			

Source: U.S. Bureau of Mines, *Commodity Summaries* (Washington, D.C.: U.S. Department of the Interior, 1982). Adapted from Patrick J. Caragata, *National Resources and International Bargaining Power: Canada's Mineral Policy Options* (Kingston: Queen's University, Centre for Resource Studies, 1984), p. 136.

Note: Reserves are known, economically recoverable resources.

a. CPEs = centrally planned economies.

b. MEs = market economies.

c. Total excludes centrally planned economies.

d. Recoverable iron.

e. Statistics for other market economies are unavailable.

f. Includes Dead Sea reserves.

The initiation of sea-bed mining on a major scale could radically alter the mineral dependency of the world's nations. According to a number of estimates, the United States, Japan and Western Europe could become almost self-sufficient in minerals if sea-bed mining were to proceed on a major scale. In the meantime, however, financial and political realities present substantial barriers to the development of these resources. Not the least of these barriers is the view that the sea-bed is common property of all nations, and that there exists an obligation to recognize the developing world's problems and interests through a fund derived from the exploitation of sea-bed resources.

Two particular concerns exist in the matter of assured access to supplies of minerals on reasonable terms. These relate to the dominant role played by a relatively few multi-national companies and the extent of nationalization of private companies that has taken place within developing countries. Misgivings concerning the commanding position occupied by multi-national companies operating in the mineral sector is engendered by their potential to limit competition.

Between 1960 and 1976, 80 mining enterprises were nationalized in the developing world, although to a lesser extent than other sectors, such as banking and petroleum. The nationalization of these sectors explains, in part, the reason that in the 1970s, over 80 per cent of the funds for new exploration and development in non-communist nations went to the United States, South Africa, Australia and Canada. Government-owned operations in the developing world expanded their share of world exports for many metals from 20 to 40 per cent by the late 1970s, a trend that is expected to continue for some time to come in many markets. Europe, Japan and the non-producer developing countries are concerned about the possibility that government-owned suppliers, for political reasons, may impose supply restrictions. For other producing countries, such as Canada, the influence of government-owned operations in the developing countries is, at the very least, a cause of some uncertainty because of their influence on prices.

On the demand side, there is general consensus that over the next decade, world consumption of minerals will increase at less than half the rate experienced since the Second World War. To a great extent, this difference reflects the fact that world economic growth is expected to be slower. It also reflects the reality that in developed countries, the quantity of industrial raw materials used in various processes has declined. Numerous factors are responsible for this decline, including the substitution of synthetic materials such as plastics and the institution of new techniques. The Mining Association of Canada told this Commission that "the rate of per capita minerals consumption is levelling off in the economically advanced countries, thus potentially shifting the geographic concentration of growth in future demand towards countries in the Third World." (Mining Association of Canada, Brief, November 23, 1983, p. 4.) Mineral markets of developing countries, aside from the NICs, are not yet clearly defined, however; nor is it certain that their mineral consumption will ever approximate that of the developed market economies. At any rate, it is projected that the one-quarter of the world's population that inhabits industrial countries will continue, for the foreseeable future, to absorb more than three-quarters of the non-fuel minerals.

As a result of technological innovation that creates new uses for minerals or leads to the development of substitute materials, changes are also expected in the relative demand for various commodities. The automobile industry provides the best-known example. There, the substitution of aluminum and plastics for steel, together with the reduction in the size of vehicles to meet fuel-consumption targets, has effectively eliminated growth prospects for a large portion of the traditional steel and iron-ore market. In the field of telecommunications, fibre optics are beginning to displace copper. By contrast, increased reliance on galvanizing for rust-proofing is expected to increase the demand for zinc. On balance, the types of changes that are likely to take place in the foreseeable future suggest that one of the chief tasks of the global minerals industry may be to develop new uses for its products.

For many years, Canada has enjoyed the distinction of being the world's largest exporter of minerals. We sell over 80 per cent of our mineral production to more than 100 countries, and these exports are significant to our well-being. The relative performance of the Canadian mining industry, however, has slipped over the last decade. Canadian production of most metals (measured by weight of output) has declined; Canada's share of world markets for some critical metals has decreased; and, even discounting the effects of the recession over the last few years, employment has stagnated. Moreover, the industry is no longer discovering and opening new mines at rates sufficient to offset the depletion of existing ore bodies and to maintain present output.

Without doubt, the most important structural change for the Canadian mining industry has been the significant reduction in long-term/growth rates for the consumption of minerals, and this trend is expected to continue to the turn of the century. Canada's adjustment problem has been compounded by the fact that low-cost developing countries are now supplying a growing market share of most non-ferrous metals. Mineral exports form a crucial part of the export goods and employment opportunities of developing countries. For this reason, during the recession of the early 1980s, these countries were less willing to reduce production, regardless of price, when demand was shrinking. The world market for minerals is expected to remain soft, and stiff competition will be inevitable.

The Forest Resource

Rough estimates indicate that through the various ages of civilization, human action may have eliminated no less than half the forests that once covered the earth. Today, forests cover 20 per cent of the world's land surface, and more than half of them are situated in the temperate climates of the industrialized world. The size of the world's timber resource is estimated at about 300 billion cubic metres.[15] It is calculated that 7.5 billion cubic metres of timber can be cut every year without reducing new growth. More intensive cultivation might, however, make it possible to double this rate of sustainable cutting. Projections of global timber consumption indicate that it will double, reaching about 5 billion cubic metres, by the year 2000. The global extraction rate today is only 2.5 billion cubic metres. There seems, therefore, little reason to doubt that the world's forests could produce double the amount of wood they are producing now. Such global figures are entirely misleading, however, because both the forests and their use are very different in the developed and the developing worlds. The practical bounds for forest harvesting in the next 25 years are considerably more restrictive than global figures would suggest. This situation, in fact, provides a sharp contrast to that of relative resource abundance in minerals.

Every year the world's tropical forests are diminishing, on average, by 11.3 million hectares or 0.6 per cent per year.[16] They are losing their millennia-long battle with civilization in countries like Tanzania, Costa Rica, Nepal, Zaire, Thailand and Malaysia. A primary cause is the continued use of slash-and-burn clearance to provide agricultural land for people attempting to stay a few steps ahead of hunger. A second cause is the garnering of wood to provide fuel. Demand for fuel wood is intimately bound up with population increases, and the stark fact is that many countries are already experiencing severe local shortages that cannot be met by importing fuel from distant areas or countries. Fuel-wood demand alone accounts for more than half of the annual destruction of forests and 80 per cent of the trees felled in the developing world. Nor is a shortage of firewood the only problem created by the cutting of forests. Over time, the felling of available trees has contributed to a serious deterioration in the productive and moisture-retaining capacity of arable land. This is particularly a result of mechanized logging, which is increasing in tropical forests. The pressures on these forests differ, of course, from one nation to another. In Southeast Asia and Africa, commercial logging and shifting colonization exert almost equal pressures. In Central America, particularly in Nicaragua, cattle-grazing is the practice most destructive of the forest. In countries like Brazil, "settlement" of the jungle has added to the problem. From the perspective of the developing world, therefore, the forests are at risk because their resources are needed for short-term survival, and because they have already suffered virtually irreversible, long-term, environmental damage.

In the developed world, concerns about the forest resource focus on timber shortages for commercial harvesting and associated environmental problems like acid rain. It is estimated that by the year 2000, the developed world will need at least twice as much industrial timber as it does today. At present, roughly two-thirds of industrial timber is softwood, which grows mainly in the northern hemisphere. North America, the Soviet Union, Europe and Oceania currently produce 75 per cent of the world's wood harvest, excluding fuel wood. As the prospect of increasing the harvest in Europe is slight, the bulk of the increase must come from Canada, the United States and the Soviet Union. It is probably on the outer edge of theoretical possibility for these countries to supply the additional amount of required timber. In fact, however, such a large supply of forest resources could be realized only through enormous investments in silviculture, reforestation and, in the Soviet Union, in new roads and settlements. Increased commercial production of softwoods, however, is already occurring in the southern United States and in the southern hemisphere, in countries like Brazil.

Although it is quite unlikely that the world's output of softwood can be doubled by the year 2000, global hardwood production can be doubled. The world's great unused reserves of hardwood are chiefly to be found in a small number of heavily-forested developing countries. To replace softwood with hardwood would require, among other changes, a significant adjustment of the technology currently used in the manufacture of paper.

The poor and the affluent countries, then, do not share similar problems with respect to the world's forest assets. Nevertheless, the long-term solution in both developing and developed regions is to replant forests. This solution, however, is not universally applicable. In reality, a tropical forest, once turned to desert, is virtually impossible to restore, and even where reforestation is possible, the financial commitment required is huge. A global reforestation strategy would, nevertheless, enhance the world's ecological system and provide an expanded forest-resource base, whether for commercial harvest or for fuel wood. China offers an example of effective action. Since the 1950s, it has made great progress in reversing the destruction of its forests, a process which had been under way for some 5000 years. Many observers of the Canadian forestry industry are concerned that the present rate of replanting and natural reforestation is not adequate to replace our annual tree harvest. We shall explore this problem more fully in Part IV of our Report.

The Environment

The physical environment of the planet Earth is a complex interactive system. Its myriad processes provide the wellspring of life for human beings and all other organisms. The natural environment forms the foundation for traditional subsistence economies just as it does for modern Western economies. In Canada today, the physical environment – the seemingly endless fields and forests and mountains, the rivers, lakes and oceans – both provides the basis for industrial activity and contributes to our cultural essence.

We Canadians have slowly come to recognize some simple, but fundamental, truths about our world. For example, its various phenomena are interconnected in many intricate ways. Air, water, land and life form an interlocking system. Climate, so important in determining the fertility of the earth, is governed by the interaction of sun and atmosphere, of oceans and forests. Industrial pollutants and the alteration of patterns of vegetation inevitably disturb these natural systems. Conversely, when we try to conduct our activities in general harmony with natural environmental processes, we reap a series of interconnected benefits. When we conserve forest regions, for example, we not only secure important supplies of timber and fuel wood, but we also conserve moisture, which helps to prevent soil loss, and reduce the danger of flooding.

Today, one of our world's most critical challenges is to find and implement ways to pursue our livelihoods without jeopardizing our planet's ability to support present and future generations. This is a new challenge, for population growth and technology have wrought pressures on the natural environment around the globe that were virtually unknown during most of the long course of history. In the developed world, short-term benefits are traded off against policies of long-term conservation to the disadvantage of future generations. In parts of the developing world, the same generation struggles daily to obtain the life-and-death necessities of food and firewood.

No one is sure to what extent our environment can accommodate a species – our own – which seems to have forgotten that it is part of a larger natural world. No one is sure just where the threshold of irreparable environmental damage lies. The vital question is: What is the long-term carrying capacity of our planet? In many situations, the threshold of irreversible damage may be relatively distant. In many instances, we do not know where the real danger points lie because we lack compelling evidence to warn of impending disaster. Nevertheless, we Commissioners think it important to consider the consequences of irreversible actions taken along the way.

The authors of *Global 2000*, a report on the prospects for the world's resources, submitted to U.S. President Jimmy Carter in 1980, believed that the present generation is nearing many dangerous thresholds in our own lifetime. They summarized their bleak vision of the environmental landscape of our planet by the end of this century:

> *There will be fewer resources to go around . . . world per capita water supplies will decline by 35 per cent because of greater population alone . . .*
>
> *The environment will have lost important life-supporting capabilities. By 2000, 40 per cent of the forests still remaining in the LDCs in 1978 will have been razed. The atmospheric concentration of carbon dioxide will be nearly one-third higher than preindustrial levels. Soil erosion will have removed, on the average, several inches of soil from croplands all over the world. Desertification (including salinization) may have claimed a significant fraction of the world's rangeland and cropland. Over little more than two decades, 15-20 per cent of the earth's total species of plants and animals will have become extinct – a loss of at least 500,000 species . . .*
>
> *The world will be more vulnerable both to natural disaster and to disruptions from human causes. Most nations are likely to be still more dependent on foreign sources of energy in 2000 than they are today . . . The loss of diverse germ plasm in local strains and wild progenitors of food crops, together with the increase of monoculture, could lead to greater risks of massive crop failures.*[17]

Some knowledgeable observers do not accept fully this gloomy view of our future. Nevertheless, the picture of our global environment is full of warning signals about the need for greater integration of economic aspirations and environmental concerns, a better balance between the needs of the immediate and the distant future. We can no longer be confident that the cumulative effects of modern industrial life are consistent with maintaining a healthy self-sustaining environment. As the Institute for Environmental Studies at the University of Toronto told this Commission, "We are entering a world in which our effects on Nature, coupled with insufficient understanding, are creating a whole new realm of uncertainty." (Institute for Environmental Studies, University of Toronto, Brief, November 1, 1983, p. 5.) Canada is not immune to the negative consequences of abuse of the environment in other countries; and we Canadians are not without fault in our own environmental practices. In reviewing the major concerns which exist with respect to the global environment, it is important to stress the increasing understanding of the interdependence between Canadian territory and the rest of the planet.

Water

Water's place in the global environment cycle is critical. Both the quantity and the quality of the world's water resources are already creating problems in many countries and are virtually certain to create more by the turn of the century, because of rapidly rising demand combined with worsening pollution. Certainly, the increasingly heavy application of pesticides, introduced with intensive agricultural practices, will further damage the world's water-supply. Industrialized countries claim that their use of long-lived chemicals such as DDT is decreasing, but the use of pesticides in the developing world may be at least four times greater by 2000 than it now is. In the less-developed countries, pollution from persistent pesticides has already reached worrisome proportions in irrigation canals, ponds and rice paddies.

In a considerable number of less-developed regions, the development of river basins to provide flood control, to generate electricity, and to facilitate irrigation is also likely to increase. Of course, the construction of large-scale dams and the undertaking of irrigation projects provide many benefits, but they can also damage both freshwater and coastal ecosystems, thus creating health problems, flooding valuable lands, damaging and destroying property, and displacing thousands of people. Coastal pollution from agriculture, industry, logging, the operation of energy systems, and the growth of coastal communities is bound to worsen in many areas.

The world's supply of fresh water is actually adequate to meet its needs, but it is commonly mismanaged and generally underpriced; local requirements and resources frequently do not match. The United Nations has estimated that the demand for water needed for irrigation, the heaviest use of this resource, will double by 2000. Population growth is also expected to double the demand for water between 1971 and 2000, in nearly half the world's countries. Still greater quantities will be needed if standards of living are to improve. Though few data exist, it seems that by 2000, several less-developed countries may be using an amount of water close to the limit of their maximum accessible supply; even before that date, they will find it expensive to develop their remaining water resources. In the industrialized countries, different interests are expected to compete more strongly for the use of water, and this competition may lead to price schedules that reflect more closely water's true value. Within the next few decades, growing demand may stimulate considerable interest in schemes to divert major rivers in China, Russia and Canada. One intervenor at this Commission's hearings recommended that because water resources are a global asset, an international monitoring team be formed to assess the global effects of these possible projects, some of which have already reached the planning stage.[18]

Canada is the custodian of roughly 20 per cent of the planet's fresh water, and Canadians have a responsibility to husband this resource for the benefit of future generations and the citizens of the world. Our effort to date – as the sorry state of the Great Lakes bears witness – has not been sufficient to make the attainment of this goal a certainty.

Acid Rain

In the northern hemisphere, perhaps the single most pressing environmental concern is the generation of acid rain. Large parts of Canada are now receiving rainfall five to 40 times more acidic than normal. During the winter and spring, a layer of haze, originating in the industrial areas of Europe and Asia, covers large parts of the Canadian Arctic, a form of air pollution which seriously reduces visibility in the winter to as little as 25 kilometres from a maximum of 300 kilometres. Wintertime Arctic air pollution has increased about 75 per cent since 1950, in correspondence with sulphur dioxide emissions from Europe and Asia, which have increased 100 per cent.[19]

Each year, world-wide emissions of sulphur oxides alone amount to 65-100 million tonnes. Emissions of sulphur oxides (SO_2) and nitrogen oxides (NO_x) originate in the smelting of sulphur-rich ores (the largest Canadian source), industrial combustion, vehicle-exhaust fumes, and the burning of coal in power plants. Oxides of sulphur and nitrogen are spread by the winds and carried across national frontiers in a global cycle. In this way, emissions affect areas hundreds of kilometres from their sources. Natural processes return pollutants to the surface of the earth; these substances are deposited directly on water, land and vegetation, or fall as precipitation containing sulphate and nitrate ions.

Acid rain is causing serious environmental and economic damage in Europe and eastern North America. For example, a 1983 study showed that 34 per cent of West Germany's forest resources had been damaged in varying degrees. The forests of Poland and Czechoslovakia have suffered similar damage. Acid rain has been cited as the major cause. In the United States, the growth rate of spruce trees in several New England mountain forests fell by half between 1965 and 1979. Acid deposition affects over 38 million hectares of forests in eastern Canada, and studies have indicated that it could be potentially damaging to germination and growth rates.

Acid rain also inflicts serious damage on bodies of water by raising acidity levels beyond the normal range. As the acidity of lakes and streams intensifies, aquatic plant and animal species begin to disappear entirely or to exist only in certain age groups. The acidic concentration can be reduced, over time, with reductions in sulphur emissions, but the natural biological processes, once damaged, cannot be revived. The effects of acid deposition on bodies of water have been observed for an extended period in Scandinavia, and their occurrence in parts of Ontario and the Adirondacks of northern New York State is also well documented. In Canada, tens of thousands of lakes in Ontario are threatened, and thousands are probably already acidic; many thousands in Quebec are also in danger. Since the 1950s, ten major rivers in Nova Scotia have become so acidic that the prized salmon has disappeared. Many more rivers in Atlantic Canada are seriously threatened.

Canada cannot afford to ignore any threat to its lakes or forests, since they are the basis for vast economic activity and form the setting for a multi-billion-dollar recreation and tourism industry. Unless action is taken to reverse the acid-rain situation, its extent and intensity are expected to increase significantly. A paper on acid rain, read at the Helsinki Conference in July 1984, suggested that this precipitation is a "time bomb" that takes some 20 years to go off.[20] It is not only the environment that is at risk from the effects of acid rain, but human health as well. Studies in recent years have confirmed a significant correlation between the level of sulphates in the air and respiratory disease. A study made for the U.S. Administration's Office of Technology Assessment, in 1984, estimated that sulphates annually contribute to 50 000 premature respiratory or cardiac deaths (that is, 2 per cent of all deaths) in Canada and the United States.[21]

There are means to prevent further pollution damage, and although they are difficult and expensive to implement, they are feasible. For Canada alone, estimates of the cost of clean-up are $2 billion in equipment and cleaner fuels, with operating and financing costs perhaps making the bill $600 million annually for 20 years. The main element so far lacking to launch remedial efforts in all the major industrialized countries, including Canada, has been political will. Progress towards amelioriating this record has been slow, but our federal and provincial governments are committed to the achievement of a 50-per cent cut, by 1994, in the sulphur emissions allowed in eastern Canada in 1980. But without American commitment to co-operate in achieving a reduction in pollution, the Canadian program cannot succeed, however vigorous it may be. This Commission views acid rain as an item high on the agenda for concrete action and urges intensive participation in international forums addressing this issue.

Degradation of Soil

Each year, in many parts of the world, approximately 200 000 square kilometres, an area half the size of Newfoundland and Labrador, turn to desert because of natural drought and because of over-cultivation, over-grazing and destruction of forests, especially in semi-arid regions. The United Nations has identified about two billion hectares of land where the risk of desertification is "high" or "very high"; this threatened area is about two and one-half times that now classified as desert. Although desertification affects some 100 countries, the process is most serious in sub-Saharan Africa, northwestern Asia, and the Middle East. Any global food strategy will have to deal with this growing problem.

While soil deterioration and desertification are especially serious problems in poorer parts of the world, the agricultural prospects of industrialized nations are also vulnerable to various forms of soil degradation, even though increasing use of chemical fertilizers, high-yield plant varieties, irrigation, herbicides and pesticides have far outweighed, in terms of crop productivity, declines in soil condition. Salinity, alkalinity and waterlogging have already damaged about half of the world's irrigated land, and while it is possible to restore damaged areas, the process is slow and costly. Much of the additional land expected to be put under irrigation by 1990 is highly vulnerable to irrigation-related damage.

Relative to its vast extent, Canada is not rich in agricultural land. Only 9 per cent of our country's land area can be cultivated, and only half of that is actually under cultivation. Soil scientists agree that there has been significant deterioration in Canadian soils in all regions as a result of water and wind erosion, compaction, salinity and loss of fertility. In our Prairie region, for instance, productivity of the native soils has decreased by perhaps 30 (some say 50) per cent since settlement, even though grain output has increased by leaps and bounds, primarily because of the development of high-yield varieties and the heavy use of fertilizers. Salt-affected soils are expanding rapidly: Alberta's damaged area has tripled over the last 10 years, and Saskatchewan's has quadrupled over the last 15 years. Other areas of Canada also offer examples of soil degradation. For instance, "60 to 70 per cent of all sediments in the Great Lakes basin originate from agricultural land." (The Honourable Eugene F. Whelan, Brief, November 24, 1983, p. 9.) According to the 1984 report of the Senate Standing Committee on Agriculture, *Soil at Risk*,[22] the overall deterioration of Canada's soil resources is serious enough to threaten the expansion of agricultural production. The kind of measures suggested by the Senate Committee are worthy of serious consideration.

Nuclear Wastes

Some observers have predicted that over the next ten years, there will be a doubling of the nuclear power generated around the world. Even in the United States, which has begun to experience cancellations, delays and lack of new orders, it is predicted that nuclear power capacity will almost double by 1995.[23] There remains considerable uncertainty about the importance of nuclear power beyond the year 2000, but the nuclear capacity of OECD countries may double or even triple between 2000 and 2025.

Nuclear power represents a high degree of hazard. In addition to the ever-present risk of a nuclear accident, an acceptable method for the permanent disposal and storage of high-level radioactive wastes has not yet been demonstrated. Some of the by-products from reactors have half-lives many times longer than the period of recorded history. The generation of nuclear power produces relatively small quantities of high-level radioactive spent fuel and larger quantities of low-level radioactive wastes. Uranium mining and processing produces substantial quantities of low-level radioactive waste and tailings. While the tailings are less potent than the original ore, they create a risk of ground-water contamination if they are not properly disposed of. In some locations, the processes of leaching and transportation of contaminants by means of aquifers could lead to contamination of surface waters.

In addition to the problem of safe disposal, nuclear power creates other environmental hazards for our modern age. Among those frequently cited are the potential diversion of research and material from the development of nuclear power reactors to that of nuclear weapons; danger to the health and safety of employees and the general public from the operation of nuclear power plants; and the continuing safety requirements of decommissioned nuclear plants. Canadian responses to these alarming possibilities have taken many forms, including our adherence to the Nuclear Non-Proliferation Treaty, the imposition of safeguards on our uranium exports, domestic regulation through the Atomic Energy Control Board, and complex research into adequately safe storage for nuclear wastes.

The potentially calamitous effects of nuclear accidents, combined with the controversies surrounding the use of nuclear energy, suggest that nuclear environmental issues deserve close attention in all countries. Since Canada is a major producer and processor of uranium, as well as a manufacturer of nuclear power-plant capability, Canadians have a particular responsibility to ensure that nuclear power production does not pose a threat to future generations. Our greater participation in international, as well as domestic, research in these areas would certainly be warranted.

Destruction of Tropical Forests

Tropical forests constitute a vital resource, not only for local populations, but also for nations far beyond their territories. As tropical forests are depleted, the environmental benefits they confer are progressively and irreversibly reduced. Local water pollution and soil erosion worsen; downstream flooding occurs; substantial climatic changes take place, and some areas become desert; moreover, there is a loss of the energy source that supplies most of the developing world. Globally, the same process causes a loss of genetic diversity, since half of the world's plant and animal life is contained in tropical forests; in addition, there is a loss of water quality and quantity in the atmosphere. Particularly in Central America, loss of the forest's genetic storehouse is a concern because a very small area contains great biological diversity.

The contribution of tropical forests to the global climate also calls for consideration. When forests are cleared, the "shininess" of the earth's surface is increased, and this change causes more of the sun's energy to be reflected back into space. Many scientists believe that this reflection can cause disruption of convection patterns, wind currents and rainfall in areas far beyond the tropics. Some scientists believe, too, that the amount of oxygen in the atmosphere is diminished when the forests are cleared.

In recent years there have been many estimates of the rate at which tropical rain forests are being destroyed. Although taking that measurement is a difficult and controversial process, many studies have concluded that forest denudation is the pervasive environmental problem of the world's tropical countries. It is very clear that because of their different ecological base, tropical forests would be unable to sustain the pattern of forest exploitation applied in North America over the past century. Once disrupted, tropical forests take anywhere from 150 to 400 years to regenerate.

In 1950, it was estimated that tropical forest covered 16 per cent of the world's land surface. That figure has now shrunk to 12 per cent, and it could drop to 7 per cent by the turn of the century. For the foreseeable future, the pressures generated by population increases, slash-and-burn clearance of forested land to be used for farming, fuel-wood gathering and rapid logging will reduce the earth's tropical forest base by anywhere from 4 million to 20 million hectares per year, according to various studies. The most thorough study, prepared jointly, in 1982, by the United Nations Food and Agriculture Organization and the U.N. Environment Program, estimated the loss of tropical forests at 11.3 million hectares, or 0.6 per cent, per year.[24] Denudation is an acute problem in Central America, most of western Africa, and southern Asia, but not in Brazil. The Ivory Coast, for example, is losing its forests at a rate of 5.3 per cent per year, compared to Brazil at 0.34 per cent per year. The forests of Thailand are all but gone. If it is not already too late, it is certainly not to soon for northern industrialized countries, including Canada, to try to help halt the razing of tropical forests.

The Greenhouse Effect

Major and minor climatic changes brought about by natural forces are not unusual in the earth's history. Projections of a significant warming of the earth over the next half century, the so-called "greenhouse effect", are not merely rare, however, but actually unprecedented because human activities, not natural forces, are the cause of the process. The total carbon dioxide (CO_2) content of the atmosphere is increasing by 3 per cent per decade, primarily as a result of the world's expanding use of fossil fuels. In 1981 alone, the concentration of carbon dioxide in the earth's atmosphere rose by about 0.5 per cent.[25] The increasing use of synthetic gases is also a contributing factor. So, too, is the rapid harvesting or destruction of tropical forests, which absorb carbon dioxide from the atmosphere; conversely, if cut down and burned for firewood, these forests add carbon dioxide to the atmosphere.

High concentrations of CO_2 do not endanger human health; indeed, they are not without some benefits, for they help crops to flourish by enriching their basic nutrients. Concentrations of carbon dioxide, however, absorb certain wave-lengths of infra-red radiation; hence, they influence the temperature of the earth's atmosphere and surface. Many experts warn that we can expect significant global warming as a result of this process, a warming which could have a dramatic and far-reaching impact on the global environment.

The advent and the degree of this warming, as well as its possible environmental effect, are matters of contention among leading scientists. So, too, are many important related matters, such as the extent to which the destruction of tropical forests will exacerbate the process, and the function of oceans in absorbing increasing concentrations of CO_2. Most scientific estimates suggest a doubling of atmospheric CO_2 from its pre-industrial level by the middle of the next century. This development would bring about a rise in mean global temperature from current levels of 1.5°C to 3°C, and the increase would be considerably higher at the poles. By 2100, the global temperature might rise by 5°C.

How significant is the projected rise in world temperatures? Even a much smaller warming can have a localized and uneven, but dramatic, impact. For example, between the 1880s and 1938, the northern hemisphere became warmer by 0.6°C, and the process caused markedly greater warming in the far reaches of the North Atlantic and the high Arctic. This effect caused codfish to move up the western coast of Greenland and transformed the local economy.[26] It is clear, then, that predictions of a rise in average temperatures of 1.5°C to 3°C are significant, especially in northern climates. If this widely used estimate approximates reality, Canada, and in particular its northern regions, will experience a profound change in climate by 2050, with an increase in average temperature of as much as 4°C to 6°C.[27]

If, as some scientists predict, climatic warming of the extent suggested should occur by the mid-twenty-first century, there will be a northward shift of climatic zones accompanied by major changes in currents, nutrients and life forms. If the temperature warms by 5°C in the climatic zones now suitable for the growing of corn and wheat, these areas could extend about 600 kilometres north of their present boundaries. This development might well prove less productive than first reaction would suggest, for soils suitable for agriculture do not exist in many northern regions, including some in Canada. Moreover, although the Canadian Prairies would gain a longer growing season, the American Midwest would become too warm for producing corn and winter wheat. The possibility of warmer temperatures in northern latitudes has led to the conjecture that the polar ice cap could melt by the latter part of the twenty-first century, leaving an open Arctic Ocean.

Significant shifts in regional precipitation would be superimposed on temperature changes. There have been forecasts of increased precipitation of as much as 7 per cent, but the net effect would undoubtedly vary by region.[28] Some model simulations indicate marked increases in run-off in high latitudes and increased aridity at middle latitudes. Run-off into the Arctic Basin would be increased, affecting Canadian marine resources, navigation and weather systems in general. A decrease of precipitation in Canada's middle latitudes could mean increased drought and dryness in the southern Prairies. In southern Ontario, increased dryness could translate into reduction in the volume of the Great Lakes by as much as 21 per cent.

Since northern warming would tend to expand agricultural zones, facilitate transportation and diminish energy demands for heating, its consequences for Canada are perceived, on balance, as beneficial. However, this same conclusion cannot be reached for all regions of the world. Canada's responsibilities as a member of the international community mean that we must be concerned about the global consequences of such a development.

In the absence of international consensus on global warming, individual nations are unlikely to take significant action to reduce CO_2 emissions. A recent American study[29] concluded that only a ban on coal by 2000 would significantly slow the rate of temperature change, but that such a ban is not politically feasible because its burden would be unevenly distributed. Certain countries appear more likely than others to promote adaptive strategies, but if such initiatives are to have any effect, much more precise and detailed information will be needed on the timing and the regional consequences of global warming.

Extinction of Species

Charles Darwin described extinction in *The Origin of Species* as the gradual, or only sometimes sudden, disappearance of species or groups of species as they are checked by unperceived hostile agencies as part of the process of natural selection.[30] In the twentieth century, humanity is responsible for causing a break in that natural process described by Darwin, and for bringing about extinctions on an unprecedented scale. We are only beginning to understand the extent and severity of this problem.

According to the International Union for Conservation of Nature and Natural Resources (ICUN), extinction threatens an estimated 25 000 plant species and more than 1000 vertebrate species.[31] These figures do not take into account the loss of thousands of invertebrate species, such as molluscs, insects and corals, and unclassified insect and plant species whose habitats are being destroyed. Several estimates suggest that when unclassified species and invertebrates are included, from 500 000 to two million species, representing a number as high as 20 per cent of all species on earth, will be extinct by the end of this century.[32]

Among major threats to species are hybridization; introduction of exotic species; exploitative hunting, fishing and commercial harvesting; and pollution. The most serious threat to wild species is habitat destruction: in particular, water pollution and the clearing of tropical forests in Central and South America. One-half to two-thirds of all extinctions projected by 2000 are expected to occur in those regions because their species diversity is greatest.

The genetic base of much modern food production has narrowed alarmingly: today four-fifths of the world's food supplies are derived from fewer than two dozen species of plants and animals. This reduction is a result of extinctions and of farmers' reliance on fewer and fewer high-performance hybrid varieties of crops. As uniformity of species increases, crops become more and more vulnerable to outbreaks of pests and diseases, and to sudden changes of climate. Since primitive varieties of crops and their wild relatives are often the only source for breeding resistance, it is imperative that their existence be maintained. Despite this necessity, varietal stocks are rapidly diminishing as wild and marginal lands are brought under cultivation.

The introduction, deliberate or inadvertent, of exotic species into an ecosystem can adversely affect the native species, with which the exotics compete for space or food, through predation, habitat destruction and transmission of diseases and parasites. For example, introduced lamprey eels have created a problem in the Great Lakes, and introduced goats and rabbits are destroying the habitats of plants, birds and reptiles on the islands of the Pacific and Indian Oceans.

Conclusions

Analysis and understanding of the global ecosystem stand at an embryonic phase. Despite the explosion of knowledge in recent decades, we still know relatively little about the natural processes that have sustained life on the earth over the millennia. Given what we do know, however, the unsettling danger signals are clear. The negative and sometimes irreversible effects of many activities are abundantly plain. Solutions cannot wait upon complete scientific understanding. It is at our peril that we base our economy on exploitation of the earth's resources at rates that exceed the capacity of the ecosystem to accommodate it.

Individual countries, such as Canada, have a responsibility to act on these global problems as far as they are able within their own boundaries. Ultimately, however, many environmental problems are global in nature, and this reality makes concerted international co-operation and action essential. Real progress on these problems may also require a fundamental change in values, to bring industrialized societies back into balance with the natural world.

Canadians have recognized the global nature of environmental problems and have experimented with institutional mechanisms such as the International Joint Commission, appointed to deal with Canada-U.S. matters relating to the quality and quantity of water. Canada also played a leading role in the Declaration of the Stockholm Conference of 1972, which launched international awareness of the environment. Our country has contributed significantly to the United Nations Environment Program (UNEP), of which a Canadian, Maurice Strong, was the first executive director; to the successful passage, in 1983, of the United Nations General Assembly's resolution creating the World Commission on Environment and Development; to a 20-country declaration concerning acid rain, which was produced at an international conference on that subject held in Ottawa, in March 1984; and to many other international agencies concerned with the global environment. Canadians thus have a national experience and, to some extent, an international record upon which to build. This Commission advocates even stronger efforts to this end.

Notes

1. Food and Agriculture Organization of the United Nations, *Agriculture: Toward 2000* (Rome: FAO, 1981), p. 123.
2. *Ibid.*, chapter 2.
3. See "People, Land, and Food Production: Potentials in the Developing World", *Options* (IIASA), pp. 1–2.
4. See Kenneth R. Farrell, Fred H. Sanderson, Trang T. Vo, and Michael F. Brewer, "Meeting Future Needs for United States Food, Fiber, and Forest Products", in Joint Council on Food and Agricultural Sciences, *Reference Document: Needs Assessment for the Food and Agricultural Sciences* (Washington, D.C., 1984), p. 29.
5. *Ibid.*, p. 91.

6. See Francis T. Christy, Jr., "Fisheries for Food: Global Developments and Special Needs", a paper prepared for the Right to Food Conference, Montreal, May 1984.
7. Shell Canada Limited, Brief, July 31, 1984, p. 6.
8. Information supplied to this Commission by Imperial Oil Limited and Exxon Corporation.
9. Information supplied to this Commission by Imperial Oil Limited and Exxon Corporation.
10. Information supplied to this Commission by Imperial Oil Limited and Exxon Corporation.
11. National Energy Board, *Canadian Energy: Supply and Demand 1983–2005* (Ottawa: Minister of Supply and Services Canada, 1984), p. 101. In this calculation, hydro and nuclear power are converted at 10.5 petajoules per terawatt hour.
12. Patrick J. Caragata, *National Resources and International Bargaining Power: Canada's Mineral Policy Options* (Kingston: Queen's University, Centre for Resource Studies, 1984), p. 40.
13. Interfutures, *Facing the Future: Mastering the Probable and Managing the Unpredictable* (Paris: OECD, 1979), p. 47. The Interfutures Group extrapolated their material from U.S. Bureau of Mines data in *Commodity Data Summaries, 1977*. This work is not frequently updated.
14. Caragata, *National Resources and International Bargaining Power*, p. 136.
15. Thomas Bertelman *et al.*, *Resources, Society and the Future*, a report prepared for the Swedish Secretariat for Futures Studies (Oxford: Pergamon Press, 1980).
16. United Nations Food and Agriculture Organization/United Nations Environment Program, *Tropical Forest Resources*, by J.P. Lanly, FAO Forestry Paper No. 30 (Rome: FAO, 1982).
17. United States, Council on Environmental Quality and the Department of State, *The Global 2000 Report to the President: Entering the Twenty-First Century* (Washington, D.C.: U.S. Government Printing Office, 1980), vol. 1, pp. 39–40.
18. See R.B. Church, University of Calgary, Transcript, Edmonton, November 16, 1983 [vol. 47], p. 9680.
19. See L.A. Barrie, D. Fisher, and R.M. Koerner, "Trends in Arctic Air Pollution Revealed by Glacial Ice Cores" (Ottawa: Department of Environment, Atmospheric Environment Service, 1984).
20. This conclusion is based on research on a 30-year collection of Finland's pine needles. The study was conducted by Professor Taisto Raunemaa of Helsinki University's Physics Department. See Taisto Raunemaa and Pertti Hari, "The Problem: Forest and the Environment, a Profound Change", a paper presented at the Club of Rome Conference on Forests and Environment, Helsinki, July 1984.
21. *Acid Rain and Transported Air Pollutants: Implications for Public Policy* (Washington, D.C.: U.S. Congress, Office of Technology Assessment, 1984).
22. See Canada, Senate, Standing Committee on Agriculture, Fisheries and Forestry, *Soil at Risk: Canada's Eroding Future* (Ottawa, 1984).
23. See Noel O'Brien, "A Canadian Viewpoint on the Outlook for Uranium", a paper presented at the Mineral Outlook Conference, Ottawa, May 15, 1984 (Toronto: Denison Mines Limited, 1984).
24. *Tropical Forest Resources*, by J.P. Lanly.
25. See F. Kenneth Hare, "Climatic Variability", *Queen's Quarterly* 85 (Winter 1978–79): 595–606.
26. *Ibid.*

27. D.F.W. Pollard, "The Carbon Dioxide/Oxygen Budget: The Global Budget from a Forestry Perspective", paper presented at the Conservation for Sustained Use Seminar, Kleinburg, Ont., March 29–30, 1984 (Ottawa: Department of Environment, Canadian Forestry Service, 1984).

28. G.A. McKay and T. Allsopp, "Climatic Change and Energy Use: A Northern Perpective on Climatic Uncertainty" (Downsview: Canadian Climate Centre, 1981).

29. Stephen Seidel and Dale Keyes, *Can We Delay a Greenhouse Warming*? (Washington, D.C.: Office of Policy and Resources Management, Office of Policy Analysis, 1983).

30. See Charles Darwin, *The Origin of the Species* (London: John Murray, 1911), pp. 458–64.

31. See Glen Lucas and Hugh Synge, *The IUCN* Plant Red Data Book (Morges: IUCN, 1978); and International Union for Conservation of Nature and Natural Resources, *Red Data Book* (Morges: IUCN, 1975)(separate, frequently supplemented or revised volumes on fish, amphibians and reptiles, birds and mammals).

32. See, for example, *The Global 2000 Report to the President*; and Norman Myers, *The Sinking Ark* (Oxford: Pergamon Press, 1979).

The Global Human and Physical Outlook: General Implications for Canada

This Commission's examination of population growth has led Commissioners to a firm conclusion: Unless the poorest countries can implement widespread family planning and parallel economic-development programs, malnutrition and poverty will certainly worsen over the next few decades. Increased disparities and tensions will follow, both intra-regional and between the developed and developing worlds, and they will lead to greater political instability for the world as a whole. Our examination of the global environment also points to frightening trends of deterioration, unprecedented and recent. These developments have re-opened the question of the earth's long-term carrying capacity. Although scientists have not fully determined the assimilative capacity of the planet, prudence would counsel immediate and serious attention to these problems, as well as better integration of economic and environmental goals. Canada's economy cannot safely be based on exploitation of natural resources to a degree that both exceeds the physical limits of the planet and strains the mechanisms of social control.

From the privileged position that Canada holds among nations, the complex and sometimes overwhelming problems facing the global community to the year 2000 and beyond seem removed, a world apart. Aside from Canadians' high standard of living, three factors distinguish Canada, even among industrialized countries. We have a small population relative to the size of our land mass. Canada is one of a handful of countries that has not had its territory ravaged by either civil or international war in the last hundred years. We have a splendid endowment of natural resources. Our economic history has evolved around our resources, as have our national identity, our international reputation, and our leisure activities. Thus, pressures relating to over-population and food supply are not problems for our country. Neither is access to minerals, fish and forest resources, fresh water, or fossil fuels and electricity. On the environmental front, however, our concerns mirror those of all other nations, as witness the widespread pollution of our Great Lakes, the damage caused our country by acid rain, and the significant decline of our readily harvestable forest resources.

Despite our relative affluence and our present freedom from crisis, any complacency concerning the global developments that Commissioners have reviewed would constitute an inappropriate and unacceptable response. First, the discrepancy in wealth between the developing world and the industrialized world gives Canadians reason enough to try to comprehend global problems and to strive to make the future better than the past. Secondly, as knowledge about the natural processes and ecosystems of the planet has increased, so too has humanity's understanding that they are truly global systems, where damage in one part can affect the whole. Similarly, advances in science and technology are weaving the nations of the world ever more tightly together. It is, therefore, both unwise and infeasible to isolate Canadians from the rest of humanity. Finally, technology has given Canadians the capacity to respond, sometimes rapidly, to crises or needs anywhere in the world.

Obviously, Canada cannot, by itself, solve or shoulder responsibility for the world's problems. We could, of course, grow more wheat suitable for sale to poorer nations, but these sales would be constrained if the receiving countries lacked the foreign exchange to buy our grain. Furthermore, our Prairies, vast as they are, cannot feed the entire world. While sharing Canadian resources through aid or commercial avenues may be a moral responsibility, we cannot make it our only contribution.

The world stands in need of concerted international efforts to find solutions for problems of health, nutrition, environmental management and the world economic and trading systems. The focus of these efforts must go beyond the technical aspects to the more important socio-economic and political aspects of our global society, to cope, in particular, with the careless tendencies of industrial civilization itself. The General Synod of the Anglican Church of Canada, for example, told this Commission that ultimately, the solution to environmental problems requires a fundamental change in global values:

> *Today we are involved in an epic struggle brought about by a deep-rooted alienation of industrialized society from the natural world . . . The environmental crisis cannot be solved by technology and science alone, for it is essentially a crisis of the spirit.* (General Synod of the Anglican Church of Canada, Brief, November 1, 1983, p. 39.)

Commissioners are advocating that Canada undertake a role of active and immediate world leadership. Canada can provide that leadership through acting within international bodies, through providing direct aid, or through offering commercially-based development assistance. A few of the most important areas where Canadians could provide effective support are agriculture, education, and facilities and funding for family planning. One intervenor proposed that Canada take similar leadership responsibility in international environmental concerns:

> *New inter-governmental understandings are required, not just about defence and trade, but also about management of the natural resources of the planet. Canada should take the lead in such endeavours.*
>
> (Institute for Environmental Studies, University of Toronto, Brief, November 1, 1983, page i.)

Canadians can also lead by example in the stewardship of our own resources, even if our actions primarily benefit ourselves. There is considerable room for improvement in our undertaking of reforestation projects and in our management of soil and water resources.

The global nature of the problems requires that even for reasons of self-interest, Canadians demonstrate a willingness to take on global responsibilities which domestic political pressure might tend to discourage. It is ethically unacceptable, however, to approach the problems of humanity from the perspective of a narrowly-defined national self-interest. Increasingly, Canadians, as well as others, will have to face the discrepancy between a global political system dominated by individual nations and the scale of problems which transcend national interests. Commissioners foresee no easy solution to this growing tension.

The Knowledge Environment: The Challenge of Change

Can Technology Solve World Problems?

Over the period of recorded history, religion and science have competed for the central role in influencing human perceptions and explanations of the world around us. In recent centuries, science has gained supremacy, and it is sometimes designated the main factor in transforming our world – for better and for worse. Modern society has witnessed advances in science and technology that contribute both to society's progress and to society's problems. Science and technology have certainly increased energy consumption, but they have helped to compensate by developing new energy sources. They have contributed to a substantial increase in the pollution of our environment, but in return, they offer a key to the elimination of the problem. They have added to the pressures on finite resources, but, conversely, they have made it possible to discover and process those resources more efficiently, and they have helped to develop substitute materials that will extend the availability of resources that might otherwise be quickly depleted. Science also offers the means of limiting the population explosion that is presently putting such strain on the world's resources.

The possibility of using science and technology to mitigate our present problems indicates that it is not the explosion of knowledge, as such, that underlies our human predicament. It is, rather, its occurrence in a civilization that has allowed science and technology to develop without adequate social control.[1] This is not to deny the possibilities open to modern societies to make intelligent use of technological change over the next century and so to modify the pattern of economic growth, vastly improve living standards, and avoid the gravest environmental hazards. The advance of knowledge can help humanity to find solutions *if* it is accompanied by determination, international co-operation, reform of international institutions, and social changes in all countries. These geopolitical elements make Commissioners less certain about the extent to which the tremendous advances in science now taking place will be used to solve the global problems reviewed in the preceding sections of this chapter.

This uncertainty was set out for Commissioners in our hearings:

> *The critical question ... is the extent to which technology determines, that is dictates, economic and social development and the extent to which it accommodates prevailing economic and social conditions and realities. To the extent that the relationship is technologically deterministic, then the question arises whether, to what extent and by what means should society control its development.* (Stephen B. Peitchinis, Transcript, Edmonton, November 15, 1983 [vol. 46], p. 9411.)

Science and Technology in the Global Context

Among the significant international effects of the enormous advances in science made in recent decades has been growing interdependence among nations, a situation created by new patterns of resource use, defence arrangements, and modern communications and transportation. The implementation of discoveries in science and technology, for example, has more and more required international trade in natural resources, particularly in the field of energy. The blending of domestic and international affairs in national policy, the increased pressure to include international concerns in the processes of decision making and management, the effect of international events on national science policies, and the expansion of international relations among non-governmental organizations and special-interest groups are more subtle indicators of the increasing global interdependence which has accompanied the explosion of scientific knowledge.

Many of the far-reaching changes resulting from scientific and technological research were not planned – or even contemplated – by their originators. Such changes were a result of interaction of scientific and technological developments with social, economic and political forces, catalysed by an element of chance. Those who contributed to the invention of television could not foresee its industrial and commercial impact nor the impact of its programs on family life, national institutions or, indeed, on world perceptions and expectations.

The shrinking of the globe, of course, cannot be attributed solely to advances in science and technology. This process is also a product of many other interrelated changes, including rapid industrialization, reduction of trade barriers, population growth, migration and increased economic specialization among nations. Still, these factors, too, have been partly determined by the forces of scientific advance. For example, science and technology have enabled the manufacture and marketing of new products in new places and have made possible the transport innovations required for expanded trade.

Particularly because it facilitates economic growth, technology has come to be transferred from nation to nation on a massive scale, further building their connections. Technological education, information, high-technology manufacturing and the "human resource" of experts have assumed considerable importance. The existence of "technological gaps" created by the attainment of different levels of technological competence in different countries has become an important political issue. There is a prospect that developing countries will continue to depend on technologically advanced ones. Governments of some developed nations have adopted industrial policies and programs to assist domestic companies to develop advanced new goods or services that are expected to be competitive abroad. This Commission was told, for instance:

> *The new wave of high technology is, paradoxically, triggering a tide of technological nationalism, uncomfortably resembling mercantilism of the eighteenth century. This time, the name of the game is not bullion, it is top-notch capability in advanced technologies. This neomercantilism – where governments are getting involved in developing the new industrial infrastructure while closing down their markets to technological product imports – is fuelled by the desire of nearly all governments to harness the cutting-edge technologies in the race towards the twenty-first century.*
>
> (Task Force on Micro-Electronics and Employment, Brief, November 28, 1983, p. 4.)

Scientific prowess itself has become a measure of a nation's status and prestige. The competition between the United States and the Soviet Union in such areas as high-energy physics, defence production, oceanography and space exploration has strongly influenced levels of funding for science and technology in both countries. Many observers believe that nations actively participating in the development of new knowledge have a head start in generating wealth. Dr. Fraser Mustard, President of the Canadian Institute of Advanced Research, told this Commission that to conduct basic research in key fields has been compared to retaining membership in a club: nations which do not pay their dues are shut out.[2] By contrast, nations with strength in one sector of a rapidly developing field have entrée to all its sectors, an opportunity which increases the overall fund of knowledge and techniques open to their industries and institutions.

While the rapid evolution of technologies has greatly affected relations among nations, it is less clear to what extent governments have come to grips with the political implications of these developments. Governments often do not anticipate national and international political repercussions of technological advance and react only belatedly and ineffectively. For example, the impact of television on public policy has been enormous. The Canadian seal hunt, placed "on trial" by the international media, or the siting of missiles in Western Europe, for example, can instantly become matters of burning, and often poorly informed, public controversy around the globe.

Advances in science and technology will clearly continue to shape our natural, human, economic and international environment. Whether they will become even more influential in the next decades is an important question and the subject of wide-ranging public discussion. It is to this subject that we now turn.

The Significance of Technological Change

In our attempt to peer into the future, Commissioners reviewed international opinion on the emerging technologies, and we asked a group of distinguished Canadian scientists to identify those developments which they considered likely to make a significant impact on human experience over the next 20 years.[3] They predicted significant developments in many fields.

In the computer sciences, the power of the micro-chip has multiplied 100-fold in the last ten years. Along with continuing exponential growth in microprocessors and telecommunications, the first fruits are emerging in artificial intelligence, a recognized field of study for only the past quarter of a century. Here, various advances in many fields are being combined in projects designed to substitute for, and improve on, human mental and physical effort. Sensory systems are now available, and laser vision will be developed in the future. Among major developments to be anticipated is computer recognition of human speech. In the next decade, we shall see "smart" robots used primarily in resource and manufacturing industries.

In astrophysics and space research, humanity's perception of its place will change as the essence of the universe is further explored. New manufacturing techniques and new (solar) energy sources in space locations are two significant advances likely to occur. Other benefits are already apparent in the fields of communication, surveillance and navigation.

In the biological sciences, developments such as the production of energy from biomass and the introduction of biological pesticides will affect the resource industries and all industrial processes. Genetic engineering will make it possible to manipulate the "information system", or genes, of all living cells. The reality of biotechnology in health care is demonstrated by the clinical use, begun in 1982, of human insulin produced in a micro-organism into which had been inserted the genes for this hormone. Advances in this field will almost certainly proceed by leaps and bounds; thus they will raise environmental risks and moral issues. In neurobiology, recent years have seen an explosive growth in knowledge about organization of the brain, and about its biophysical, biochemical and physiological functions, and their role in affecting behaviour and associated mental illness.

In physics, revolutionary discoveries are taking place which will allow us to begin to comprehend the substructure of the atom and the characteristics of all matter. The materials sciences, too, are undergoing a revolution that will provide substitutes for, or add new properties to, metals, glass and wood. The future role of materials science lies less in developing new materials *per se* than in developing new and more efficient ways to process existing materials so that they will embody new properties. Such efforts will provide us with strong and tough ceramics, extremely corrosion-resistant metals with outstanding strength-to-weight ratios, more durable concretes for road use, and electrically conductive and self-reinforced polymers. Industry sources project that up to 65 per cent of the structures of commercial aircraft will be made from composite materials by the mid-1990s.

In electro-optics, a multi-billion-dollar market has developed in the past few years, and further exponential growth is expected. Laser applications range from aerial surveillance, metals discovery and assay, welding and surgery, to high-definition television, printing and fibre-optic communications.

In the field of energy, the technology for producing solar, nuclear, photovoltaic, biomass and hydrogen power are all available, and each one of these forms will increase in use within the energy mix. Of these sources of energy, however, only nuclear forms are likely to be used to a significant degree until well into the twenty-first century.

In ocean sciences, development of ocean-bed hydrocarbons and mining of sea-bed nodules are restrained less by technology than by economics and policy decisions concerning the Law of the Sea.

The pace of technological change and the rate of expansion of knowledge are often said to have increased dramatically in recent years, driven chiefly by exponential growth in micro-electronics, as well as by rapid advances in materials science, biology, space and ocean science, and the social sciences. The Canadian Manufacturers' Association expressed this view in its submission to this Commission:

> *The micro-electronics revolution has reached the state of widespread application to industrial tasks ... The automation of all industries, in the*

factories and in the offices, is very much upon us . . . Further, innovations in communications and computer technology have accelerated the rate of change by increasing the speed and efficiency of communication. Thus micro-electronics are not only the source of profound change, but are also accelerating the rate of change.
(Canadian Manufacturers' Association, Brief, September 6, 1983, p. 3.)

Other observers, however, consider recent advances in science and technology as part of a continuing improvement in productivity, rather than as representing any fundamental departure from the achievements of the past. The disagreement stems from confusion over the terms 'technological change', 'technical change' and 'revolution', and from the sheer difficulty of constructing measures of change. Widely-varying research traditions and a lack of interdisciplinary exchange tend to characterize this field of study.

Technology, as American economist Edwin Mansfield has defined it, is society's pool of knowledge with respect to the industrial, agricultural, and medical arts.[4] It deals with more than machines: it relates to the skills and knowledge and ability of people to develop and use tools – in the broadest sense of the word – that make their lives more enjoyable and productive. Technology, in other words, is "know-how" and "know-why", often embodied in the soul of the inventor and motivated by the thirst for knowledge. It is a social, cultural and educational phenomenon that we cannot consider in isolation from its human sources.

Technological change, then, is the advance of knowledge in technology. It takes the form of new ways of manufacturing existing products and new designs that enable the production of goods with important new characteristics, and it is often combined with innovative techniques of organization, marketing and management. Technical change, by contrast, is simply a new technique or an alteration of equipment, products and organization already in use. The transfer of technology (that is, the pool of knowledge) is thus a much more complex process than the diffusion of new machines embodying technical change.

Those who believe that the current era of technological advance is only a stage in a continuing process tend to view technological change in the narrower sense. They see it, that is, as representing adjustments and innovation in the technical apparatus and processes of production or, more properly, as technical change. They do not necessarily seek to measure the rate of expansion in knowledge, nor do they place much emphasis on science and technology as the driving force of the economic process. These observers have reached the conclusion that there is no convincing evidence of acceleration of the pace of technological change. As one piece of evidence, they cite the decline in total factor productivity. Total-factor productivity grew much more slowly in all industrialized countries in the mid- to late 1970s. A decline in patenting or research activity is offered as further evidence of slower innovative activity in recent years.

Critics of this evolutionary view of scientific and technological progress cite major problems with its measurements of change. The slower growth of productivity apparent in the 1970s, they maintain, might be taken as evidence of a generalized slow-down in the processes of innovation and new discovery. No one, they point out, seems to have drawn this conclusion. Again, many observers contend that patent statistics do not provide convincing evidence of broad technological change because many discoveries are not recorded in a patent office. Furthermore, R&D statistics may be a poor measure of technological change because no fixed relationship exists between research costs and results.

Historians of science have tried to measure the rate of expansion of scientific knowledge. Among these scholars, there is general agreement that the normal mode of growth for science is exponential: that is to say, the more extensive it becomes, the faster it will grow. Over the last two or three centuries, scientific knowledge has doubled every 15 years. One eminent scholar, Derek de Solla Price, said in 1962 that young scientists starting work in the 1960s would find that only 10 to 20 per cent of all scientific work ever achieved would antedate their career, and that 80 per cent of scientific knowledge would, therefore, be contemporary.[5] If the theory of exponential growth is valid, then the fact that the greater part of scientific work has been produced within living memory is true of scientists living in earlier centuries, too. Indeed, the Royal Commission on Canada's Economic Prospects (the Gordon Commission) maintained 30 years ago that "the most remarkable feature of world progress in recent years in science and technology has been the acceleration of pace."[6] What explains our keen awareness of the pace of technological change in our own era, however, is the cumulative effect of the steady doubling of scientific knowledge at such short intervals.

Many contemporary scientists also accept the theory that the pace of accumulation of knowledge is increasing. They often cite anecdotal evidence of the closing of the time lag between basic research and technological application. Examples given are the rapid creation and use of lasers; the quick exploitation of new scientific insights such as the discovery of recombinant DNA; the discovery of peptides that act as neuro-transmitters in the brain; and the emergence of a biotechnology- related industry that relies principally on research done over the past ten years.

Many businesses and their associations appearing before this Commission spoke of the changing pace of the acquisition of knowledge in the business world. Gulf Canada Ltd., for example, stated:

> *Since the mid-1970's we have witnessed a rapid acceleration in the pace of technical advance, which has shifted significantly the positions of competitors in various industries throughout the world. Prospects are for a continuation of this trend towards rapid changes in products and production processes, led by microelectronics and communications technologies but broadening into many fields; and for an accelerated rate of diffusion of these technical advances to other industries and other countries as a result of facilitating government policies. Consequently, the pressure on Canadian industry to keep up to the international pace of technical advance is more likely to intensify rather than slacken.* (Gulf Canada Ltd., Brief, November 18, 1983, p. 11.)

The National Research Council argued before this Commission that the rapid pace of change is the significant factor in adjustment:

> *The problems we face today result not from technological change per se but from the rapidity with which such changes are now being thrust upon us. It appears that the pace will continue to quicken, and that there is no way in which we can isolate ourselves from world events.*
>
> (National Research Council of Canada, Brief, October 31, 1983, pp. 6-7.)

The Honourable Michael Wilson, Minister of Finance, put forward the same thesis in his first economic statement, *A New Direction for Canada*:

> *Canada's future economic performance will in large part be determined by how successfully Canadians respond to the challenge of an ever-quickening pace of technological change and an increasingly competitive world trading environment.*[7]

Former Prime Minister the Right Honourable Pierre Trudeau addressed a major technology conference during the course of this Commission's mandate, saying, "It is in our common interest to prepare for the impact of the technological revolution, for it will effect changes in our world more profoundly than any other peaceful movement in history, and at a phenomenal pace."[8]

Professionals, politicians and laypersons alike brought their views on this matter before this Commission. Feeling their way on unproved ground, most told Commissioners that the new knowledge and technologies surrounding us may be of an entirely unprecedented sort. Typical of the testimony were the remarks of the Honourable Larry Grossman who declared, in submitting to this Commission the brief of the Government of Ontario, that "the Canadian economy is . . . in the midst of a major industrial and economic transformation." (Government of Ontario, Transcript, Toronto, December 5, 1983 [vol. 58], p. 12189.) Again, the brief contributed by A.W.R. Carrothers, Dean of Law of the University of Ottawa, emphasized that "the modern technological revolution is upon us, and we are just beginning to become sensitized to the reality that out there somewhere is a whole new electronic world that is as incapable of description as was the world of steam." (A.W.R. Carrothers, Brief, November 10, 1983, pp. 9–10.)

Those who predict for our era revolutionary change springing from scientific advances usually refer to knowledge and technology in their broadest sense and attempt to study how they might affect all facets of life. These observers foresee dramatic changes in the nature of work, in employment, in communications, in education, in leisure, in democratic institutions, in power relationships, and in global interaction, as well as fundamental alterations in the processes of production. Among members of this school are economists and historians who have revived interest in the theory of "long waves" of economic development,[9] a theory which we describe here not as advocates, but to illustrate the broader concept of technological revolution. This theory sees the last quarter of the twentieth century as the beginning of a third industrial revolution.

As the theory goes, an industrial revolution requires the simultaneous appearance of innovations in energy sources, transport, tools and the manufacturing process. Another essential ingredient is a surplus pool of labour. An industrial revolution is the amalgam of this combination of activities which initiates the prolonged process of expansion that continues until each new product has saturated all the terrain open to it. A revolution has pervasive effects throughout the entire economic system.

According to the "very long-wave" concept, there have been two industrial revolutions which transformed human societies since the agricultural revolution of some 10 000 years ago. As shown in Table 2-6, the first industrial revolution – based on coal, steel and steam power – did not reach its peak until the mid-nineteenth century. The second industrial revolution – based on fossil fuels, the automobile, the aeroplane, sheet metal, organic chemistry, plastics, the electrical industry and mass production – was the first revolution of the twentieth century. According to this theory, a third industrial revolution, conceived just decades after the fossil-fuel revolution, is now in its embryonic phase. This revolution is rooted in developments in electronics; biotechnology; nuclear, biomass and solar power; space and ocean sciences; and new materials. Some of its innovations are already visible today; they include integrated networks of telephones, automatic couriers, facsimiles, video conferencing and the space shuttle. It is projected that this revolution will reach its peak sometime in the next century, as Figure 2-4 indicates.

Industrial revolutions are usually divided into four phases: infancy, characterized by weak growth; adolescence, marked by rapid growth; adulthood, displaying slower growth; and maturity, a period of zero growth. From the perspective of the long-wave theorists, the slow growth of the years from 1975 to 1985 has been the result of the combination of two phases: the maturity and decline of the major industries developed during the second industrial revolution, and the weak growth of activities characteristic of the infancy of the third industrial revolution.[10] If the long-wave theory continues to apply, a new phase of rapid growth should begin about 1990.

While the view of the long-wave theorists is unique in its determinism, they are not the only observers who have described the dimensions of the new technologies as profound. The 1979 report on the future, published by the Organisation for Economic Co-operation and Development (OECD), also described developments in electronics and micro-processors as "a decisive qualitative leap forward":

> *In the longer term, however, the electronics revolution will change the face of advanced industrial societies ... These developments contain the seeds of a completely new accounting technique and also of a reorganized society ... it will change the technical context in which choices are made: the choice of freedom and decentralization, and the choice of participation and, more generally, the choice of life styles.*[11]

Those who predict that profound change will occur in the next few decades foresee that this current "revolution" will contribute to prosperity, but that it may also be the source of social conflict. While serious unemployment in

TABLE 2-6 Characteristics of the Industrial Revolutions

	Energy	Transport	Tools	Basic Production	Characteristics
Neolithic	Wood Charcoal	Wheel	Hand	Cereals Textiles Stone	
First Industrial Revolution (19th century)	Coal	Rail	Mechanical industry	Steel ingots Mineral chemicals Manufactures (textiles, etc.)	Substitution of *mechanical* capital for human labour Decreased demand for skilled labour Increased demand for unskilled labour Key invention: the steam engine Key resource: energy (coal) Substitution of mechanical for human and animal energy
Second Industrial Revolution (20th century)	Oil Electricity	Car Aircraft	Electrical industry	Sheet steel Organic chemicals Plastic	Substitution of *mechanical* capital for human labour Key innovations: harnessing of electricity; the internal combustion engine Key resources: hydro power, petroleum Substitution of mechanical for human and animal energy

TABLE 2-6 (cont'd.)

	Energy	Transport	Tools	Basic Production	Characteristics
Third Industrial Revolution (20th century)	Nuclear Solar Other new forms	Rockets Telecommunication Dirigibles Sailing cargo ships	Electronics Computing Robotics Office automation Genetic engineering	Synthetic products Aquaculture (neolithic marine) All production affected	Substitution of *information* capital for human labour Decreased demand for skilled labour Decreased demand for unskilled labour Decreased demand for physical capital Decrease in demand for energy capital Key invention: the computer chip Key resource: information

Sources: Adapted from André Piatier, "Innovation, Information and Long-Term Growth", in *Long Waves in the World Economy*, edited by Christopher Freeman (London: Butterworth, 1983), p. 228; and Yves Rabeau, "Tele-Informatics, Productivity and Employment: An Economic Interpretation" (Montreal: Gamma, 1980).

FIGURE 2-4 The Three Industrial Revolutions

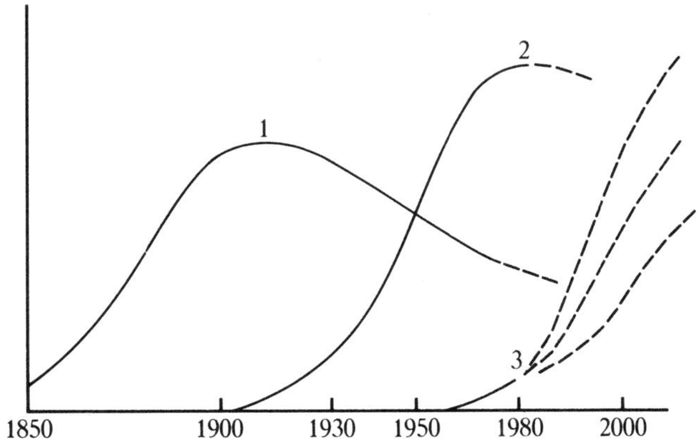

Source: André Piatier, "Innovation, Information and Long-Term Growth", in *Long Waves in the World Economy,* edited by Christopher Freeman (London: Butterworth, 1983), p. 228.

Notes 1 = Coal, steel, rail, textiles, chemistry.
2 = Oil, cars, steel (sheet), mechanical industry, air transport, organic chemistry, electricity.
3 = New energy sources (including nuclear), oceanic development, biomass, genetic engineering, electronics, telematics, automation.
The dotted lines represent three potential trajectory paths, depending on the speed of change in this wave.

particular sectors or regions may be associated, in the short term, with dislocations caused by technological change, the labour force will take up new and different jobs over time. Is there, then, any feature of this current wave of knowledge and technologies, even if it is considered a third industrial revolution, that is qualitatively different from those of earlier periods? Is there anything in this current wave to which our institutions – national and global – will be unable to adjust? Gerard Piel, publisher of the *Scientific American,* has written that "we are living in a revolution . . . yet we manage to fit the changes in the way we live and make our livings into the picture of the society we grew up with, suppressing any recognition of the impact of change on those values and institutions."[12] As Piel suggests, whether the same pattern of progress will continue is a matter of considerable debate in the industrialized world, and it is a question inherent in conflicting views about the significance of change.

We Commissioners cannot be certain where the rapid increase in knowledge will lead, or what will be its social, political and economic implications, nationally and internationally. We *can* be sure, at least, that the rapid advance of science and technology is bringing about far-reaching changes which will require adjustments, in the short and the long terms, in virtually all aspects of our society. In Part III of this Report, Commissioners examine the less exotic theories of the relationship between technology, growth and jobs. There, while we are mindful of the broader concerns addressed in this section, we express optimism that society, as in the past, will be able to use a variety of mechanisms to cope with the implications of future change. We cannot, however, stop there. The challenge posed by technology also has a global aspect – both economic and political – which will, of itself, force the rethinking of traditional solutions. It is to the subject of the changing international economic environment that we now turn.

Notes

1. See Robert L. Heilbroner, *An Inquiry into the Human Prospect* (New York: Norton, 1980).
2. See Canadian Institute for Advanced Research, Brief, January 10, 1985, p. 1.
3. Canada, Royal Commission on the Economic Union and Development Prospects for Canada, Emerging Technologies Conference, Alton, Ontario, August 19–21, 1984. A summary of the conference is available in the Public Archives.
4. Edwin Mansfield, "Technological Change and the International Diffusion of Technology: A Survey of Findings", in *Technological Change in Canadian Industry*, vol. 3, prepared for the Royal Commission on the Economic Union and Development Prospects for Canada (Toronto: University of Toronto Press, 1985).
5. Derek J. de Solla Price, *Little Science, Big Science* (New York: Columbia University Press, 1963).
6. Canada, Royal Commission on Canada's Economic Prospects, *Final Report* (Ottawa: Queen's Printer, 1957), p. 25.
7. *A New Direction for Canada: An Agenda for Economic Renewal*, statement by the Minister of Finance, Ottawa, November 8, 1984.
8. Address by the Right Honourable Pierre Trudeau to the Canada Tomorrow Conference, Ottawa, November 7, 1983.
9. A particular version of long-wave theory involves the so-called "Kondratieff cycles", named after the economist who, during the 1920s, identified and analysed long-term trends in economic activity, based on approximately 50-year cycles. Joseph A. Schumpeter gave a new twist to the long-wave concept in 1939, when he explained the Kondratieff cycles in terms of periods of major technical innovations and accompanying flurries of entrepreneurial activity. The current long-wave theory further hones this concept, concluding that a cluster of innovations may be of such significance that it can fundamentally alter existing economic and social processes. According to those who support the theory of very long-waves, when several major innovations appear simultaneously, their combination takes the form of an industrial revolution.
10. André Piatier, "Innovation, Information and Long-Term Growth", in *Long Waves in the World Economy*, edited by Christopher Freeman (London: Butterworth, 1983), p. 229.
11. Interfutures, *Facing the Future: Mastering the Probable and Managing the Unpredictable* (Paris: OECD, 1979), p. 114.
12. Gerard Piel, "Re-entering Paradise: The Mechanization of Work", *Challenge* 26 (September/October 1983), p. 4.

The Economic Environment: Structural Shifts and Long-Term Trends

Interdependence at a Crossroads

Economic nationalism of the inter-World War period has given way, in the post-Second World War period, to a much more open international economy. While this development represents the general trend, it must be acknowledged that autarky, that is, the desire for self-sufficiency and an independent national economy, remains a powerful force. The international trade environment also retains vestiges of mercantilism: some countries still seem inclined to drive, at the expense of others, for expansion of exports and large balance-of-trade surpluses. It is worthwhile to trace briefly the evolution of this international environment and to outline the current state of OECD interests, for the global forces at work have considerable momentum and will assuredly do much to shape Canada's prospects for economic development.

Dominating the post-war evolution of international relationships has been the struggle between the two super-powers to contain the influence of the other. The military and economic power of the United States gave that country a decisive influence in shaping the international environment that lies outside the large segment of the globe controlled by the Soviet Union. Immediately after the Second World War, the United States applied the full weight of its considerable influence to create a liberal international economic order. The establishment of the International Monetary Fund (IMF), the International Bank for Reconstruction and Development (World Bank) and the General Agreement on Tariffs and Trade (GATT) were manifestations of this emphasis on drawing the "free" world into a network of interdependent trade partners.

This grand scheme for trade liberalization, however, overlooked the practical short-term requirements for reconstruction in Europe and Japan. Thus, the United States shifted gears in fairly quick order: the Truman Doctrine and the Marshall Plan inaugurated a new approach that promoted social stability. The Bretton Woods monetary regime, with its emphasis on full currency convertibility, was suspended, at least in part; massive financing was provided through the Marshall Plan. Trade liberalization was to become a much more incremental process. The United States exercised its unchallenged supremacy in the Western world in many ways, including the management of pegged exchange rates so as to allow Europe and Japan to acquire a competitive advantage for their exports in world markets. As the crisis of reconstruction was overcome, the initial plan of the United States was applied: the IMF became increasingly active and, in the 1950s, currency convertibility was restored, and the Bretton Woods monetary regime went into operation. While all this activity was going on, the control of Saudi Arabian oil by American companies provided the lubricant so necessary for industrial growth.

In this environment, trade and growth were mutually reinforcing. The results were impressive. Trade during the period from 1948 to 1973 expanded at the rate of 7 per cent annually, while world output expanded at the rate of

5 per cent. These gains are all the more impressive when compared to those made in the period from 1913 to 1948, when trade expanded by only 0.5 per cent annually and world output by 2 per cent. Over the past decade, the expansion of world trade has slowed. Still, by 1980, more than 20 per cent of world output of goods and services crossed national boundaries.

Increased trade is only one manifestation of post-war national interdependence. Improved transportation, better means of communication, and the rapidly growing world pool of knowledge caused the Western nations to tighten the knot of shared experience. Trade in the form of services, travel and investment became more and more important. Interdependence became more strongly institutionalized: some one hundred international organizations were established in the 1960s and 1970s, and more than 150 countries now belong to the United Nations. The private sector, too, especially as represented by financial intermediaries and multi-national corporations, has vastly expanded its international network.

The age of trade liberalization and global interdependence challenged traditional American hegemony and, hence, the paternalistic system that made it flourish. Liberalization of trade was the means of transmitting prosperity within the Western world during the 1950s and 1960s. In the 1970s and 1980s, however, the same process became a transmitter of inflation and recession. Inflationary financing of the Vietnam War led the United States ultimately to abandon a fixed relationship between the dollar and gold, and to withdraw the Bretton Woods currency arrangement. Flexible exchange rates became the norm.

In the face of increasing inflation and erosion of the real returns on its oil resources, the Organization of Petroleum Exporting Countries (OPEC) successfully challenged the post-war energy regime. World oil prices increased by some 1500 per cent during the 1970s, greatly intensifying the earlier inflationary forces. Major oil-importing countries made co-operative, but largely unsuccessful, efforts to contain the consequences of this development. The United States severely tightened its monetary policy in order to break the upward spiral of inflation. This U.S. policy quickly led to rising interest rates, slower economic growth, and rising unemployment through much of the world. Those Western countries that sought, by stimulating their economies, to act independently of U.S. policy came under intense pressure to return to an "orthodox" position.

Full employment has become more difficult for the industrialized nations to achieve. The spectacular rise in oil prices of the 1970s produced a massive transfer of wealth from industrialized nations to primary producing countries. Real income fell because of worsening terms of trade for industrialized countries and reduced aggregate demand that resulted from restrictive monetary policies. During the 1970s, governments made some attempt to shift the burden of adjustment from labour to capital by redistributing income through the tax system: the relative level of taxes on workers declined, while those on business increased. The attempt proved counter-productive, however, when private investment declined: indeed, its consequences for employment were serious.

State intervention was once a comfortable ally of international openness. In the expansive 1950s and 1960s, economic policies, designed to align aggregate demand and supply conditions, appeared capable of smoothing out the vagaries of the business cycle. Moreover, social service policies and programs, including governments' commitment to balanced regional growth, appeared both affordable and provisory of basic social justice in an increasingly affluent world. However, the realities of the 1970s and the early 1980s raised profound questions about old assumptions.

The scope for independent national policies appears to be more and more limited. Economic summits of the "Group of Seven",[1] held during the late 1970s and early 1980s, proved incapable of producing more than bland statements exhorting joint action. These countries turned to the United States for leadership, not having observed that it could no longer provide a solution. Their problems were aggravated by the monetary restraint of the U.S. Federal Reserve Board, but restrictive U.S. monetary policy was not the sole cause of poor economic performance in Western industrialized nations.

The expansion of capitalism from its North American and Western European core to Japan and developing countries has been a factor contributing to the adjustment problems of the late 1970s and early 1980s. The rapid increase in exports from Japan and newly developing countries tended to be concentrated in particular sectors. Developed countries began to protect themselves by tightening restrictions on imports. And as competition increased, so did the general reaction against trade liberalization. The tariff reductions initiated under the GATT began to give way, through more state intervention, to non-tariff barriers (NTBs) to trade.

Differences between the advanced countries and the newly industrializing countries (NICs) are alleged to give an unfair advantage to the latter. Western Europe supports advanced welfare systems, and the United States makes large defence expenditures. By contrast, the NICs, where employers pay very low wages and can copy Western production techniques, appear to enjoy a competitive edge over traditional industries in Western industrialized countries. The multilateral non-discriminatory principles of post-war trade liberalization have been severely strained.

Industrial nations must decide whether they will continue down the road of global interdependence or withdraw into a protective shell. International openness to the exchange of goods and services is still a valid principle: gains are available through enhanced trade, and these gains need not be made by one nation at the expense of others. The world economic pie is enlarging, and while the North American slice may shrink compared to that of other areas, it will still grow in absolute terms. Economic theory has been bruised by events, but its fundamentals remain intact.

Even so, doubts remain. A maturing international economic order imposes severe demands: international forces will affect national policies. Nations will share technology and production techniques with rivals. The "club" of achievers will draw in new members, a process that often imposes substantial adjustment costs on veteran members. Fortunately, the strength of the post-recession economic recovery has made adjustment much easier. Indeed, it is likely that future trends in world trade and general interdependence will be governed, to a very great extent, by world economic growth. Only if the world achieves a balanced and sustained pattern of growth is it likely to proceed with trade liberalization and promote interdependence among nations.

Although newly industrializing countries have been able to participate aggressively in the growth of world trade, many developing countries have so far found themselves unable to adopt production techniques that would substantially raise their standard of living and overall competitiveness. For many years, developing countries have sought reforms in the global institutions which regulate both trade and international finance. "Trade, not aid" was their slogan in the 1960s. In the 1970s, following the breakdown of the Bretton Woods exchange-rate regime and the first oil shock, those countries pushed actively for a "New International Economic Order" (NIEO).

In 1975, the United Nations formally adopted a resolution favouring moves towards the proposed reforms. Although a Conference on International Economic Co-operation was held in 1975-77, little progress was made, in the 1970s, towards accommodating the concerns of developing countries. The Common Fund for commodities, once the centre-piece of the thrust toward the NIEO, finally won agreement in a watered-down form of the original proposal. This agreement has still not been ratified by a sufficient number of developing countries for it to be implemented. By the end of the decade, the "Southern" diplomatic effort was directed at a "Global Round" of negotiations on international economic issues at the United Nations. This effort was brought to a halt, however, by continued unwillingness among the industrialized countries to have monetary issues discussed in that forum rather than within the specialized agencies which usually deal with these matters: that is, the IMF and the World Bank. Later, the second oil shock, the international debt crisis and the recession deflected international attention from matters of structural reform to more immediate concerns.

The seriousness of the economic situation in the developing world and many of the difficulties of its countries reflect internal policy making rather than weaknesses within the global economy. Nonetheless, institutional reform at the global level is urgently required. Over the next 20 years, the problems of the developing world are likely to become a major issue facing the global economy. It may even be that the ideological hostilities of the East-West factions will recede, to be replaced by substantial conflicts of interest between a rich North and an impoverished South. To make the present global institutions work and to ensure that they will respond to the problems besetting the developing world is a distinctive and important contribution Canadians can make.

Economic Performance over the post-War Period

Since the end of the Second World War, the global economic structure and the pattern of international trade have changed dramatically. Of particular interest and importance to Canada are changes that have occurred among our major trading partners. Still, events in other countries with which Canadians have no close trade connections can also have an important bearing on the performance of our economy. The operations of the countries making up OPEC and the effects on the international financial system of the plight of some heavily-indebted less-developed countries (LDCs) serve to illustrate the point.

The crisis in international debt management which surfaced in 1981 endangered the international banking system and, according to some experts, created the threat of a world-wide depression. Debtor countries had become fundamentally overextended, while lending institutions had failed to diversify adequately against the risk that debtor countries might be unable to meet their obligations. Sky-rocketing oil prices during the 1970s contributed to this outcome, for they made more credit available (from major oil producers in the Middle East) at the same time that they made more credit necessary (particularly for developing nations dependent on oil imports). In addition, some oil-producing countries, notably Nigeria, Mexico and Venezuela, greatly increased their foreign borrowing, on the assumption that future oil revenues would provide the means for repayment.

The collapse in international oil prices, together with the sharp escalation in U.S. interest rates, greatly altered the ability of some debtor countries to meet their debts. The contraction of world trade and export earnings further exacerbated the problem. Fortunately, the International Monetary Fund, with extensive co-operation from the international banking community, has successfully contained the debt crisis. Still, the experience serves as a sharp lesson about the potential vulnerability of the international economic system and the implications for individual countries. It has left a legacy which will take many years to resolve fully, even with extensive international co-operation and assistance.

Aside from such international 'shocks' as these, the world economy, from a Canadian perspective, is dominated by the bloc of 24 countries (including Canada) that comprise the Organisation for Economic Co-operation and Development (OECD). Although OECD countries represent only 19 per cent of the world's population and 24 per cent of its land area, they account for over 65 per cent of world production. Figure 2-5 shows that the world map looks very different when country size is represented in proportion to gross national product (GNP).

Most developed market economies experienced similar broad trends in their post-war economic performance: relatively rapid real growth rates and productivity growth until 1973, followed by a slow-down; rising unemployment rates and inflation rates in the 1970s until the onset of the deep recession of the early 1980s; a sharp recession-induced drop in inflation rates; and, despite widening recovery, persistent high rates of unemployment. Table 2-7 sets out the main economic indicators of these occurrences. It illustrates that real growth rates dropped appreciably in OECD countries after 1973, falling from 5 per cent, between 1968 and 1973, to 2.7 per cent between 1974 and 1979. The first three years of the 1980s were a period of even more marked slow-down. Growth in productivity followed the same pattern.

FIGURE 2-5 World GNP and Trade, 1980
(Region size in proportion to GNP)

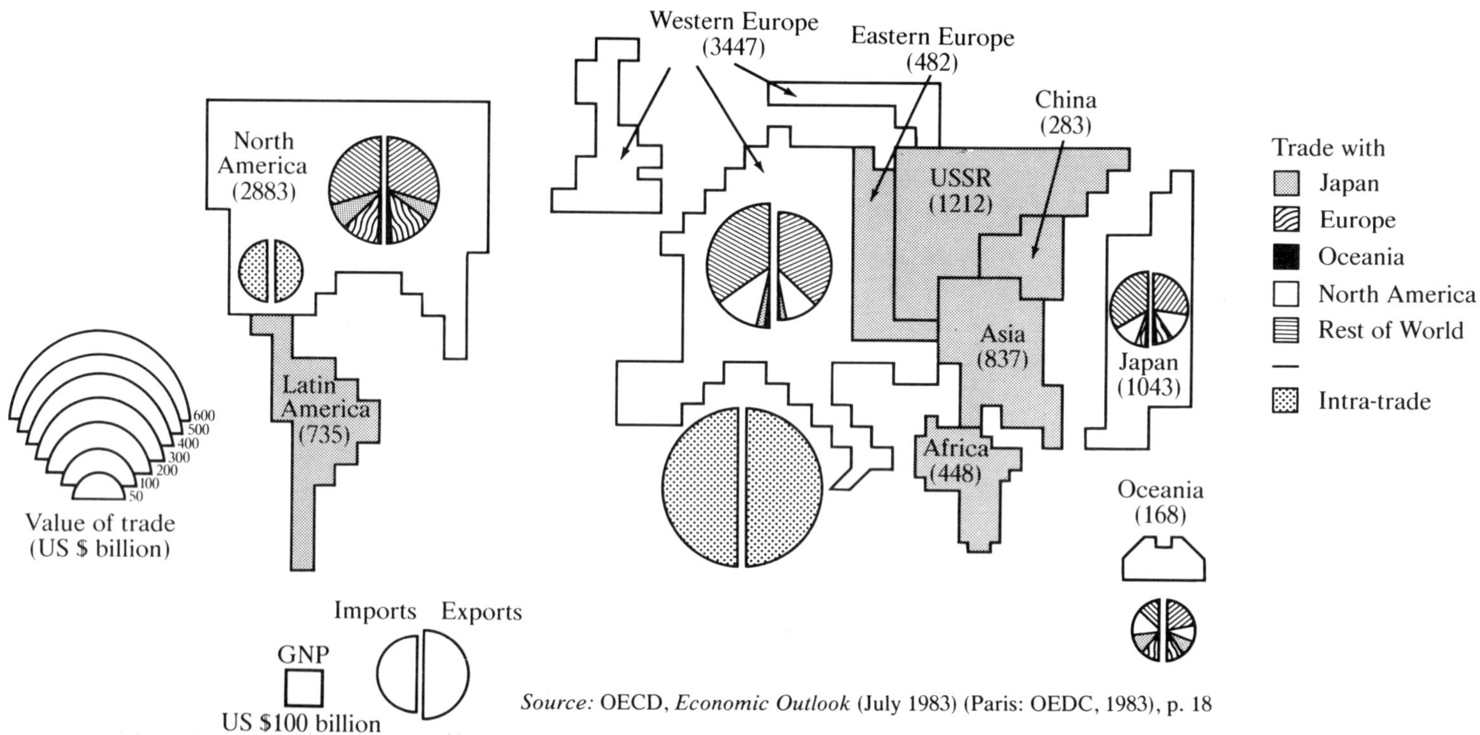

Source: OECD, *Economic Outlook* (July 1983) (Paris: OEDC, 1983), p. 18

Note: (...) = *GNP figure in billion $U.S.*

TABLE 2-7 International Comparisons: Main Economic Indicators

	(averages in per cent)							
	1961–67	**1968–73**	**1974–79**	**1980**	**1981**	**1982**	**1983**	**1984**
Growth in real GNE/GDP								
United States	4.6	3.7	2.8	−0.2	2.5	−2.1	3.7	6.8
Japan	10.2	9.5	3.6	4.9	4.0	3.3	3.0	5.8
Germany	3.9	5.3	2.4	1.9	−0.2	−1.1	1.3	2.5
France	5.5	5.6	3.1	1.1	0.2	2.0	0.7	1.8
United Kingdom	2.9	3.4	1.4	−2.0	−1.5	2.5	3.2	2.0
Italy	5.6	5.0	2.6	3.9	0.1	−0.4	−1.2	3.0
Canada	5.5	5.7	3.2	1.0	3.4	−4.4	3.3	4.7
Total OECD	5.1	4.9	2.7	1.2	1.7	−0.3	2.6	4.8
Growth in productivity[a]								
United States	2.8	1.4	0.2	−0.8	1.4	−1.3	2.4	2.6
Japan	8.6	8.3	2.9	3.3	3.2	2.2	1.3	5.3
Germany	4.0	4.8	3.0	0.9	0.6	0.7	3.1	3.0
France	5.0	4.7	2.9	1.1	1.0	1.8	1.5	2.8
United Kingdom	2.4	3.4	1.2	−1.4	2.0	4.1	3.6	1.0
Italy	6.3	5.2	1.6	2.4	−0.3	0.0	−1.3	3.0
Canada	2.3	2.4	0.4	−1.7	0.5	−1.2	2.5	2.1
Total OECD	4.0	3.8	1.6	0.6	1.4	0.2	2.2	3.3

TABLE 2-7 (cont'd.)

	(averages in per cent)							
	1961–67	1968–73	1974–79	1980	1981	1982	1983	1984
Employment growth								
United States	1.8	2.3	2.5	0.5	1.1	−0.9	1.3	4.1
Japan	1.5	1.0	0.7	1.0	0.8	1.0	1.7	0.5
Germany	−0.3	0.5	−0.6	1.0	−0.8	−1.8	−1.7	−0.3
France	0.9	0.9	0.2	–	−0.8	−0.1	−0.8	−1.0
United Kingdom	0.5	–	0.2	−0.6	−3.4	−1.5	−0.4	1.0
Italy	−0.7	−0.2	1.0	1.4	0.5	−0.4	−0.1	0.0
Canada	3.1	3.2	2.8	2.8	2.8	−3.3	0.8	2.5
Total OECD	1.0	1.2	1.1	0.6	0.4	−0.5	0.4	1.5
Standardized unemployment rates[b]								
United States	5.0	4.7	6.8	7.1	7.6	9.7	9.6	7.5
Japan	1.2	1.2	1.9	2.0	2.2	2.4	2.6	2.8
Germany	0.6	1.0	3.2	3.0	4.4	6.1	8.0	8.1
France	1.7	2.5	4.5	6.3	7.3	8.0	8.0	9.1
United Kingdom	2.5	3.4	5.3	6.9	10.6	12.8	13.1	13.4
Italy	5.1	5.7	6.6	7.4	8.3	8.9	9.7	10.0
Canada	5.0	5.4	7.2	7.5	7.5	11.0	11.9	11.3
Total OECD	2.7	3.2	4.9	6.0	6.7	8.2	8.7	8.2

TABLE 2-7 (cont'd.)

	(averages in per cent)							
	1961–67	1968–73	1974–79	1980	1981	1982	1983	1984
Consumer price inflation								
United States	1.7	4.9	8.5	13.5	10.4	6.1	3.2	4.3
Japan	5.7	6.7	10.0	8.0	4.9	2.7	1.9	2.2
Germany	2.7	4.3	4.7	5.5	6.3	5.3	3.3	2.4
France	3.5	5.9	10.7	13.6	13.4	11.8	9.6	7.3
United Kingdom	3.4	7.0	15.6	18.0	11.9	8.6	4.6	5.0
Italy	4.4	5.0	16.3	21.2	17.8	16.6	14.6	10.8
Canada	2.2	4.5	9.2	10.1	12.5	10.8	5.9	4.3
Total OECD	2.7	5.4	10.0	12.9	10.5	7.8	5.3	N.A.[c]

Sources: Organisation for Economic Co-operation and Development, *Historical Statistics, 1960–1981* (Paris: OECD, 1983); and *Economic Outlook* (December 1983) (Paris: OECD, 1983) for 1983 forecast values except 1983 consumer price inflation increases, which are actuals.

Note: Canadian and U.S. figures are updated for latest actual data available (Department of Finance Estimates for 1983). Average growth rates are compound annual rates from level in year before first year of period specified to level in final year of period specified.

a. Productivity increased as real GNP/GDP per member of the civilian labour force.

b. Standardized unemployment rates for all countries but the United States and Canada are based on the latest OECD forecast of recorded data for 1983, adjusted by the percentage-point difference between OECD reported actual and standardized rates for 1982. The rates for the United States and Canada are actual and correspond closely to the OECD standardized concept.
   Average standardized unemployment rates are for 1960–67, rather than 1961–67.

c. N.A. = not available.

The data given in Table 2-7 indicate that the post-1973 fall-off in productivity growth was greatest for Japan and next greatest for Italy. The measure of productivity growth used in this table, however, is real gross national expenditure (GNE) per employed person. More important, from a standpoint of international trade, is output per hour worked in the manufacturing sector. This measure of productivity for the seven major OECD countries is provided in Table 2-8. Again, the break after 1973 appears to have been particularly sharp for Japan, although that nation continued to out-perform European and North American countries by a wide margin.

The slow-down in productivity growth experienced by OECD countries explains most of the parallel slow-down in overall growth of output. As Table 2-9 shows, though employment growth also slowed after 1973, the effect of that slow-down on overall economic growth was minor compared to the effect of the slow-down in productivity growth.

According to the laws of market demand and supply, the reduction of the growth in output and productivity of OECD countries produced a slow-down in the growth of total demand for goods and services. The massive increases in world oil prices precipitated by OPEC in 1973–74 and 1979–80 siphoned off considerable disposable income and caused general economic belt-tightening. In addition, capital investment was weak in European countries throughout the 1970s, and it weakened further with the onset of the recession in the early 1980s. Capital investment in Canada dropped by 26 per cent in real terms between 1981 and 1982, while in the United States, the decline was a more modest 16 per cent. Capital investment in the United States, however, has rebounded sharply since the economic recovery began; the current U.S.

TABLE 2-8 Labour Productivity in Manufacturing in Major OECD Countries

Years	U.S.A.	Canada	Japan	France	Germany	Italy	U.K.
		(average annual percentage growth rates)					
1951–1973	2.8	4.3	10.0	5.3	5.8	6.6	3.4
1967–1973	3.1	5.0	11.9	6.0	5.3	7.1	4.7
1974–1981	1.5	1.1	6.2	4.2	4.4	3.6	2.2
		(percentage change)					
1967–1973 to 1974–1981	(−1.6)	(−3.9)	(−5.7)	(−1.8)	(−0.9)	(−3.5)	(−2.5)
		(annual percentage growth rates)					
1979	0.7	1.7	8.9	4.9	4.9	7.3	3.3
1980	0.2	−3.3	6.8	1.6	1.4	5.8	0.6
1981	2.8	0.3	3.2	1.6	2.7	3.4	5.9

Source: U.S. Department of Labor, Bureau of Labor Statistics, Office of Productivity and Technology, *Output per Hour, Hourly Compensation and Unit Labor Costs in Manufacturing, Eleven Countries, 1950–81* (Washington, D.C., December, 1982).

Note: Labour productivity = output per hour worked.

TABLE 2-9 Basic Components of Growth in Output

	Average Annual per Cent Increase		Change between 2 Time Periods
	1961–1973	1973–1981	
OECD			
Output	4.9	2.4	2.5
Employment	1.0	0.7	0.3
Output per worker	3.9	1.7	2.2
OECD Europe			
Output	4.6	1.9	2.7
Employment	0.3	−0.2	0.5
Output per worker	4.3	2.1	2.2
United States			
Output	4.2	2.3	1.9
Employment	2.0	2.1	−0.1
Output per worker	2.2	0.2	2.0
Canada			
Output	5.6	3.0	2.6
Employment	3.0	2.8	0.2
Output per worker	2.6	0.2	2.4

Source: Organisation for Economic Co-operation and Development, *Historical Statistics 1960–1981* (Paris: OECD, 1983).

capital boom is, at least in part, the result of tax cuts and increased defence expenditures.

The economic growth averages shown in Table 2-9, for time periods spanning 1961 to 1981, cloud the volatility of the business cycle over the past two decades. Since 1960, industrial production and gross national product have oscillated more and more widely from their long-term/growth trends. These swings are especially worrisome because, as Figures 2-6 and 2-7 demonstrate, successive peaks and troughs appear to leave behind progressively higher levels of inflation and unemployment.

Inflation in most OECD countries appears to be under much better control now than it has been for many years. Unemployment, however, is a deeply worrisome problem in Europe and Canada. The United States, in contrast, has experienced rapid economic recovery and a sharp improvement in its employment rate. For the 24 OECD-member countries, unemployment averaged almost 9 per cent in 1983, and 8.5 per cent in 1984; it is expected to remain at that level in 1985, despite continued economic recovery.

Since the mid-1970s, there has been a wide divergence between North American and other OECD countries in the growth of unemployment. This divergence is dramatically portrayed in Figure 2-8. The very marked divergence in unemployment trends, essentially those of Western European countries, the United States, Canada (although to a lesser degree) and Japan,

FIGURE 2-6 Average Rate of Inflation for the Seven Major OECD Countries, 1960–1985

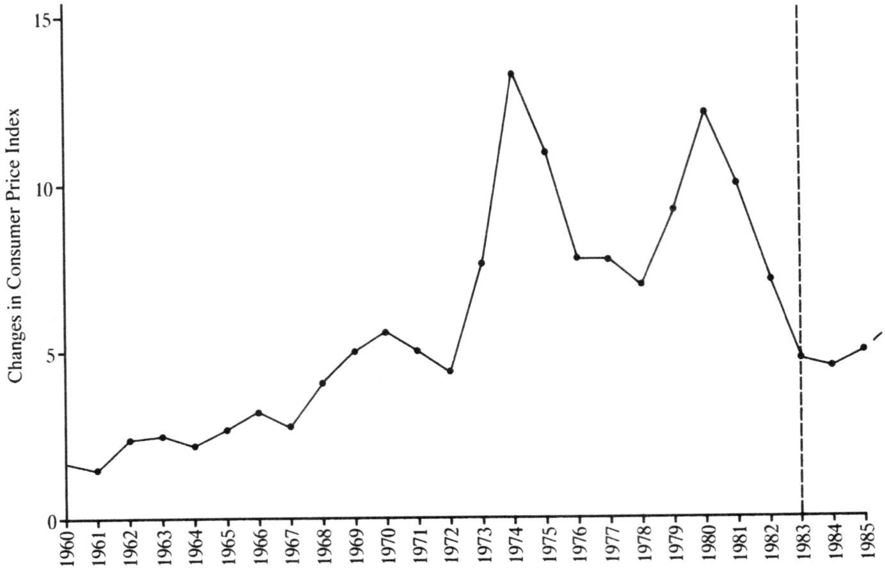

Sources: OECD, *Economic Outlook* (December 1977) (Paris: OECD, 1977), p. 125. OECD, *Economic Outlook* (December 1984) (Paris: OECD, 1984), p. 175.

FIGURE 2-7 Average Rate of Unemployment for the Seven Major OECD Countries, 1960–1985

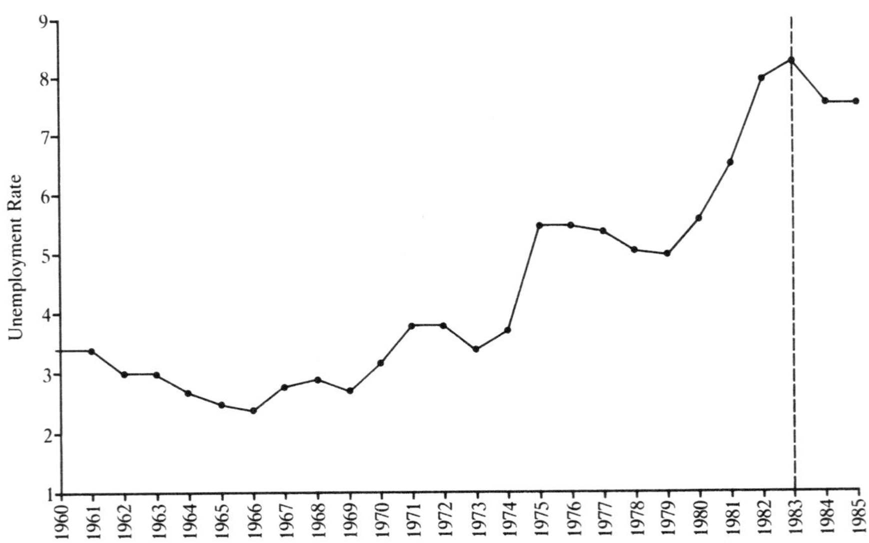

Sources : OECD, *Towards Full Employment and Price Stability* (Paris: OECD, 1977), p. 42. OECD, *Economic Outlook* (December 1984) (Paris: OECD, 1984), pp. 51, 177.

stems from marked differences in employment growth. Total employment in Europe actually fell between 1973 and 1983, while in North America and Japan, employment growth has been quite strong. The United States experienced a net creation of 15.8 million jobs between 1973 and 1983, in sharp contrast to a net loss of 1.5 million jobs in Europe. As a result, several European countries are experiencing critical unemployment problems, particularly among young job applicants.

FIGURE 2-8 Number of Unemployed

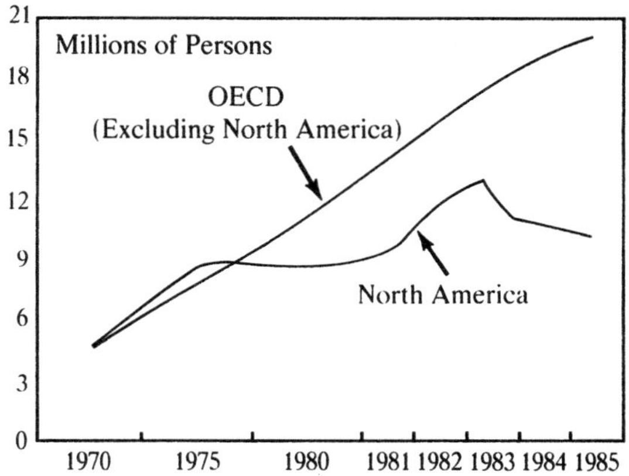

Source: Conference Board of Canada, reproduced in Shell Canada Limited, *Perspective on Energy Policy Directives.* Submission to the Royal Commission on the Economic Union and Development Prospects for Canada, July 31, 1984, p. 1

Table 2-10 indicates the extraordinarily high youth-unemployment rates in France, the United Kingdom, Italy and Spain. More than 10 million young people are unable to find jobs in the 12 countries represented in the table. In total, more than 31 million workers of all age groups are unemployed in OECD countries; some 10 million of these workers live in North America. The OECD *1984 Annual Report* states that "three of the most vulnerable groups are workers affected by large-scale employment dislocations, young workers, and the long-term unemployed."[2]

Prospects for resolving the severe unemployment problems of so many countries are uncertain at best. The overriding worry is the level of interest rates, which is very high both in nominal and real terms. Figure 2-9 indicates that in the United States, real interest rates (that is, nominal interest rates less the rate of inflation) have stood at exceptionally high levels for the past three years. Real interest rates in excess of 8 per cent are some four times higher than the average rate of little more than 2 per cent that prevailed throughout most of the period from 1945 to 1980. Because of the integration of capital markets, the high interest rates in the United States have caused high rates throughout OECD countries.

TABLE 2–10 **Youth Unemployment in Selected OECD Countries**

Youth Unemployment Rates[a]	(per cent) Actual 1980	1981	1982	1983	Prelim-inary 1984	Forecast 1985
United States	13.3	14.3	17.0	16.4	13.0	12.5
Japan	3.6	4.0	4.4	4.5	4.8	4.8
Germany	3.9	6.5	9.6	10.8	10.3	9.5
France	15.0	17.0	20.2	21.0	24.8	28.5
United Kingdom	14.1	18.1	23.1	23.2	23.8	23.5
Italy	25.2	27.4	29.7	32.0	33.8	35.3
Canada	13.2	13.3	18.7	19.9	19.0	18.3
Total of above countries	12.2	13.7	16.6	16.7	15.5	15.5
Australia	12.3	10.8	12.9	18.0	16.0	14.8
Finland	10.0	10.9	11.7	12.5[b]	12.0	10.8
Norway	5.4	5.8	8.1	9.8	9.5	9.0
Spain	28.5	33.7	36.9	38.9	42.8	44.5
Sweden	5.1	6.3	7.6	8.0	7.5	7.5
Total of twelve countries	12.9	14.5	17.4	17.7	16.8	16.8
Youth unemployment levels (millions)						
Seven major countries	6.8	7.7	9.2	9.2	8.5	8.5
Twelve countries	8.0	9.1	10.7	10.9	10.3	10.3

Source: Organisation for Economic Co-operation and Development, *Employment Outlook* (July 1984) (Paris: OECD, 1984), p. 44.

a. Aged up to 24 years. Data refer to the total youth-labour force in all countries except Canada and Australia, where Armed Forces personnel are excluded from the labour force aged 15 to 24 years.

b. The 1983 figure for Finland is an estimate.

Although opinion about the sustainability of world economic recovery tends to focus on interest rates, other factors may prove more troublesome in the long run. These include trends in productivity growth; the technology race and its implications for job displacement; the sectoral shifts in economic structure; the demands for flexibility and adaptability; and changing trade patterns, particularly the competition offered by Japan and newly industrializing countries (NICs).

Structural Shifts in Economic Activity

Most countries have experienced wide-ranging structural changes over the post-war period. This is particularly true of Western industrialized countries, where the government sector has grown markedly and the service sector even more, while the manufacturing and resource sectors have tended to shrink in relative importance. Table 2-11 reflects these structural changes in output for

FIGURE 2-9 Real Interest in the United States[a]

(per cent per annum)

Average U.S. Real Interest Rate

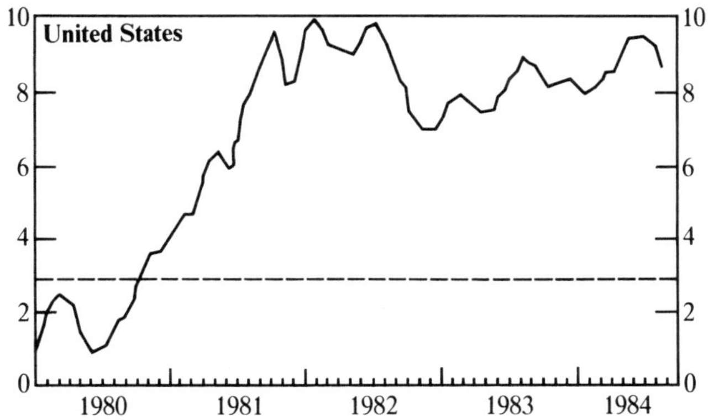

Source: International Monetary Fund *World Economic Outlook, September 1984* (Washington, D.C.: International Monetary Fund, 1984), p. 20

Note: The dashed line represents the average value of the U.S. real long-term interest rate during the period 1974 to 1983.

(a) Monthly average weekly yields on long-term government bonds deflated by the rate of inflation.

Canada, the United States, the United Kingdom, Germany, Japan and Sweden. Table 2-12 gives similar information on the distribution of employment.

These two tables demonstrate that the structural changes have related predominantly to employment. With the exception of Japan, which has rapidly reduced the relative importance of its agricultural sector to bring it more in line with those of other foremost countries, major OECD countries have made only modest changes in output composition over the past 20 years. Output accounted for by the service sector, for example, increased, on average, by only 2 percentage points between 1964 and 1981. Japan's service-sector output actually fell, in relative-share terms, while its manufacturing sector accounted for another 12 percentage points of total output. Agriculture's contribution to total output decreased in all countries, while the manufacturing share of GNP increased in the late 1950s and early 1960s, and then decreased during the late 1960s and 1970s in all countries except Japan. It is important to note that the structural changes in output summarized in Table 2-11 are expressed in real dollar terms rather than in nominal dollar terms. If they are expressed in the latter terms, these changes closely parallel the much more marked structural changes in the composition of employment.

The employment shifts, as already noted, have been much more marked. The primary-sector share of employment fell from 17.5 per cent in 1956, to 5.4 per cent in 1981, a decline of almost 70 per cent. Over the same period, Japan's primary sector share of employment fell even more dramatically,

TABLE 2-11 International Comparison of Share Distribution of Real GDP

	(per cent)					
	Primary	Mining	Manufac-turing	Construc-tion	Utilities	Services
Canada						
1960	5.8	3.7	21.1	7.6	10.2	51.6
1970	4.3	4.0	22.8	6.7	11.7	50.6
1981	3.4	2.7	21.7	6.2	13.8	52.2
United States						
1960	4.6	3.0	23.2	6.9	7.4	54.9
1970	3.4	2.9	24.0	5.7	8.4	55.7
1981	3.0	2.5	23.8	4.1	9.0	57.6
United Kingdom						
1960	2.9	3.2	28.5	8.3	7.4	49.8
1970	2.8	2.1	30.1	8.6	8.0	48.4
1981	3.2	5.1	24.2	5.9	8.8	52.8
Germany						
1960	4.7	3.1	34.4	8.4	7.8	41.6
1970	3.3	1.8	37.9	7.3	8.3	41.4
1981	2.8	1.0	34.8	6.0	10.0	45.4
Japan						
1964	9.9	0.8	23.9	8.4	7.3	49.6
1970	6.1	0.7	29.8	9.3	8.3	45.9
1981	3.4	0.5	35.9	7.4	7.3	45.5
Sweden						
1964	7.0	0.9	28.3	9.4	7.3	47.1
1970	5.6	1.0	29.8	9.1	7.7	46.8
1981	4.5	0.6	26.2	7.8	10.4	50.5
Six-country average						
1964	5.4	2.3	27.4	8.3	8.0	48.6
1970	4.2	2.1	29.1	7.8	8.7	48.1
1981	3.4	2.1	27.8	6.2	9.9	50.7

Source: Michael F. Charette, Robert P. Henry, and Barry Kaufmann, "The Evolution of the Canadian Industrial Structure: An International Perspective", in *Canadian Industry in Transition*, vol. 2, prepared for the Royal Commission on the Economic Union and Development Prospects for Canada (Toronto: University of Toronto Press, 1985).

from 38.5 per cent to 10.0 per cent. Relative to other major industrialized countries, Japan still employs a high percentage of its labour force in primary production, mainly agriculture. While we Canadians tend to think of ourselves as heavily dependent on our resource sectors, employment shares indicate that we have a distribution of employment broadly similar to the patterns of our major trade partners.

Although the movement out of agriculture was essentially complete in North America by the early 1970s, Europe (most particularly, West Germany, France and Italy) lost 1.6 million agricultural jobs between 1973 and 1981, while Japan lost 1.5 million. Even middle-income economies

TABLE 2-12 International Comparison of Share Distribution of Employment

	(per cent)					
	Primary	Mining	Manufacturing	Construction	Utilities	Services
Canada						
1956	16.4	2.1	25.7	7.4	8.9	39.5
1960	13.2	1.6	24.7	7.0	8.6	44.8
1970	7.7	1.6	22.7	6.0	8.8	53.3
1981	5.5	1.8	19.4	5.9	8.3	59.1
United States						
1956	11.2	1.4	29.2	5.1	7.2	45.9
1960	9.1	1.2	28.1	4.8	6.7	50.0
1970	4.7	0.8	26.0	4.8	6.1	57.7
1981	3.7	1.1	21.3	4.4	5.5	64.0
United Kingdom						
1956	4.6	3.7	37.1	6.7	9.1	38.8
1960	4.3	1.7	34.7	6.8	8.3	45.3
1970	3.2	1.7	34.7	6.8	8.3	45.3
1981	2.6	1.4	26.2	6.5	8.0	55.3
Germany						
1956	16.9	3.1	36.5	7.6	8.7	27.2
1960	14.0	3.1	36.7	8.5	6.5	31.2
1970	8.6	1.2	39.4	7.9	6.4	36.4
1981	5.5	1.4	33.6	7.5	7.0	45.0
Japan						
1956	38.5	1.0	19.2	4.4	4.7	32.1
1964	26.8	1.1	24.3	6.2	6.5	35.6
1970	17.4	0.4	27.1	7.7	6.9	40.4
1981	10.0	0.2	24.9	9.8	6.7	48.4
Sweden[a]						
1964	12.8	0.6	28.5	9.1	7.5	41.6
1970	8.4	0.5	26.5	9.5	7.4	47.8
1981	5.3	0.4	22.0	7.4	7.8	57.1
Six-country average						
1956	17.5	2.3	29.5	6.2	7.8	36.8
1964	12.2	1.4	30.0	7.0	7.4	42.1
1970	8.3	1.0	29.4	7.1	7.3	46.8
1981	5.4	1.1	24.6	6.9	7.2	54.8

Source: Michael F. Charette, Robert P. Henry, and Barry Kaufmann, "The Evolution of the Canadian Industrial Structure: An International Perspective", in *Canadian Industry in Transition*, vol. 2, prepared for the Royal Commission on the Economic Union and Development Prospects for Canada (Toronto: University of Toronto Press, 1985).

a. The sample average for 1956 excludes Sweden.

experienced a significant shift away from agriculture. As Table 2-13 shows, only in low-income economies does agriculture continue to provide the principal means of employment.

TABLE 2-13 Industry Sector Distribution of Labour Force

	(per cent)					
	Agriculture		Industry		Services	
	1960	1980	1960	1980	1960	1980
United States	7	2	36	32	57	66
Canada	13	5	34	29	52	66
France	22	8	39	39	39	53
West Germany	14	4	48	46	38	50
Japan	33	12	30	39	37	49
Italy	31	11	40	45	29	44
United Kingdom	4	2	48	42	48	56
Industrial market economies	18	6	38	38	44	56
Non-market industrial economies	42	18	30	45	28	39
High-income oil exporters	62	46	13	19	25	35
Middle-income economies	62	46	15	22	23	34
Low-income economies	77	72	19	15	14	15

Source: World Development Report 1984 (New York: Oxford University Press for the World Bank, 1984), pp. 258–59.

Tables 2-14A and 2-14B indicate that the manufacturing share of civilian employment in OECD countries has been reasonably stable over the past two decades. Manufacturing employment figures most prominently in West Germany, the United Kingdom and Japan and, of the major industrialized countries, least prominently in Canada. Some 79 million people were employed in this sector in OECD countries in 1981, but as a consequence of the recession, only 75 million were so employed in 1982. In that year, manufacturing employment fell by 7 per cent in the United States and by more than 9 per cent in Canada. While these drops caused considerable concern, the rebound in 1983 and 1984 underscores the need to look at long-run trends rather than at short-term gyrations.

Growth in manufacturing employment has been greater in the United States and Canada than in most OECD countries. Indeed, France, West Germany, the United Kingdom and Italy suffered absolute declines in manufacturing employment of 3.3 million jobs between 1973 and 1981. Even in relation to Japan, North American economies have done well in providing employment, although much of the difference in performance is related simply to faster growth in this continent's labour force. Manufacturing accounts for a much higher percentage of gross domestic product in Japan than it does in Canada and the United States, yet Japan's allocation of labour to manufacturing is not much higher, proportionately, than that of North America.

Employment in the service sector grew rapidly in Western industrialized countries during the 1960s and 1970s. On average, the service sector accounts for 55 per cent of total employment in OECD countries. This is a marked increase from 37 per cent in 1956. The United States and Canada have large service sectors, considerably larger, indeed, than has either Germany or Japan.

TABLE 2-14A Employment in Manufacturing as Percentage of Civilian Employment

	1960–67	1968–73	1974–79	1980–82	1960–82
United States	26.8	25.8	23.0	21.4	24.8
Japan	23.7	26.9	25.4	24.7	25.1
West Germany	35.3	36.6	35.1	33.7	35.4
France	28.4	27.9	27.2	25.2	27.6
United Kingdom	37.4	36.1	32.5	28.2	34.6
Italy	26.8	29.1	28.9	27.3	28.0
Canada	25.0	23.8	21.7	20.8	23.3
Total of above countries	28.2	28.4	26.3	24.5	27.3
Total OECD	26.9	27.2	25.4	23.7	26.1

Source: Organisation for Economic Co-operation and Development, *Historical Statistics 1960–1982* (Paris: OECD, 1984), p. 37.

TABLE 2-14B Civilian Employment in Manufacturing: Average Annual Percentage Changes

	1960-68	1968-73	1973-79	1979-82	1960-82
United States	2.3	0.2	1.1	−3.3	0.7
Japan	4.1	2.0	−1.3	1.2	1.7
West Germany	0.3	0.9	−1.3	−1.9	−0.3
France	0.4	1.6	−1.1	−2.0	−0.1
United Kingdom	−0.3	−1.0	−1.4	−7.1	−1.7
Italy	0.7	0.9	–	−0.7	0.4
Canada	2.8	2.1	1.5	−2.0	1.6
Total of above countries	1.7	0.8	−0.3	−2.2	0.4
Total OECD	1.6	0.9	−0.4	−2.1	0.4

Source: Organisation for Economic Co-operation and Development, *Historical Statistics 1960–1982* (Paris: OECD, 1984), p. 28.

The growth of the service sector reflects the growth of government over the post-war period. Figure 2-10 indicates the growth in government expenditures in OECD countries between 1960 and 1982. To help put Canada's position in perspective, we have shown its experience and that of the United States separately. The growth of Canada's public sector has closely paralleled that of Europe's. Figure 2-10 makes it clear, however, that Canada's public sector represents a larger percentage of gross domestic product than does that of the United States. Still, as we shall see in Part III of this Report, comparisons between countries are difficult, and conclusions should be cautiously drawn.

Government expenditures exceed revenues by a considerable margin in the major industrialized countries. Table 2-15 indicates the resulting growth in budget deficits. Financing these deficits absorbed more than 50 per cent of net private savings of the seven major industrialized nations in 1982 and

FIGURE 2-10 Expenditures by General Government

(as percentages of GDP[a])

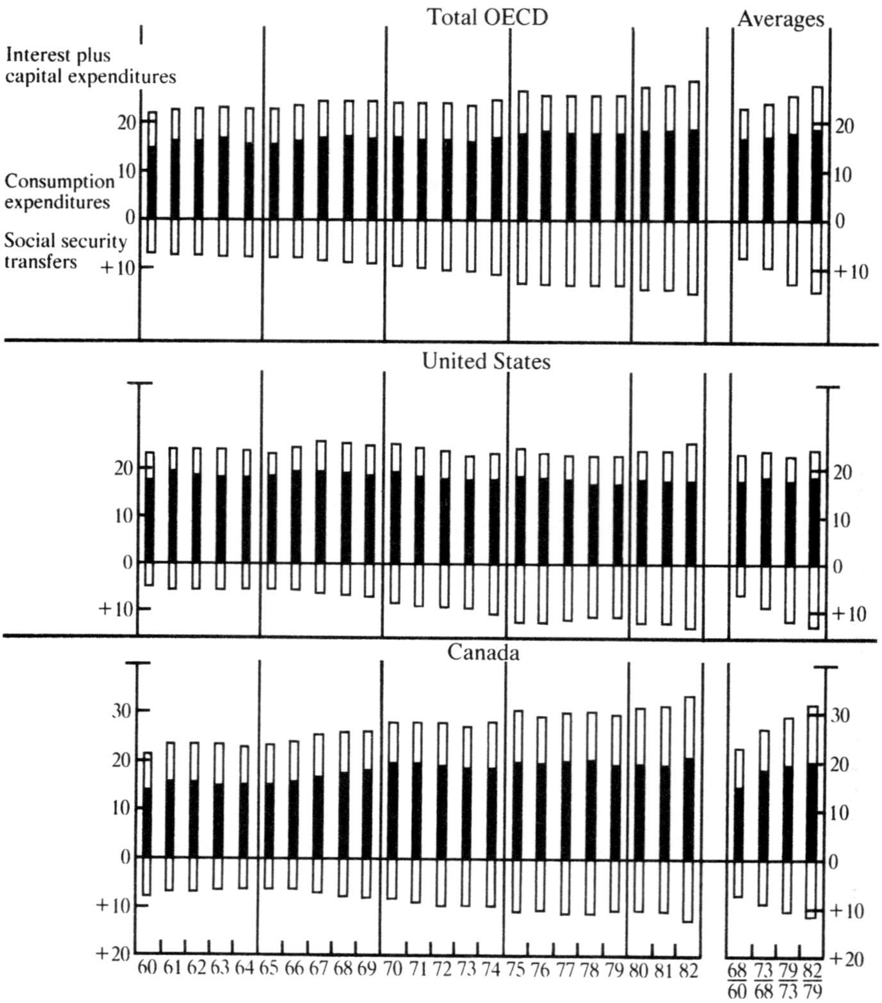

Source: OECD, *Historical Statistics 1960–1982* (Paris: OECD, 1984), pp. 150 and 152.

a. The total height of each bar measures total government outlays as a percentage of GDP.

1983. In addition, total government debt of that group of nations now exceeds 50 per cent of their collective output.

From 1973, governments ceased to be a net source of savings and became increasingly heavy net users. This shift in savings, as indicated in Table 2-15, can be interpreted as evidence that private investment, which has been at low levels in Europe and Canada in the 1980s, is insufficient. A review of the deficit and debt positions of major OECD countries shows that the largest

TABLE 2-15 Public-Sector Claims on Private Savings and Government Indebtedness

(per cent)

A. Ratio of budget deficit to gross private savings[a]	1973	1974	1975	1976	1977	1978	1979	1980	1981	1982	1983[b]	1984[b]	1985[b]
United States	−3.4	2.0	22.9	12.3	5.5	−1.1	−3.5	7.2	5.3	22.2	22.9	18.1	21.5
Japan	−1.6	−1.2	9.5	12.1	13.1	18.2	16.6	15.6	14.2	12.5	12.2	9.1	6.6
Germany	−6.0	6.4	27.2	17.0	12.9	12.5	13.2	15.7	19.3	17.0	12.9	6.4	1.7
France	−4.4	−3.1	10.7	2.5	4.2	8.8	3.4	−1.2	10.0	14.4	18.6	19.3	18.9
United Kingdom	14.1	23.8	28.8	28.7	17.0	20.5	16.4	18.4	15.6	12.2	21.7	17.3	14.6
Italy	32.6	31.7	43.5	33.4	29.9	35.1	33.9	30.6	45.4	48.8	47.9	48.9	47.8
Canada	−5.3	−9.8	12.5	8.5	12.6	15.5	8.3	11.2	5.3	25.0	26.4	24.1	20.9
Total	−0.3	4.2	21.2	14.1	9.9	8.6	6.1	11.0	11.5	20.3	21.2	17.4	17.7
B. Ratio of budget deficit to net private savings[a]													
United States	−7.0	4.8	52.4	30.4	13.7	−2.6	−9.3	22.0	15.0	71.4	68.2	49.7	61.2
Japan	−2.7	−2.1	17.1	20.6	23.0	31.0	29.8	28.2	26.5	24.7	26.9	20.3	15.2
Germany	−11.8	12.9	55.9	35.5	28.9	26.2	27.8	35.4	46.2	40.6	30.5	15.8	4.3
France	−7.5	−5.9	20.2	5.8	8.5	16.7	6.7	−2.6	24.2	35.2	47.0	47.2	43.0
United Kingdom	26.4	61.4	76.1	68.5	37.8	40.7	35.8	42.8	40.5	30.8	56.3	48.1	39.8
Italy	47.2	48.7	69.4	52.4	47.9	54.2	51.4	47.5	73.0	78.0	82.9	85.1	82.2
Canada	−10.5	−19.1	24.1	16.8	26.7	30.6	15.3	20.8	10.4	50.5	49.8	44.0	37.5
Total	−1.6	9.1	45.6	30.6	20.5	15.2	10.0	25.2	25.7	54.0	54.8	42.7	44.7

TABLE 2-15 (cont'd)

C. Ratio of general government debts[c] to nominal GDP	1973	1974	1975	1976	1977	1978	1979	1980	1981	1982	1983[b]	1984[b]	1985[b]
							(per cent)						
United States	42.5	41.3	44.9	45.2	43.8	42.0	39.8	41.0	39.0	43.2	45.7	46.0	47.8
Japan	17.1	17.9	22.5	28.2	33.6	42.2	47.6	52.9	58.1	62.3	66.5	67.7	67.7
Germany	18.6	19.7	24.9	27.0	28.4	29.8	30.6	32.5	36.3	39.4	41.0	40.7	39.4
France	16.9	24.7	25.8	24.7	25.2	26.3	26.3	25.1	25.9	28.7	32.4	36.6	40.7
United Kingdom	70.9	70.3	65.6	64.7	63.2	60.3	56.0	55.5	55.5	54.1	55.0	55.3	55.3
Italy	60.6	57.7	65.0	63.1	62.3	68.4	68.1	65.3	68.4	74.3	79.7	85.3	92.8
Canada	46.8	44.4	44.7	42.5	44.4	48.5	46.7	45.9	45.5	50.6	54.9	58.1	60.5
Total	37.5	37.0	40.1	41.1	41.4	42.5	42.0	42.9	43.9	47.5	50.5	51.6	53.2

Source: Organisation for Economic Co-operation and Development, *Economic Outlook* (July 1984) (Paris: OECD, 1984), p. 29. 1973 figures from (December 1983), p. 43.

a. General government financial deficit as a percentage of private savings. A minus sign indicates a financial surplus. Gross private savings = household + business gross savings, net of stock appreciation where data are available (for the United States, the United Kingdom and Canada), but before allowance for capital consumption. Net private savings = gross savings, net of capital consumption.

b. OECD estimates and forecasts.

c. General government gross financial liabilities at the end of calendar year.

increase in the ratio of government debt to GNP occurred in Japan, where this ratio rose from 17 per cent in 1973 to 68 per cent in 1984. The smallest increase occurred in the United States where, between those years, the ratio of government debt to GNP rose from 43 per cent to 46 per cent. Canada's increase, which brought our government-debt ratio from 47 per cent of GNP in 1973 to 58 per cent in 1984, was the second-smallest among the seven major OECD countries.

The structural shifts among the primary, manufacturing, service and government sectors, noted in this section, stem from a wide range of causes. Productivity advances in the agricultural sector have brought great increases in output with a fraction of the original labour force. This change in the labour-force/productivity balance has prompted rapid urbanization. Almost 80 per cent of the population of Western industrialized countries lives in urban centres. This figure constitutes an increase of 10 per cent over the urban-rural mix of 20 years ago. Less than 20 per cent of the population of many low-income countries lives in urban centres. More generally, productivity gains have led to much higher per capita incomes and consequent changes in the demand for goods and services. The labour force has adapted to these changes and, in the process, has changed its composition and institutional organization.

One striking feature of the post-war period has been the rapid increase in women's participation in the labour force. Some 56 per cent of working-age women in the seven major industrialized countries now work outside the home. Consequently, women now make up 40 per cent of the work-force, compared to 35 per cent in 1960. In the majority of families, there is now more than one breadwinner.

Labour-force growth in OECD countries averaged 0.9 per cent annually between 1960 and 1968, increasing to 1.4 per cent for the following decade. Since 1979, there has been a marginal decline in the growth rate. Growth in Canada's total labour force has considerably outpaced that of other OECD countries, rising at a rate of more than double the average. The sharp rise in women's participation has been an important contributing factor, as has the sharp increase in the birth rate after the end of the Second World War.

Another striking feature of the post-war period was the growth of unionization. With the 1981-82 recession has come a considerable drop in the proportion of the labour force working under union contracts, but it is too early to tell whether this signifies a trend or simply represents a short-term aberration.

One manifestation of the rise in living standards in OECD countries has been more leisure time, which has taken the forms of a shorter work-week and earlier retirement. A recent phenomenon in some countries has been the substitution of part-time workers for full-time workers. The higher proportion of women in the work-force, together with higher education and training requirements and the independence of youth at earlier ages may explain this shift to part-time work.

Over the post-war period there have been pronounced changes in the ways that labour is employed and in the composition and organization of the labour force. The service sector, including government, is the predominant source of employment in industrialized countries. The shift from resource-based industries, particularly those related to agriculture, has facilitated rapid urbanization and specialization, as well as unionization and a greatly enhanced role for women in the labour force. Moreover, the growing interdependence of different sectors within the labour force, both domestically and internationally, together with the demand for publicly organized health and other social services, has given government a major influence in creating and allocating the national income.

Productivity, Living Standards and Competitiveness

Some observers of the different productivity performances noted in the preceding sections are quick to draw conclusions about the relative international competitiveness of various nations. Those countries with a relatively weak productivity performance, such as the United States and Canada, are thought to be losing their ability to compete. The relationship between productivity and international competitiveness, however, is less straightforward than it might appear at first.

Productivity is usually defined, in general terms, as the total output of a nation per unit of labour input. While this definition appears to stress labour productivity, it implicitly includes the overall efficiency of resource use, including capital. Competitiveness is more narrowly related to those goods – particularly manufactured goods – and services that are traded internationally. Thus a nation could maintain a reasonably strong overall productivity performance, yet suffer a decline in competitiveness because of a relatively weak productivity performance in sectors that trade internationally. Alternatively, a nation could have a weak overall productivity performance, yet remain competitive because of a relatively strong performance in sectors that trade internationally. Competitiveness is influenced, too, by factors other than productivity.

Figure 2-11 indicates the relative competitive position of the manufacturing sector of each of the seven major industrialized countries; the trend lines of particular significance are those showing per-unit labour costs expressed in constant U.S. dollars. While the trends shown in this figure are approximations, the broad directions for each country are considered reasonably accurate. The figure suggests that over the period from 1973 to 1984, there have been significant shifts in the relative competitive positions of the manufacturing sectors of the seven major OECD countries. The positions of the United States and the United Kingdom have deteriorated considerably, while Japan's position has strengthened notably. There have been no significant changes, however, in the position of the other four countries shown, including Canada. Most of the dramatic changes shown for the United States, the United Kingdom and Japan have occurred since 1978.

These shifts in relative competitiveness are not solely the result of differences in productivity performance. Exchange rates are also a major determinant of the competitive position of a given country, and they may be influenced by a wide variety of factors, including domestic monetary policies,

FIGURE 2-11 Measures of Relative Competitive Position

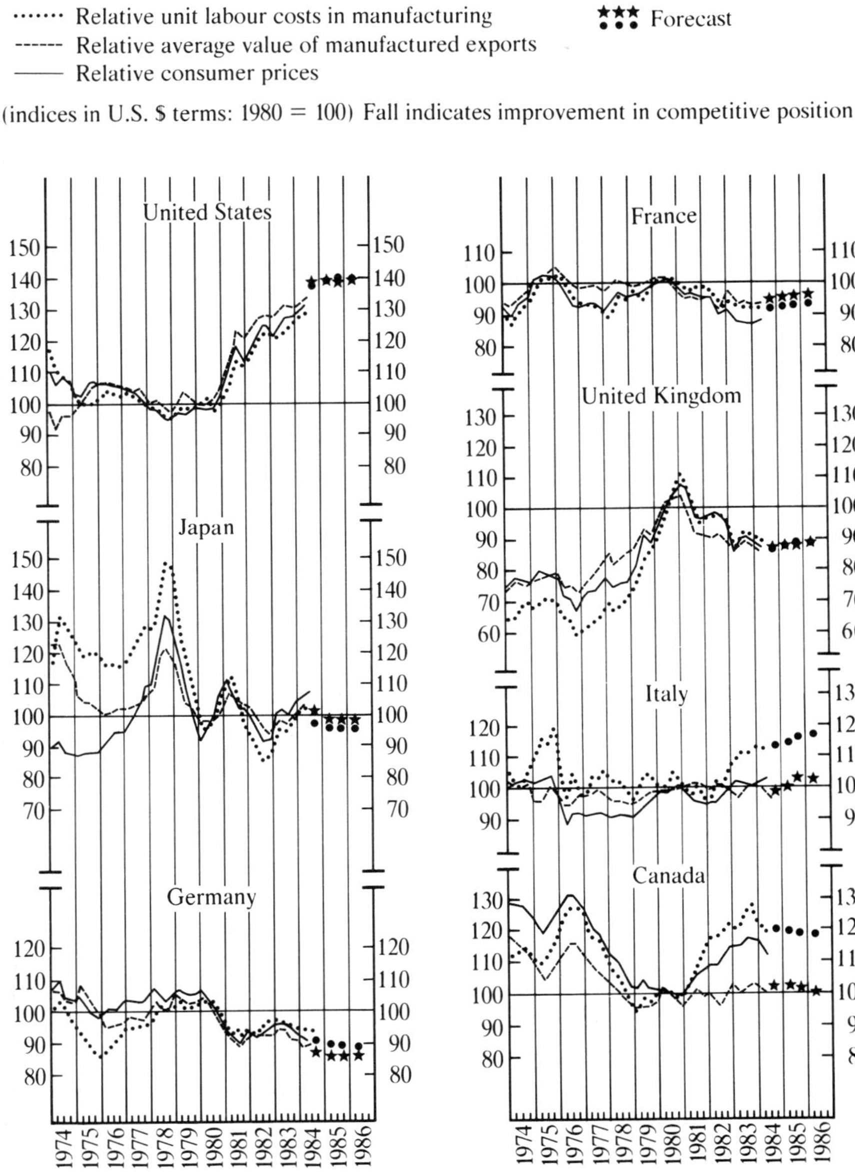

Source: OECD, *Economic Outlook* (December 1984) (Paris: OECD, 1984), p. 74.

rates of inflation, and changes in the terms of trade. The sharp deterioration in the position of the U.S. manufacturing sector that is evident in Figure 2-11 is more the result of the considerable appreciation of the U.S. dollar, induced by the high level of U.S. interest rates, than of any other single circumstance.

Competitiveness at the level of individual firms involves the relative costs and prices of two producers for an identical or very similar product. International trade, however, is based on specialization: that is, countries produce goods and services in which they have some form of comparative advantage. Such an advantage may be natural in origin (the result of climate, for example) or it may be "engineered" (that is, derived from superior organization, more advanced technology, innovation or some other such factor or factors). A comparatively high-cost producer of certain manufactured products may continue to compete effectively in domestic and international markets simply because other countries have more productive ways of employing their limited human, capital and other resources. Although a company or a whole industry in a particular country may be forced out of business because of inability to compete with foreign suppliers at home or abroad, such a fate does not threaten a nation's existence.

While there is a distinction to be made between productivity and international competitiveness, it should not be overstated. Generally, a strong productivity performance relative to other trade partners should allow gains in real income and in export sales, support an appreciating exchange rate, and give a further boost to real income. Some countries may choose to realize real-income gains associated with productivity growth by expanding export sales and achieving a stronger currency. Some observers claim, for example, that Japan has been using part of its productivity gains to reduce the relative prices of its exports, and that this strategy has increased the competitive standing of its products and enabled it to expand its markets.

However realized, the real-income gains from productivity growth are the foundation for rising living standards. Table 2-16 provides an approximate measure of the improvement in living standards during the 1960s and the 1970s. To allow for international comparisons, all figures are expressed in U.S. dollars, using 1975 exchange rates. Furthermore, to abstract the effects of inflation, all aggregates are expressed in 1975 prices. To facilitate comparison with current prices and exchange rates, a column has been added for 1982.

Because the early 1980s were such abnormal years for many countries, it is advisable to focus on the period from 1964 to 1980. Canada's standard of living improved by 62 per cent over this period, compared to 38 per cent for the United States, 139 per cent for Japan, 75 per cent for France, 60 per cent for Germany, 74 per cent for Italy, and 33 per cent for the United Kingdom. Although the United States' rate of improvement is relatively low, we must remember that it started from a substantially higher living standard than most countries. The great disparities in performance of the twenty-four countries shown in Table 2-16 can be explained in many ways, but rates of productivity growth certainly provide one explanation. On this score, Japan has greatly outperformed other major industrialized countries during the past two decades.

TABLE 2-16 Gross Domestic Product, per Capita, in Constant U.S. Dollars at the Exchange Rates and Price Levels of 1975

	1964	1970	1980	1982	1982[a]
Canada	4 940	6 033	8 014	7 809	12 104
United States	5 762	6 637	7 974	7 870	13 106
Japan	2 292	3 834	5 485	5 806	8 966
Australia	4 599	5 697	6 789	6 785	10 371
New Zealand	3 642	3 992	4 372	4 480	7 520
Austria	3 232	4 183	5 940	5 945	8 835
Belgium	4 288	5 467	7 265	7 257	8 552
Denmark	5 743	6 926	8 408	8 657	11 017
Finland	3 770	4 966	6 803	7 014	10 175
France	4 236	5 486	7 409	7 477	9 961
Germany	5 009	6 200	8 058	7 958	10 691
Greece	1 234	1 851	2 671	2 619	3 917
Iceland	4 253	4 679	6 965	6 844	11 265
Ireland	1 828	2 281	3 003	3 106	5 062
Italy	2 365	3 176	4 111	4 086	6 133
Luxembourg	4 926	5 798	7 333	7 083	9 137
Netherlands	4 469	5 718	7 020	6 776	9 615
Norway	4 850	5 845	8 826	8 736	13 648
Portugal	895	1 317	1 934	1 988	2 338
Spain	1 756	2 365	3 090	3 090	4 778
Sweden	6 509	7 927	9 311	9 281	11 907
Switzerland	6 985	8 321	9 245	9 147	14 928
Turkey	566	687	946	999	1 132
United Kingdom	3 366	3 784	4 482	4 527	8 523
OECD (Total)	3 946	4 899	6 181	6 184	9 571
OECD (Europe)	3 336	4 148	5 229	5 203	7 517
EEC	3 754	4 693	6 030	6 014	8 700

Source: Organisation for Economic Co-operation and Development, *National Accounts, 1953-1982*, vol. 1 (Paris: OECD, 1984), p. 86.

a. Gross domestic product, per capita, in U.S. dollars at current prices and exchange rates.

While Japan's performance has been remarkable, its overall share of OECD production has not changed dramatically. Table 2-17 shows the relative shares of OECD output from 1970 to 1982, adjusted for the purchasing power of each country's currency. The United States has maintained its overwhelming dominance, while Japan's share has improved by some 3 per cent, at the expense of the European Community (EC).

Table 2-18 indicates that growth rates of non-industrialized countries have been greater than those of Western countries. Until recently, growth was skewed in favour of high-income oil-exporting countries, but it was by no means limited to them. Low-income and middle-income developing countries achieved healthy annual increases in their gross domestic products during the 1960s and 1970s. Despite these growth rates, however, per capita incomes remain very low for roughly half the world's population.

TABLE 2-17 Shares in OECD Totals: GDP in Current Dollars Using Current Purchasing-Power Parity

	(per cent)												
	1970	1971	1972	1973	1974	1975	1976	1977	1978	1979	1980	1981	1982
United States	38.76	38.53	38.52	38.29	37.72	37.52	37.51	38.01	38.29	38.00	37.43	37.82	37.03
Canada	3.31	3.15	3.00	2.94	3.27	3.42	3.55	3.53	3.50	3.55	3.59	3.65	3.45
Japan	12.40	12.51	12.92	13.24	12.99	13.32	13.37	13.55	13.69	13.96	14.46	14.76	15.27
Belgium	1.26	1.26	1.26	1.26	1.30	1.28	1.29	1.25	1.24	1.23	1.26	1.22	1.24
Denmark	0.74	0.73	0.73	0.72	0.70	0.70	0.71	0.70	0.68	0.69	0.68	0.66	0.68
France	6.85	6.96	6.99	6.94	7.10	7.13	7.13	7.09	7.09	7.10	7.09	6.97	7.09
Germany	8.75	8.71	8.61	8.48	8.46	8.34	8.38	8.33	8.26	8.34	8.39	8.23	8.17
Greece	0.56	0.58	0.60	0.61	0.58	0.62	0.63	0.63	0.64	0.65	0.65	0.64	0.65
Ireland	0.23	0.23	0.24	0.23	0.24	0.25	0.24	0.25	0.25	0.25	0.26	0.26	0.26
Italy	6.08	5.96	5.83	5.88	6.07	5.86	5.92	5.81	5.74	5.84	5.99	5.88	5.88
Luxembourg	0.06	0.06	0.06	0.06	0.07	0.05	0.05	0.05	0.05	0.05	0.05	0.05	0.05
Netherlands	1.86	1.87	1.83	1.82	1.87	1.85	1.86	1.84	1.81	1.80	1.79	1.74	1.72
United Kingdom	7.22	7.14	6.92	7.01	6.89	6.84	6.76	6.60	6.57	6.50	6.25	6.05	6.20
European Community	33.61	33.50	33.08	33.01	33.29	32.92	32.99	32.53	32.33	32.44	32.39	31.69	31.93
Austria	0.88	0.89	0.90	0.89	0.92	0.91	0.91	0.92	0.89	0.90	0.91	0.90	0.91
Portugal	0.47	0.48	0.49	0.52	0.51	0.49	0.50	0.51	0.51	0.53	0.54	0.53	0.55
Spain	3.05	3.08	3.16	3.21	3.37	3.41	3.35	3.34	3.27	3.17	3.18	3.13	3.17
Other Countries	7.52	7.85	7.93	7.90	7.93	8.00	7.82	7.62	7.53	7.46	7.48	7.52	7.68
OECD Total	100.00	100.00	100.00	100.00	100.00	100.00	100.00	100.00	100.00	100.00	100.00	100.00	100.00

Source: Organisation for Economic Co-operation and Development, *National Accounts, 1953–1982*, vol. 1 (Paris: OECD, 1984), p. 98.

TABLE 2-18 Population, GDP and GDP per Capita in 1980, and Growth Rates, 1960–83

Country Group	1980 GDP (billions of dollars)	1980 Population (millions)	1980 GDP per Capita (dollars)	GDP Growth Rates (average annual percentage change)					
				1960–73	1973–79	1980	1981	1982	1983[a]
Developing countries[b]	2 118	3 280	650	6.3	5.2	2.5	2.4	1.9	1.0
Low-income countries	549	2 175	250	5.6	4.8	5.9	4.8	5.2	4.7
Asia	497	1 971	250	5.9	5.2	6.3	5.2	5.6	5.1
China	284	980	290	8.5	5.7	6.1	4.8	7.3	5.1
India	162	675	240	3.6	4.3	6.9	5.7	2.9	5.4
Africa	52	204	250	3.5	2.1	1.3	1.2	0.5	−0.1
Middle-income oil importers	915	611	1 500	6.3	5.6	4.3	0.9	0.7	0.3
East Asia and Pacific	204	183	1 110	8.2	8.6	3.6	6.7	4.2	6.4
Middle East and North Africa	28	35	800	5.2	3.0	4.2	−2.4	5.5	2.0
Sub-Saharan Africa[c]	37	60	610	5.6	3.7	5.5	3.9	1.1	0.3
Southern Europe	201	91	2 210	6.7	5.0	1.5	2.3	0.7	−0.9
Latin America and Caribbean	445	241	1 840	5.6	5.0	5.8	−2.3	−0.4	−2.2
Middle-income oil exporters[d]	654	494	1 320	6.9	4.9	−2.4	2.4	0.9	−1.7
High-income oil exporters	228	16	14 250	10.7	7.7	7.4	0.0	N.A.	N.A.
Industrial market economies	7 463	715	10 440	4.9	2.8	1.3	1.3	−0.5	2.3

Source: *World Development Report 1984* (New York: Oxford University Press for The World Bank, 1984), p. 11.

a. Estimated.

b. Data for 1982 and 1983 are based on a sample of 90 developing countries.

c. Does not include South Africa.

d. The estimated 1983 data exclude Angola, Iran, and Iraq.

Emerging Trade Realities

In the post-war period, the world has become heavily dependent on trade. The proportion of goods and services that crosses national boundaries has more than doubled, rising from 11 per cent of world output in 1950 to 21 per cent in 1980. This expansion of world trade has included significant shifts in trade structure and pattern, and these changes have important implications for Canada. Figure 2-12 illustrates, in a very general manner, the changing shares of world trade. It shows that both the United States and Canada have lost part of their former shares of world trade, although both countries have experienced increases in the proportion of their gross national product accounted for by trade.

Rapid technological change, the discovery of raw material supplies around the world, intense Japanese competition to sell industrial goods in international markets and, more recently, the influence of developing countries have

FIGURE 2-12 Shares of World Trade, 1960–1980

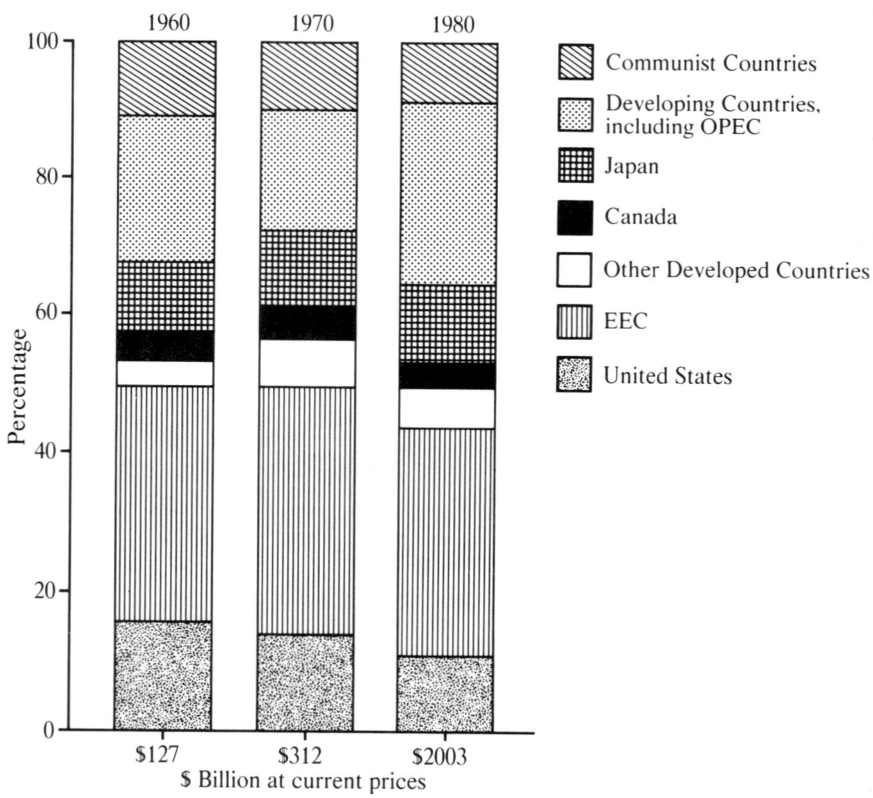

Source: U.S. Department of Commerce, International Trade Administration, *U.S. Competitiveness in the International Economy,* October 1981, as cited in Bruce R. Scott, *American Competitiveness: Concepts Performance and Implications,* Harvard Business School 75th Annual Colloquium on United States Competitiveness in the World Economy, 1984.

all generated a new sense of urgency to address some fundamental questions about Canada's economic future. Notable developments in post-war trade include the overwhelming importance of the U.S. market for Canadian products, especially end-products; the growing importance of manufacturing for Canada's trade sector; and the dominance of foreign-controlled firms in influencing Canada's imports. Again, developing countries have experienced considerably faster growth rates for their exports of manufactured goods than have the North American or European economies. Developing countries account for a growing share of OECD imports. For example:

> *In 1970, only 5% of manufactured imports of countries of the OECD came from the developing countries. In 1981, the share was almost 10%. This competition can be expected to increase and spread, adding to the existing pressures to adjust output and employment in traditional labour-intensive industries.*
>
> (Bank of Montreal, Brief, November 17, 1983, p. 24.)

During the 1960s and 1970s, as Figure 2-13 demonstrates, several Asian countries dramatically increased their share of total exports of manufactured goods. More particularly — and most worrisome, according to some observers — Japan appears to be gaining a strong hold on the world's rapidly expanding high-technology markets. (See Figure 2-14.) In consequence of these trends, the challenges facing Canada are clear.

Traditionally, the doctrine of comparative advantage between nations has served as the foundation of economic theory relating to international trade. Canada, for example, has a relative abundance of fertile land and efficient production and transportation systems which have enabled it to become a major exporter of agricultural products. Unfortunately, however, the doctrine of comparative advantage fails to account adequately for a good deal of the international trade that is presently going on around the globe. The basis of trade in manufactured products, for example, appears to be provided by factors much more subtle than a country's relative endowments in human, capital or natural resources.

Attention has turned more and more to technology's contribution to economic growth. The United States no longer has exclusive claim to the unique set of factors that so stimulated its research and development (R&D) programs in earlier years. Other countries, such as Japan and Germany, have the wealth, the capital and the human-resource skills to produce many new products. Furthermore, experience has shown that newly industrializing countries can readily adapt quite sophisticated technology. The pace of technological change, adjustments in relative prices for goods, and growing government involvement in industrial development are reshaping the manner and the terms of international trade.

Given the opportunities afforded by developments in micro-electronics and other fields such as biotechnology, international trade competition is, and will remain, intense. Moreover, technological diffusion to new competitors is seriously challenging some of the "traditional" industries of the developed countries. The automobile industry offers one example. In Canada, businesses and governments alike are particularly concerned about new factors that

FIGURE 2-13 Manufactured Exports as Share of Country's Total Exports, 1960–1979

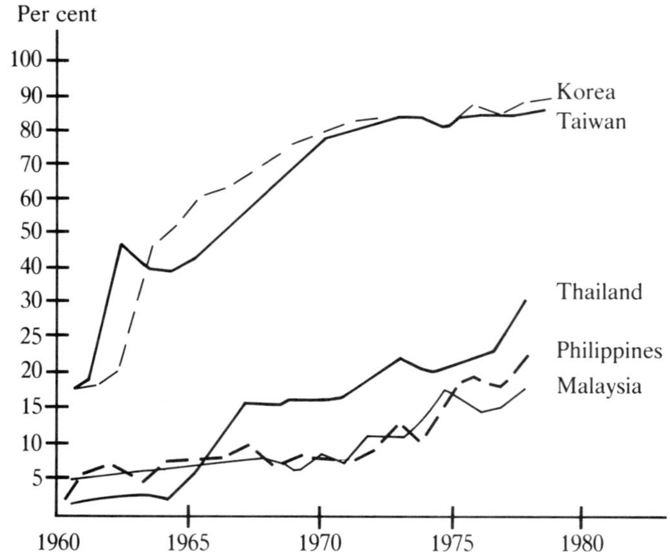

Source: Miyohei Shinohara, Industrial Growth, Trade and Dynamic Patterns in the Japanese Economy (Tokyo: University of Tokyo Press, 1982), p. 100.

might change the relative ability to compete of Canadian resource-based industries. The Government of Nova Scotia has warned, for instance, that:

> *New suppliers of natural resource commodities are emerging and the location of manufacturing activity is changing to reflect international differences of labour and other costs. New materials are being substituted for the traditional ones as in the case of the glass fibres in place of copper wires. Generally less growth will occur in the primary resource industries and more is expected in manufacturing and the service sector.* (Government of Nova Scotia, Brief, January 23, 1984, p. 41.)

Further automation is often seen as a possible solution to the problems of cost competition confronting industrial nations. The adoption of new technologies that reduce costs, such as computer-aided design and manufacturing (CAD/CAM), or that increase the efficiency of smaller-scale operations, also serve to enhance their competitive position. From the point of view of a particular company or industry, however, another possibility is simply to transfer production from high-cost developed countries to low-cost developing countries. In fact, there are plenty of examples of resort to both the automation and the transfer options. Traditional "smoke-stack" industries such as steel, which are less mobile because of heavy unrecovered capital investment, may resort to other options. They may, for instance, appeal to the state for increased protection and/or subsidies to meet foreign competition; or they may pressure labour to accept reductions in real compensation. At this time, it is not clear to what extent these various options may be put to use.

FIGURE 2-14 Market Shares of High-Technology Exports

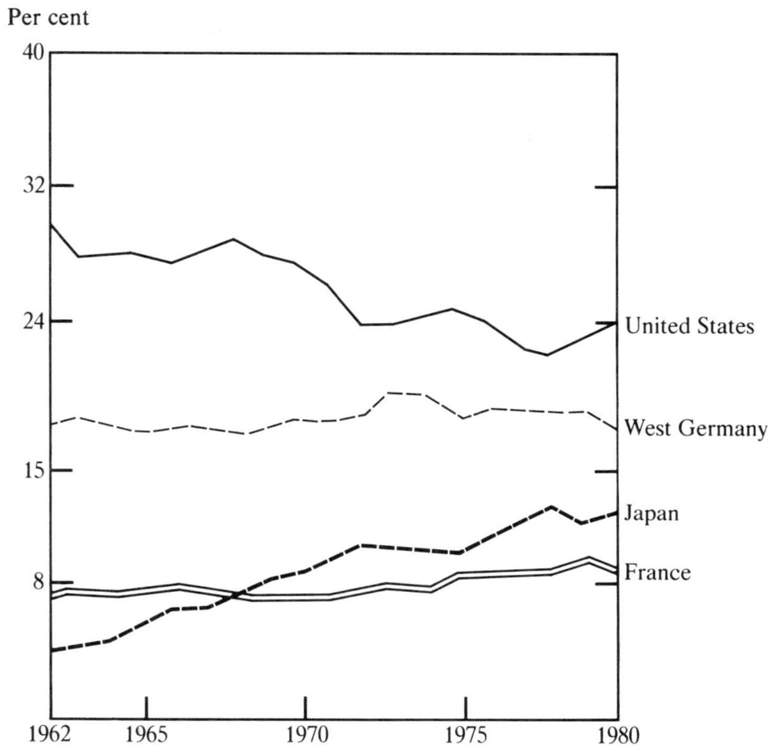

Source: Department of Commerce/International Trade Administration, from U.N. Series D Trade Data, as cited in U.S. Department of Commerce, International Trade Administration, *An Assessment of U.S. Competitiveness in High Technology Industries* (Washington, D.C.: U.S. Department of Commerce, February 1983), p. 9.

Over the past several years, considerable debate has taken place over the part that governments might play in facilitating or "engineering" new developments through which their countries might gain some comparative advantage over the producers of other nations. The Honourable Donald Johnston described the concept of engineered comparative advantage to this Commission:

> *Essentially, as we move into the so-called "information society", the application of know-how and skills can give a country a major comparative advantage that was usually not the case in the past. In other words, the comparative advantages arising from natural resources and other advantages of that kind have changed.*
>
> (The Honourable Donald Johnston, Transcript, St. John's, September 21, 1983 [vol. 12], p. 2877.)

The debate over the appropriate role of government in industrial policy is inconclusive. Some observers claim that Japan's industrial success stems from highly co-ordinated public/private-sector initiatives which, through determination and commitment, have enabled its producers to take a leading place in the market. Whatever the reality, it is impossible to know whether Japan would have succeeded to the same degree if its public and private sectors had practised a more North American style of interaction.

The concept of "engineering" long-term comparative advantage is nonetheless intriguing if for no other reason than that it seems to be the practice of a number of countries. By investing heavily in education and skills-training programs, for instance, a country might promote its high-technology industries. Its investment would only produce a comparative advantage, however, if it achieved an improvement, relative to that of other countries, in some particular factor of production. Although the risk of such an enterprise is considerable — for the market might evaporate before an engineered comparative advantage materialized — not to join the race is to concede the market to others. An Air Canada executive assured Commissioners:

> *The fact of the matter is that our environment has changed drastically in recent years, while in many respects we have not yet adapted our industrial relations systems and philosophies to account for these changes. Today much more than in the past, we are a part of what is becoming an integrated global economy. Thus, we are engaged in a world-wide competition in which the standard of living in our country will be largely determined by our ability to compete for our share of this newly emerging world economy.*
>
> (Bernard F. Miller, Brief, November 23, 1983, p. 2.)

Increasingly intense international competition has underscored the importance of many dimensions of industrial organization. Key variables are an economic infrastructure, a skilled labour force, and economic integration aimed at increasing efficiency, which might be attained, for example, through rationalization of production to achieve economies of scale. The transportation and communication system, which facilitates the flow of goods, services and people, as well as the flow of information, is vital to the organization of production and exchange.

Changes in the governmental framework of relationships among countries and regions may make possible the introduction of extensive economies of scale, especially for a small economy; the evolution of the European Community provides an example. The growth of large, tariff-free, internal markets is a new trade reality: the integrated European market, made up of the EC and the European Free Trade Association (EFTA), represents over 300 million people; the U.S. market represents 230 million people; and Japan has 120 million people. Of the major industrialized countries, only Canada and Australia have free-trade markets of substantially fewer than 100 million people.

International competition may be even keener in the future because of CAD/CAM technology and flexible manufacturing processes. In some circumstances, CAD/CAM technology will lead to the scaling down of a large number of manufacturing processes, but it is impossible to predict whether, on average, economies of scale will increase or decrease. The "information revolution" has considerably reduced the cost and increased the efficiency of managing large and diverse operations, including those of conglomerate organizations. A trend toward vertical and horizontal integration may develop, with an increase in the size of the most efficient firm. If the latter possibility occurs, it could mean the imposition of entry barriers to export markets. It may become more difficult for a domestic firm located in a small market, such as Canada represents, to enter a foreign market, particularly if the corresponding world industry is highly concentrated. Economies of scale may also derive from "learning by doing": that is, the time-consuming process of discovering the most efficient production methods. Whatever the source of its economies of scale, a firm that successfully pre-empts a competitor in the short term may sometimes retain the lead for a long time.

Whether world trade will again offer the bonanza it did in the 1950s and 1960s is open to question. As the Western industrialized nations move to become service-oriented societies, their non-trade sectors may actually increase. Services are traded, but to a much smaller extent – at least up to the present time – than are primary commodities or manufactured goods. Thus, the slow-down experienced in the growth of world trade since 1973 may reflect, at least in part, the rapid growth of the service sector.

More important, there has been a troublesome degree of protectionism creeping back into world trade. The reduction in tariffs since the Second World War has been remarkable, but the 1970s witnessed a trend toward greater use of non-tariff barriers (NTBs). Moreover, the 1981-82 recession intensified the pressures on the world's governments to adopt protective measures. Government procurement policies, favourable tax provisions, assisted export financing, contingency provisions, and a number of other measures, including barter trade, have been woven into the commercial policies of major trading countries. The North-South Institute has explained the pressures towards protectionism as follows:

> *These trends of growing interdependence and the dispersion of economic actors and activities have themselves produced strong pressures for adjustment, much intensified by rapid technological change and diminishing productivity and growth. In recent years, in particular, the growth of protectionism has been symptomatic of the political and/or economic inability of industrialized countries to adjust so fundamentally and rapidly.*
>
> (North-South Institute, Brief, August 31, 1983, pp. 3–4.)

Since more than 70 per cent of Canada's exports are destined for U.S. markets, developments in that country are of particular interest to Canadians. It has been estimated that the proportion of U.S. manufactured goods protected by non-tariff restrictions, including quotas and other import barriers, has risen from 20 per cent in 1980 to 35 per cent in 1983. This strengthening of protectionist policy makes some observers question whether world trade, in general, and Canada-U.S. trade, in particular, will continue to grow as it has in the past. The substitution of NTBs for tariff barriers and, especially, the threat of countervailing duties have prompted some Canadian firms to open branches in the United States. Canada's National Policy of 1879 is, according to some observers, in the process of being turned on its head.

Job Security in a Rapidly Changing World

The structural shifts and expansion of world trade described in the previous sections have had profound implications for job security in Western industrialized countries. These developments have underscored a striking feature of post-war economic development: the need for a highly adaptive and flexible labour force. This need is clearly illustrated by the performance, in recent years, of many newly industrializing countries (NICs). Not only have these countries made new technological breakthroughs, but they have also quickened the pace at which they are adopting state-of-the-art production techniques. This latter dimension of technological progress has enabled the first wave of NICs, such as Hong Kong, South Korea, India, Mexico, Brazil and Argentina, to break into the textile, apparel and footwear markets. A second wave of NICs, including Malaysia, Thailand, the Philippines, Sri Lanka and China, is now moving not only into these markets, but also into new ones, such as electronics. At the same time, the more prosperous of the first-wave NICs are diversifying their manufactures to include steel, chemicals and automotive products. Worker displacement in Western industrialized countries has inevitably resulted. As consumers, these countries have benefited greatly from low-priced imports, but these imports have also intensified the need for sound adjustment policies, including retraining of the labour force.

Many observers claim that Western societies are in the midst of a major and fundamental transformation based on an increase in the pace of technological progress. The quite extraordinary discoveries in microelectronics and the availability of that technology to many users through cost reductions are at the heart of this sense that we are experiencing a new industrial revolution. The economic system is constantly churning, because of both domestic and international developments. A good deal of this structural change is accommodated by job mobility within fairly limited geographic confines; much is accommodated by normal attrition and retirement. The scale of these shifts can be large, as in British coal-mining, where employment figures fell from over 600 000 in 1960 to fewer than 300 000 in 1970; and in the U.S. Postal Service, which lost more than 10 per cent of its jobs during the 1970s. In both sectors, relatively few workers were laid off because most of the reduction was achieved through attrition.

Such examples and the even more dramatic reduction of agricultural jobs should remind us just how flexible and adaptive Western societies have been over the post-war period. Still, some Canadians argue that our society has shown a growing resistance to change. Furthermore, there have been institutional and social developments tending in the same direction: families with two breadwinners and liberal unemployment-insurance systems may discourage or impede adaptability. The non-inflationary unemployment rate (that is, the rate of unemployment below which the rate of inflation begins to accelerate) has steadily crept upwards in OECD countries. In North America, the non-inflationary unemployment rate now appears to be about 7 per cent, compared to roughly 4 per cent in the 1960s.

The post-war realignment in employment that has taken place throughout OECD countries has resulted as much from the necessities imposed by competition as from the natural inclination of workers to seek better employment prospects. Some indication of the extent of realignment is provided in Table 2-19. The table shows employment changes in seven countries for the textiles, basic iron and steel, shipbuilding and repair, and motor-vehicle industries. The 1970s and early 1980s were turbulent years. Between 1974 and 1980, some 100 000 jobs were lost in the U.S. steel industry. In the same period, some 710 000 fewer workers were employed in the European textile industry. Nor was Japan spared large-scale adjustments: its shipbuilding industry dropped 117 000 employees between December 1974 and June 1979. The most dramatic realignment, however, resulted from the loss of production, sales and employment in the U.S. automobile industry between 1979 and 1980. An estimated 750 000 jobs were lost throughout the U.S. economy as a consequence of the drop in production. These adjustments occurred before the onset of the 1981–82 recession.

Some observers believe that Western industrialized nations are caught in a fundamental dilemma: technology is being diffused and adapted so quickly that sufficient replacement jobs often appear elusive; yet no country can afford to opt out of the technology race. Moreover, technological diffusion to developing countries, often through the channels of multi-national corporations, allows these countries to combine modern production techniques with low-wage structures. The effect is devastating, at least in the short term, for some Western firms and industries. Although this general trend has not had a major effect on Canadian jobs to date, the pressures are expected to increase dramatically in the future.

These developments are cause for considerable concern. While historical experience leads to the belief that adjustment can and will accommodate such developments, the current pace of change challenges this conventional wisdom. The improvement in output through technological advance in developed and developing countries should be the basis for significant improvements in living standards; and these improvements, in turn, should form the basis for many new employment opportunities. This is the logical conclusion to draw from past experience. But is the future likely to be a continuation of past and present experience? Is it possible, in fact, that the world is in the midst of a global realignment that threatens Western living standards and employment structures?

Some alarming forecasts point to looming unemployment problems as serious as those of the Great Depression. Reports from Britain forecast an unemployment rate as high as 25 per cent by 1990. A French report indicates that 30 per cent of bank and insurance-company employees could be redundant within 10 years.[3] An American study predicts that in 25 years, the U.S. manufacturing sector will employ few more people than does the present agricultural sector.[4] Equally alarming forecasts have appeared in Canada. One Canadian author has claimed that there is "ample reason to fear that informatics could contribute to severe job displacement and reduced

TABLE 2-19 Employment Changes, Selected Industries, 1975–1983

(per cent change from peak employment year, as indicated)

Country	Textiles		Iron and Steel		Shipbuilding and Repairing		Motor Vehicles	
	Peak Year	% Decline	Peak Year	% Decline	Peak Year	% Decline	Peak Year	% Decline
Canada	1975	–20	1979–80	–32	1981	–12	1978	–3
United States	1978	–16	1979	–38	1979	–29	1978	–23
Japan	1975	–5	1975	–5	1975	–8	1983	0
Sweden	1975	–22	1975	–19	1975	–29	1980	–13
Germany	1975	–23	1975	–40	1982	–7	1979–80	–20
France	1975	–13	1975	–12	1982	–1	1977–78	–17
United Kingdom	1975	–21	1975	–38	1975	–16	1978	–33

Source: Organisation for Economic Co-operation and Development, *Indicators of Industrial Activity* (Paris: OECD, 1979–84).

employment prospects among female clerical workers."[5] Labour Canada's report entitled *In the Chips*[6] reached a similar conclusion. The Organisation for Economic Co-operation and Development suggests that some 32 per cent of all jobs are at risk.[7]

Many observers believe that fears of widespread job dislocation as a result of technological progress are ill-founded. Perhaps the most authorative study expounding this point of view is the recent work by Faye Duchin and the Nobel prize-winning economist Wassily Leontief. Concerning the effects of automation on the U.S. economy and society, these authors concluded:

> *The intensive use of automation over the next twenty years will make it possible to conserve about 10% of the labor that would have been required to produce the same bills of goods in the absence of increased automation. The impacts are specific to different types of work and will involve a significant increase in professionals as a proportion of the labor force and a steep decline in the relative number of clerical workers. Production workers can be expected to maintain their share of the labor force; direct displacement by specific items of automated equipment (like robots and numerically controlled machine tools) will, at least in the initial stages, be offset by the increased investment demand for all sorts of capital goods, especially computers ... Whether or not the smooth transition from the old to the new technology can actually be realized will depend to a large extent on whether the necessary changes in the skill structure of the labor force and its distribution between different sectors of the economy (and geographic locations) can be effectively carried out.*[8]

The findings of Leontief and Duchin are similar to the findings of the Economic Council of Canada, published in its 1984 *Annual Review*. The Council concluded that technological change in the 1970s slowed employment growth by about one per cent per year, but increases in living standards and overall demand far exceeded those needed to offset the effect of technological change:

> *The pace of technological change and diffusion will affect jobs and the work place but probably should not cause undue worry. Some occupations will be eroded, but many will be enriched; the process will be evolutionary, in line with market-determined decisions, with the indirect demand-induced employment growth, particularly in many traditional occupations, more than offsetting the loss of jobs as a result of technological change.*[9]

Although the Council's conclusion is contrary to many predictions concerning the effect of technological change on Canada's future employment opportunities, as well as to a good number of the submissions made to this Commission, it nevertheless, represents mainstream thinking among economists. While this more optimistic view is salutory, it does not detract from the need for flexibility and adaptability in our economic system. Intensified international competition and the faster pace of technological progress have drawn increasing attention to the adequacy or inadequacy of adjustment policies in Western industrialized countries.

The World Economic Outlook

The world economy strengthened appreciably in 1983 and 1984, in marked contrast to its deterioration at the outset of the 1980s. While the major industrial countries, including, notably, the United States, have been at the forefront of this recovery, developing countries have also been experiencing strong growth rates. In fact, 1984 marked the first time in five years that output in developing countries grew significantly faster than population.

With economic recovery, a number of critical problems are beginning to ease. For example, the net export/import-trade position of developing countries and their credit-worthiness have both improved. Nevertheless, a number of problems threaten recovery: the high level of real interest rates; the still-precarious financial position of many heavily indebted developing countries; the sizeable deficits of some governments; disparities in growth performance among industrial countries; serious imbalances in the current-account positions of some major countries; and the pressure for protection of domestic industry from foreign competition.

Figure 2-15 portrays the way in which the world's general economic situation has unfolded over the past few years, together with the most recent pertinent data. The figure indicates that there has been a wide disparity of output performance among industrial countries, with robust growth in North America (particularly in the United States), moderate expansion in Japan, and a much less definite recovery in Europe. Growth rates among the industrialized countries are expected to become somewhat more uniform in 1985, and real gross national product is expected to increase, on average, by some 3.5 per cent.

Part III of this Report addresses the longer-term outlook for Canada. It also draws attention to the perils of long-term forecasting. While forecasting involves reckoning with obscurities, it is, nonetheless, an indispensable tool for managing both national and international affairs. However sharply disputed the outlook may be, it would be less than sensible to argue that one can rest content without taking any long-term view. Among the many expectations placed upon this Commission is, in fact, the task of assisting Canadians to gauge the long-term outlook. To that end, we Commissioners have supplemented our hearings and the many submissions we have received with special seminars and research projects designed to clarify the cloudy images in the crystal ball. At the outset, the complexity of the subject matter must be underscored. There are a great many models to draw from, and each is supported by many different assumptions and structural components. To assimilate these various models into a single economic outlook for the entire world is a daunting task. Yet not to try is to confuse the outlook so much that it ill serves those who want and need at least some indication of what the future is likely to hold. This latter consideration prevailed.

In looking forward to the decades ahead, Canadians must keep in mind some key relationships between people and resources. Commissioners draw attention to three of these:

FIGURE 2-15 General World Economic Situation

Major Industrial Countries: Industrial Production and Real GNP, 1979 to June 1984 (Indices, fourth quarter 1982 = 100)

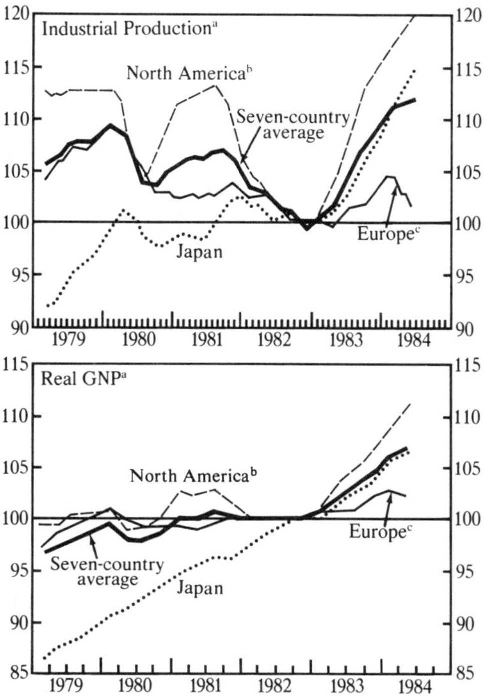

a. Seasonally adjusted.
b. The United States and Canada.
c. The Federal Republic of Germany, France, Italy, and the United Kingdom.

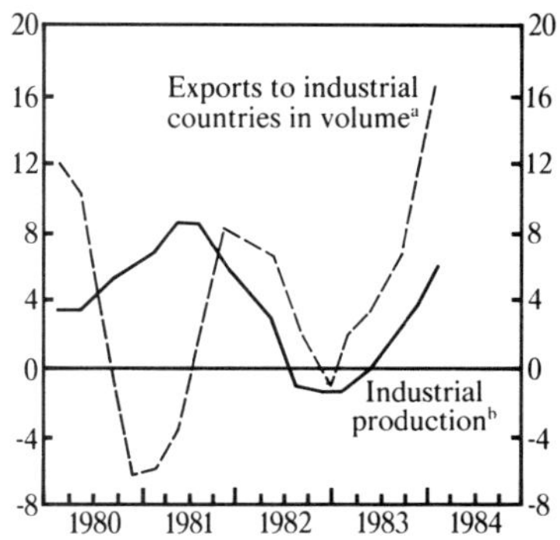

a. Imports of industrial countries from non-oil developing countries, as reported in the International Monetary Fund's *Direction of Trade Statistics,* deflated by export-unit values for non-oil developing countries.
b. Sample of 13 countries for which up-to-date monthly industrial production data are shown in the Fund's *International Financial Statistics.* Country indices weighted by the dollar value of GD in 1979-81.

Source: International Monetary Fund, *World Economic Outlook* (Washington, D.C.: International Monetary Fund, 1984) pp. 2, 8.

Note: Industrial production = average for three months ending in month indicated.

- As we consume non-renewable resources, we are forced to seek out more distant and poorer-quality resources. This tendency involves progressively higher extraction costs and progressively higher resource costs. New discoveries, especially in developing countries, may provide an exception to this process.
- Advancing technology offsets this trend to a greater or lesser degree, depending on the nature of the advances. Efficiency in extracting resources and in using resource materials continually improves.
- Overriding most factors is the institutional framework for resource supply and resource use. For example, food shortages on a global scale are related to income-distribution problems. Similarly, conditions governing the

undertaking of trade can either promote or frustrate the gains from international specialization.

The world's material well-being is highly dependent on these factors, although models of global economic developments have often ignored or oversimplified them.

This Commission has not attempted to enter the formal process of global modelling, but has reviewed the work of the major contributors to this literature.[10] The global economic outlook presented in the next few pages borrows heavily from the report prepared for the Japanese government, *Japan In The Year 2000*.[11] This work represents, in an easily understandable format, a good deal of mainstream thinking, and it is one of the very few attempts to present global projections of this type. The authors of the report assumed that countries would continue to promote international trade, although the trade climate would be less expansionary than it was in the 1950s and 1960s. Further, they assumed that industrialized countries would be able to correct the faults that led to the 1973-83 economic slow-down, particularly in respect to productivity, but that, nonetheless, demographic factors would weigh against rapid growth. Finally, they assumed that after a period of hesitation, energy prices would show moderate increases.

The report predicts that the share of world output accounted for by industrialized countries will continue to fall, to the advantage of developing countries. This development would simply reflect a gradual catch-up for the developing countries. As Table 2-20 and Figure 2-16 of this Report show, the socialist countries are expected to retain their current share of world output. The shares estimated here are, of course, highly speculative. Even so, it is important that they not be misinterpreted. Industrialized countries, particularly the United States, are shown as having growth rates considerably lower than those of developing countries, with a consequent reduction in their share of world output. This does not mean that the standard of living in industrialized countries will fall. On the contrary, the projections foretell a steady improvement. Developing countries have a population explosion to contend with, and the faster growth of their gross national product stems, in large measure, from this fact.

The changes shown in shares of world output among European, North American and Asian countries are worthy of note for trade reasons. It is projected that European and North American countries will lose 13 per cent of their relative share of world output between 1980 and 2000, while Asian countries, including Japan and China, will improve their relative shares by 20 per cent. This forecast is especially important for western Canada, which accounts for some two-thirds of all Canadian exports to the Asia Pacific. This view was shared by several intervenors at this Commission's hearings, particularly those from western Canada:

> *The role of Asia in the affairs of the world will increase. The relative role of Europe will decrease. Our economic ties with, and our understanding of, the Pacific Rim countries must be reflected in our economic and technological strategies. We must increase our understanding of the Asian societies in which*

TABLE 2-20 World GNP Composition in 2000

(per cent)

	GNP Composition in 1960	Present GNP Composition[a]	Real Economic Growth Rate (Annual Rate): Latest 10 years (1970–1979)	Real Economic Growth Rate (Annual Rate): Composition 1980–2000	GNP Composition in 2000
Industrialized countries					
Japan	3	10	5.2	4.0	12
United States	33	22	3.1	2.5	20
EEC and other OECD members	26	34	3.1	2.5	26
Total	(62)	(63)	(3.3)	(2.8)	(58)
Developing countries					
Newly industrializing countries[b]	3	4	8.0	6.0	7
Other LDCs	11	11	5.7	4.0	13
Total	(14)	(15)	(6.3)	(4.6)	(20)
Socialist countries					
Soviet Union	15	13	5.1	—	12
East Europe, et al.	4	5	5.9	3.0	5
China	5	5	5.8	4.0	5
Total	(24)	(22)	(5.4)	(3.2)	(22)
World total	100	100	4.3	3.2	100

Source: Japan, Long-Term Outlook Committee, Economic Council, Economic Planning Agency of Japan, *Japan in the Year 2000* (Tokyo: The Japan Times, 1983), p. 40.

a. The present GNP composition is at 1978 prices in $ U.S.

b. Newly industrializing countries are South Korea, Hong Kong, Singapore, Brazil, Mexico and Taiwan.

FIGURE 2-16 World Economic Map

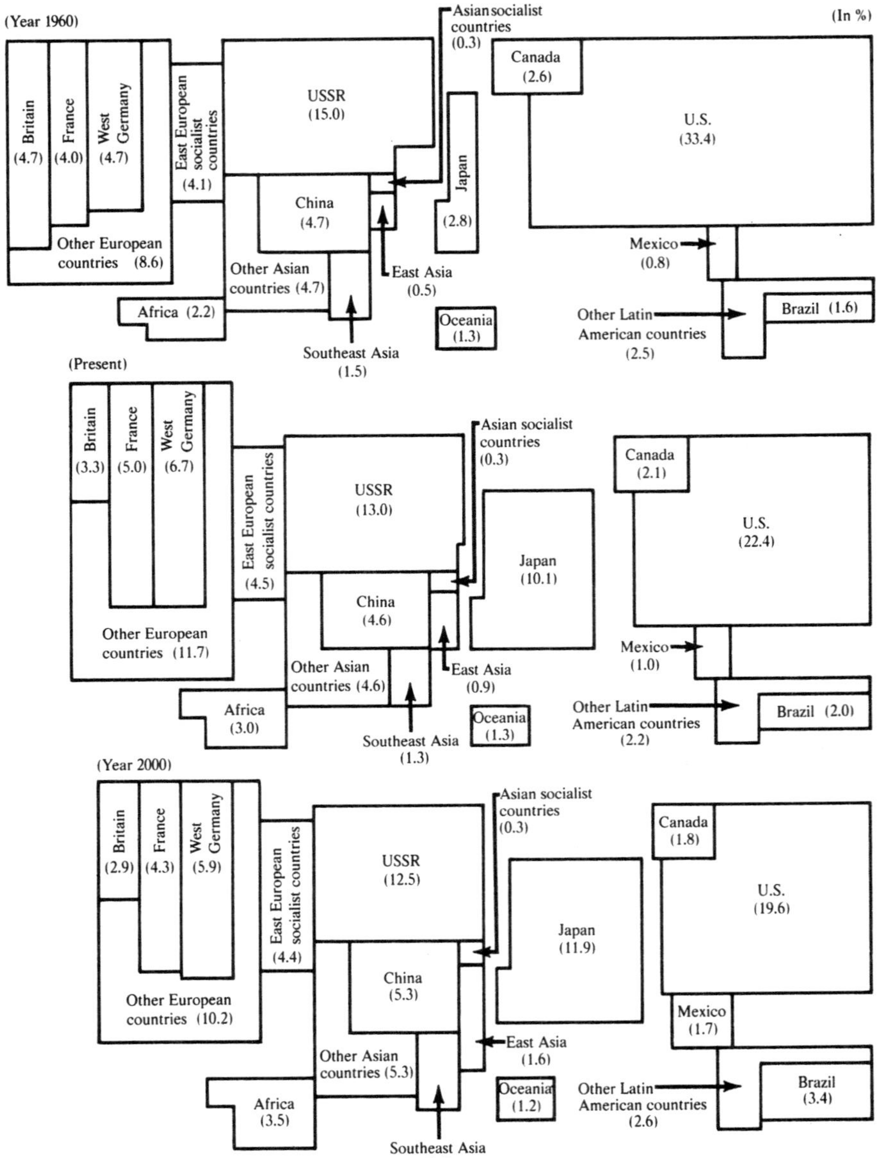

Source: Japan, Economic Council, *Japan in the Year 2000* (Tokyo: The Japan Times, 1983), p. 42.

Note: National GNP shares in the year 2000 are based on the figures given in Table 2-20.

The maps are based on the assumption that the GNP growth rate of a group of countries is identical to that of each country. It is inappropriate to attempt an international comparison of growth rates.

Figures in parentheses denote national or regional shares in world GNP.

the majority of humans collectively reside. The sleeping giants of China and India are awakening and their economies will have a profound effect on Canada.

(Len T. Bruton, Brief, September 2, 1983, p. 6.)

Real-growth rates over the next two decades are expected to be somewhat slower than those experienced during the years from 1970 to 1979, but not markedly so. If this expectation is realized, the prospects for a healthy world economic environment appear reasonably good. How individual countries fare will depend on their domestic policies, especially in relation to improvements in productivity.

Notes

1. The "Group of Seven" consists of: Canada, France, Japan, Italy, the United Kingdom, the United States, West Germany.
2. Organisation for Economic Co-operation and Development, *Employment Outlook* (Paris: OECD, 1984), p. 33.
3. Cited in Science Council of Canada, *The Impact of the Microelectronics Revolution on Work and Working*, Workshop proceedings (Ottawa: The Council, 1980), p. 16.
4. Cited in Giles Merritt, *World Out of Work* (London: Collins, 1982), p. 71.
5. Heather Menzies, *Women and the Chip: Case Studies of the Effects of Informatics on Employment in Canada* (Montreal: Institute for Research on Public Policy, 1981), p. 65.
6. Canada, Labour Canada, *In the Chips: Opportunities, People, Partnership*, Report of the Task Force on Micro-Electronics and Employment (Ottawa: Minister of Supply and Services Canada, 1982).
7. Merritt, *World Out of Work*, p. 74.
8. Wassily Leontief and Faye Duchin, *The Effects of Automation on Employment, 1963–2000* (New York: Oxford University Press, 1984), pp. 1–2.
9. Economic Council of Canada, *Steering the Course*, Twenty-First Annual Review (Ottawa: Minister of Supply and Services Canada, 1984), p. 83.
10. See A.R. Dobell and B.R. Kennedy, "Global Futures and Canadian Prospects: A Review of the Global Modelling Literature", in *Economic Growth: Prospects and Determinants*, vol. 22, prepared for the Royal Commission on the Economic Union and Development Prospects for Canada (Toronto: University of Toronto Press, 1985).
11. Japan, Long-Term Outlook Committee, Economic Council, Economic Planning Agency of Japan, *Japan in the Year 2000* (Tokyo: The Japan Times, 1983).

The Global Political Environment

The global environment has three important aspects: the physical, the economic and the political. The global political environment, in turn, has two major components: first, international institutions such as the United Nations, the General Agreement on Tariffs and Trade (GATT) and the World Bank and, secondly, individual nation states. The roles which the nation states play on the global stage are determined, to a significant degree, by their own domestic political and economic environment.

What developments does this Commission discern, at least in broad outline, within the domestic political and economic environment of several major countries and blocs? And what projections can Commissioners suggest from our observations about the future roles of these nation states, played singly or in concert, on the stage of world politics? Our observations will not, of course, permit us to provide a detailed assessment: indeed, we must admit that our crystal ball is at least as cloudy as that of any other prognosticator. Moreover, the limitations of space prevent us from doing justice to the richness and complexity of any of the units which we shall consider. We proceed, however, because we believe that domestic developments within major powers or groups of powers will ultimately affect Canada, and that Canadians cannot afford to disregard them.

A number of questions, therefore, call for consideration:

- What are some of the major domestic political and cultural strengths and weaknesses of each country or group of countries?
- What are the major economic factors that contribute to these strengths and weaknesses?
- How might these factors evolve over the next two decades?
- How will this evolution affect the likelihood of various countries' working together to deal with their common problems?
- What are some of the commonalities and differences between their situation and that of Canada?

The United States

Predictably, Commissioners have encountered a considerable range of opinions on the general political health of the United States. Some observers propose the highly optimistic view that America's national purpose has been greatly strengthened by a clear and visionary political leadership, a major realignment of political forces, and a return to traditional values that emphasize the work ethic, the home, family, religion and "good old Yankee ingenuity". At the other extreme is the highly pessimistic view that political stalemate and instability are about to reappear; that the economy is flying high in the mid-1980s only because incipient stress fractures have not yet torn off its wings; that society is fraught with racial and social divisions which will soon reappear; that the political institutions of American democracy are quite incapable of dealing with these problems. There is no doubt that the truth lies at a point somewhere between these two extreme opinions. Unquestionably, a significant series of problems does beset the United States. Observers have seen these as including political, social, economic, domestic and foreign-relations difficulties. Since over 20 per cent of Canada's gross national product (GNP) is directly tied up in trade with the United States, and since Canadians have developed an open relationship with our giant neighbour that is virtually unparalleled in recent history, it is important to speculate about where that truth might lie.

Structural Problems

In the late 1970s, it was fashionable for observers of the United States to paint a picture of a once-powerful nation on the point of being brought to its knees because of its vulnerability to other countries' technological advances and to dissenters and even saboteurs at home and abroad. After the Organization for Petroleum Exporting Countries (OPEC) imposed its oil embargo in 1973, some analysts saw the United States as a victim of self-delusion, convinced by its own assurances that it was capable of adjusting to far higher costs for oil and for credit. Even if such adjustments could be made, it was argued, they must surely require important changes in the traditional American way of life, both public and private.

Other observers have queried whether the maintenance of liberal democracy as we know it depends on ever-increasing prosperity. This question is particularly relevant in view of the contention that no major industrialized nation can maintain the pace of economic growth that was enjoyed in the first few decades that followed the Second World War:

> *Sustained economic growth in the 1950s and 1960s concealed issues of relative income distribution which now confront policymakers as affluence has created rising expectations that can no longer be met simultaneously for all strata of the population. Inflation rather than growth became the vent for distributional pressures in the 1970s.*[1]

The conclusion follows that unless some consensus can be reached on income distribution, political conflict is likely to increase substantially.

Many of the proponents of these views made their statements in the late 1970s or early 1980s. In the mid-1980s, their voices seem to have a curiously anachronistic ring as the U.S. economy completes its best period of economic growth in half a century, and as the first two-term President since Dwight Eisenhower takes office after a landslide victory. In fact, the U.S. economy does appear to have adjusted to costly credit and costly energy without forcing disruptive changes on the American way of life and American institutions. Yet this "sea-change" in the climate of American government and the U.S. economy should not blind Canadians to the possibility that still another reversal could occur, and that the structural problems which surround all economies and all political systems at all times could again dominate American life.

Growing Inequality

There is some evidence that economic inequality in the United States is increasing rather than declining. The proportion of U.S. citizens living below official poverty lines has increased from 1979 to the end of 1984, reversing a trend of some 20 years' standing and paralleling the situation in Canada. Inequalities of income in the United States are wider than the average in countries belonging to the Organisation for Economic Co-operation and Development (OECD) and have increased in the 1980s; they are also slightly greater by standard measures than those in Canada. Another indication that significant social problems may be emerging is to be found in the slight decline in health-status indicators in the United States. That country is virtually alone among industrialized nations in having experienced, in recent years, some increases in morbidity and mortality indicators and in infant mortality.

Declining Relative Wealth

Per capita income and living standards are extremely sensitive to the measures used to assess them and to assumptions made about exchange rates and non-monetary components of well-being. Still, the United States, in common with Canada, has demonstrated some disconcerting tendencies in the past decade. The growth of productivity has slowed remarkably during recent years, in both absolute and relative terms. The extent, nature and cause of this impairment of productivity growth is, however, a matter of some dispute. Although, over time, the rate of increase in productivity has been faster in Japan and West Germany than in the United States (and Canada), the actual level of productivity remains significantly higher in North American economies. In the late 1970s, an index of productivity that put the United States at 100 would have recorded 91.6 for Canada, 84.7 for France, 79.8 for West Germany, 63.2 for Japan, 55.8 for Britain, and 54.3 for Italy. According to this scale, it would have taken ten workers in Germany to produce what could have been turned out by eight workers in the United States. Indeed, throughout most of the 1970s, the rate of increase in productivity was slowing down around the globe, a problem that was compounded by the economic recession of the early 1980s.

While some observers contend that the slow-down in U.S. productivity growth is a result of "deindustrialization" of heavy industries, others insist that this is only a myth. They hold that the effect of foreign competition on U.S. manufacturing industries has been relatively small, and that there has been no absolute decline in the U.S. industrial base, although there have been declines in the employment share of certain industrial sectors. The shift to service industries, where advances in productivity may be harder to achieve, may have been a factor in this decline, as may the increased importance of knowledge industries, for some of the real value of the latter is never captured in productivity statistics. Others argue that what problem there is stems largely from an over-valued U.S. dollar.

Increasing World Interdependence

Over the years, observers point out, the U.S. economy has become increasingly integrated with that of the world. While this development has conferred undoubted benefits on the United States, it has also increased that nation's vulnerability to forces over which it has little or no control. In 1938, U.S. exports and imports combined amounted to 4 per cent of the gross national product; from 1976 to 1978, they amounted to 10 per cent. More than 20 per cent of U.S. industrial output is exported; the job of one in six workers in manufacturing depends on sales abroad; and two out of five acres of farmland are devoted to the growing of produce for export. One-third of U.S. corporate profits comes from international activities; some 70 per cent of all American goods are exposed to international competition. Although the United States was paramount when the world adopted the open, market-oriented, international trading system that prevails today, its ability to dominate the global economy has declined. Certainly, a number of sectors in the U.S. economy have a vital interest in the preservation of the liberalized trade and investment order; other domestic industries, however, exposed to mounting competition from abroad, have been applying pressure for a retreat into protectionism.

The Political Foundations

Some observers, who are inclined to be pessimistic about the future of the United States, consider that the problems outlined above would be manageable if the American political system had not become so fragmented and so paralysed by the division of powers that it is no longer capable of coming to grips with the kinds of problems that will confront it over the next several years. According to this school of thought, the effects of these developments have been pervasive. There has reputedly been a sharp decline in confidence in the U.S. government since the mid-1960s, and this decline has reflected adversely on Congress, on the Executive, and on non-governmental institutions. Business and labour unions, as well as government, have been targets of this growing negativism. In February 1983, U.S. pollster Lou Harris reported that 63 per cent of Americans expressed "sad and bitter alienation toward their own society and felt powerless to do anything about it."[2] This decline in confidence has not, however, caused complete loss of faith in the fundamental elements of the U.S. political system. Indeed, belief in the basic soundness of that system is still high. The current U.S. leadership has, it may be argued, been able to capitalize on this reservoir of goodwill to restore faith in the performance and the potential of government.

It may be that observers see less of a consistently negative trend in American opinion than of an increase in its volatility. This response may be nowhere more evident than in the field of international relations. Thus an earlier trend that favoured a "retreat from world power" has been replaced by a massive shift in public support for a much more assertive stance that favours the strengthening of U.S. military forces and the direction of their use to uphold American domestic interests. This assertiveness—and, perhaps, volatility—also appears clearly in international economic relationships. The see-saw battle within the United States over protectionism may be an indication of this situation which is particularly important for Canadian interests.

In the opinion of some observers, this general volatility reflects the fact that the broad consensus that once served to govern the conduct of both domestic and foreign affairs has dissolved and has been replaced by a number of different schools of thought that cling to convictions often mutually exclusive and sometimes internally inconsistent. As one or another view gains the lead, the conduct of affairs may shift radically. Sharp differences have developed in the foreign-policy sphere between domestic reindustrializers, egalitarians and quality-of-lifers who overlap Cold War internationalists, post-Cold War internationalists and the neo-isolationists.[3] Not surprisingly, these divisions of opinion are also reflected among occupants of positions of power at all levels. This lack of unity, it is claimed, impairs the effectiveness of the decision-making process of the U.S. Administration with respect to both domestic and international issues. It must also be recognized, however, that other observers see these divisions as the normal and healthy ferment of ideas which has always served to strengthen American democracy.

Observers have also expressed concern over the "disintegration" of the U.S. political party system. This is not to suggest that the parties no longer play any significant role, but rather that they no longer provide the bridge they once did to connect the separate elements of government. Once again, however, some observers hold a contrary and more optimistic point of view: the present situation, they contend, is evidence of a salutary realignment of political forces and the emergence of a majority coalition reflecting new industrial and regional balances. They see the situation as a reflection of the American ability to adapt political institutions to a changing reality.

Looking Forward

Given the problems confronting the United States, it is possible to develop a series of scenarios. In the "worst case", one which Commissioners do not anticipate, the United States would be unable to develop an effective and reasonably consistent consensus on domestic and foreign-trade issues. Slowly but steadily, it would turn inward and partially abandon its traditional stabilizing role in the world economy. It would increase its protective trade barriers and resort more and more to the making of *ad hoc* industrial policy as its Administration experienced progressively greater difficulty in establishing compromises among competing groups, to further the national interest. The President would provide economic leadership, especially in foreign trade and aid, as Congress increasingly thwarted the Executive in the matter of international agreements that threaten special domestic interests. Concern for international institutions would decline, and there would be increased emphasis on the military power required to assert U.S. national interests. Cut-backs in social assistance and growing inequality of income would augment domestic conflict. Political turmoil would be exacerbated by slow economic growth, a continued decline in profits, and inadequate structural adjustment that increased social tension. Canada would have less opportunity to exercise autonomous economic and political initiative in the face of U.S. demands for "better terms" as compensation for the military protection it receives and for special arrangements allowing Canadian access to the U.S. market. The United States would attempt to reinforce Canada's provision of a resource hinterland and a market for its manufactured goods, and the result would be the reliance of a fragile Canadian economy on a less co-operative and more erratic American economic and political system.

At the opposite extreme, it is possible to hypothesize that the United States will continue to experience strong economic growth, at least to the end of this decade. Its President would maintain forceful executive leadership, and Congress would show a responsible and co-operative attitude. The nation would achieve a gradual reduction in its budgetary deficit, reach arms-control agreements with the Soviet Union, and move simultaneously towards less military and more domestic expenditure. It would display a more open attitude toward the rest of the world, a greater willingness to share a new plenty both at home and abroad, and a more open approach to international trade.

Of course, neither of these polar opposites represents a most probable outcome. Instead, a more realistic scenario offers a continued reasonable rate of growth in the U.S. economy, marked by some modest pauses and downturns. The United States would generally retain its economic leadership of the world, but without exercising dominance. No dramatic changes would occur in its rate of economic transformation or its ability to accommodate change. American political leadership of the global economy would be tentative at times, lacking a clear sense of direction, but it would generally tend to become more open than it has been in the last few years. In trade relations, a generally open attitude would prevail, but protectionist pressures would never be far below the surface.

U.S. military expenditures would be maintained at a high level in the short term, and they would thus conflict with the need to improve the social services of government. They would tend to decline, however, as both the United States and the Soviet Union recognized the immense costs, in terms of foregone domestic growth, of pursuing the arms race. In the short run, at least, some strains could be created between Canada and the United States if the latter puts increasing pressure on its allies to bear a larger share of the defence burden. In the opinion of some observers, the need to strengthen international organization, especially the need for a new world monetary system will become more and more apparent. Pressure in this direction, however, could meet strong U.S. resistance because such a move might reduce American power on the world stage. Nevertheless, the United States might slowly and gradually agree to strengthen the multilateral development banks. The emphasis might be on bilateral, not multilateral or global, agreements.

American domestic politics would be tense at times, just as they have always been. However, in this middle-range scenario, new party and political alignments would be fairly firmly established, and they would extend a strong stabilizing influence over developments of the next two decades. These new alignments might also make it easier for Congress and the President to agree on the broad outlines of policy, and this trend, in turn, would make the United States, as our major trading and cultural partner, easier and more stable to deal with. In order to remain aware of these changes and to cope with them, the Canadian government would have to maintain a very strong continuing presence in Washington and continue to develop special Canada-U.S. relations. There is little in this most plausible scenario to prevent us from following this path.

Western Europe and the European Community

The economic problems faced by Western Europe have been broadly similar to those experienced by Canada and the United States; they include modernizing the economy, adapting to technological change, reshaping the energy-supply system to adjust to new realities, reducing the environmental impact of industry, improving working conditions, and gearing up to meet the challenge from the less-developed countries (LDCs) in such fields as textiles, steel and vehicles. By the 1970s, virtually all of Western Europe found itself facing serious setbacks in the form of slower economic growth, increasing inflation and unemployment, and a fiscal situation that some observers termed a "crisis". This situation was created by the difficulty of reconciling with the maintenance of a developed and costly welfare state, a "managed" market economy confronted with severe competition from abroad, and especially from the newly industrializing countries (NICs).

Various circumstances have been identified as the specific cause of this weakening of the economy. The economic decline has been attributed to the wage policies of organized labour, strong increases in non-wage/labour costs, the emergence of competition from the less-developed world, increases in the costs of raw material, and the inherent instability of European market economies. Partly because of these factors, profits were squeezed, the return on capital decreased, capital investment declined, and state revenues were reduced. It has been contended, too, that government fiscal and monetary policies and industrial plans have significantly reduced the influence of market forces in directing the vast European economy. The result has been a system that is neither capitalist nor socialist, but one in which "the corporatist state tries to exercise direct control over the internal decision-making of companies and over the bargaining strategies of unions."[4] This close marriage of market capitalism and public management has not always worked well. Members of the European Community (EC) have faced the same difficulties as Canada and the United States in forming a coherent industrial strategy. For this reason, market intervention by governments has tended to be piecemeal and sometimes internally contradictory, aimed less at building a viable economic base than at easing crises of the moment, at protecting the income shares of various economic groups, and at responding to changes in the economic cycle in order to win short-term political advantage.

Conversely, the fiscal regime in the European Community, with important exceptions, has been considerably more conservative than that in North America. Moreover, during the 1980s, EC productivity increases have been larger than those of North America, and trade deficits are not the problem that they are in the United States. The condition of government finances, then, appears to be a significant "plus" for EC nations.

That optimistic note, however, should not hide the possibility that other major structural problems exist. Western Europe, some observers claim, has been weakened by over-reliance on traditional energy sources and by lack of preparation of the fundamental technical and social challenges confronting it. Its physical plant is aging rapidly, and its education system may be too specialized and segmented to cope with the "third industrial revolution" on which the world has embarked. From the late 1970s, only 11 to 17 per cent of Western Europeans aged 20 years and over were engaged in higher education, as compared to 29 per cent of Japanese and 25 per cent of Americans.

Unemployment poses a particularly serious problem in many EC nations. In the period from 1973 to 1983, Europe created only 2 million jobs, compared to Japan's figure of 5 million and the United States' 19 million. Unemployment rates in Europe quadrupled between 1973 and 1983, compared to a doubling of the figure in the United States. In 1982, 33 per cent of unemployed Europeans had been out of work for more than 12 months; in the United States, the figure stood at only 8 per cent. Youth unemployment is a particularly difficult problem. Canadians consider an existing and projected youth-unemployment figure of 18 per cent as alarming, but comparable 1985 projections for Britain stand at 23.5 per cent; for France, the projected figure is 28.5 per cent, and for Italy, a stunning 35.3 per cent.

Some writers maintain that a change is under way in Europe from the material values that so dominated the post-war period to the "post-materialist" values of the new generation of youth. Although a changing values system might serve to provide some consolation to unemployed youth, it could also lead to growing political friction by adding to the numbers of those who support the environmental protection, zero-population/growth and anti-nuclear movements, in opposition to those who give priority to strengthening European industry and military defences.

During the late 1960s, in Europe as in North America, the view developed that differences among the major political parties had been reduced to those of degree rather than of kind. The power of legislatures was believed to have declined, yielding to a "cartel of élites" made up of interrelated public and private bureaucracies. Decisions were made by a network of committees closely aligned with the central administration, a style of decision making that encouraged the identification of issues as technical problems. What emerged, in short, was a corporate system of governing that brought all the main centres of power, public and private (and particularly those of business and labour), into the decision-making process. In fact, European politics vary a great deal more than this simple analysis would imply. However, those countries that have developed a "corporatist" structure of policy making and management may deal more effectively than others with social and economic exigencies. Where corporatist structures are lacking, social and economic conflicts increase.

The corporate approach, for example, has achieved some significant success in mediating conflicts among various interests and in enhancing the ability to conceive and institute policies aimed at effectively serving the national interest. In particular, corporatism has produced some notable results in reducing conflicts over income distribution among various groups. Some observers believe that those West European countries that have embraced corporatism – particularly Austria, Norway and West Germany – have significantly outdistanced, by several standards of measurement, those countries that have clung to traditional approaches; these include Britain, Ireland, Spain and Italy.

Another study of OECD countries, covering 1960–1975, served to demonstrate the strong link between political structures and processes and economic developments:

- Those countries with strongly organized unions and union-supportive political parties, a centralized state and a centralized economy were characterized by low inequality of income and high increases in productivity. (Examples are Sweden and Norway.)
- Those countries with weak trade unions in a centralized state and a centralized economy displayed higher inequality of income and high increases in productivity. (Examples are France and Japan.)
- Those countries with strong trade unions and union-supportive political parties, with a centralized state, but a decentralized economy, rated low in equality of income and had low increases in productivity.
- Those countries with weak trade unions, a decentralized state and a decentralized economy were marked by high inequality of income and a low increase in productivity. An example cited was the United States, which was characterized as having a fragmented, decentralized, political/economic system with little economic planning and few controls on investment; it was also thought to be influenced in the determination of its economic policy more by the political exigencies of election years than by macro-economic policy or market considerations.[5]

The European Community itself faces a number of issues. Most significantly, the basic concept of European unity began to experience a crisis in the 1970s. Among both political leaders and the public at large, support for unification has declined almost steadily, largely because of the economic crisis that confronted EC members in the mid-1970s and the continuing enlargement of the organization. Although there was some reversal in the decline of popular support for the idea of integrating Europe in the early 1980s, the economic expression of that change, in the form of the Common Market, continues to decline in public favour.

Conflict has also developed between those Europeans who played a part in rallying support for the European Community and the national political leaderships whose coalition brought the Common Market into being. While the former are now to be found concentrated in the European Commission, the latter are represented on the Council of Ministers. The Council currently occupies a dominant position. Its members appear to have a strong concern for the enhancement of the national interests of the individual countries they represent, and this concern tends to fragment the union. For the first time, there is also a strong political élite, basically opposed to the EC, to be found in Denmark, the United Kingdom and Norway.

A report by the so-called "three wise men"[6] on the problems of the European Community maintained that the treaty structure was not at fault, but that the political circumstances and attitudes were blameworthy. It contended that the Council of Ministers was mismanaged, and that the

Commission had no coherent policy orientation. These institutional insufficiencies have become worse with the passing years. In the view of many observers, the enlargement of the Community has proved indigestible, and the Parliament is ineffective and virtually invisible.

Many observers regard the disintegration of the Community at some time in the foreseeable future as a very real, if highly regrettable, possibility. Major fluctuations among its chief currencies have been destabilizing, while volatile movements in the price of energy and the international credit system have created emergencies for both Europe and the less-developed world. The EC does not appear to have been very useful in helping members to deal with these recurrent crises. Conversely, however, it is well to emphasize that member states have a very considerable investment in the Community, and that the concept of European economic unity has achieved strong legitimacy, in many quarters at least.

Although the future of the European Community and of Canada's relations to it are of less direct importance to Canadians than are our relations with the United States, a very considerable part both of our trade relations and of our diplomatic ties are with the EC and its member states. The existence of the Community has represented an important bulwark of the post-war world, and Canada should seek to support its continuity as strongly as possible.

Japan

"When one looks at the Japanese political scene" observed former U.S. Ambassador Edwin Reischauer in 1977, "it is hard to find clouds, whether political, economic or social, that really threaten the parliamentary democratic system."[7] In fact, there may be some clouds on the Japanese horizon, but to Canadian observers they appear to be small fluffy ones.

Japan's gross national product per capita is still well below that of Canada, but it is increasing at a faster rate than ours. New social and economic problems will probably develop as a result of a number of demographic changes now in progress: the increase in the average life span (now 80 years); the trend towards an aging labour force (for the proportion of the labour force aged between 54 and 65 is projected to increase from 11.6 per cent to 16.9 per cent between 1980 and 2000); and a growing concern to achieve greater social equality, shorten the work week, and improve the "quality of life".

A number of Japanese have expressed concern about the possible effect of these factors on a maturing economy. Over the medium term, it is expected that the economy will continue to move towards a knowledge and service base requiring a high degree of individual innovative capacity. There is some fear, however, that Japan's less "individualistic" culture may not adapt well to such different requirements.

Japan's economy has now become much more open to competition, and there is some real uncertainty about the ramifications of this exposure. Political cynicism and a lack of trust in the political system appear to remain at a high level, in the view of a number of analysts. This attitude is offset by the fact that the Japanese people exhibit considerable satisfaction with non-political facets of their lives. In recent years, there has also been an apparent increase in nationalist sentiments, and this change of outlook may reduce the willingness of the Japanese to contribute sufficiently, in future, to the accommodation of global problems.

Japan's basic system of government remains one in which there are close financial and social ties among business interests, the ruling Liberal Democratic party that has long formed the government, and the government bureaucracy. The "old boy" network is also a reinforcing link, for 80 per cent of the senior bureaucrats and 40 per cent of leaders in the nation's top 300 companies have graduated from the University of Tokyo. These ties are strengthened by a hierarchy of major trading companies and financial groups that exist at the summit of a pyramid of cross-directorships and joint-stockholding entities, which enables the large corporations to control the smaller ones lower down in the pyramid.

The Japanese bureaucracy is more powerful than that of most countries. For instance, administrative vice-ministers (akin to our deputy ministers), openly make policy declarations. Moreover, retired bureaucrats tend to enter Parliament because of the rule requiring senior officials to retire at the age of 50. (Six of Japan's last ten Premiers were former bureaucrats.)

This pattern of tight political, economic and social integration and cohesion is changing, however, and a much more pluralist and competitive system is gradually emerging. Bank and bureaucratic controls have weakened, as companies can now raise equity capital more freely. Business no longer speaks and acts only through major trade associations, and there is now somewhat broader access to positions of leadership from universities other than the University of Tokyo. Problems of co-ordination have become more significant in recent years as a result of increased conflict between key government departments over competing policy proposals. Overall, however, Japan's social structure still ensures a strong commitment to the work effort and, at least for the upper tier of the economy, a deep loyalty to place of work. Important, too, is a highly competitive education system, an effective banking system, a high rate of personal savings, and a high level of corporate ability to co-operate on research, in conjunction with strong competition in marketing and production. There is still a strong and widespread commitment to the foundation stones of Japanese industrial policy: the development of key industries, the special public-private linkages, and the assumption by the state of a significant share of the risks of capital investment through the provision of extraordinarily high tax assistance.

The most hopeful prospect for Japan is one in which it plays an active role in strengthening the international order by taking on more of the costs of development and diversification of the LDC economies; by providing stronger support to the international development banks; and by assisting in global efforts to solve the problems of environmental degradation, the need for alternative energy services, and the lack of sufficient foodstocks. This outward focus would be reinforced by a greater willingness on the part of Japan to open its domestic market to international competition, while tolerating restrictions in trade on the part of other economies requiring more time to make structural adjustments. All these activities would also be reinforced by a steadily growing and changing economy and social structure. Canada should also be alert, however, to tendencies in the other direction on the part of Japanese governments, since there has been some historical tendency for Japan to be more self-focused than is desirable from an internationalist point of view.

The Soviet Union and China

The Soviet Union and China share certain communistic roots and have demonstrated some similarity of development since those dedicated to communism came to power. There are, however, vast dissimilarities in the background, history and culture of the two nations, and these explain, in part, the estrangement that separates them. In addition, there are significant differences in the problems and challenges the two face for the future.

The principal problems with which the Soviet Union must contend in the years ahead are:

- A marked decline in the rate of economic growth, which fell sharply during Brezhnev's tenure of office, at the same time that growth was declining among all developed nations
- Serious problems in agriculture, which have compelled the country to purchase sufficient grain from abroad to meet 25 per cent of its needs. This necessity has made the Soviet Union the world's largest importer. Although these imports drain foreign-exchange reserves, they remain politically imperative in view of the rising number of work stoppages and consumer protests that shortages have provoked in recent years.
- Failure to become a technological society, despite its considerable progress towards becoming an industrial society. Continuing imports of required technology tend to perpetuate and exacerbate existing weaknesses in the domestic development of innovative technologies.
- A severe economic drain created by the fact that its outlay of resources on military activities is almost equal to that of the United States, while its total national output is little more than half as much
- Declining work productivity, perhaps more marked than that in the West
- Difficulties within its satellites in Eastern Europe, which in recent years have resulted in high costs. In the 1970s, the Eastern Bloc countries were driven into a "debt trap" that compelled them to borrow very heavily merely to pay off the interest on past loans; this necessity, in turn, distorted intra-Bloc trade and development. In 1981, gross debt owed to the West amounted to $88.1 billion (in current U.S. $). This situation put pressure on Eastern Europe to pursue a less centralized course than it had in the past, in order to produce the better-quality goods required to achieve the increased export sales needed to repay foreign debts. This development, in turn, weakened the Communist Party in a number of East European states. As West European loans dried up at the end of the 1970s and in the early 1980s, the Soviet-satellite countries had to turn once again to the U.S.S.R. for further aid.

The present political structure of the Soviet Union is based on what might be called the "Brezhnev consensus", after the former Russian leader who brought it to maturity. This structure is a corporate form of government that fuses within a single ruling group all the major functional power centres in the state, in order to confine any centrifugal forces within an internal system of bargaining and trade-offs. This system, however, is now in some jeopardy. Such systems depend for their success on the maintenance of healthy economic growth, which serves as the necessary lubricant to reduce friction among the competing corporate groups that make up the whole. As growth slackens, economic constraints make stringent trade-offs necessary, and this process puts severe strains on the integrity of a system in which the military is still able to make dominant claims on whatever additional resources become available.

Some observers have suggested three possibilities pertaining to the nature and structure of the Russian government in the future. One is a perpetuation of the current centralized corporate system; another is the institution of a system modified by technocratic reforms imposed from the top, such as is presently in place in China; and the third is change in response to the kind of grass-roots pressure for reform that, at least for a time, succeeded in Poland.

The last possibility is the least likely to become reality. Poland is not a model for Russia. The Soviet Communist Party is simply too thoroughly integrated with every facet of society to make possible a popular uprising. The likelihood of a continuation of the present structure is more difficult to evaluate. Economic and social problems in the U.S.S.R. are immense, and there are indications that the new and younger Soviet leadership recognizes the necessity for fundamental structural reform. Thus, imposition of a technocratic reform from above is well within the realm of possibility. As in China, this reform would require a gradual disengagement of the state from a number of sectors of the economy, a reduction in the Party's dominant position, integration of market forces with some form of democratized planning, economic decentralization, and greater constitutional legality. The unforeseen consequences of changes, whether initiated from the top or from the bottom of the political pyramid, could be explosive if the processes of internal reform were to get out of control.

China is further along than the Soviet Union in the process of change imposed by the new leadership. On October 16, 1984, the Central Committee of the Chinese Communist Party issued a 16 000-word statement on reform of "every aspect" of the country's economic structure. It stipulated that half of the economy was to be freed from compulsory planning and pricing, and made subject, instead, to price, tax and interest-rate controls. Since 1979, collective agriculture has been all but dissolved, and crop decisions and profit making have been returned to individual families. Since proposed industrial reforms affect the 80 million Chinese who produce 80 per cent of government revenue, they may prove costly. They will also have profound effects on members of the Chinese Communist Party apparatus, who play an important part in running the country's factories. The medium-term result of this transformation of the system may be political turmoil generated by declining food subsidies, labour unrest prompted by pressure on workers to work harder and accept greater income differentials, and strong resistance on the part of disaffected Party members.

The Communist Parties of the Soviet Union and China have both matured beyond the despotic phases that followed their respective revolutions. By now, both are governed by bureaucratic oligarchies. Domestic politics are no longer marked by severe ideological conflicts, but by disparate pressures for economic modernization along with bureaucratic inertia. The Soviet Union will probably be increasingly preoccupied with internal politics and more inclined to support international stability (unless internal faction encourages movement in another direction). To the degree that trade is seen as limiting autonomy, it will be restricted, as it is currently, but this restriction will be offset by the imperatives of technological modernization, by the demands of consumers, and by the need to participate in global trade to finance part of the country's economic modernization.

The longer-term effects on a world trading and economic order of an invigorated, industrialized and trade-seeking China are incalculably great. It may be that the next generation of Canadian Royal Commissioners will look back on the last decades of the twentieth century as ones in which the emergence of China was the most important single factor on the world scene. Obviously, Canada must pay very close attention to the possibility of this outcome and support it wherever possible, to the mutual advantage of the two nations.

The Less-Developed World

Most observers agree that immense difficulties confront the less-developed world, particularly in those countries lagging furthest behind in development. Nevertheless, there is very considerable debate about the causes of these problems and effective means of dealing with them. Table 2-21 shows a mixed picture, indicating perhaps that the existing pattern of development has, in a sense, worked not too badly. In fact, however, the contrast between the less-developed countries and the rich industrialized states is still extremely stark.

Taken together, the less-developed world makes up 70 per cent of the earth's population, but accounts for only about 12 per cent of the global output of goods and services. More than 80 per cent of the world's trade and capital investment is undertaken by the industrialized nations. Although Asia's food production increased by some 26 per cent in the last decade, Africa's rose by only 1 per cent. While food has made up an increasing proportion of the imports of a number of less-developed countries, several of them could not afford to import the food they required to meet their needs, nor were they able, for a variety of reasons, to expand significantly their own agricultural production. In sub-Saharan Africa, per capita food production has steadily declined since 1961, and food output is currently increasing at only half the rate of the 3-per cent annual increase in population. Most devastating and discouraging is the fact that this deterioration in the situation has come about despite the expenditure of some $8 billion a year to provide international aid in Africa.

TABLE 2-21 National Patterns of Development 1960–1979

	Low-Income Economies	Middle-Income Economies (excluding capital/surplus oil producers)	Industrialized Market Economies
Average annual growth rate GDP	4.6%	5.8%	4.2%
Per capita GNP	1.6%	3.8%	4.0%
Population growth	2.2%	2.4%	0.9%
Life expectancy at birth (1960–1979)	42–57 yrs.	53–61 yrs.	70–74 yrs.

Source: World Development Report 1981 (New York: Oxford University Press for The World Bank, 1981), Tables 1, 2, 17, 21.

The problems of many less-developed countries (LDCs) have been compounded by their accumulation of foreign-owed debts of massive proportions. These debts originated in the early 1960s, when a number of countries borrowed heavily abroad to finance capital investment aimed at promoting economic growth. The borrowers incurred much of their debt load on the assumption that increasing exports abroad would provide the foreign exchange they required to amortize their debts. Several LDCs also found themselves compelled to import increasing amounts of food from abroad to meet their needs; subsequently, they were forced to borrow substantial sums in order to cover the vastly increased cost of oil imports, following the two price shocks the world experienced in the 1970s.

A development even more severe in its impact than all of these has resulted from the fiscal and monetary policy pursued by the United States since 1980. Although the American policy has reduced inflation, it has also contributed to the development of world-wide recession and to a sharp drop in international trade and in commodity prices. This drop has led, in turn, to a fall in the foreign-exchange earnings of the LDCs, a problem seriously aggravated by the increase in real interest rates. In 1982, the total LDC debt hovered close to $650 billion, and interest payments alone exceeded the total cost of oil imports. The exposure of the private banks that had loaned money to the LDCs was over $350 billion dollars, twice the amount of their capital holdings.[8]

As of 1983, two-thirds of all LDCs were in receipt of foreign loans that had been advanced only on their acceptance of certain policy conditions. While these conditions varied, the standard requirement of the International Monetary Fund (IMF) called for spending restraints, reduced domestic consumer subsidies, higher user fees, establishment of price levels that would promote exports, reduced tariffs, and adoption of more market-oriented policies. These stipulations have not been domestically popular, and they have often resulted in social unrest.

These generalizations should not obscure the fact that the political and economic systems of the individual LDCs vary greatly. The variations are natural, since they reflect different economic opportunities and constraints and, often, distinctive interactions among factors of history, population size, education, culture and industrial base. In 1975, the newly industrialized countries (NICs) – South Korea, Taiwan, Hong Kong, Singapore, Brazil and Mexico – together accounted for 62 per cent of the LDCs' manufacturing exports. Between 1965 and 1978, the first five of these countries achieved annual growth rates in gross national product (constant prices) of between 8 and 11 per cent. Yearly increases in manufacturing exports rose as high as the 20 to 40 per cent range. These LDCs also dominate South-South trade as much as they dominate the South's trade with the North: five of the NICs account for approximately 65 per cent of the South-South trade in capital goods. LDCs also differ in the way they have dealt with the debt crisis, for the East Asian NICs have coped with it far better than have the others.

It is difficult to be certain what combination of factors explains the surge in the development of certain of the less-developed countries. Some observers believe that this pattern of development is most likely to occur in countries where a strong authoritarian government is able both to maintain political stability and to impose an export-oriented industrialization strategy. By way of example, they point to the progress of certain East Asian nations that have followed this model. These countries moved from the production, in the 1950s, of basic, non-durable, consumer goods for the domestic market alone, to marketing abroad in the 1960s. In the following years they shifted gradually into the production of more technologically advanced, capital-intensive goods initially intended for the domestic market and, subsequently, for the export market. This strategy, it has been argued, enabled them to achieve high rates of economic growth, restrain inflation and limit their foreign borrowing. By contrast, the LDCs in Latin America sought to maintain rapid growth rates by resort to heavy borrowing abroad, from sources which were no longer available after the early 1980s. Some students of LDC development maintain that no country has established the advantages of pursuing an export-oriented strategy over an alternative course based on industrialization that is geared to the replacement of imports by domestic goods. The export-oriented/ industrialization strategy has been successful in some countries, they argue, because of a unique combination of circumstances involving exchange rates, capital investment and export opportunities.

Other observers believe that political cohesion and sense of nationhood among newly self-determining countries are important prerequisites for achieving sustained economic development. To attain such political unity is often difficult for new states where significant ethnic, religious and linguistic differences exist, creating problems that may be intensified when a core group occupies a dominant position. The problems caused by such differences may be overcome, some scholars think, if the state is able to see that a fair share of the rewards of economic growth is made available to all groups, and if the government is regarded as prepared to act as an honest broker.

The problems of the developing countries are often viewed from three different perspectives. One views those problems as primarily internal in origin, because of such factors as low capital formation, underdeveloped infrastructure, and policies that fail to allow for the operation of market mechanisms. Consequently, it is contended, the solution must also be primarily internal. Moreover, these internal problems are often aggravated by the policies and practices followed by the advanced industrialized nations. These include import restrictions and restraints imposed by multi-national corporations on technology transfers, which hobble the development of infant industries in the LDCs. Extensive state intervention and subsidization are required to deal with these latter problems.

The second perspective is aligned with the concept of a New International Economic Order (NIEO). It takes the view that a change is required in the basic principles and practices that govern the international allocation of resources. Under this new approach, the liberal market-based system established by the United States after the Second World War to determine the distribution of resources would be replaced by a system in which equal sovereign states, sometimes acting through international organizations, would intervene directly in the process of resource allocation. Equity would replace efficiency as the system's governing criterion, and the goal would be to accelerate economic growth in the South.

A third, quite different, perspective on the position of the LDCs sees the population explosion as leading to uncontrolled migration and severe pressure on the world's limited resources. It is argued that extreme poverty will lead to political instability in the South, which will in time be transmitted to the North. Since world stability is indivisible, it is maintained, the North can only secure its own future by intensifying its efforts to promote the orderly development of the nations of the South. The policy implications emerging from this perspective are that if domestic policy in developing countries is to be improved, impediments to those countries' exports must be removed. The poorest countries need large-scale resource transfers, and for this reason, thought should be given to restructuring international economic institutions in order to allot the South more influence and responsibility. International commodity agreements should be considered as means of stabilizing the prices of raw material.

Taken separately, the problems of the LDCs appear severe, but possibly manageable; taken together, they appear unmanageable, especially in the light of forecasts of generally slower growth and escalating domestic problems accruing from rising consumer demands. The most that prudence can probably expect from the international system is continual patchwork and *ad hoc* holding operations. The LDCs, therefore, face enormous tasks of engineering fundamental domestic reforms in the face of an international system that they may consider hostile or, at the very least, unconcerned with their problems.

Conclusions

There is one respect in which the preceding sketches tend to share a common and disquieting theme: the tendency for nearly all of the world's major nations to become more self-focused and more preoccupied with domestic problems. This tendency has two related implications for these nations' conduct of their foreign affairs: first, they pay less attention to the needs of others, and secondly, perhaps even more than in most periods, they tend to use international politics to press their own advantage. The golden age of international altruism, if ever one was with us, now seems a mere memory.

To some extent, this development may be viewed as inevitable. There is, after all, some inherent tension between sovereignty of individual nations and international co-operation. Moreover, one major incentive for co-operation among nations is bound to be the pursuit of self-interest; nations cannot be expected to behave differently from individuals in this respect. Nations, however, like individuals, ought also to be able to recognize that to maximize long-term and short-term advantages sometimes requires two different sets of behaviour patterns. Like individuals, they may also, we hope, occasionally be motivated by altruism.

In the international sphere, altruism and long-term self-interest may well coincide. This coincidence derives from the probability that ultimately, the distributional implications of the developed nations' short-term pursuit of maximum national self-interest is likely to turn out quite perversely, both for themselves and for others. Blocked from affluent markets, deprived of capital, technology and, most important, of demand for what they can produce, the underdeveloped nations will develop and grow far more slowly than they would in a more open and co-operative international environment. Thus stunted in its growth, the less-developed world will not become a major market for the advanced goods and services of the developed world. This means that the entire world market for advanced goods will not grow as quickly as it could, and every nation will be worse off. A more open approach by developed nations might protect the world from experiencing that unpleasant possibility.

Of course, international co-operation and openness can affect matters other than the distribution of income and opportunities in the less-developed world. These policies have ramifications for the growth of the developed world as well. Part II of this Report deals with these issues. Here Commissioners' objective is to point out that there are some domestic political and economic trends among our major world partners that bear watching as possible impediments. In all countries of the world except China, which, in any case, cannot yet be considered a developed nation, the indications for increased international co-operation are neutral, at best, and sometimes quite negative. The overall international stance of the United States is fairly unpredictable in the long run; in the shorter term, self-conscious pursuit of the national interest seems predominant, sometimes demonstrating less than full regard for the effects of its activities on the interests of others. While Commissioners have expressed considerable hope about the future stance of Japan, it must be recognized that that country's history shows it as tending to self-absorption and ethnocentrism. Western Europe still appears preoccupied with its own problems and, in any event, the world may be better off if European nations concentrate on shoring up the foundations of European unity. The Soviet Union is always an unpredictable actor in Western eyes, and it scarcely needs stating that altruism has not been a hallmark of Soviet foreign policy. The NICs remain preoccupied with their own growth, nor do they yet produce economic surpluses which would allow them to do otherwise.

Commissioners do not wish to leave our readers with an unduly pessimistic view of international prospects. The preceeding sketches suggest a substantial degree of uncertainty and seem to predict a disquieting world political environment incorporating the array of problems faced by most of the actors on the international stage. Although it certainly appears that there are many problems to be faced in dealing with a world of nation states, we Canadians will find it worth reminding ourselves that we have managed to cope with very serious causes for concern in the past. Over the last four decades, we have seen the appearance of over 100 new nations. We have witnessed the birth of the European Community and its Common Market; the capture and, later, the partial loosening of the bonds of Eastern Europe; the emergence of Japan as a major industrial power; the weakening of American world leadership; the re-emergence of China on the world scene; the creation of new centres of power in NICs; the rise and – to some extent, at least – the fall of OPEC; the rise of the welfare state; a major arms race; and a list of other changes that could fill many pages. The international economic and political order has gained and declined in stability several times over this period, but Canada has managed, with a considerable degree of alacrity, to adapt its stance to these changing forces. There is no reason that we cannot continue to do so.

This brief survey, then, suggests that Canada holds a unique position among the nations of the world, since we Canadians have both the capability and, more than most, the inclination to play a leading role in building a more co-operative international order. Both our short-term and our longer-term self-interest contrive to make that role a highly desirable one for us to play.

Notes

1. Norman J. Vig, "Post-Keynesian Economics and Politics: Toward an Expectationist Theory of Democracy?", *World Politics* 34 (October 1981), p. 80.
2. Lou Harris, "Alienation Rises To Record Levels", *The Harris Survey* (March 17, 1983), p. 1.
3. James N. Rosenau and Ole R. Holsti, "U.S. Leadership in a Shrinking World: The Breakdown of Consensuses and the Emergence of Conflicting Belief Systems", *World Politics* 35 (April 1983): 368–92.
4. J.T. Winkler, "The Coming Corporatism", in *The End of the Keynesian Era*, edited by Robert Skidelsky (New York: Holmes and Meier 1977), p. 82.
5. J. Rogers Hollingsworth, "The Political-Structural Basis for Economic Performance", *The Annals of the American Academy of Political and Social Science* 459 (January 1982), pp. 28–45.
6. See A.N. Duff, "The Report of the Three Wise Men" (Barend Biesheuvel, Edmund Dell and Robert Marjolin), *Journal of Common Market Studies* 19 (March 1981).
7. Edwin Reischauer, *The Japanese* (Cambridge, Mass.: Harvard University Press, 1977), p. 330, cited in James W. White, "Civic Attitudes, Political Participation, and System Stability in Japan", *Comparative Political Studies* 24 (October 1981), pp. 372–73.
8. Richard S. Weinert, "International Finance: Banks and Bankruptcy", *Foreign Policy* 50 (Spring 1983): 138–49.

Global Options

The preceding sections have described five different aspects of the world environment:

- The human environment, particularly the world-population explosion
- The physical environment, particularly as it involves the food, energy, raw material and environmental consequences of the population explosion
- The knowledge environment and the communications "revolution"
- The economic environment, especially the widespread structural changes and the changing nature and pattern of trade
- The geopolitical environment, dominated by trends in the United States, Western Europe, Japan, the Soviet Union, China and the developing countries.

How do these five dimensions interact? What are their combined effects likely to be for the global community in the year 2000 and beyond? Is the world economic outlook portrayed earlier in this chapter too optimistic, particularly in light of the population pressures and the rapidly evolving international political economy? Can we expect a smooth adjustment process? Or are the challenges and changes likely to be so sweeping that they will call into question some of the fundamental relationships that have—at least until the latest recession—served to enhance humankind's standard of living? More particularly, can Western industrialized countries count on a positive climate for growth over the next 20 years?

To suggest definitive answers to these questions would be to overstep the proper bounds of humility. Fatalistic or extremely pessimistic pronouncements on the future of humanity have often been made, only to be proved unfounded with the passage of time. Some advocates, contemplating the future, have pointed out the path that would lead to Utopia, if only their policies were adopted. In truth, no one can foretell the future with any degree of accuracy. Nonetheless, governments, like individuals, must try to anticipate the future, either in order to prepare for some expected development or in order to attempt to shape world affairs in a preferred fashion. Thus, for those who wish to form a more coherent view of the future, it is instructive to review briefly the evolution of global forecasting.

Historians of past civilizations have drawn the seemingly irrefutable conclusion that while there is a minimum level of satisfaction of human needs, below which life is impossible, there is practically no limit to human desires. The important question is not the extent of demand, but whether future supplies will be adequate to meet future requirements:

> *At the beginning of the twentieth century some economists advanced the idea that mature economies are bound to stagnate because consumption cannot expand as production does. The crisis of 1929 and subsequent events seemed to support the theories of the stagnationists. There is no doubt that on occasion demand can fall short of productive potential and damage the economy for more than five or ten years—the span of a business cycle.*
>
> *There may also be long-term disequilibria with overtones of excessive*

production in some specific sector of the economy. But on the whole, in the long view of history, economic difficulties of mature empires [countries] apparently do not stem from insufficient consumption. Quite the contrary! Even if their economic analysis is not unremittingly rigorous, historians have always felt instinctively that the main economic troubles of mature empires [countries] stemmed from the side of supply.[1]

Even early forecasters saw supply-side limitations as cause for great concern, if not for alarm. Malthus' *Essay on the Principle of Population*[2] was received as a prophecy of doom and provoked considerable debate. Almost 200 years later, the Club of Rome burst onto the forecasting scene with much the same message, but one fortified by the mystical device of the computer. The message was stark: global collapse could only be avoided by a marked deceleration in overall growth and by great emphasis on conservation. *The Limits to Growth*, published by Dennis Meadows and his colleagues in 1972,[3] reflected the Club of Rome's conjectural extrapolations of past trends into the future. Yet it does not require a computer to predict the consequences of maintaining an exponentially increasing population characterized by exponentially increasing per capita consumption on a planet with finite resources.

The Global 2000 Report to the President, commissioned by President Carter in 1977 and released in 1980, represented a more sophisticated attempt to understand the future. Again, the report took a very gloomy view:

If present trends continue, the world in 2000 will be more crowded, more polluted, less stable ecologically, and more vulnerable to disruption than the world we live in now . . . Despite greater material output, the world's people will be poorer in many ways than they are today.

For hundreds of millions of the desperately poor, the outlook for food and other necessities of life will be no better. For many it will be worse. Barring revolutionary advances in technology, life for most people on earth will be more precarious in 2000 than it is now—unless the nations of the world act decisively to alter current trends.[4]

While the report has become a bible of futurism, it is not without critics. A study entitled *The Resourceful Earth*[5] disputes the assertions and conclusions of *Global 2000*. Contrary to the views expressed in the 1980 report, the authors of *The Resourceful Earth* claim that the world's population pressures are not serious, that energy supplies are virtually limitless, that the prices of industrial raw materials will decline, and that atmospheric pollution is decreasing.

Clearly, these two outlooks represent a schism. It derives, in large part, from our manner of viewing the role of humanity in shaping its own destiny. Global modelling over the last 15 years has given more and more emphasis to human shortcomings, as compared to the limits of natural resources. Technological progress and institutional organization are held to be the dominating variables which ultimately determine the concurrence between future supplies and future requirements. Unfortunately, many futurists and economic philosophers contend that in a mature society, institutional change inevitably moves towards decreasing efficiency. For others, the institutional factor is the independent variable, the "handle" by which we grasp the time bomb.

Thus there are at least two theories underlying growing national interdependence. On the one hand, the concept is supported by the international trade theory of comparative advantage, although there are "new" interpretations even of this doctrine, explaining how its principle can be manipulated to a country's advantage. On the other hand, it is supported by a theory of political economy or, at least, by a premise institutionally derived from that theory. The latter premise views the world's states as actors in the international system they have constructed. For states, boundaries are important. Institutional networks have been created to manage the international economy in terms of states' multiple objectives. States are not exclusively interested in maximizing domestic economic growth, let alone global economic growth. The world economy, therefore, exists in conjunction with a world political system of states.

Whatever one thinks of the proper role of states in the domestic economy, the international economy must be managed – and it must be managed by states, using both domestic and international machinery. The duty of states, on the one hand, is to see that the political anarchy of the world state system does not destroy the benefits of world economic interdependence. On the other hand, states must simultaneously pursue innumerable non-economic objectives.

Depending on the assumptions used in formulating a global model, predictions will be either pessimistic or optimistic. To illustrate, two scenarios are set out below. The first presents a global community where adjustment is orderly, and where growth in the world economy proceeds in an open and constructive manner. The second represents a global community where change cannot be accommodated within existing institutional frameworks, where nation-states are not able to resolve the problem of the external effects of one another's actions, and where isolated spheres of interest become the established order.

The Future as a Continuation of Past and Present Experience

Barring a catastrophe, either natural or induced by war, the future as a continuation of past and present experience presents a reasonably optimistic vision. After all, in the post-Second World War period, humanity has managed not only to survive, but to prosper. Despite the population explosion and the plight of so many millions, overall progress has been made in advancing living standards. Moreover, the ecological balance, while seriously threatened by acid rain, deforestation, desertification and a variety of other ills born of over-population or human ignorance, has not yet deteriorated to the point where control has been lost. On the contrary, argue the optimists, human ingenuity can and will be applied to resolve those problems that threaten human well-being. More positively, humanity will continue to advance living standards. Technological advances in micro-electronics, biotechnology and other fields promise future strides in productivity and solutions to many ecological problems. Growing bureaucratic complexity and a decline in investment can be corrected, and economic performance can be greatly improved.

The North-South dichotomy will no doubt continue, but even this division might well be moderated through education and improved communications. Developing and less-developed countries are rapidly adopting the production techniques of Western industrialized nations, and this evolution holds the potential for greatly improving the distribution of production world wide. While lower-priced goods will jeopardize industries in some countries, consumers will benefit and will demand wholly new goods and services. These demands, when combined with increased leisure made possible through increased wealth, will ensure that sufficient employment is generated – at least in Western societies – to leave unchallenged both the work ethic and current means of income distribution.

Moreover, the optimism of this outlook extends to the sustainability of the welfare state. Indeed, societies possessed of greater wealth might well choose to enrich their welfare and social security programs. Some may see this move as a logical way to fortify the economic system; others may see it as a public good for which they are willing to give up private consumption.

In this world of steady growth, the current international debt problems that now seem so intractable should recede. The enormous deficits of governments should decline also, since a modicum of increased fiscal care should result in a rough balance over the long run. Severe inflation will no doubt recur from time to time, but it will not cause economies to collapse. Some nations are likely to experiment with institutional solutions to inflation, while others are likely to try to make more market-determined adjustments.

With steady growth, world trade will continue to expand and with it, the benefits of a higher degree of specialization. The temptation will always remain strong for nations, or a group of nations, to break rank and try to lever a favourable trade advantage for themselves. Furthermore, all nations will engage in subterfuge in an effort to disguise what would otherwise be termed "protectionist policies". At some point, however, the substitution of non-tariff barriers (NTBs) for tariffs and quotas will give rise to sufficient costs for a halt to be called.

Industrial strategies may be a form of protectionism or export promotion, especially if they are targeted at specific industries or firms. Over-zealous attempts by governments to engineer comparative advantage can prove highly disruptive to traditional concepts of "fair" trade, for there is little doubt that a state has the potential – if it is willing to dedicate sufficient resources – to capture a significantly greater share of a particular market. Countries are experimenting with new methods of competition, but to the extent that a country's competitive position can be enhanced by some form of industrial strategy or targeted approach, other governments might seek to counteract such advantages by special measures of their own. Moreover, to the extent that income gains can be derived from avoiding counter-productive competition, future GATT or bilateral efforts might be dedicated to managing the problem.

Interest groups will hone their skills in extracting some particular advantage, and their attempts may tie the decision-making process into knots. Alternatively, they will try to expedite decisions that are to the disadvantage of the nation or nations concerned. Again, however, there is little reason to believe that the resource misallocation that might result from these activities would extend beyond the cost of modifying them.

Guardians of a future that is meant to represent a continuation of past and present must place considerable reliance on the rationality of people. Although many challenges threaten our future well-being, a rational optimism suggests that they will be surmounted by technological progress and institutional adjustments, domestically and internationally.

The Future Marked by Discontinuity

According to this discontinuous global oulook, the future threatens to be much more difficult. Our second scenario adopts the underlying premise that the population pressures, resource constraints, ecological problems and technological changes which we are now witnessing, and which are expected to compound, cannot be accommodated by a simple extension of past and present approaches.

In this Commission's hearings, Environment Canada described such a future in extreme terms as the "Doomsday Scenario" and explained its cause this way:

> *The Doomsday Scenario for the future is based on the premise that nation states will not be able to gain and apply the understanding, the imagination and the political and moral will necessary to deal effectively with the set of global mega-problems confronting human societies ... The scenario predicts major disruptions to world trading patterns, international monetary collapse and severe world-wide depression accompanied by rising crime, terrorism and eventually thermonuclear and/or environmental disaster.*
>
> (Environment Canada, Brief, February 14, 1984, pp. 10–11.)

To understand this way of looking at the world, several issues must be addressed. The North-South dichotomy is one such issue. Rates of population growth that vary widely between developing and developed countries create a problem unique to the developing nations: how to sustain minimum standards of living when many of their populations will double over the next 20 to 40 years. The size of the problem is staggering—so staggering, in fact, that it threatens to overwhelm the means of control. In the struggle for survival, ecological damage will become so extensive that it will ultimately undermine survival for many, many millions of people. Cutting of the tropical forests, overgrazing and desertification, a "greenhouse effect", and many other forces already in play will continue to interfere seriously with the global ecological balance.

Western industrialized countries will not escape the consequences. Indeed, they will be a major source of the problem, as their smoke-stacks continue to spew pollution and sulphur dioxide. Acid rain is already wreaking havoc, yet there is little evidence of a determined effort to address this problem. Although rich agricultural land is being degraded by some current farming technologies, their use continues. Misuse of our forests is a widely-acknowledged problem, but Canada, for one nation, has failed to take corrective measures.

What this global outlook foresees, therefore, is a short-sighted humanity, one that discounts the needs of future generations in order to "live better" now. In the struggle for the good life, or for mere survival, we waste our land, our resources and our environment. Obviously, policies that may be designated as selfishness in Western societies cannot be so described in the developing and low-income countries. There, mere day-to-day survival leads to the relentless over-exploitation of nature's limited ability to support life.

The technology race is another factor contributing to a possible discontinuity between the past and present and the future. Trade advantages that reward the first nation's efforts to develop and/or adapt new technology drive other countries to accelerate their technology-related efforts. Inevitably, the productivity advances that are associated with these new technologies displace more and more workers. Some concerned observers foresee that robotics and other new production techniques will, for the first time in the history of humankind, create a "demand" limitation to growth as opposed to "supply" limitations. Unemployment will soar, and new ways of distributing income will be required.

Because technology and modern methods of production are so readily transportable, the spectre of "unfair" competition from low-income and developing countries calls into question the post-war tradition of non-discrimination and multilateralism. Furthermore, the extraordinary will of Japan to put itself at the forefront of industrialized nations has shaken North American and European faith in freer trade. Western industrialized countries have been striving to protect themselves from these "shocks", despite seeming compliance with the provisions of the General Agreement on Tariffs and Trade (GATT). Since there is every reason to assume that these external shocks will continue to assault the economic foundations of industrialized nations, there is every reason to believe, too, that protectionism will increase rather than decrease.

Canada's Stake in the Alternative Outlooks

In reality, there is no choosing between the optimistic and pessimistic scenarios set out above, not, at least, within the next twenty years. The preferred future will incorporate elements of both. Clearly, although it is very much in Canada's interest that the optimistic global outlook materialize, we cannot be sure which direction the global community will take, nor whether traditional relationships and values will hold for the future. Even within the optimistic scenario, there are very real questions about how society will confront the challenges ahead. Will it be sufficient to rely on the more traditional solutions of "growth through technology"? Or is there something more fundamental at stake here?—something which will require a major transformation on the scale of the industrial revolution if we are to advance into a world where people place greater emphasis on the understanding of the human condition and its relationship to the natural environment.

No one, surely, can help but be overcome by the enormous challenges described in the previous pages. Many countries will continue to suffer severe deprivation. The quality of life for a large number of the world's citizens is likely to deteriorate, even though aggregate income levels may continue to rise. Thus, on a global scale, Commissioners cannot be generally optimistic, for we have been profoundly saddened by the growing danger signals which have helped to outline for us the contours of future human experience.

For the few, such as most Canadians, the opposite will be true. Our abundance places a very heavy moral responsibility on us to manage our own affairs with increased concern for our fellow global citizens. In considering how we can best marry this positive view of Canadian prospects with a more discouraging outlook for the global community, Commissioners have drawn from an emerging consensus of the global modelling literature:[6]

- Social, political and institutional structures, values, norms and world views are responsible for unsatisfied basic needs; physical scarcity is not the problem at a world level.
- There appears to be a good deal of latitude for accommodating population growth, although strenuous, international, co-operative effort will be required.
- Current policies will result in an increasing gap between the rich and the poor, problems with resource availability and environmental destruction, and worsening economic conditions for most people.
- Technological progress is not a panacea for the world's problems. To restructure social, economic and political systems is vital to bringing about a desirable future. We should expect a transition to some world order that will be both quantitatively and qualitatively different from the present, just as the world today is a very different place from the world of 40 years ago.
- Global interdependence is greater than commonly imagined. It demands that decisions be made within the broadest possible context, with longer-term goals firmly in mind. Further international co-operative approaches are required to achieve individual, national and international goals.

These principles provide a context for strategic decision-making. They do not supply a context for complacency. Indeed, the core message here is that real changes are necessary to overcome our current problems. To see the breadth and scope of the required changes, we have stepped back very far, in this chapter of our Report, from immediate Canadian problems so that we may gain sufficient perspective on our country and our institutions to keep options open for discussion. Yet many of the more radical options inherent in our analyses that relate to two types of problems – the profound uncertainty with respect to the risk of major irreversible change consequent on human activity and the nature of the social contract – are, in a way, beyond the scope of even this Commission's mandate. Nevertheless, we do maintain that further debate on many of these issues is critical if we are not to foreclose future options.

Canada's rich natural resource base, its access to extensive capital, its well-educated and well-trained labour force, and other advantages, as well, are no guarantee of a prosperous future. Fundamental choices confront Canadians, choices that are highly interdependent with policy directions taken by our major trading partners and competitors. Our starting point as Commissioners has been to ask whether the global outlook is generally optimistic or pessimistic and, more narrowly, whether or not the international environment is likely to be conducive to our overriding goal of growth in the well-being of Canadians.

At best, Commissioners are able to conclude only that global prospects are uncertain. While we have a good deal of faith in the resilience and adaptability of capitalism, this potential has little application to much of the world's economy. Even within our major trading partners, institutional and social lethargy are major impediments to increasing efficiency. In such circumstances, Canada has no choice but to pursue policies that place greater emphasis on flexibility and adaptability, both with respect to our socio-economic goals and also with respect to the reform of our institutions, through which many of our goals are pursued. Canadian experience in the past 40 years has shown our nation to be capable of responding to challenge both domestically and internationally. It is to this latter challenge to our foreign policy more generally that we now turn.

Notes

1. Carlo M. Cipolla, ed., *The Economic Decline of Empires* (London: Methuen, 1970), p. 7.
2. Thomas Robert Malthus, *An Essay on the Principle of Population, as It Affects the Future Improvement of Society* (London: J. Johnson, 1798).
3. Donella H. Meadows, Dennis L. Meadows, Jorgen Randers, and William W. Behrens III, *The Limits to Growth: A Report for the Club of Rome's Project on the Predicament of Mankind* (New York: Universe Books, 1972).
4. United States, Council on Environmental Quality and the Department of State, *The Global 2000 Report to the President: Entering the Twenty-First Century* (Washington, D.C.: U.S. Government Printing Office, 1980), p. 1.
5. Julian L. Simon and Herman Kahn, eds., *The Resourceful Earth: A Response to Global 2000* (Oxford: Basil Blackwell, 1984).
6. See Donella Meadows, John Richardson, and Gerhart Bruckman, *Groping in the Dark: The First Decade of Global Modelling* (Proceedings of the Sixth Conference on Global Modelling of the International Institute for Applied Systems Analysis) (New York: Wiley, 1982).

Implications for Canadian Foreign Policy

The minor- and middle-power states of the global community have a particularly strong interest in promoting multilateral procedures and institutions for resolving international problems. This interest derives partly from the general advantage that accrues when nations can pursue economic and other goals abroad in a secure, stable and predictable environment. It stems also from the fact that if multilateral institutions and procedures are effective, they can help to weaken the ability of the greater powers to act entirely on their own, either singly or together. At the same time, they create opportunities for smaller countries to increase their influence by co-operating to achieve their common objectives. Just as anarchy sometimes works to the particular advantage of the strong, so maintaining order among members of institutions can especially benefit the weak.

We Canadians are geographically isolated on the North American continent, in the close company of a dynamic super-power which has at its disposal unprecedented military, economic and cultural resources. In these circumstances, Canadians have been preoccupied historically with the problem of maintaining the freedom of manoeuvre we need to preserve a separate and satisfying political identity. For these reasons, we have been exceptionally open to arguments in favour of conducting international relations multilaterally, particularly since the end of the Second World War. These arguments were all the more attractive because they offered a happy way of combining altruism and enlightened self-interest. These motives unite Canadians' genuine and praiseworthy desire to contribute constructively to maintaining a peaceful international environment for all nations, with a political and diplomatic strategy clearly calculated to strengthen Canada's hand in world affairs.

As the agenda of international politics have grown more crowded and complex, and as the interests of individual states, including Canada, have become increasingly subject to foreign influences, it has become more important than ever for nations to encourage the development of effective problem-solving institutions in the international community. The strengthening of such institutions is not, in fact, a matter of choice, nor should the need for this action be viewed as applying too narrowly. It is necessary for sovereign states to negotiate their purely economic transactions – their exchanges of labour and capital, and their trading of goods and services – and often to conduct them according to international regulation, as well. Here, as elsewhere, economics and politics are interlocked. Peace may depend on prosperity; prosperity certainly depends on peace. Without peace, all else fails. This Commission, therefore, supports a reinvigoration of Canadian diplomatic traditions that were especially well established during the two decades immediately following the Second World War. These traditions often have been described as "internationalist" and commonly identified with the concept of Canada as a middle power; they are now more relevant than ever before, and for this reason they receive explicit treatment in this Report.

The concept of Canada as a middle power was first developed in a way that was linked to international organizations and multilateral diplomacy during the final years of the Second World War. Its appearance in Canadian statecraft was partly a reflection of the growth of Canada's real capabilities, in both absolute and relative terms. The devastation of Europe and the eventual military defeat of Italy, Germany and Japan demoted, at least briefly, many of the other players in the international hierarchy. At the same time, Canada's military and economic contributions to the war itself won us a very substantial claim to prominence in world affairs. After France fell, and before the Soviet Union and the United States entered the war, Canada had ranked second only to the United Kingdom among the allied powers. At the end of the war, some analysts ranked Canada fourth among the nations in terms of real international capabilities. Even the United Kingdom, its resources stretched beyond their limits, had come to depend on Canada for the assistance it required not only to finance its war effort, but also to bring about its ultimate post-war economic recovery. Moreover, in some of the newer fields of international concern – atomic energy, civil aviation and food production, for example – Canada had resources and expertise that placed our nation in the front rank.

Canadian policy makers, confident of Canada's relative strength and potential, were well aware that if they failed to initiate an active multilateral diplomacy, the great powers alone would be left to conduct global affairs. These powers had run the war; they might easily fall into the habit of running the peace. Canadian statespersons were not so naïve as to think that the management of international affairs could be based on the principle of state equality. Indeed, realism led quickly to the conclusion that any system which attempted to distribute responsibilities in a way that was grossly at odds with the distribution of capabilities was bound to fail. Plainly, the greatest powers would wield the strongest influence.

If, however, the great powers could be encouraged to act within the confines of multilateral negotiating and decision-making institutions, the constraint imposed by these bodies could qualify their supremacy and modify their activities in accordance with the insistently-expressed needs and demands of the lesser powers. Furthermore, the principle that influence in multilateral organizations ought to correspond to power could be applied at more than one level and could work to the advantage of more than one category of state. If the great powers were to exercise great influence, then the middle powers could be expected to wield medium influence. If the latter were not accorded this right as a matter of course, the principle gave them the right to claim it, and wisdom would suggest that the claim be honoured. Moreover, if a power that was otherwise modestly endowed happened to control a leading share of important resources – as Canada, for instance, held an impressive position in relation to atomic energy and aviation – it might reasonably aspire to exercise an outstanding degree of influence, rather than a modest one.

Still another belief buttressed the Canadian position. This was the conviction that the creation of a secure and peaceful international order ultimately depended on two eventualities: the effective operation of collective security agencies and the gradual development of practical and functional co-operation among the various members of the international community. Some

Canadians went so far as to claim that unless this approach was adopted, and unless it was given formal expression in such institutions as the International Civil Aviation Organization (ICAO) and the Food and Agriculture Organization (FAO), any attempt to deal more directly with the problem of preventing war and containing conflict was bound to fail.

These ideas appeared most plainly in Canadian attempts to strengthen the position of middle powers in the United Nations in 1944–45, while the United Nations Charter was being negotiated. They were visible, as well, in the prominent part that Canada's representatives took in forming such specialized agencies as the United Nations Atomic Energy Commission. In later years, they could be detected, too, in Canada's approach to the creation of the North Atlantic Treaty Organization (NATO) and, particularly, in our government's repeated attempts to strengthen and formalize arrangements for ensuring that the Allies consulted one another in the making of NATO policy. Enthusiastic Canadian participation in the ill-fated discussions of the late 1940s, which were aimed at establishing an International Trade Organization (ITO) and, later, in the early negotiations relating to the General Agreement on Tariff and Trade (GATT), demonstrated the same strategic interest, supported by the same diplomatic philosophy.

Much of this multilateral activity pertained, of course, to matters that were far too specialized to attract the close attention of the general public. By the mid-1950s, however, Canadian diplomatic activity was beginning to acquire a new gloss that made it at once more visible and more dramatic. It was a gloss that had a particular appeal because it seemed to express an almost unique capacity to make a constructive and apparently disinterested contribution to the maintenance of international peace and security. It therefore helped to define a distinctive Canadian identity abroad while, at the same time, it provided reassuring grounds for self-esteem. It originated, of course, in the mediatory diplomacy of Canadian statesmen and diplomats, Lester Pearson notably among them, and in their conflict-resolution activity. It became actual in the assignment of Canadian peace-keeping forces to various trouble-spots around the world. In retrospect, its outworking was discernible in Canadian responses to the Middle East conflict of the late 1940s; to issues relating to the evolution of the Commonwealth in the same period; to diplomatic questions that arose in connection with the Korean War; to the dispute over Kashmir; to the Indo-China problem that followed French withdrawal in 1954; and to a number of other problems, as well. It was most dramatically expressed in the Suez Crisis of 1956 and the establishment of the United Nations Emergency Force, an enterprise that was to be repeated in the Congo, Cyprus and elsewhere. As these experiences accumulated, Canada's role as a middle power came to be more widely recognized and to be seen as more than the exercise, in multilateral contexts, of a medium degree of influence based on medium-level capabilities. It was also viewed as a moral disposition to act pragmatically, imaginatively and with moderation, in attempts to resolve third-party disputes peacefully.

Canadian statespersons were able to perform these functions as a result of a variety of factors. These included their status as representatives of a middle-sized power, which gave them sufficient diplomatic and military resources to meet the requirements of the task. Moreover, they were not generally so prominent or so intrusive in international politics as to arouse the anxieties of disputing parties or to cause suspicion that they might be acting from ulterior motives.

While many Canadians were tempted to assume that their country's reputation for detachment in international matters was the product of a special virtue, the reality was that it was also the result of happy circumstances. There may, however, be some truth in the notion that the diversity underlying Canadian politics generates a pragmatic, flexible and open-minded approach to resolving differences, which can be of special service in international affairs. Canada is geographically isolated from the areas where conficts seemed to be most prevalent. Moreover, Canadians are concerned to preserve an international environment that is conducive to peaceful economic exchange. These circumstances combined to give us a fundamental interest in maintaining global order, rather than in seeing one side victorious over another in any particular instance. Thus Canada was more deeply preoccupied with the fact than with the terms of any given settlement. Since many of the international disputes occurred in areas now associated with the less-developed nations, it was helpful, too, that the Canadian reputation, unlike that of many European countries, was not perceived as tarnished by a history of colonialism.

Much of the post-war world was divided into two hostile camps, each anxious to deny to the other any expansion of leadership or influence, and each prone to view every local conflict as a potential incentive to dangerous mischief on the part of its opponent. This circumstance created a widespread interest in containing the scope of local conflicts and in forestalling any direct involvement of great powers that could magnify small wars into large ones. In effect, the bipolar structure of the international community itself created both the need and the opportunity for Canadian conflict-resolution activity.

Canada's support of multilateral mechanisms and procedures for handling international problems was developed at various stages as a carefully calculated strategy. In addition, the Canadian position in particular situations may have reflected a consistent set of views concerning the best ways to deal with political conflict. Nevertheless, our government's responses to the various international crises with which it attempted to grapple were *not* initially conceived as expressions of a continuing "role". Rather, they were practical reactions to specific problems and circumstances, undertaken on the implicit premise that "internationalist" activity of this kind was very much in Canada's national interest. The notion came much later that peace-keeping and mediatory diplomacy were indications of an ongoing Canadian "policy", with characteristics that were, in some respects, unique to Canada, and that reflected the special attributes of a middle power.

When this notion did arise, it proved to be a popular and satisfying concept, since it could be regarded as constructive and benign – even altruistically humanitarian – and since it was clearly distinguishable from roles played by most other countries, including the United States, the nation to which Canada was most commonly compared. Additional encouragement for this view came in the form of the Nobel Peace Prize awarded to Lester Pearson. It was not surprising, therefore, that in due course, Canada's claim to the peace-keeping role should come to have a prominent place in our government's official declarations on external affairs. So attractive did that role appear that by 1964, peace-keeping was identified as one of the principal objectives of Canadian defence policy, and the special military requirements it entailed were being put forward as part of the rationale for the integration of our three armed forces. In short, Canada's conflict-resolution activity, which had begun as a series of practical responses to particular international disputes – responses which were founded in an enlightened self-interest – had evolved into a standing feature of our foreign policy. It was a policy which had widespread support at home, and which, through precedent, seemed to have created expectations abroad that our government would readily act on it at international request.

The domestic popularity of the middle-power role, however, was a two-edged sword. It certainly enabled the Canadian government to help maintain a stable external environment by taking modest "internationalist" initiatives. Nonetheless, it gave rise to a national belief that Canada would play the role with almost automatic regularity on "suitable" occasions. This expectation was unrealistic, and it became increasingly so as the structure of international politics developed. During the 1960s, Canada's relative importance in matters relating to international security seemed to recede as Europe and Japan recovered from the catastrophe of the Second World War.

Moreover, the appearance in the international community of a large number of newly independent states transformed such institutions as the United Nations and the Commonwealth: it did not merely alter the balance of political forces within them, but changed the nature of the various agenda with which they were attempting to deal. In these new circumstances, Canada became a less prominent power with fewer opportunities to exercise effective diplomatic leadership. On many of the newer issues, especially those with a "North-South" dimension, Canadian delegates in the United Nations had become members of a targeted minority. They represented a rich, privileged and developed country of which new demands might reasonably be made – or so it seemed to disadvantaged nations – in order to achieve a fairer distribution of welfare around the globe.

In addition, the Cold War, which had provided the background for much of Canada's most visible conflict-resolution activity, appeared to moderate, and its participants seemed to become less rigidly polarized. This development, too, helped to weaken whatever measure of indispensability Canadians had previously enjoyed. Of course, Canada continued with many of its peace-keeping enterprises and related diplomatic activities, but they were interspersed with developments which offered food for disillusionment. These included, most notably, the withdrawal of the United Nations Emergency Force from Egypt, over Canadian objections, in advance of the 1967 Six-Day War, and the repeated failure of Canadian diplomatic attempts to promote an end to the Vietnam War.

Understandably, concern arose that these changing conditions would make it difficult for the Canadian government and its diplomatic service to continue to perform in accordance with the public's high level of expectations. It was partly for this reason that Canada's role as a "helpful fixer" was explicitly downgraded, in 1970, in *Foreign Policy for Canadians.*[1] Moreover, Canadian policy statements gave less emphasis to the internationalist orientation of our foreign activities. For a long time that outlook had been nourished by the view that Canada's interest would ultimately be served best by attempts to contribute broadly to maintaining, under multilateral auspices, a peaceful external environment. Instead, our government highlighted the pursuit of goals that were more directly and narrowly founded in specific domestic needs. Even in the field of defence, peace-keeping was demoted to last place in the official rank-ordering of the objectives of Canada's military establishment. The military dues that were being paid to NATO, partly as the price of admission to a multilateral decision-making forum, were substantially reduced.

A nation has every reason to tailor its foreign-policy aspirations to its actual capabilities. Canada's move in this direction attracted unusual attention. Since the decline in Canadian capacity in external affairs (relative, at least, to that of other powers) was particularly evident in the peace and security fields, the dramatic character of the issues gave it unusual visibility. The change, therefore, had a special impact on public perceptions of what Canada could really do on the international scene. Certainly, Canada's share of world trade has declined since 1945, as the participation of other countries in the international economy has increased, and as the total volume of world trade has grown. However, the original concept underlying Canada's post-war policy was that our real influence as a middle power would vary with the issue, and that it could be especially strong in some of the more specialized areas of practical co-operation. A multilateral strategy remains, in any case, an attractive option for powers that are not in the first rank. This contention, as it applies to Canada, is strengthened by the massive imbalance of power inherent in our all-important relationship with the United States. In such circumstances, the potential advantage of dealing with issues on a multilateral, rather than a bilateral, basis cannot lightly be dismissed.

Given these considerations, it is not surprising that analysts of Canada's external relations should have devoted further thought to the potential sources of Canadian influence abroad. Perhaps our country lowered its international aspirations in the 1970s because of an excessive preoccupation with our government's capacity to contribute to the resolution of issues directly related to peace and security, to the neglect of other promising fields of international activity. For example, Canada had played a leading role in the lengthy, intricate and vital negotiations concerning the development of the Law of the Sea. Was this intervention really the mark of a declining power in world affairs?

Some observers have obviously thought not. One of them, in an analysis first published in 1975, drew attention to Canada's plentiful store of energy, raw materials, food and technological expertise, and pointed out the weakening of the United States' former position of global supremacy. On the basis of these observations, he argued that Canada has the potential to become not just a middle power, but a "foremost" power.[2] Similarly, two scholars, who tried, in 1979, to locate Canada on an international scale of capabilities (as measured by military and economic strength, availability of natural resources, and diplomatic representation) concluded that our country should not be ranked with such middle powers as Australia and Sweden, but with major powers like the United Kingdom, France and West Germany. Through interview research, however, they also showed that this ranking was not commonly perceived by members of the foreign-policy community, either at home or abroad, nor did it correspond to the view of independent foreign-policy analysts. Both groups seemed to subscribe to a more modest opinion of Canada's place in the world. The authors explained this marked discrepancy between perception and reality largely in terms of the contention that "Canada is a regional power without a region", its capacity for visible initiative overshadowed by its proximity to the United States.[3]

A more recent analysis has taken the argument further. It suggests that the decline of American supremacy and the tendency, in recent years, for power to be more diffusely distributed in the international system at large have combined to promote Canada from middle- to principal-power status. The authors hold that this expansion of Canada's relative capabilities has led to the adoption of a more autonomous style of foreign policy. This development reflects our government's increasing awareness of its ability to pursue distinctive Canadian interests and values by bilateral means and in competition with other states. In these circumstances, the necessity for internationalist multilateralism declines, and policy makers can more freely undertake unilateral initiatives as they attempt to drive hard bargains. They can also adjust their diplomatic alliances pragmatically, to suit their short-term opportunities and needs. Bilateral diversification becomes at once more appropriate and less constricting than multilateralism as a means of maximizing influence. Participation in the process of engineering a world order takes place through joint actions with other principal powers, rather than by way of effective international institutions.[4]

When taken together with the actual evolution of Canadian policy, these comments show that in an increasingly integrated world, populated by diverse and proliferating states and plagued with constantly changing issues that are both technically intricate and politically difficult, no single strategy will do. Appropriate measures will vary with the situation. If we consider the Law of the Sea, for example, where Canada has important economic, environmental and security interests, both long-term and short-term, it is clear that there can be no substitute for a multilateral approach, although this approach may be complemented (as, in fact, it has been) by unilateral initiatives and bilateral bargaining. We can say the same of trade negotiations, aid policy, environmental diplomacy, international discussions relating to the exploitation of outer space, and a host of other matters. Moreover, the balance of advantage as between multilateral and bilateral approaches will vary, not merely with the issue, but with time, as circumstances change and different political forces prevail. The available opportunities for forming diplomatic alliances are just as variable. States that are allies in the security field may be rivals in trade; the most natural market for the export of energy may also be the principal external source of environmental pollution.

It follows indisputably from all this that Canada cannot afford to adopt a passive posture in world affairs. Our government must devise an active foreign policy that incorporates ingredients of both the internationalist and the "realist" approaches. It is not appropriate, in any case, to view these as competing orientations. Canada's support for international institutions and its role as helpful fixer were always tempered by realistic assessments of the possible, and they reflected a strong sense of the vested environmental interests of a *status quo* power. They also demonstrated the belief that a "regional power without a region" had better cause than most others for diversifying its contacts abroad and for nourishing the growth of multilateral decision-making systems. Paradoxically, as we Commissioners shall argue in Part II of this Report, greater efforts to establish a North American economic region reinforce the traditional Canadian foreign-policy strategy of diversification.

Moreover, many current international problems cannot be managed or resolved, even technically, by other than multilateral mechanisms. Even if unilateral or bilateral approaches were effective, the powers that are strong and secure – middle, major, foremost, and principal alike – court danger for themselves, as well as for the world at large, if they seek, in administering global affairs, to exclude the less fortunate, inconvenient though the involvement of weaker states may sometimes appear to be. We Canadians, in any case, have repeatedly expressed our desire to make constructive contributions to the world order. This desire reflects, in part, our happy geopolitical circumstance, but it also expresses the finer ingredients of our political culture, as well as our need to play a distinctive role in the international community as one means of maintaining our faith and trust in ourselves.

This review suggests a number of practical implications for Canada: vigorous and visible support for the multilateral system represented by the United Nations and its specialized agencies, in spite of the limitations of the United Nations Security Council as a collective security institution; strong specific support for the GATT, the International Monetary Fund (IMF) and other agencies of international economic co-operation as the preferred approach to promoting secure conditions of international trade, but not necessarily to the complete exclusion of bilateral initiatives, including those with our key partner, the United States; participation in the North Atlantic Alliance as the best vehicle for promoting Canada's capacity to influence Western security policy and the prospects for moderating East-West relations, and for confirming the general stability of the international community; aggressive joint initiatives, with other developed countries of like mind, to promote the welfare of less-developed states through a more realistic and enlightened form of development assistance, improved access to Northern markets, and relief of external debt; and more aggressive participation in world forums dedicated to the concerns of the natural environment and the need to integrate environmental decisions with those related to economic development.

Notes

1. Canada, Department of External Affairs, *A Foreign Policy for Canadians* (Ottawa: Information Canada, 1970).
2. James Eayrs, "Defining a New Place for Canada in the Hierarchy of World Power", *International Perspectives* (May–June, 1975). Later reprinted in *International Perspectives* (November–December 1981).
3. As cited in Peyton V. Lyon and Brian W. Tomlin, *Canada as an International Actor* (Toronto: Macmillan, 1979). See especially pp. 56–76. Herman Kahn's argument is also cited in a brief discussion of the same issue in Peter C. Dobell, *Canada's Search for New Roles in Foreign Policy in the Trudeau Era* (Toronto: Oxford University Press for the Royal Institute of International Affairs, 1972). See especially pp. 1–5.
4. See David B. DeWitt and John J. Kirton, *Canada as a Principal Power: A Study in Foreign Policy and International Relations* (Toronto: Wiley, 1983). The argument is briefly summarized on p. 4.

Conclusions and Recommendations

As we peer into the future, there is only one central fact about which we can be reasonably certain: there are powerful forces loose around the globe that will profoundly affect the lives of all of us here in Canada. The global outlook is full of danger signals; a majority of the world's citizens are facing very troubled prospects.

Commissioners have noted two very distinct trends in world affairs which are disturbing when viewed together. The world today has become more interdependent in economic, social and technological matters. We all share problems and opportunities as global citizens. However, the political will and international institutional machinery have not kept pace with this growing interdependence. While Commissioners are not alarmed by this divergence, we are concerned that it be recognized, and that steps be taken to rebalance altruism and self-interest on the international stage.

In entering what may well be a very turbulent period, Canadians occupy a privileged position that may make the prospective problems of the global community appear quite remote. We enjoy a comparatively high standard of living; we possess abundant natural and human resources; and we have in place a political fabric and institutions that up to now have proved themselves reasonably capable of providing the framework of laws and regulations, policies and programs required to serve our national interest best.

But, "no man is an island, entire of itself", as John Donne astutely observed more than three and a half centuries ago. As Commissioners noted at the outset, Canada is more exposed than most nations to developments taking place in the world, because of far-reaching links of trade, aid and diplomacy. Canadians are highly vulnerable to adverse impacts, both direct and indirect, but we are also in a favoured position, in many ways, to seize opportunities as they arise.

In addition, however, the very breadth and depth of Canada's involvement in affairs around the world appear to impose upon Canadians a special responsibility to take up the important role that may be available to us: to contribute to a resolution of some of the more critical global problems that will arise in the years ahead. This view is based on Commissioners' deep belief that the major problems facing the global community are rooted in social, political and institutional structures, values and norms. In part, Canada's contribution might be made in material forms and by way of education, training and technology. Conceivably, however, we could play an even more important role as a catalyst, in bringing other nations together to work in concert for the resolution of global challenges and problems.

As Commissioners stressed at the beginning of this section, and as we reiterate now, we can at best perceive only dimly how the future will unfold. Undoubtedly, many current projections of prospective developments and their likely consequences will prove wrong in degree or in kind. It is crucially important, however, that Canadians should carefully search out the primary forces in play around the world, constantly monitor their action and interaction, and stand ready to respond, as circumstances require, either alone or in combination with other nations. While many future developments abroad will certainly have a direct impact on our nation, in many instances we may well have greater cause for concern about the indirect consequences for us of global impacts on other countries.

This Commission underlines the importance of recognizing five critical features of the global system:

- The degree of interdependence will continue to increase in the foreseeable future, causing the domestic policies of any one country to be significantly affected and, in some instances, dominated by global forces and the policies of larger countries.
- While the eradication of poverty and famine is within the grasp of most developed nations and certainly of Canada, it is not even on the horizon for most of the world's peoples.
- The dangers and challenges identified in the physical, economic and political global environment are so significant that the general increase in well-being of all dwellers on the planet is at risk.
- The principal limits to growth are not physical, but political, social and institutional. The major challenge thus lies in the fruit of technological and institutional ingenuity.
- Global interdependence demands that decisions be based on long-term goals and be made in the broadest possible context.

■ In view of this assessment of the global environment, Commissioners urge that the fundamental global priority within the context of peaceful co-existence become the general increase of the well-being of all nations and peoples, and the urgent eradication of malnutrition and starvation.

- Given the high degree of global uncertainty that this Commission has identified, it is important that Canadians understand both the privileged position we occupy on this planet and the human imperative this places on Canada to provide leadership in those areas of critical concern to the world, where our nation has a capacity to provide that leadership. Commissioners recommend that as a matter of high priority, Canada pursue a more activist foreign policy based on the concept that Canada now occupies a more responsible position as one of the principal powers. Combining humanitarian and pragmatic interests, Canada should:
  - Seek to broaden Canadian and world understanding of the meaning of interdependence and the threats and opportunities which confront civilization. This approach includes giving higher priority to issues relating to the natural environment and especially to the implications for global well-being of the continuing population explosion.
  - Vigorously support reform of the multilateral system represented by the United Nations and its specialized agencies to bring the institutional machinery into line with the substantive problems and opportunities of the future

- Pursue bilateral and regional initiatives where these are appropriate and essentially outward-looking in a multilateral context.

■ This Commission has reviewed the broad sweep of global interdependence in an effort to identify those areas where Canadians will be offered both challenges and opportunities over the next quarter century. We Canadians must take account of this interdependence in designing our own national policies. In particular, Commissioners recommend that:

- In the decades ahead, Canada's policy makers integrate environmental decisions with those on economic development. This policy will be essential, for there is, in this Commission's view, no ultimate trade-off between economic development and the preservation and enhancement of a healthy environment and a sustainable resource base.
- Canadian economic policies be developed increasingly in a global context. This process requires a fuller recognition of the long-term and structural changes evolving, particularly in the areas of trade, technology and the role of governments, in the struggle for competitiveness. The incentives for work effort and productive contribution should be enhanced in a more flexible market environment.
- Canadian social support mechanisms and programs be designed more efficiently to accomplish the feasible task of removing the blight of poverty within Canada and to establish our national economy on a flexible, but secure, social infrastructure
- Parliament be reinforced as the principal forum for national debate and reconciliation of international, national and regional interests. □

PART II

CANADIAN OPPORTUNITIES IN AN OPEN WORLD

PART II

Contents

Chapter 3 **Retrospective** *213*
Chapter 4 **Canada in the Global Economy: The Present Situation** *231*
Chapter 5 **Canada and the General Agreement on Tariffs and Trade** *277*
Chapter 6 **Freer Trade with the United States** *297*
Conclusions and Recommendations *378*

CHAPTER 3

Retrospective

Introduction *215*
Note *217*
The Formative Years: From Colonial Times to 1945 *218*
Notes *224*
The post-War Years: Predominance of the International System *225*
Development of International Institutions *226*
Bilateral Relations *227*
Canada's Trade Policies 1945–1980 *228*
Looking at the Past and Looking to the Future *229*
Note *230*

CHAPTER 3

Retrospective

Introduction

The global environment presents an enormous challenge to Canada today, and that challenge will increase over the next two decades. In political terms, it is one of managing international interdependence and of building new relationships that will accommodate the growing importance that nations have for one another. In legal terms, it is one of adjusting existing structures to new realities. In economic terms, it is one of accommodating and mastering new technologies and of adjusting to a more competitive world economy than has ever been known before. In sum, the challenge is one of change, adaptation and adjustment. It constitutes one of the most difficult problems faced by modern nations and their governments.

The challenges of the global environment bear on all countries, and Canada is not alone in facing them. Nor are the problems more severe for Canada than for other countries. Today many nations are going through an exercise of soul-searching to determine how modern global relationships will affect their futures. The task involves examining the nature of the global challenge and then exploring how particular national institutions and processes can respond to that challenge. This undertaking is first of all a task of analysis, one that takes account of the historical development of a nation and its people, and of the unique institutions and processes that it has established to govern itself. Secondly, it is a task of decision and action, one that adjusts national practices to the realities of the global environment.

Any analysis of Canada and the global environment must take account of the themes of the Canadian historical experience. These themes distinguish our experience from that of other nations. They appear in the history of our country from its earliest beginning, and they must be addressed in any program for future change. One such theme is that Canada's domestic economy is largely defined by its relation to the global economic system. Most

Canadians or their ancestors are or were immigrants from Europe, and they brought with them customs and culture from the "old" countries. Once in North America, Canada's immigrants found their culture profoundly affected by the economic geography of their new land. Trade with their mother countries and with industrial centres in Europe and the United States sustained economic activity in Canada and, in turn, shaped the institutions of the new country. As Canada's eminent political economist Harold Innis has observed, Canada emerged as a political entity with boundaries largely determined by the fur trade. In his words: "The lords of the lakes and forest – the beaver – have passed away, but their work will endure in the boundaries of the Dominion of Canada and in Canadian institutional life." Today the image of Canada is less romantic, but our nation's economy is still deeply influenced by external economic relations, as reflected in the fact that foreign trade accounts for over 30 per cent of Canada's gross national product. In this dimension, Canada ranks among the most trade dependent of the nations belonging to the Organisation for Economic Co-operation and Development (OECD).

A second theme is that of Canada as a hinterland and resource-producing economy. In the colonial period, Canada was situated on the margin of European civilization, and its economic relations with the centre were driven by its exports of staples: fish, fur and, later, timber and wheat. As the nation grew, and as a changing technology came to demand increased use of metals, Canada's vast riches of minerals and ores were developed for export to more highly industrialized nations. Today Canada is a fully-industrialized nation producing a wide range of manufactured goods. While resources continue to be an important building block in the Canadian economy, their relative function will not be as great in the future as it has been in the past. In pursuing resource-development opportunities, Canada will continue its long-standing policy of seeking to extend the further processing of resource products beyond the primary stage.

A third theme is that of industrial development. Since Canada's beginning as a nation, our governments have sought to promote the growth of a manufacturing industry so that Canadians would have opportunities to earn their living in ways other than as "hewers of wood and drawers of water". The cornerstone of these efforts was the National Policy announced by Sir John A. Macdonald in 1878 and implemented by his government in 1879. This policy instituted a protective tariff for Canadian manufacturers and provided east-west transportation links meant to build a strong national economy. The goals, and to some extent the means, of the National Policy have been maintained to the present day; they are reflected in the fact that Canada's tariffs are some of the highest among those applied by the OECD nations. At a time when nations have been debating the appropriate form of industrial policy with which to face the problems of the 1980s and the years beyond, it is useful to recall that Canada's industrial policy has undergone major changes since the National Policy was introduced in 1879. It is also important to remember that the cornerstone of Canada's industrial policy has been its trade policy.

A fourth theme is that of the role of the state in the economy. Because Canada historically exported raw materials, the Canadian government became closely involved in economic activity through providing transportation, finance and other support services. It spent heavily on railroads and canals, and provided large grants and subsidies to support other infrastructural development. Government involvement in the economy began in earliest colonial times with the trade in fur and fish, and the pattern reinforced itself with each new staple commodity Canadians produced. In our own day, governments, both federal and provincial, are major players in our national economy, and any attempt to analyse and make recommendations to improve Canada's economic performance must necessarily take account of this fact.

A fifth theme concerns Canada's relations with the United States. In historical terms, the United States constitutes a central problem for Canada because it provides such a strong engine of growth for our exports, and yet, on account of its strength, may pose a threat to our Canadian identity.[1] Much of Canadian domestic and foreign policy has been heavily influenced by the Canada-U.S. relationship. For example, the National Policy was both a domestic policy of economic development and also a foreign policy designed to stem the southward flow of emigrants from Canada to the United States. Moreover, it was promoted, in part, on its appeal to anti-Americanism. In modern times, economic events have deepened Canada's economic relations with the United States, and this development, in turn, has magnified Canadian concern with the problem of renewing and strengthening our national identity. Today Canada-U.S. relations are an unavoidable issue on our nation's economic-policy agenda, and it is certain that their handling will be as deeply politicized in the future as it has been in the past.

These, then, are five themes that have influenced Canada's economic development. In the 1980s and beyond, Canada will face new problems, but its response will blend old institutions and procedures with adjustment to new realities. These themes will help to define the new problems Canada faces, and they will set the parameters within which our nation will take future action. The task for Canada is to retain its character and identity while meeting the challenges that a changing economic environment will place before it.

Note

1. See J.L. Granatstein, "The Issue That Will Not Go Away: Free Trade Between Canada and the United States", in *The Politics of Canada's Economic Relationship with the United States*, vol. 29, prepared for the Royal Commission on the Economic Union and Development Prospects for Canada (Toronto: University of Toronto Press, 1985).

The Formative Years: From Colonial Times to 1945

From the earliest stages of European settlement, economic activity in Canada has been based substantially on trade. As, first, France and, subsequently, England founded settlements in the northern half of North America, the economies of the various political units established there followed widely-recognized patterns of colonial development. The colonies supplied the mother country with their most valuable and readily accessible raw materials and were, in turn, supplied with manufactures. This interchange, which some Canadians have come to view as an exploitive connection, was originally a relationship of convenience and even of necessity. The investors who sponsored settlement of the colonies relied on returns from natural resources to make their enterprise profitable. The European settlers relied on manufactured goods from "home" to make their life in the new world tolerable.

Canada's early development, like that of other colonies, was based on the export of a small number of staple goods: first, furs and fish, and subsequently, timber and wheat. Later, Canada's international economic relations reflected both continued reliance on extensive trade in staple products and the desire to develop a manufacturing sector; manufacturing was seen as necessary to ensure long-term national stability and prosperity. Historically, the first of these two thrusts has been the major force behind Canada's policy of liberalizing trade. The second has provided our motive for adopting protective trade measures.

In the late 1840s, Canada's economy began its evolution from the old colonial system to a regime in which trade with the United States has become increasingly important. The repeal of the Corn Laws in Great Britain, in 1846, sparked some Canadian interest in trade reciprocity. The shift in British policy from mercantilism to free trade confronted Britain's colonies with the necessity for changing their own trade policies. Coupled with this pressure was the economic damage that the world depression of the early 1850s inflicted on British North America: businesses went bankrupt, public debt increased, and unemployment grew. It was under these circumstances that the British North American colonies, in pursuit of renewed economic prosperity, turned to trade with the United States.

Although the Americans had rejected the British North American Colonies' earlier offers of reciprocal free trade, the United States signed a Reciprocity Treaty with these five colonies in 1854. By the terms of this treaty, all signatories gained rights of reciprocal free trade in natural products, free navigation of the St. Lawrence and Great Lakes water systems, and fishing rights off the Atlantic coasts. Predictably, the Reciprocity Treaty increased trade between the colonies and the United States. From 1854 to 1855, the volume of trade between the United States and the British North American Provinces more than doubled.

By 1866, however, the U.S. Administration realized that imports from the BNA colonies were beginning to outweigh corresponding American exports, thus creating an unfavourable bilateral trade balance for the United States. In addition, bitterness developed south of the border about certain tariff increases on goods manufactured in the colonies, which were not covered by the Reciprocity Treaty. Finally, and perhaps most important, ill feeling was generated against the colonies during the U.S. Civil War, partly because of Britain's apparent support of the South against the Union, as evidenced, for example, by the seeming British and Canadian laxity in controlling Southern representatives in Canada during the war and by incidents like the St. Albans raid. For these and other reasons, on March 17, 1866, the United States exercised its right under the Treaty to terminate its agreement.

In that same year, Sir Alexander Galt, the then Minister of Finance, introduced the Tariff of 1866, which represented a direct reversal of the high-tariff policy that he had proposed in 1858. The Act of 1858 had, for the first time, advocated protectionist principles in Canada; the Tariff of 1866 reduced the average duty on imported goods. These reductions were intended to help secure the union of the British North American Provinces in Confederation. Few British North Americans, however, supported the idea of uniting the economy of the proposed Confederation with a common tariff. In the Maritime colonies, which traditionally had favoured free trade, one of the strongest arguments put forward against entering Confederation was the high level of duties imposed by the Province of Upper Canada. Many Maritimers feared that their prosperity would be seriously undermined if their trade were to be effectively restricted to the "two or three millions of people who live in the rear".[1] Furthermore, they believed that rapid expansion into the West, which the proponents of Confederation living in the Canadas hoped to achieve, would impose additional and onerous financial burdens.

For the Fathers of Confederation, the creation of a viable and integrated national economy was a prime goal. Representatives of Canada at the pre-Confederation meetings, especially John A. Macdonald and George Brown, gave this aim an especially high priority. They believed that their objective of an effective economic union could be achieved only through the integration of the diverse resources and industries of the various provinces. The colonies could no longer rely on a single resource or industry: if the Maritime fisheries encountered difficulties, for example, agriculture in Upper Canada would be a dependable resource to help restore the economic balance.

Inherent in this objective was the goal of increased trade both inside and outside the proposed union. There was hope that the removal of tariffs among the provinces-to-be and the improvement in their communication would eventually result in increased trade when the provinces entered Confederation. It was expected, too, that union would result in increased international export trade, and that the new nation of Canada would achieve a prominent place in international markets. Although manufacturers and politicians expected Confederation to stimulate growth in trade and economic development, it was apparent that:

> *There was no general demand that Confederation should be strengthened by a national policy of protection ... It was not upon protection, but upon geographical position, natural resources and widened markets that the manufacturing interests of the different provinces based their hopes.*[2]

Shortly after Confederation, in the early 1870s, Canada tried to negotiate a new Reciprocity Treaty with the United States; the attempt failed. In 1878, Sir John A. Macdonald, with the same objectives in view that he had held earlier, decided to adopt a policy of protectionism. On March 7, 1878, Macdonald made his intentions known in the House of Commons. He moved that:

> *. . . the welfare of Canada requires the adoption of a National Policy, which, by a judicious readjustment of the Tariff, will benefit and foster the agricultural, the mining, the manufacturing and other interests of the Dominion; that such a policy . . . will prevent Canada from being made a sacrifice market, . . . and moving (as it ought to do) in the direction of a reciprocity of tariffs with our neighbours, so far as the varied interests of Canada may demand, will greatly tend to procure for this country, eventually, a reciprocity of trade.*[3]

Canada's continuing desire for reciprocity was, then, a major force behind Macdonald's proposal. At the time, Macdonald believed that the low tariff Canada had imposed was benefiting the United States to the detriment of Canadian economic interests, especially in manufacturing. He argued that since Canadian markets were already open to the Americans, there was no incentive for the United States to negotiate a new Reciprocity Treaty. "It is only by closing our doors" he claimed, "and by cutting them out of our markets, that they will open theirs to us."[4] Macdonald's policy was, in many ways, a second attempt to achieve the economic goals which the Fathers of Confederation had hoped to attain through Union, but which so far had not been reached.

Macdonald had other reasons, directed to the same end, for the introduction of a protectionist tariff. First of all, he considered the tariff a means of controlling emigration, believing that it would retard the outflow of Canadians to the United States. Under the new tariff, he was sure, Canada's industries would flourish, and employment would increase; thus Canadians would no longer have to move south of the border in search of jobs. Secondly, he saw the introduction of high tariffs as a means of fostering industrial development in Canada. If manufacturers enjoyed reasonable protection, they, like their American counterparts, could develop their own resources and gain control over a number of key industries within their particular sectors. This development would stimulate investment which, in turn, would provide revenues to finance new transportation facilities and generally expand the Canadian economy.

Macdonald and others saw protection, too, as representing a policy of "nation building" through import substitution. Tariff adjustment, they contended, would increase trade among the provinces and send products to eastern and western areas of Canada, instead of to the United States or to England. It would also encourage manufacturers and consumers to buy from Canadian suppliers. The increased duty on certain articles would be especially significant for goods that Canadians could produce and manufacture themselves. The device worked: the new tariffs fostered and encouraged interprovincial trade. The result was much to be desired, for even after

Confederation, the provinces had had little connection with one another, except for a common allegiance to Great Britain.

The tariff was put to its first popular test in the election of 1891. Export trade had been traditionally important to Canada, and it had always proved difficult to maintain a balance between measures which expanded trade and those which protected domestic industries. Moreover, the 1880s had been difficult years for our country. As a result, many Canadians had begun to question the protectionist approach and, indeed, to look again at Canada-U.S. reciprocity as a likely source of renewed economic prosperity.

The Liberal party, now under the leadership of Wilfrid Laurier, adopted as an election platform "unrestricted reciprocity", a Canada-U.S./free-trade arrangement which allowed both countries to set their own tariffs. Sir John A.'s Conservatives had, indeed, briefly explored the possibility of reciprocity with the United States, but when their overture was rebuffed, they quickly labelled the Liberal position "virtual treason". In the opening speech of the 1891 election campaign, Macdonald made his now-famous statement: "A British subject I was born, a British subject I will die." His purpose was to evoke patriotism to Queen and Empire in order to defeat the French, Roman Catholic-led Liberals. The Liberals dropped the issue of reciprocity, at least publicly, and subsequently won the election of 1896.

In 1904, the then Minister of Finance W.S. Fielding, in defending Canada's tariff levels, clarified the industrial development goals of the tariff:

> *I think, Sir, as to whether or not it is adequate protection we have some evidence of a gratifying character that the tariff, without being excessive is high enough to bring some American industries across the line and a tariff which is able to bring these industries into Canada looks very much like a tariff which affords adequate protection. If my honourable friends opposite wish to see some of the good results of the tariff let them go up to the city of Hamilton and look at the vast industries which have been established there by American capitalists who have come across the line under the operation of this tariff, and who are now engaged in carrying on very large businesses. Let them go to the city of Toronto and they will find similar organizations of American capital starting in the manufacturing business. So, we are able to say that not only has the tariff been a great revenue tariff, but one which has afforded a reasonable degree of incidental protection and one which has brought about, as far as these industries are concerned, very gratifying results.*[5]

Between 1900 and 1910, Canada's average annual manufacturing-growth rate was 5 per cent. Growth at this pace had been unprecedented in British North America. Although the tariff had achieved some apparent success in promoting Canadian manufacturing and interprovincial trade, the issue of Canada-U.S. reciprocity was still in the air. The Liberal government continued to put out feelers in Washington. It was encouraged in this undertaking by the pro-free-trade sentiments of Western farmers, who resented paying artifically high prices for farm implements and manufactures produced in central Canada.

In December 1910, farmers besieged the Parliament buildings in Ottawa to press their case. The government was impressed by these demonstrations, not only because of their vehemence, but because of the continuing importance of staple products and their producers to the Canadian economy. As vital as the manufacturing sector was becoming, staples – wheat, fish, timber and minerals – continued to be the backbone of the economy, especially in western and eastern provinces. Thus the growth of manufacturing in central Canada, combined with the continued prominence of staples production in the Atlantic and western provinces, made the reciprocity debate a regional conflict. This geographic dimension of the free-trade issue has subsequently contributed to the growth of regional conflict in Canada, as well as to the sense of alienation in the less populous Western and Maritime regions.

In January of 1911, an election year, Finance Minister Fielding announced to Parliament that a reciprocity agreement had been concluded with the United States. That agreement provided for free trade in a wide variety of primary products and for tariff reductions on many other goods, notably farm machinery and implements. It was clearly aimed at supporting the agricultural community, but it also retained considerable protection for manufactured goods. Nonetheless, as Conservative leader Robert Borden considered how to oppose the agreement, he found willing and active support in the central-Canadian business and financial community. Business people, including many disaffected Liberals, feared that free trade in primary products was just the beginning of a process that would soon engulf their firms and remove the protection they had enjoyed. They resolved to support the Conservatives in their fight against the Liberals on reciprocity and in the election. Their support, however, was conditional: Borden secretly agreed that if he were elected, he would bring in ministers from outside Parliament and consult a group of prominent, formerly Liberal, business leaders on the composition of his Cabinet. These conditions met, the business community put its substantial resources into the fight against reciprocity, through the Canadian National Association and the Canadian Home Market Association, which was sponsored by the Canadian Manufacturers' Association.

The resounding defeat of Laurier's Liberals in 1911 came about, in part, because of the strength of Henri Bourassa's *Nationalistes* in Quebec, but to an even greater extent, because of the reciprocity issue. The latter reason made that defeat significant on two counts. First, the Liberal loss demonstrated the power and resolve of central Canada's manufacturing interests, which had grown and thrived behind the protective wall of the National Policy. Secondly, the Conservatives won the election because of the popular appeal of the anti-reciprocity argument, based on a carefully orchestrated campaign of anti-Americanism and, implicitly, of British and Canadian nationalism. The election campaign of 1911 demonstrated the strength of Canada's new nationalism, particularly in the context of the presumed threat to Canadian sovereignty, posed by the possibility of free trade with the United States. This perception of looming American economic domination has since promoted an appeal to Canadian nationalism whenever the issue of Canada-U.S. trade has surfaced in debates on these matters.

In spite of Canada's rejection of reciprocity in 1911, its trade with the United States continued to grow. The growth was hastened by the First World War, which generated increased economic integration and co-operation between the two North American Allies. The United States emerged from the War with the world's strongest economy, but Britain had declined in economic strength. For Canada, this development resulted in an inevitable change in foreign-investment patterns. Capital investment from the United States rapidly equalled and soon surpassed the traditionally dominant investment from British sources. In a country which has always relied heavily on foreign capital to finance its economic development, this change was of profound economic and political importance.

In 1921, the trend towards Canada-U.S. economic integration was temporarily halted by the passage, in the United States, of the Emergency Tariff Act. This Act initiated a decade of steadily increasing American tariffs, matched turn for turn by Canada, and culminating in the Smoot-Hawley Tariff of 1930, which set the record of American trade protection. Combined with the market crash of the Great Depression, this escalating protection crippled Canada-U.S. trade. Prime Minister Bennett retaliated against the Smoot-Hawley Tariff by trying to extend British Imperial preferences to compensate for lost U.S. trade. Such measures, however, were plainly inadequate, and the unprecedented protection imposed by the United States was clearly harmful. In 1933, Franklin D. Roosevelt became president. With his predisposition to lower tariffs, he and Bennett soon agreed, under the U.S. Reciprocal Trade Agreements Act of 1934, to begin a search for means to increase the exchange of commodities between their two countries.

By the early 1930s, Canada, for the first time, had a small team of trade experts in the civil service. Nevertheless, progress towards trade liberalization was slow, and talks with the United States stalled in August 1935. They were enthusiastically resumed, however, after Mackenzie King defeated R.B. Bennett in the federal election of the same year, and on November 15, 1935, the first Canada-U.S. trade pact since the Reciprocity Treaty of 1854 was signed. By the terms of the new treaty, each nation extended most-favoured-nation (MFN) status to the other and agreed to a few more specific provisions. The result was to roll the tariff back almost to its 1920 level.

Both Canada and the United States, however, regarded this agreement as only a first step, especially in view of their bitter experiences during the Great Depression. "Our stake in world trade," wrote External Affairs counsellor Norman Robertson, in 1937, "and the peculiar degree of dependence of our industries on export markets have identified Canada's real national interest with the revival and liberation of international trade."[6] It was not possible at the time, however, for the Americans to make further tariff cuts, since political constraints and the U.S. Reciprocal Trade Agreements Act prevented them from cutting their tariffs by more than 50 per cent. Nor could we Canadians cut our tariffs unilaterally because we were committed to maintain a margin of trade preference with other British Empire countries. The system of Imperial preferences meant that further Canada-U.S. trade negotiations would, of necessity, have to involve trade negotiations with

Britain and other Dominions. It was, in fact, in the course of British-American trade talks, in 1937, that the next round of Canada-U.S. talks was initiated. These talks were held in response to British requests that Canada abandon certain preferences in order to facilitate British-American tariff cuts.

The talks that followed were important. Like the first multilateral trade negotiations, they set the pattern for the international conduct of trade policy during the post-Second World War era. For each commodity under consideration, Canada had to hold separate discussions with the United States and Britain and, frequently, with Australia, New Zealand and South Africa, as well. Although the discussions were frustratingly slow, they yielded an agreement, signed on November 17, 1938, whereby Canada gained easier access to the United States for 129 of its commodities, and the United States removed or reduced most of its remaining import quotas. The United States, for its part, gained improved access to Canada for a variety of its manufactured goods. By way of further concession, Canada was forced to relinquish British preferences on a number of its primary products.

These negotiations set the precedent for the multilateral trade-liberalization discussions that have dominated the post-war trading system. Predictably, the lowering of Canadian tariffs on U.S.-manufactured goods raised opposition from the Canadian Manufacturers' Association. The talks, however, resulted only in tariff reductions: free trade was not extended to any new items. The avoidance of free-trade terminology may well have been an important feature in preventing any widespread, emotionally based, nationalistic opposition to the agreements. Presented as a simple attempt to get trade moving again and to create jobs, the agreements disarmed the critics; any complaints sounded like special pleading.

Notes

1. Cited in D.G. Creighton, "British North America at Confederation", study prepared for the Royal Commission on Dominion-Provincial Relations, Appendix 2 (Ottawa: J.O. Patenaude, 1939), p. 41.
2. *Ibid.*, p. 47.
3. Canada, House of Commons *Debates*, vol. 1, 1878, p. 854.
4. *Ibid.*, p. 862.
5. Canada, House of Commons *Debates*, vol. 3, 1904, p. 4351.
6. Cited in J.L. Granatstein, *A Man of Influence: Norman A. Robertson and Canadian Statecraft, 1929–68* (Ottawa: Deneau, 1981), p. 66.

The post-War Years: Predominance of the International System

The Second World War marked Canada's coming of age as a sovereign nation. Canada contributed significantly to the war effort, built up its manufacturing sector to produce war materiel, and established lasting relationships with a growing range of countries. By the end of the war, it was ready to assume an important and influential role in world affairs, particularly in the areas of trade and finance. Despite these ambitions, the period immediately after the war was one of stagnation for Canadian external trade as our overseas customers struggled to recover from years of destruction and subsequent balance-of-payments difficulties. These problems were particularly serious for the United Kingdom, and they caused further deterioration in the relative position of the United Kingdom among Canada's trading partners.

The economic effects of the war did not last long, however, and by 1950, production and trade had revived in the North Atlantic area. World trade grew steadily after 1950, averaging about 6 per cent per year and outpacing world growth in production. The proportion of world output of goods and services that crossed national boundaries almost doubled over this period, rising from 11 per cent in 1950 to 21 per cent in 1980. The change in composition of trade has been as significant as its absolute growth. Trade in industrial products and services has grown steadily, compared to trade in agricultural products and raw materials. Manufactured goods now account for a much larger share of trade than they did in the immediate post-war period.

Between 1950 and 1970, trade grew most rapidly among the Western industrialized countries and with Japan. Post-war reconstruction and the formation of the European Community (EC) were among the processes that contributed to this development. While relative shares of total trade changed, all Canada's chief trading partners experienced substantial growth in the volume of their foreign trade, relative to domestic production. Among them, Germany, Japan and some other nations made spectacular gains; still others, such as the United States and the United Kingdom, were faced with substantial declines in their shares of world trade. The U.S. share of world exports, for example, dropped from 22 per cent in 1950 to 10 per cent in 1980, while its exports as a proportion of U.S. gross national product (GNP) rose from about 5 per cent to 10 per cent over the same period.

During these years, the European Community emerged as the world's largest trading bloc; its external trade now equals the combined shares of the United States and Japan. The developing world also made gains: by 1983, the developing countries' share of world trade had reached almost 30 per cent. As for Canada, between 1951 and 1960, its exports grew, in real terms, at an average annual rate of about 4 per cent for the decade after 1951. This rate is low compared to that of the 1960s, when Canada's exports attained an annual average growth rate of over 9 per cent.

During the 1950s, Canada's economic infrastructure also developed extensively: the building of pipelines, the construction of the St. Lawrence

Seaway, and a major expansion in oil, metals and minerals paved the way for the increase of exports in the 1960s. Much of this development was secured through foreign investment.

Rising exports of finished manufactured goods accounted for the expansion of Canadian trade that took place in the 1970s. Canadian exports of this type of goods nearly doubled in volume between 1971 and 1981. Primary manufactured goods, generally consisting of fabricated materials, were sold to foreign markets in quantities slightly more than 40 per cent above the total of 1971 shipments. In addition, Canada exported almost 40 per cent more foodstuffs. Between the early and late 1960s, Canadian exports of fabricated materials and finished manufactured goods rose from about 60 per cent to nearly 70 per cent of our total export trade, and they have remained at this level. The relative increase has been greatest for our exports of fully-finished manufactured products and especially, under the Auto Pact, for our foreign sales of autos and parts.

Development of International Institutions

A significant feature of the period from 1945 to 1980 has been the development of international institutions that influence the global trade environment. The disruption of the world financial and trade systems that occurred in the 1930s and 1940s, first through depression and then through war, had made confirmed multilateralists of Canada's post-war political leaders. They believed that strong multilateral institutions would reduce the risks of world protectionism and isolationism; that they would encourage the evolution of an open-world/trade and /payments system within which the Canadian economy would prosper; and that they would provide an opportunity for Canada to influence directly the policies of the major powers in ways favourable to our further development as a nation. The multilateral systems that were created, and their institutions, rules and procedures were also expected to affect profoundly the relationships Canada would forge with a growing number of bilateral trading partners.[1]

The world trade and economic institutions founded in the 1940s, largely within the broad framework of the United Nations, were dedicated to the establishment of a liberal multilateral order based on the free flow of goods and services, and on convertible currencies that would permit multilateral settlement of national accounts. Central to the system were the twin pillars of the General Agreement on Tariffs and Trade (GATT) and the International Monetary Fund (IMF). These two institutions were founded on the proposition that a liberal trade system based on agreed rules would lead to prosperity and growth for its members and thus contribute to global peace and stability. They were based on the economic theory of comparative advantage, and on the premise that the competitive forces at work in international trade and the effective operation of the price system would benefit the world economy and the economies of individual countries. The post-war planners realized that to create a world of strong multilateral institutions would entail some sacrifice of national sovereignty, but they considered this disadvantage a small price to pay for a system that could help to prevent a recurrence of the chaos and disorder of the previous 20 years. Generally speaking, the system they planned has worked well and has contributed to the increasing international division of labour, to a rapid growth of world production and international trade, and to extensive interdependence among nations.

In the post-war period, then, Canada has expended a great deal of effort in defining, refining and pursuing its interests through these multilateral institutions. This activity reflects many factors, but above all, it demonstrates Canada's interest in, and commitment to, developing a sound international framework for its international trade and payments. Canada has used its involvement in the building of multilateral institutions as one way to avoid becoming overly dependent on exclusive two-way relationships with more powerful nations. Moreover, it has maintained a strongly multilateral policy in the post-war decades, in the hope of encouraging the United States to increase its commitment to multilateral frameworks and, subsequently, to join other nations in an attempt to establish counterweights to American power. This multilateral approach seemed, in the past, to offer the best means of protecting and advancing Canada's international interests.

Bilateral Relations

For a period of almost forty years, Canada and its major trading partners have generally pursued their international economic relations multilaterally. The nature of international transactions, requires, nonetheless, that Canada use bilateral, as well as multilateral, instruments to pursue its trade interests. The prevalence of bilateral arrangements based on mutual economic interests and political ties shows that a growing number of nations insist on dealing with one another within a bilateral, government-to-government framework. This framework appeals, in particular, to the newly industrialized countries (NICs), which are becoming ever more important to Canada.

Canada's best-known bilateral agreement is the Canada-U.S. Automotive Products Trade Agreement (Auto Pact). This agreement, signed in 1965, has had the effect of integrating North American auto sales and production into a single market. Through a series of safeguards and incentives, it ensures that the value of production in Canada is guaranteed as a proportion of auto sales in the Canadian market. Indeed, the Auto Pact has substantially increased Canada's automotive exports. The recent increase in our exports of fully finished goods has stemmed, in large part, from the rationalization of the Canadian and American auto industries under the Pact. In 1984, for example, the auto industry accounted for exports worth almost $30 billion, or nearly 27 per cent of our total foreign sales of goods; this compares to a share of only 2.3 per cent in 1964. Rationalization has also produced increases in Canadian imports of automotive products, which reached a value of nearly $26 billion in 1984.

In addition to the Auto Pact, Canada has negotiated, from time to time, a wide range of other bilateral economic agreements. It has struck bilateral agreements relating to taxes, air travel, general economic co-operation, science and technology exchange, export credit and insurance arrangements, anti-trust measures, trade restraint (particularly in the textile and clothing sectors), international aid (establishing levels and types of assistance, and linking aid to the purchase of Canadian goods), nuclear energy (including the provision of nuclear fuel and technology, the sale of a CANDU reactor, and commitments to safeguards), and any other matters which a particular bilateral relationship may involve. The bilateral rights and obligations represented in these agreements forge additional links between Canada and its various trading partners and define more closely the constraints and opportunities Canada faces in the global environment. They also provide an additional framework, beyond those provided by multilateral institutions, for the resolution of disputes.

Canada's Trade Policies, 1945–1980

In the post-Second World War period, Canada has participated actively in the multilateral trade negotiations conducted under the GATT. Most early GATT negotiations were relatively limited in scope. Substantial progress toward tariff liberalization in multilateral trade was first achieved in the Kennedy Round negotiations (the sixth in the series), which came to an end in 1967. Canada's participation in that round presented our government with a clear choice: Was Canada to maintain its traditional use of protective tariffs under the National Policy, or should it co-operate in a multilateral attempt to liberalize trade, especially trade in manufactures? We resolved this dilemma by adopting a middle course designed to support the liberal international aims of the round and still retain some protection that our growing industries required. Other participants in the round introduced a formula or "across-the-board" approach to tariff reductions, in an effort to maximize achievements in this area. Canada, Australia and New Zealand rejected this approach. Canada maintained that most of its exports were primary products on which tariffs were low, while its imports consisted of industrial products on which tariffs were much higher. Hence, if our government accepted a formula reduction of tariffs, it would extend more benefits than it received. Instead, it negotiated tariff reductions with its major trading partners on an item-by-item basis, in order to achieve an exchange of concessions.

The Kennedy Round left Canada with a higher average level of tariffs than the United States or the European Community. Naturally, this led our major trading partner to make representations to our delegates in the next GATT negotiations, the Tokyo Round of 1973–79. Participants in that round again adopted a formula approach to tariff cutting, and they strongly urged Canada to do the same. After extensive internal discussions, the Canadian government tabled offers consistent with a formula approach. In the end, Canada made a generous offer which will leave our average weighted tariff on dutiable imports at about 9 to 10 per cent in 1987, when all Tokyo Round cuts are phased in. Taking into account duty-free imports, the overall incidence of the tariff should be about 4 per cent, a level of tariff protection similar to that maintained by the United States, the European Community and Japan. Thus Canada's actions during the Tokyo Round, which were prompted by a desire to proceed towards an open and liberal world economic environment, moved our country a further step away from the protectionism of the National Policy. Trade negotiation, however, is a matter of give and take, and the Tokyo Round produced benefits for Canada that were decidedly in our national interest. For one thing, we received an attractive tariff offer from the United States, especially on our exports of semi-processed goods. Most of the Tokyo Round agenda concerned non-tariff barriers (NTBs), and in this area, too, Canada was a net beneficiary. A GATT code was written on government procurement that will increase the capacity of Canadian firms to supply products to foreign governments. Technical problems relating, for example, to product standards and import-licensing arrangements were reduced. Our most important objective, to encourage the United States to adopt a realistic injury test before levying countervailing duties, was achieved as part of negotiations on a multilateral code governing subsidies and countervailing duties. Already this injury test has been important for Canada in the matter of litigated trade disputes in the United States. It has helped us to reduce the harmful effects of one form of U.S. "contingent protection", which has been described by Canadian trade negotiator Rodney Grey as "legal protection when and where you need it". This intermittent protection has been, and continues to be, one of Canada's main concerns in trade relations with the United States.

Looking at the Past and Looking to the Future

Over the past 120 years, then, Canada has matured as a nation and as an economic entity. The process has been most rapid during the last 40 years. A recurrent theme throughout our history has been the important influence exercised by external forces. It could be suggested, indeed, with only slight exaggeration, that Canada was formed in reaction to mid-nineteenth century British and U.S. trade policies, and that the gradual development of our nation was shaped, to a great extent, by external influences. Our foreign economic policy has been based, in large part, on a desire to channel these forces in directions beneficial to natural growth. Since Confederation, Canada has adopted a pragmatic policy stance, born out of recognition that our country was neither strong enough nor large enough to chart a wholly independent course.

Since the mid-1940s, multilateral institutions have provided the principal means of imparting stability and predictability to Canada's external relations and the outside influences that affect them. By participating in these global institutions, Canada has become an influential partner in their management and a nation well integrated into world economic systems. The multilateralism practised over the past 40 years has served our country well: it has nurtured a trading nation with a much stronger industrial base, more capable of confronting the pressures emanating from the international economic environment. Even in this post-war era of multilateralism, however, Canada has experimented effectively with bilateral negotiations aimed at achieving specific objectives compatible with broader international concerns.

Note

1. The development of multilateral institutions and their influence on Canadian economic development are discussed in M.M. Hart, *Canadian Economic Development and the International Trading System,* vol. 53, prepared for the Royal Commission on the Economic Union and Development Prospects for Canada (Toronto: University of Toronto Press, 1985).

CHAPTER 4

Canada in the Global Economy: *The Present Situation*

Introduction *233*

Canadian Trade in the 1980s *235*

Challenges from the Global Environment *239*

International Competition *239*

The Challenge to Adjust *241*

International Investment *242*

Growth of Regionalism *244*

Notes *246*

Trade with Our Principal Partners *247*

Trade with the United States *247*

Trade with Western Europe *248*

Trade with the Asia-Pacific Region *250*

Trade with Other Developing Countries *256*

Canadian Aid Performance *258*

Trade with Other Regions *260*

Notes *261*

The Choices Before Us *263*

Policy Choices *268*

Notes *274*

CHAPTER 4

Canada in the Global Economy: *The Present Situation*

Introduction

Canada entered the world of the 1980s as a developed industrial state which has derived benefits from post-war liberalization of international economic relations. Canadian trade has faced decreasing duties abroad while managing to develop, with the help of foreign capital, a strong industrial base further consolidated by the gradual removal of tariffs and by the gradual exposure to international market forces. In recent years, Canada has carefully charted a middle course between the familiar shore of its long-standing protectionist policy and the far harbour of a more open, liberal and international, economic environment.

In the decades to come, however, Canadians should not assume that the policies of the past will ensure our nation's adaptation to the new pressures deriving from the global environment and, especially, from our country's close relationship with the United States. Indeed, this Commission believes that Canada stands at a turning point in its economic history, and that a new era demanding innovative foreign and domestic economic policies is about to dawn for Canadians. This new era will require our governments to develop and implement policies which will facilitate adjustment in the Canadian economy to a rapidly changing and increasingly interdependent world. Canada needs policies which will provide the flexibility to adapt rapidly to changing external influences. Without such policies, Canadians will not achieve the sustained growth necessary to maintain our present standard of living. This challenge confronts us across the broad spectrum of foreign economic policy, which must take account of trade, foreign investment, aid, immigration, and other areas of responsibility. In all these fields of global economic activity, we Canadians will need to define our place, exert our influence, and pursue responsive domestic policies. Of greatest moment, however, will be our future trade policies.

Trade has always been of prime importance to Canada's economic development; it is the vital link between the Canadian economy and the international competitive environment. Successive governments have emphasized the function of trade in strengthening our Canadian economy, in promoting the continued development and expansion of our resource-based industries, and in building our industrial capacity to achieve a competitive position in specialized international markets. It is through the gradually increasing exposure of Canadian producers to competitive world-market forces that the Canadian economy, as a whole, has become more productive. Trade and trade policy have also helped to improve Canadians' standard of living by expanding the markets for Canadian producers and hence the economic scale of their operations, by providing us with imported goods that would be more expensive to produce domestically, and by improving the quality of employment.

In a technical sense, trade policy is the collection of laws, regulations and government decisions which affect the export and import of goods and services. These individual policy documents have been conditioned and, to a large extent, determined by our perception of the sort of trade environment that would best suit Canada's economic interests. In broad terms, Canadian trade policy has been the art of the possible. Throughout our history, the Canadian economy has depended heavily on world markets. As a basic proposition, successive Canadian governments have tried, through trade negotiations, to obtain the most favourable terms of access to foreign markets, while maintaining some measure of protection for Canadian production. Canadian trade policy has thus been developed as a compromise between the objective of improved access to foreign markets and the desire to provide protection for important Canadian industries. Our trading partners must also consider a similar set of factors in determining how they will negotiate with us and with others.

Even a brief consideration of the range of our international responsibilities and opportunities makes it plain that we must increasingly recognize that Canada's trade performance is affected by the whole range of our domestic economic policies. Foreign policy, export-trade policy and marketing issues all influence Canada's trade performance, but they need to be related to our government's industrial and economic development strategies. We must take into account that domestic and international issues affect one another, and that government-policy considerations affecting these issues should not be viewed in isolation, but rather should be so constructed as to reinforce one another. A strong domestic foundation is vital to Canada's future trade and economic performance. To achieve more efficient and internationally competitive Canadian resource, manufacturing and service industries will require close co-ordination and coherence between trade policy and domestic framework policies. Taking account, then, of the full range of our domestic policies, Canada's private sector must seek out and develop markets at home and abroad. Canadians will thus need to reach strong national consensus about the kinds of framework and support policies needed so that individuals can confidently plan and pursue their interests. Commissioners consider these policies in Part V of our Report.

Canadian Trade in the 1980s

Between 1950 and 1980, world trade grew at about 6 per cent per year, outpacing the growth of world production as national economies became more open and thus more integrated. Figure 4-1 documents this greater trade exposure of the industrialized economies and shows that Canada is among the most open of the large economies of the Organisation for Economic Co-operation and Development (OECD).

FIGURE 4-1 Exports of Goods and Services by Country, as Percentage of Gross Domestic Product, 1960 and 1980

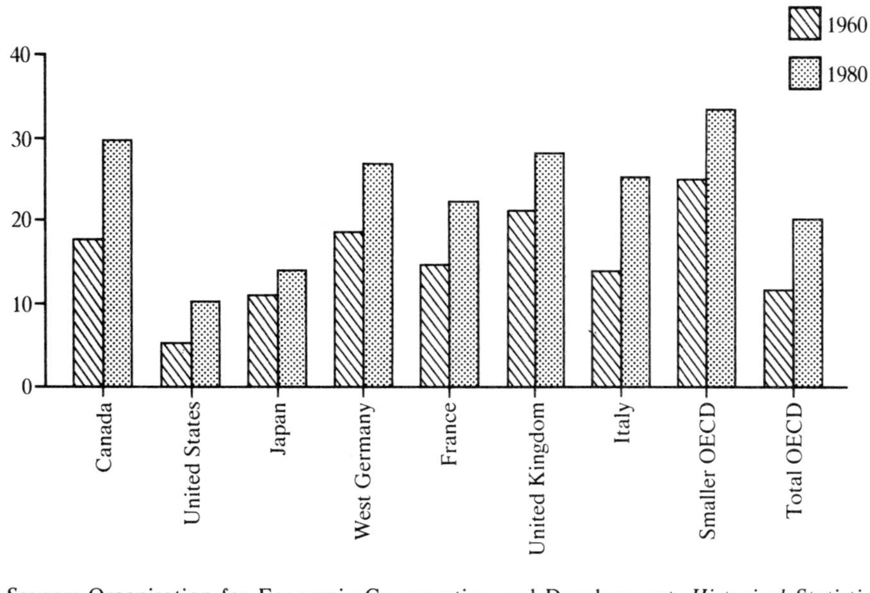

Source: Organisation for Economic Co-operation and Development, *Historical Statistics 1960-1981* (Paris: OECD, 1983), Table 6.12, page 67.

The nature of the commodities that Canada imports and exports has undergone significant change since the end of the Second World War. As Figures 4-2 and 4-3 demonstrate, trade in end products has become more important while, relatively speaking, that in raw materials and farm and fish products has shrunk. As a result of the 1965 Automotive Products Trade Agreement (the Auto Pact) with the United States, the import and export of motor vehicles and parts has expanded greatly, accounting for much of the growth in end-products trade. In 1954, these products accounted for only 7.6 per cent of Canadian imports, but they represented 27.3 per cent of that total in 1984. Similarly, automobiles and parts comprised a mere 1 per cent of Canadian exports in 1954, but amounted to 26.4 per cent in 1984. Over the same period, there has been a decline in the relative importance of Canadian exports of metals and minerals, but significant growth in our exports of

FIGURE 4-2 Canadian Merchandise Imports by Commodity, 1954 and 1984 (percentage distribution)

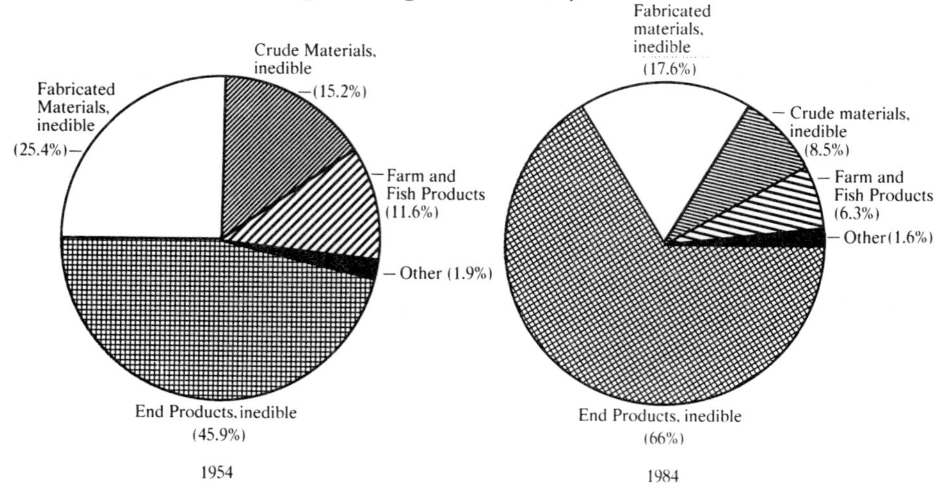

Source: Statistics Canada, *Historical Statistics of Canada*, 2d ed. (Ottawa: Statistics Canada, 1983), Series G429, G431, G433, G435, G437, G439, G441.
Statistics Canada, *Summary of External Trade, December 1984,* Cat. No. 65-001 (Ottawa: Minister of Supply and Services Canada, 1985), Table 3.

Note: Unallocated balance-of-payments adjustments were added to total imports in the calculation for 1984.

FIGURE 4-3 Canadian Merchandise Exports by Commodity, 1954 and 1984 (percentage distribution)

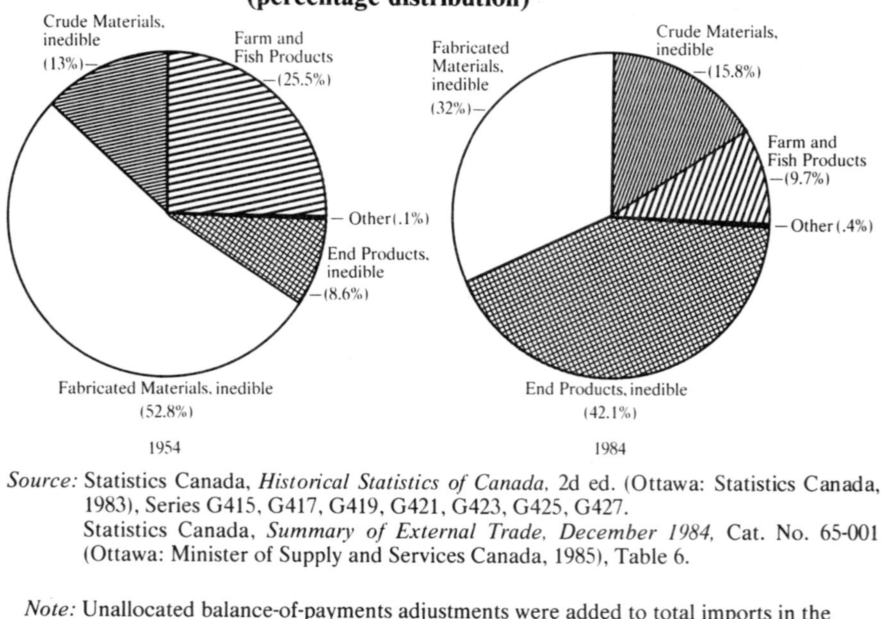

Source: Statistics Canada, *Historical Statistics of Canada*, 2d ed. (Ottawa: Statistics Canada, 1983), Series G415, G417, G419, G421, G423, G425, G427.
Statistics Canada, *Summary of External Trade, December 1984,* Cat. No. 65-001 (Ottawa: Minister of Supply and Services Canada, 1985), Table 6.

Note: Unallocated balance-of-payments adjustments were added to total imports in the calculation for 1984.

energy materials. The relative decline of exports of fabricated materials reflects, in part, the shrinking importance of forest products. These accounted for 34.8 per cent of Canadian exports in 1954, but only 12.5 per cent in 1984.

While the product composition of Canadian trade has been changing, so, too, has the identity of our chief trading partners. Figures 4-4 and 4-5 illustrate this change. The increasingly predominant position of the United States as Canada's principal trading partner is evident, as is the growing importance of our trade with Japan. The importance of our trade with the United Kingdom has continued its long decline from the days when it was Canada's largest export market.

FIGURE 4-4 Canadian Merchandise Imports by Countries and Trading Areas, 1954 and 1984

(percentage distribution)

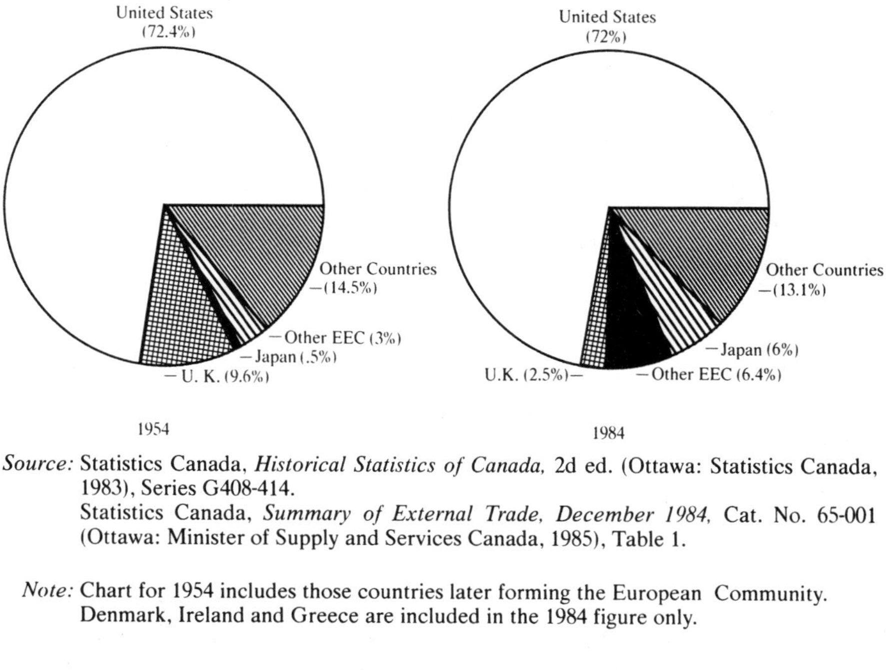

Source: Statistics Canada, *Historical Statistics of Canada,* 2d ed. (Ottawa: Statistics Canada, 1983), Series G408-414.
Statistics Canada, *Summary of External Trade, December 1984,* Cat. No. 65-001 (Ottawa: Minister of Supply and Services Canada, 1985), Table 1.

Note: Chart for 1954 includes those countries later forming the European Community. Denmark, Ireland and Greece are included in the 1984 figure only.

If exports and imports of both goods and services (including transfers) are considered, the relative importance of the United States and Japan decreases slightly. In 1984, for example, merchandise and non-merchandise receipts from the United States amounted to 71.4 per cent of total receipts. This figure compares with a U.S. share of Canadian merchandise exports of 76.3 per cent. On the import side the United States accounted for 67.9 per cent of payments abroad, compared with their 72.4 per cent share of Canadian merchandise imports.

FIGURE 4-5 Canadian Merchandise Exports by Countries and Trading Areas, 1954 and 1984 (percentage distribution)

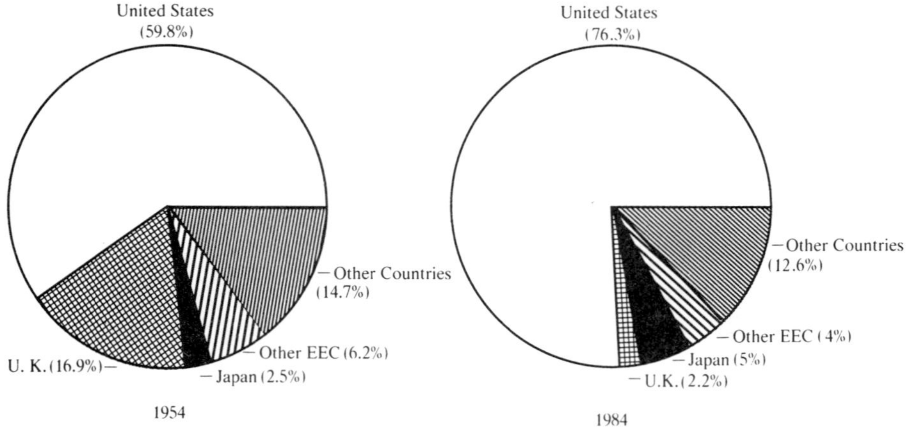

Source: Statistics Canada, *Historical Statistics of Canada*, 2d ed. (Ottawa: Statistics Canada, 1983), Series G401-407.
Statistics Canada, *Summary of External Trade, December 1984*, Cat. No. 65-001 (Ottawa: Minister of Supply and Services Canada, 1985), Table 2.

Note: Chart for 1954 includes those countries later forming the European Community. Denmark, Ireland and Greece are included in the 1984 figure only.
Figures on 1984 Chart do not sum to 100 because of rounding.

Challenges from the Global Environment

A major problem for most nations today is to find a means of reinvigorating economic growth that will help them reach the high-growth levels that were the norm through most of the post-war period. Nor is slow recovery from the severe recession of the early 1980s the only problem facing the world economy. Substantial change, especially industrial change, is occurring, and it reduces stability and predictability for governments and their constituents. High interest rates in one nation affect interest rates and exchange values in another country; high exchange values create pressures on trade balances; and falling trade balances can expand problems of international debt. This interplay of forces, creating a sense of greater risk and uncertainty makes national governments less secure in the control of their economies than they were in the 1950s and 1960s.

Canada, of course, shares this world-wide problem, the general sense of uncertainty and loss of control. Moreover, it faces specific challenges arising from the international environment that bear particularly on our future aspirations and opportunities. As we have seen in Chapter 2, these challenges emerge from growing international competition; the need to adjust to the new competition; the changing nature of international capital flows; intensified regionalism; and more discriminatory trading arrangements.[1]

International Competition

International specialization based on comparative advantage, which eased the way for trade liberalization in the early post-war years, has changed over the past two decades. In the earlier period, trade liberalization was made easier by the fact that only the Western industrialized countries were seriously involved in the process. The developing countries, often still in colonial status, provided raw materials and only rarely competed with the industrialized countries in exporting manufactured goods; the East European countries were generally excluded from the trading system by the Cold War. It was plain that comparative advantages among the industrialized countries depended on differences in their supplies of capital, labour and natural resources, as well as in their technology. While it was expected that comparative advantage would vary, it was assumed that changes would be evolutionary and predictable, and that their pace would allow time for countries to make adjustments.

Current rapid changes in trade patterns tend to impose much greater burdens on mature industrialized countries and therefore to cause much more serious domestic political opposition to imports than occurred in an earlier period. Japan, for example, has caught up with or surpassed the United States as the international leader in industrial technology in many sectors. Its competitive drive has been so strong that North American producers have found it extremely difficult to adjust rapidly enough: the domestic markets of some have withered, and they have been unable to secure export opportunities which would offset this erosion. Canadian manufacturing industries have faced strong competition from Japan in a variety of advanced manufacturing sectors, such as those producing cars and electronic equipment. Some of our exporters have lost foreign markets to the Japanese, although their loss has been limited by the fact that Canada has never had a significant export presence in many of the sectors in which the Japanese have been strong. The most severe direct loss of Canadian export markets occurred in the late 1970s, as a result of Japanese auto exports to the United States.

There is a tendency to assume that the imbalance of Canadian-Japanese trade in manufactures originates solely in Japanese protectionism. Certainly, Japan did impose overt protection in the first two decades after the Second World War. Today, however, Japanese protection does not *appear* to be appreciably greater than that of other industrialized countries, at least as assessed under the rules of the General Agreement on Tariffs and Trade (GATT). Nevertheless, for many products it continues to be very difficult to penetrate the Japanese market. The challenge posed by Japan today stems both from its trade policy and from the competitive economic performance of its whole society. Government policy plays a part in promoting this performance, but it is unrealistic for Japan's trading partners to attribute Japanese success wholly to government intervention and protection. At the same time, Japan is under growing pressure to open up its own economy or to face stronger retaliation against its exports in the European Community (EC) and the United States.

The emergence of the newly industrialized countries (NICs) made another post-1960s change in the international structure of comparative advantage. This change will be profoundly important for Canada in the future. The NICs are highly competitive producers and exporters of certain high-volume, standard-technology, manufactured goods, the production of which requires relatively large numbers of low-skilled workers, but comparatively little capital and raw material. Textile, clothing and footwear sectors were among the first affected by competition from these new producers, but the NICs have since become competitive in steel, ships, automobile parts and household electronics. Meanwhile, other developing countries have become exporters of resource-based products in increasingly serious competition with Canada.

Canadians should be careful not to exaggerate the past effect of competition from NICs. So far, trade with those countries has probably had little, if any, net effect on rates of employment in the Western industrialized countries, since growing exports to them have compensated for employment losses in certain sectors that compete with NIC imports. The real test, however, is yet to come. In 1977, NICs accounted for only 8.1 per cent of all manufactured goods imported by members of the Organisation for Economic Co-operation and Development (OECD) and for just over 1 per cent of total OECD consumption of manufactures. These shares have increased somewhat since 1977, but the effect of NIC competition on overall manufacturing production and employment in the industrialized countries, while still relatively small, was perceived to enlarge as a result of the 1981-82 recession.

Although the absolute trade volumes and overall effects of the NICs have been small, the unemployment problem associated with competition from NIC exports has been concentrated in certain sectors, such as textiles and clothing. The low-skill level of the displaced workers, their age and other characteristics make it difficult for them to find other employment. The concentration of the threatened industries in specific regions of our country has heightened the political sensitivity of the problem.

The Challenge to Adjust

An open-trade stance relative to both imports and exports may impose substantial transitional costs on both capital and labour in sectors affected by externally initiated changes. If Canada further relaxes import restrictions, jobs are likely to be lost in sectors under import pressure. Moreover, where that pressure stems from lower-wage newly industrializing countries or less-developed countries (LDCs), a disproportionate share of the burden of domestic adjustment is likely to fall on lower-income, lower-skilled workers. This effect will rightly strike many Canadians as unfair and unacceptable.

Some industries, of course, will have to face structural adjustments in order to exploit fully the new opportunities occurring in export markets. These changes, in turn, will require even more extensive inter-sectoral adjustments within the labour force if firms are to benefit from the economies of scale and the specialization needed to make Canada effectively competitive in either a North American or a world market. Conversely, freer trade will increase Canada's output and, probably, its manufacturing-employment levels, as well. The challenge, therefore, will be to facilitate, rather than to frustrate, adjustment.

In the past, Canadian policy towards sectors threatened by imports has been designed, in large measure, to postpone, rather than to facilitate, adjustment.[2] For some industries, such as textile, clothing, and footwear manufacturing, this policy has meant high-tariff and quota protection supplemented by subsidies to enable firms to modernize. Much more modest subsidies have been paid to displaced labour. These policies have retarded Canada's process of adjustment, even in buoyant economic times, when alternative economic opportunities for displaced labour and capital were more abundant than they have been in recent years.

Dynamic growth strategies are born of dynamic adjustment strategies. The success of Canada's adjustment strategies must be measured according to the speed with which they enable our industries to adapt to changing economic opportunities, and not according to their capacity to postpone adjustment. This contention was supported in a number of briefs submitted to this Commission. For instance:

> *Protectionism is not a valid answer to the fundamental changes occurring in international trade. Conserving outdated production, protecting against the less expensive goods of the NICs, subsidising high energy consumption production and production methods, only delay the essential changes.*
>
> *The principle must be that any help to industries or sectors hit by sudden and heavy structural changes is transparent and given on a reducing basis* with a clear and final time limit. *There must be consensus on this point. An open economy like Canada's must embrace flexibility.*
>
> (International Business Council of Canada, Brief, November 28, 1984, pp. 2–3.)

The key is to facilitate rather than to resist change, to widen access to large export markets and to avoid an excessive preoccupation with defending smaller domestic markets against imports.

The importance of successfully meeting the adjustment challenge is also expressed in the following observations in one of this Commission's research studies:

> *It may be tempting to delay adjustment, and indeed, such measures as quotas or subsidies bring immediate relief and political benefits—but they entrench the problem. A non-competitive activity in an open economy needs an ever-increasing battery of aid, as has been amply demonstrated in the case of textiles and clothing. Labour, management, machinery and materials all become locked into a marginal activity, perversely drawing resources from more efficient activities to pay for maintaining a non-competitive sector. Short-term help to ease adjustment may be readily defensible, but too often it rapidly evolves into long-term help to avoid adjustment. Policies must thus be carefully designed and implemented to avoid crossing the line from one to the other.*[3]

In the years ahead, an integral and key part of Canada's trade policies must be a set of adjustment measures which compensate Canadians disadvantaged by trade-related developments, but which also facilitate, rather than resist, change. A flexible, adaptable, economic structure is essential if we are to make full use of the opportunities available to us through interactions with our global environment.

International Investment

Increasingly, international trade occurs between related parties, especially international firms and their affiliates; this fact, in itself, raises questions about the consequences of non-arm's-length international transactions. Furthermore, the location of affiliates has an important bearing on trade flows. The location of major foreign investments is more and more often negotiated between governments and international firms, and motivations on both sides are often political. To attract foreign investment, most governments regularly provide investment incentives, such as direct subsidies, or "tax holidays" (that is, exemption from corporate taxes for either a specified or an indefinite period). In addition, they often impose performance requirements to influence the economic behaviour of firms that establish themselves within their jurisdiction. These practices open the door to considerable competition among governments for attracting foreign investment.

For their part, international firms have shown a capacity to adapt their investment decisions to the practices of host governments, and they have varied their investment patterns in ways that could produce trade flows different from those based solely on factor costs or market opportunities. The principle of comparative advantage has thus been subject to reinterpretation in light of modern investment practices. Comparative advantage has traditionally depended on resource endowments or on slowly accumulating capital stocks; today, however, it depends increasingly on major investment decisions, on research and on the development of human capital through training. It is now easier to acquire a comparative advantage in a particular sector through manipulation, and this development offers countries a greater opportunity to influence their own trade patterns. As a result, the composition of trade flows is becoming more subject to the actions of governments. Members of the General Agreement on Tariffs and Trade (GATT) assume that governments generally act by imposing restrictions, and GATT rules attempt to regulate the manner in which governments may apply those restrictions. Modern foreign-investment policies give governments greater scope to create trade, and except in the matter of subsidies, GATT rules generally do not regulate this aspect of international activity.

The high degree of foreign ownership within the Canadian economy has strong influences, both negative and positive, on Canada's export patterns and prospects. Combined with the trend toward the "internationalization" of business, extensive foreign ownership now accounts for the high proportion of Canadian trade that consists in intra-corporate transfers: that is, transfers of goods and services among branches of a single transnational corporation. A survey covering about half the sales of foreign-owned firms in Canada showed that by the late 1970s, about 80 per cent of their exports to and imports from the United States were intra-firm transactions.[4] Much of this was in the form of petroleum exports or trade under the Auto Pact. While comparably precise figures for Canada's trade with other regions are not available, indications are that intra-corporate transfers account for a smaller, but still significant, part of our overseas trade. Conversely, producers may be prohibited from exporting – or restricted in the markets to which they can export – by administrative arrangements with the parent corporation, arising out of the latter's strategy for supplying various world markets. Even Canadian-owned firms, if they are licensed to make use of foreign technology, may similarly be restricted to our domestic market.

World product mandates may provide one possible solution to the problem of externally-imposed export limitations on foreign-owned manufacturing subsidiaries in Canada. Federal and Ontario government policies encourage such subsidiaries to specialize in a small number of product lines and to export a portion of their output to all of the parent company's markets. This procedure is intended to replace some companies' current practice of reproducing all of the parent company's product lines on a small inefficient scale and restricting sale of their products to our protected domestic market. In return for rationalizing production and increasing exports, the federal government offers duty-remission schemes, whereby the subsidiary with a world product mandate is permitted to import, at reduced rates of duty, required goods needed to enlarge its product line. Such schemes, while not yet widely applied, are proving attractive to a growing number of companies seeking to make better use of their Canadian investment. The technique may well prove of great value as part of a more general trend towards rationalizing productive facilities along North American lines. However, Canadian subsidiaries seeking a world product mandate must still demonstrate that they are competitive. In today's open market, no company can afford to carry a non-competitive branch or affiliate.

While the high degree of foreign – especially U.S. – ownership of industry in Canada may have contributed to the lack of diversification in our export trade, it would be a mistake to view foreign ownership as a negative factor. The use of a foreign parent's technology, brand name and marketing organization can enhance a subsidiary's opportunities to make foreign sales, and sales orders generated by the parent may be filled, in whole or in part, by the subsidiary. Those enterprises may provide better markets for exports from the Canadian subsidiary, and these may be less risky than those acquired through arm's-length dealings. Rationalization and specialization thus lead to greater trade flows, albeit within a corporation. This type of trade, however, is equally sensitive to secure access.

Canada, like other countries, is trying to develop productive high-technology industries. The global nature of technology in these industries often means that if Canada is to participate, it will have to do so in partnership with foreign firms. Furthermore, if Canada is to attract investment, it will have to compete with other countries. Such competition, however, enables foreign companies to play off one government's offers against another's. In the late 1970s, for example, the major North American automobile manufacturers successfully played off the various provincial and state governments against one another as these authorities provided investment incentives for new plants, the locations of which might already have been decided. Obviously, the cost to governments of subsidizing foreign investment can quickly accumulate, yet there is considerable evidence that incentives are not the determining factor. Nevertheless, the perception of Canada held by potential foreign investors *is* an important factor in our nation's ability to attract future investment.

Growth of Regionalism

The multilateral trade and payments system is founded on the principle of non-discrimination. In practice, this principle requires that GATT-member nations apply the same regulations and restrictions on trade to all their trading partners. The principle of non-discrimination, which is the foundation on which any multilateral trading system must be based, has been deeply threatened by the establishment of preference areas or regional trading blocs. These blocs have become more important since the 1950s, despite the commitment of all GATT members to accord non-discriminatory treatment to their trading partners. By far the most important is that formed by the European Community (EC) and its many associates. This bloc now includes a number of Mediterranean countries, as well as developing countries in Africa, the Caribbean and the Pacific. The countries of the European Free Trade Association (EFTA) are linked to the European Community by industrial free-trade agreements. Roughly one-fifth of total world trade now takes place within the huge, EC-centered, preferential trading system. Other notable preferential trading systems include the Association of South-East Asian Nations (ASEAN), the Caribbean Common Market (CARICOM), and the Generalized System of Preferences, which most Western industrialized countries apply on a non-reciprocal basis to imports from developing countries. These systems are all discriminatory, through tariffs and non-tariff barriers, in favour of trade among their members. Although this discrimination virtually always departs from the spirit of the GATT, it has been legitimized, in most instances, either by waivers from GATT obligations or by application of Article XXIV of the General Agreement.

The trend towards regionalism in the world trading system holds considerable dangers for our nation. Because Canada is not a member of any preferential trading bloc, it is one of the few major industrial countries lacking free access to a market of over 100 million people. The relatively small size of our domestic market puts us at a competitive disadvantage with the EC countries, the United States and Japan, since all those nations have sufficiently large domestic markets to provide a strong base for developing competitive exports.

The European Community's discrimination against non-associated suppliers has directly affected Canadian exports to Europe. Resource exports have suffered most severely, since Canada has never developed a strong export trade with Europe in manufactures. Wheat offers a notable example: the EC's Common Agricultural Policy (CAP) has severely reduced Canadian access to what were once large markets in Britain and certain continental European countries. Newsprint exports have also been threatened by the preferential trade agreements negotiated between the EFTA countries and the Community. In addition, some Canadians have expressed concern that tariff and non-tariff/barrier preferences granted to developing countries associated with the EC could cut into our exports of minerals and processed mineral products. To date, however, there is no evidence that this has happened, since few of the developing countries associated with the EC produce significant quantities of the minerals Canada exports to the Community.

Another negative consequence for Canada of the trend to regionalism is the growing tendency for issues of world trade policy to be settled in trilateral negotiations involving the United States, Japan, and the European Community. When these giants reach a settlement, Canada may be given limited opportunity to voice its concerns on the issue in question. Furthermore, even when Canada is fully involved in negotiations, the development of units of the EC and, to a lesser extent, the EFTA reduces our opportunities to influence the outcome by allying ourselves with other medium-sized countries. Among smaller industrialized countries, only Canada, Australia and New Zealand stand alone. There is a tendency, too, in such tripartite negotiations, to throw Canada arbitrarily into the U.S. orbit, and the decision to do so involves assumptions that impede Canadian efforts to establish a distinct voice in international economic relations.

Alarming as this situation may be, Canada, in the last analysis, can do little to reverse the trend towards regionalism in the world political economy because the process essentially involves relationships among third parties. However, this trend does increase the urgency for Canada to define its role in the international trading system of the future.

Notes

1. These themes are discussed in more detail in Michael C. Webb and Mark W. Zacher, "Canadian Export Trade in a Changing International Environment", in *Canada and the International Political/Economic Environment*, vol. 28, prepared for the Royal Commission on the Economic Union and Development Prospects for Canada (Toronto: University of Toronto Press, 1985).
2. See Department of Regional Industrial Expansion, "Experience in Canada with Adjustment Policies", and Matthew Robertson and Alexander Grey, "Trade-related Worker Adjustment Policies: The Canadian Experience", in *Domestic Policies and the International Economic Environment*, vol. 12, prepared for the Royal Commission on the Economic Union and Development Prospects for Canada (Toronto: University of Toronto Press, 1985).
3. M.M. Hart, *Canadian Economic Development and the International Trading System: Constraints and Opportunities*, vol. 53, prepared for the Royal Commission on the Economic Union and Development Prospects for Canada (Toronto: University of Toronto Press, 1985).
4. Reported in Economic Council of Canada, *On the Mend*, Twentieth Annual Review (Ottawa: Minister of Supply and Services Canada, 1983), p. 22.

Trade with Our Principal Partners

Over the years, Canada has developed mutually beneficial trade and investment links with a range of trading partners. In order fully to assess the choices before us, we need to ask and answer a number of questions: What is the nature of our ties with our major trading partners? How are our relations likely to evolve over the next few decades? Is the multilateral trading system still the best means to manage relations with such a diverse group of countries? Will future multilateral negotiations result in better and more secure access to these markets?

Trade with the United States

The United States and Canada are each other's principal trading partners. Three-quarters of Canadian trade is now directed to the United States, representing a total of $156 billion-worth of exports and imports in 1984. Recent global economic developments – the challenges of freer trade, the pace of technological change, the restructuring of Western economies, the emergence of the new Japan – point to a future in which the importance to Canada of our U.S. relationship may well increase further, not decline. We Canadians are being driven still closer to our neighbour by factors which we have difficulty controlling. No matter which way we direct our future policies, our relations with the United States will continue to constitute a primary, even a predominant, factor in the determination of our foreign, defence and economic policies. The success of the goal of economic renewal in Canada will thus depend, in no small way, on the nature of Canada's ties with the United States.

This Commission has been impressed by the view of many Canadians that the time may now be ripe for a new approach to Canadian trade relations with the United States. These men and women believe that Canada can no longer rely on the policies and practices of the past; that the intimate and extensive links between the two countries, as much as the state of our economy and of the international trading system, no longer allow Canadians room to manœuvre; rather, they make us more vulnerable.

One of the factors which brings home the degree of our vulnerability is the protectionist legislation poised for passage in Congress. This legislation is being driven by concern about the size of the U.S. merchandise-trade deficit and the strength of the U.S. dollar, as well as by a perception that only the United States plays by the international rules and has become a victim of its past generosity. The threat of protection imposed by the U.S. Congress is of particular concern to Canada. Any increase in protectionist legislation could hold serious implications for job-creating investment. Even where we are not the principal target, we risk being the major victim of a spate of protectionist legislation before Congress. No realistic amount of diversification can offset the degree of Canada's vulnerability to unilateral action by the United States.

The issue is more than a potential threat. Existing U.S. trade legislation already allows American companies constantly to harass their foreign competitors. These laws include provisions for imposing countervailing duties against subsidized imports, anti-dumping duties, emergency relief from seriously injurious imports, retaliation against "unfair" trade practices, and relief from imports deemed prejudicial to U.S. national security. Rules formulated in the General Agreement on Tariffs and Trade (GATT) may prevent the final imposition of duties or quotas unless the case is strong and proper procedures are followed, but they do not prevent frivolous complaints and strong Congressional pressure on the Administration to agree with the complainant. The American penchant for litigation guarantees that at any one time, Canadian governments and exporters are fully engaged in preventing the imposition of a special duty or quota of one kind or another. Some Canadian industries are wondering whether they can afford many more victories. Others have not been so lucky.

Canadian well-being thus depends substantially on our relations with the United States. There is significant scope for the reduction or removal of barriers to cross-border trade in goods and services, and for improving the management of bilateral issues in a variety of areas. Discord in Canada-U.S. relations can place significant constraint on Canadian policy making; mutual commitment to common goals can open substantial opportunities.

Our past policies have indicated our general tendency to resist the forces driving us closer to the United States. One of the reasons for this resistance has been the belief that Canadian policy decisions should be made as though we could and should counter the American presence. This stance has abetted only to a limited extent our efforts to hold back the forces driving us to a closer economic relationship with the United States. What is more important, it has frustrated efforts to seize opportunities arising from our close ties.

This Commission's public consultations highlighted a perception shared by the Canadian business community that:

> *When you are protected at home, something happens to your costs, something happens to the structures that automatically means you are not going to be competitive on a world scale . . . If Canadian industry can be competitive with U.S. industry, you could almost feel quite comfortable about multilateralizing the result.*
>
> (Howard Hart, Transcript, Montreal, May 31, 1984 [vol. 2] p. 338.)

Furthermore, though the degree is hard to measure, it seems that policies designed to resist the attraction of the United States may have left Canada less open to consideration of trade-offs and potential new areas of co-operation from which both Canada and the United States might have benefited.

Commissioners see a clear need to take a new direction. We Canadians now have a stronger sense of confidence in our own institutions and in our ability to safeguard discernible differences between the two countries than they may have had in years past. We are ready for and are expecting such a change.

Trade with Western Europe

The European Community (EC)[1] is the world's largest trading body and a key player in both international trade relations and in the GATT system. It has participated actively in past GATT negotiations which have resulted in a considerable lowering of its external barriers to trade, particularly in industrial goods. To a large extent, however, the EC is preoccupied with its own internal problems. These problems are partly the result of its enlargement to include other European countries than those which formed the original Community, and partly a consequence of its management of the relations with its key trading partners in Europe and the Mediterranean area. The EC is less enthusiastic than it once was about any new efforts to strengthen multilateral discipline, although it is playing its part in efforts to formulate an agenda for future trade negotiations.

Writing almost thirty years ago, on the eve of the formation of the European Economic Community, the last Royal Commission on Canada's Economic Prospects noted:

> *If it were to be successful in creating a common market in Western Europe, efficiency would be improved, output increased, and the ability of the whole area to trade with the rest of the world, including North America, raised to a higher plane. On the other hand, if the project were to be only partially successful, it might prove to be only another engine for discriminating against dollar imports.*[2]

Experience shows that both observations have turned out to be true. European economic integration contributed in no small measure to growth and prosperity in Western Europe. Greater prosperity contributed to making Europe an attractive export market. European discrimination, however, has frustrated Canadian traders seeking to penetrate that market. Europe's share of Canada's exports has steadily declined since 1965, as the U.S. share steadily rose.

Dana Wilgress, one of the principal architects of Canada's post- Second World War trade policy, observed some twenty years ago that the advantages for Canada of European integration would be long-term and intangible, while the disadvantages would be immediate. He went on to say:

> *All that can be said with safety at the present time is that the long-term advantages appear likely to compensate for the short-term disadvantages – although if the United Kingdom becomes a Member of the Community, the long-term advantages will have to be very great to compensate Canada for the loss of the preferential position now enjoyed in the U.K. market.*[3]

Entry of the United Kingdom in 1971 had the effect Wilgress feared. By 1984, the U.K. market took up only 2.2 per cent of Canada's exports, compared to 41 per cent in 1938, 27 per cent in 1947, and 18 per cent in 1955. European integration accelerated a trend already apparent in the 1950s. The Community as a whole – indeed Europe as a whole – does not provide the market for Canada that the United Kingdom represented only a generation ago.

Our federal government sought to reverse this trend a decade ago by establishing a "contractual link" with the Community. A considerable amount of political will and negotiating effort was expended and eventually culminated, in 1976, in a Framework Agreement providing for consultations, industrial co-operation, technology exchanges and other techniques to foster stronger economic ties. The Agreement is supplemented by a number of consultative mechanisms with individual member states, including France and the United Kingdom. These and the Framework Agreement, however, have produced little direct effect. They have not opened Community markets; they have not given Canada a privileged position; and they have never caught the imagination of the private sector. They have proved, indeed, to be largely a vehicle for bureaucratic contacts and consultations. The realities of distance, lack of intra- and inter-corporate links, and the continuing high levels of trade barriers which protect European processing and manufacturing industries all reduce the likelihood of a major expansion in trade. A realistic assessment of the relationship, ten years after the signing of the Framework Agreement, suggests that Canada's economic opportunities in Europe are limited.

Nevertheless, the Community is still Canada's second-largest trading partner, accounting for 7.8 per cent of our trade in 1984. As with the corresponding Canada-U.S. relationship, Canada depends more heavily on its trade with the EC than does the Community on its trade with Canada. There would appear to be significant areas in which economic co-operation and trade between Canada and the EC could be further developed. In a number of these areas, however, it will be necessary for Canada to negotiate further adjustment in the Community's import system before the benefits of such co-operation can be fully realized. This is particularly true for trade in fisheries' products, further-processed resource products, and sophisticated end products, such as telecommunications equipment. European agricultural policies remain of considerable concern to Canadian agricultural producers. These policies, which involve the Community's use of large export subsidies, both inhibit our prospects for agricultural sales in Europe and endanger our position in third-party markets.

In their trade and economic policies, the non-EC countries in Western Europe tend, as does the Community, to be preoccupied with the issues centered on European integration. The members of the European Free Trade Association (EFTA), are now firmly linked to the Community through industrial free-trade agreements. Spain and Portugal will enter the EC in January 1986, and Turkey has an association agreement. These preferential arrangements have reduced Canada's access to these markets. Trade with these countries is largely similar in composition to that with the Community: Canada exports resource-based products and imports specialty-manufactured and agricultural products. The volume of goods exchanged is modest. Canadian access to these markets is governed by the GATT, and the General Agreement provides the contractual basis for the conduct of relations. For Europe, however, GATT has been reduced to a secondary status. That area's most important trade agreements are now those which provide for preferential relations between the various European trading partners.

Trade with the Asia-Pacific Region

In recent years, Canadians have variously perceived the Asia-Pacific rim as a boundless frontier of economic opportunity, as a threat to the well-being of many of our domestic industries and communities, or as marginal to many of our mainstream economic concerns. It has proved difficult to describe our economic relations with Asia-Pacific without either exaggerating or discounting the region's importance, or without establishing a myopic focus on either import competition or export opportunities.

Canadians' apparent inability to get a clear perspective on Asia-Pacific is primarily a result of the newness and uncertainty which many Canadians associate with this relationship. We lack a balanced and mature appreciation of our economic links with the Asia-Pacific countries. Much more readily, if not instinctively, we accept the benefits and the costs of economic interdependence with our traditional trading partners; we comprehend the dimensions and probable future scope of these relationships much more easily.

The Asia-Pacific region is now the most dynamic in the world economy. As Table 4-1 indicates, Asia-Pacific is by no means a homogeneous entity, yet the developed and developing countries of the region have been commonly distinguished by rapid economic and trade growth. Together they have forced a considerable shift in the focus of international economic activity from the Atlantic to the Pacific, and their economic ascendancy may result in the next century becoming the "century of the Pacific".

TABLE 4-1 Economic Indicators of Asia Pacific Countries

	Population (in millions) mid-1982	GNP per Capita U.S. $ 1982	GNP per Capita Annual Growth 1970–82	Merchandise Trade Average Annual Growth	
				Exports 1970–82	Imports 1970–82
Japan	118.4	10 080	6.1	8.5	3.5
China	1 008.2	310	5.0	—	—
Hong Kong	5.2	5 340	7.0	9.4	11.9
South Korea	39.3	1 910	6.6	20.2	9.8
Indonesia	152.6	580	4.2	4.4	12.3
Thailand	48.5	790	4.5	9.1	4.3
Malaysia	14.5	1 860	4.3	3.8	7.3
Philippines	50.7	820	2.8	7.9	2.1
Singapore	2.5	5 910	7.4	—	—
(Canada)	24.6	11 320	3.1	4.0	4.3
(United States)	231.5	13 160	2.2	5.6	3.8

Source: World Development Report 1984 (New York: Oxford University Press for The World Bank, 1984), pp. 218–21, 234–35.

For Western Canada, of course, and particularly, for British Columbia and a small number of major firms throughout Canada, the Pacific has long loomed large in economic terms. British Columbia exports more goods across the Pacific than to the United States. Many Canadians, however, have only recently come to appreciate the economic might and potential of the Asia-Pacific countries. These countries have also become the main source of troublesome import competition and the special targets of most of Canada's recent protectionist measures.

The countries of the Asia-Pacific region differ widely in terms of their size, resource base, level of development, and political, cultural and linguistic characteristics. In economic terms, they can be divided into four groups: the resource-poor, advanced industrial state of Japan; the resource-rich, vast but underdeveloped, continental economy of China; the resource-poor, rapidly and newly industrializing countries (NICs) of South Korea, Taiwan, Hong Kong and Singapore; and the more richly endowed, "near-NICs" of Southeast Asia: Indonesia, Thailand, Malaysia and the Philippines.

Important differences, as well as some similarities, exist within these groups; the city states and *entrepôt* centres of Hong Kong and Singapore, for example, differ from the somewhat larger and more diverse economies of South Korea and Taiwan. Despite these distinctions, the four can be grouped together, not just because of their geographical proximity, but by virtue of their rapid economic growth during the 1970s and 1980s. The Asia-Pacific countries, with the exception of China, also have in common a high dependence on trade and market-oriented economies. In recent years, economic growth in the Asia-Pacific developing countries has greatly outpaced that in Canada and the United States – and in the developed world generally – and Japan's economy similarly outperforms its industrial-country peers.

At present, Canada's economic relations with the Asia-Pacific rim can be characterized in the following ways:

- The Asia-Pacific countries are Canada's fastest growing trading partners and have recently replaced Western European countries as our most important non-U.S. trade region. There has not been any radical shift, however, in overall Canadian trading patterns and our Pacific trade, while buoyant, has not been booming.
- In aggregate, the traditional dichotomy in our trade relations with the Asia-Pacific – primary commodity exports derived, for the most part, from Western Canadian provinces and end-product imports which compete with central Canadian manufacturing industries – remains relatively unchanged.
- Canadian investment in the Asia-Pacific is dominated by the activities of a few major Canadian corporations and is underdeveloped relative to Canada's current trade profile in the region. Asia-Pacific investment in Canada is at an embryonic stage.
- Canadian financial institutions have extensive links in the Asia-Pacific region and represent a necessary bridge for Canadian exports.
- Canada's aid relations are significant to only a few Asia-Pacific developing countries, and even there, are of less economic importance – and probably even of less political consequence – than our trade relations.

Canadians are probably most familiar with Japan's rapid economic transformation. They have watched as Japan's export basket ceased to be filled predominately with light manufactures, as in the 1950s and 1960s, came to include more capital-intensive industrial products such as automobiles, steel and ships in the 1970s, and has been stocked with more knowledge-intensive products in the late 1970s and 1980s. By North-American and European standards, economic restructuring in Japan has been swift while the use of forward-looking industrial plans and the function of government-business co-operation have been unique. The imperatives of managing a resource-poor country and reducing its inherent vulnerabilities have driven this rapid and ongoing economic transformation. They also underlie the growing vertical integration and internationalization of the Japanese economy typified by increasing overseas investments in resource supplies and product markets. However, Japan's import profile has remained relatively unchanged and continues to be dominated by fuels and other mineral and agricultural commodities.

Canadians have been frustrated by their lack of success in penetrating the Japanese market with more sophisticated products. In spite of major efforts on the Canadian side and assurances from the Japanese government that it also is committed to economic and industrial co-operation with Canada, concrete results have been few. Examples of frustrated efforts by Canadian exporters in the face of Japanese restrictions of one kind or another are many. Nevertheless, some hopeful signs are appearing that Canadian business interests may achieve progress in gaining access to the Japanese market for certain sophisticated products, including telecommunications.

Dealing successfully with Japan is more than a GATT problem. Of equal importance is the impact of Japanese trade and industrial policies and practices on other countries, particularly the United States. U.S. concerns are not dissimilar to those of Canada, but U.S. leverage, both in economic and political terms, is considerably greater than Canada's. Japan has become aware of foreign frustration with its import regime and foreign dissatisfaction with the lack of penetration of their manufactured and processed goods into its market. A number of recent decisions by its government show that this concern is being translated into concrete action. A number of packages of specific unilateral trade concessions have been put forward in response to foreign pressure largely imposed by the United States and the European Community, and these concessions have been of limited benefit to Canada. The possibility that Japan might accommodate U.S. interests in ways that could be discriminatory and detrimental to Canadian trade is therefore of special concern to Canada.

While Japan is generally committed to the multilateral system, it tailors its export and import practices to the needs of the moment and often prefers bilateral accommodation to pursuit of its rights under GATT. It has never, for example, sought compensation for safeguard actions by its trading partners which largely affected its interests, nor has it resorted to the GATT dispute-settlement procedures to solve its bilateral trade problems. Nonetheless, it has frequently been the object of GATT complaints, resort to conciliation, and safeguard actions.

The Japanese share the general perception that it is important to maintain and strengthen the multilateral trading system. Their approach, however, is more directly based on their own bilateral trade problems with the United States and the European Community. At times these problems have translated into a heightened determination to develop a positive and forward-looking multilateral trade agenda which will divert attention from specific bilateral irritants. The Japanese did not formulate any particular suggestions during the preparations for the Kennedy and Tokyo Rounds and frequently develop their ideas on the basis of suggestions from the United States, the Community, and Canada. Japan can usually be expected to be co-operative in addressing a wide variety of topics and to delay reaching any definite decisions until the views of most other major participants have become clear. It has therefore been somewhat surprising, but encouraging, that the Japanese have been more active lately in initiating multilateral discussion.

Canada's trade relations with the Asia-Pacific are still dominated by our two-way trade with Japan: commodity based exports, on the one hand, and increasingly sophisticated manufactured imports, on the other. However, without exaggerating their absolute importance in terms of size, our most dynamic two-way Pacific trade is with the fast-growing NICs, and to a somewhat lesser extent, ASEAN. These countries tend to import a more diversified mix of goods from a wider cross-section of the Canadian economy than does Japan. At the same time, however, the Asia-Pacific developing countries are also beginning to export more capital and skill-intensive products, widening their range of import competition in the Canadian market.

There are a number of reasons to believe that Canada's economic relations with the Asia-Pacific rim will continue to strengthen and diversify in the decades ahead. The single most important of these reasons is the relatively high growth rates projected for the region and, particularly, for the "newly" and "nearly" industrializing economies of East and Southeast Asia. The growth in output and trade of these countries is likely to continue to outpace significantly that of Canada's traditional trading partners, the United States and Western Europe. The dynamism of the Asia-Pacific countries will result both in new export opportunities for Canadian industries and in intensified import competition across a wider spectrum of industries. It is less certain, however, whether Canada's business interests will be able to expand beyond their present areas of market penetration in the Asia-Pacific, and how readily they will adjust to new import pressure at home. It *is* certain, however, that competition will continue to be very stiff. Canada is a relative late-comer to Asia-Pacific trade, and most other industrial countries are also looking to this dynamic region for opportunities to increase exports and expand employment. Not only must we Canadians become more familiar with the region and with Asian ways of doing business, but we must also commit ourselves to developing, over time, a solid business relationship: familiarity and trustworthiness are important elements of business relations in Asia.

As part of its "Third Option" of diversification adopted early in the 1970s, the federal government sought to develop government-to-government arrangements which would enhance the opportunities available to Canadian business. With the exception of China and Taiwan, all the countries in the region are members of GATT, and the General Agreement provides the contractual basis for our trade relations with these countries. In addition to GATT, however, Canada has entered into a Framework Agreement with Japan and a number of industrial co-operation agreements with smaller countries. Canada has a bilateral trade agreement with China, but does not recognize Taiwan. The thrust of all these agreements is to facilitate government-to-government contact which, in turn, provides an umbrella for private sector co-operation.

In the longer term, Canada should be prepared to devote greater effort bilaterally to enhance our trade relationship with Japan. Although this Commission has not accepted the proposal[4] for a bilateral free-trade agreement with Japan, made by a noted Canadian economist, Robert Mundell, Commissioners have been sufficiently intrigued with the notion and sufficiently concerned with the issue to ask our researchers for advice. It may be that over time, Canada and Japan could develop a stronger formal or contractual relationship bilaterally, regionally or within the context of multilateral negotiations. The key is to recognize the importance of the relationship and to give it the priority it deserves.[5]

In policy terms, therefore, there will be ongoing need for co-ordination and co-operation between Canada's government and the private sector in developing a greater awareness of business opportunities in the Asia-Pacific region. Business-government relations are usually quite close in this part of the world, and national governments are often heavily involved in major business projects. Increasingly, too, some of the Asia-Pacific countries, such as Indonesia and Malaysia, in an attempt to manage balance-of-payments problems, are attaching growing importance to bilateral trade balances and to counter-trade agreements. Given the nature of its political and economic system, China, too, is prone to monitor closely bilateral trade accounts, and counter-trade fits well with its institutional exigencies. Nevertheless, while there is an important role for the Canadian government to play in providing information, facilitating contacts, "catalysing" export contracts, and raising Canada's profile in the region, the role of government must be kept in perspective: it is ultimately up to the private sector to make itself competitive and to take advantage of these new market opportunities.

Canada's policy of domestic protectionism will be of growing importance to our future relations with Asia-Pacific, particularly in relation to the region's developing countries. Canada is not, of course, the only developed country that has imposed special trade restrictions on key manufactured exports from Asia-Pacific countries, nor is it necessarily the most restrictive. Neither, however, has Canada the market power of some of the other industrialized countries. For this reason, we could stand to lose more than others if the developing countries should choose, in the future, to take issue with developed-country protectionism. Canada has already had one sobering experience of this sort when, in 1984, Indonesia resisted Canadian efforts to curtail certain of its clothing exports and threatened to scuttle some major Canadian export contracts involving substantial Canadian commodity and capital goods exports.

It takes experiences such as this to establish the important relationship between import and export policies. Unfortunately, this link is forged too infrequently, and the connection is hampered by the bureaucratic separation, within government, of much import- and export-policy making. Canada sometimes treats "trade policy" as a synonym for "export policy", and our governments, when they come to make decisions, often take inadequate account of the wider economic and trade implications of import-policy moves. This lack of appreciation of the two-way nature of trade is most evident in our dealings with our new, developing-country, trade partners. In the future, these partners can be expected to offer more forceful resistance to our protectionist actions, particularly those which discriminate against them in areas such as textiles and clothing.

Trade with Other Developing Countries

In the years since the Second World War, Canada has played a special role in global affairs through its interaction with the developing world. As a middle-level power with no territorial or military ambitions, Canada has been accepted by developing countries as genuinely interested in helping the development process in less-developed countries (LDCs), even though our policy actions on trade and aid issues have not always matched this image. Some Canadians, for instance, are concerned about LDC demands for selective treatment in their favour in some of our key export markets, where their products provide the competition. Nevertheless, the generally favourable view of Canada, held in the developing world, reflects our belief in the use of quiet, but active, diplomacy, along with a willingness to discuss and help with the problems of the developing world. This approach to world problems has been reflected, in recent years, in Canada's active participation in the ongoing debate on North-South issues.

Canada has a much more precise interest in the developing world than can be reflected in general humanitarian considerations. We have, for instance, interests in particular issues that are similar to those of the developing countries. These interests include trade in resources, price stability for primary products, and transfer of technology. Moreover, Canada shares the interests of all smaller, trade-dependent countries in the healthy functioning of the international trade and payments system. Most important of all, the developing countries are our future and, to some extent, existing trade partners. The potentially vast markets of the less-developed countries, while still relatively untapped by Canadian exporters, are becoming increasingly important. Thus, while our present relationship with the developing world may still be dominated by humanitarian considerations, the foundations are now being laid for a mutually beneficial commercial relationship in the future.[6]

Compared with that of other members of the Organisation for Economic Co-operation and Development (OECD), Canada's share of trade with developing countries is relatively small, in proportion to our total international trade. In 1983, for example, 7.5 per cent of our imports and 7.1 per cent of our exports were with non-oil/exporting developing countries, while 28.9 per cent of U.S. imports and 29.4 per cent of U.S. exports were with these countries. Our relatively smaller share of trade with developing countries may be partially explained by the fact that as a major exporter of resources and agricultural products, Canada tends to compete with developing countries in third-party markets. While this competition may somewhat constrain our opportunities to export to developing countries, it also gives us some community of interest in certain aspects of trade policies.

Canadian trade with developing countries is concentrated in the Asia-Pacific and Latin American regions. Our imports from Latin America consist largely of fuels and primary products, while those from East and South Asia are mostly manufactured products. Conversely, Canadian exports to Latin America consist largely of manufactured products, but fuels and primary products are somewhat more important in our exports to East Asia.

Although the total amount of Canadian exports to the developing nations is relatively low, those nations represent a fast-growing export market. The high-growth countries of the developing world, especially the Pacific Rim countries, offer considerable export potential. In the years ahead, these countries will provide growing markets for our services in such areas as high-technology industries, aircraft production and engineering management. Other developing countries are likely to provide a market for Canadian expertise in engineering consulting, the construction of nuclear and hydro facilities, and communication and transportation infrastructure. Experience in extracting and processing resources will enable Canadian firms to help the developing nations to undertake these activities. Canada is also in a position to provide educational services to these countries.

Canada retains the same sort of economic protection against the developing countries as do the other members of the OECD. In the mid-1970s, non-fuel imports to Canada from developing countries faced a weighted-average tariff of 11.4 per cent, as against only 6.7 per cent for imports from other developed countries. For manufactured imports, the average Canadian tariff faced by developing countries was over twice as high as that encountered by developed countries: 15.5 per cent for the LDCs as against 7.2 per cent for the others. Tariff reductions negotiated in the Tokyo Round again treated "sensitive" Canadian industries with special care, and this caution further accentuated the existing bias favouring protection for unskilled-labour/intensive products.

Canada has implemented preferences in favour of developing countries through the Generalized System of Preferences (GSP), introduced in the early 1970s within the United Nations Conference on Trade and Development (UNCTAD). Under this program, the developed countries are allowed to grant special tariff preferences on products from developing countries, without receiving reciprocal concessions from the latter. Canada implements the GSP under the Canadian General Preferential Tariff (GPT). In practice, this concession is of limited importance, as most textiles, footwear and some electronics products are ineligible. Imports under the GPT amount to only about 4 per cent of all Canadian imports from developing countries and 0.2 per cent of total Canadian imports.

Non-tariff barriers (NTBs) against developing countries became increasingly important in the 1960s and 1970s as Canada, along with other developed countries, adopted policies to slow and control penetration of its domestic market by imports of textiles, clothing and footwear from these countries. Prominent among these global undertakings is the GATT Multi-fibre Agreement, the origins of which go back more than twenty years. While Canada is certainly not alone in pursuing these policies, neither has it been a leader in the effort to develop an alternative to increasing protection of this type. The trade restrictions imposed on these items were intended as temporary measures to allow the industries producing them to adjust to new competitive conditions. Unfortunately, this method of achieving adjustment has been ineffective, as restrictive policies have remained in place and have taken on a degree of permanence. These measures are costly to Canadian consumers and to those developing countries attempting to expand their export-oriented manufacturing activities.[7] Many developing countries are already struggling under other heavy debt burdens. While developed countries have a considerable stake in maintaining conditions under which LDCs can service their debts, discriminatory protectionist measures often act against these interests. They are also inconsistent with the desire of Canadians to help the development process of the LDCs. One Canadian company told Commissioners:

> *International aid to the Third World should be directed toward increasing their ability to stand on their own, with Canada providing a market opportunity for resulting products, as they, in turn, provide a market opportunity for Canadian products.* (George Weston Limited, Brief, September 18, 1984, p. 2.)

Quebec and Southern Ontario would probably be the regions most seriously affected by more liberal Canadian trade policies towards the developing world. Our governments should, of course, provide effective adjustment assistance for retraining and relocating workers affected by a removal of protective trade measures. In the past, adjustment assistance has been given to firms to enable them to modernize and thus retain workers in their previous jobs. An adjustment-assistance program which facilitates, rather than prevents, relocation of workers may ultimately prove to be the key for improving our trade policies towards the developing world.

Canadian Aid Performance

Foreign aid, or "official development assistance", has long been considered an important means by which Canadian government policies affect the developing countries. Despite the importance of aid as a policy tool, it is scarcely the only link between developed and developing countries. Such interactions are dominated by commercial relationships. The value of trade flows, together with commercial capital flows, dwarfs the importance of foreign aid in all but exceptional developing countries. "Official transfers" to non-oil developing countries totalled only $11.7 billion in "special drawing rights" (SDRs) in 1982, while their total exports of goods and services amounted to nearly $400 billion SDRs as Table 4-2 shows. Similarly, Canada's trade flows with developing countries are much larger than our aid flows.

TABLE 4-2 Major Elements in the Aggregate Balance of Payments of the Non-Oil Developing Countries, 1982

	(billions of SDRs)	
Current Account		
Merchandise exports	295.7	
Other goods and services exports	103.7	
Subtotal		399.4
Merchandise imports	–340.0	
Other goods and services imports	–154.6	
Subtotal		494.6
Capital Account		
Private transfers	21.4	
Official transfers	11.7	
Direct investment	10.7	
Portfolio investment	5.3	
Other long-term capital inflow	35.6	

Source: International Monetary Fund, *IMF Survey 13* (January 9, 1984), p. 13.

In 1980, the federal government announced its intention of raising the annual amount of Canada's foreign aid to 0.5 per cent of gross national product (GNP) by 1985 and to make its "best efforts" to achieve an aid/GNP ratio of 0.7 per cent by 1990. The present government has announced that aid will be 0.6 per cent of GNP by 1990, and that the 0.7 per cent target will not be met until 1995. In the past, such longer-term targets have not always been taken seriously enough. The 1984 federal budget, for example, announced our government's intention to use up to one-half of the increase in future aid allocations to stimulate Canadian exports to developing countries. The question raised by this plan is how much aid will actually reach the developing countries. Norway, the Netherlands and Sweden have all stated their intention of keeping their aid flows at 1 per cent of their GNP. Since these countries have already achieved this level of aid performance, the credibility of their promises is greater than ours in the developing world.

In 1975, the Government of Canada pledged to "untie" its bilateral development loans to the extent of permitting developing countries to compete with Canadian companies for contracts let by the Canadian International Development Agency (CIDA). It has not yet taken this step. A recent study of Canadian aid to Bangladesh concluded that "tying" regulations constitute an important operational constraint on the activities of CIDA in that country.[8]

These regulations inhibit activities in the rural and social sectors, which have ostensibly been made priority areas for Canadian assistance. Because untied resources have been reserved for aid to rural activities, projects in other sectors have frequently suffered most from the effects of tying. In a study of Senegal, for instance, the effectiveness of CIDA projects was evaluated as significantly reduced by the intrusion of Canadian commercial and other interests into the consideration of their choice and design.[9]

The degree of public support for effective international aid programs is also a major element in determining national aid performance. One measure of this support is the extent of voluntary private giving to developing countries. The share of GNP voluntarily directed to overseas aid has fallen in Canada over the past decade, as it has both in the United States and in the OECD as a whole. Conversely, a striking feature of the data on official aid performance is that generous governmental aid is reflected in private aid performance. The strong aid performance of the Dutch, Swedish and Norwegian governments seems to reflect a more positive perception of developing countries among their citizens than is discernible in North America. This situation implies that a prerequisite to improved foreign aid performance in Canada may be increased public awareness of the need for aid. This imperative was brought home to Commissioners by the Canadian Association for the Club of Rome:

> *Canadian policy belongs in a global context—a context that recognizes a changing world and its impact on Canadian policy and potential . . . An integral part of establishing the future in an international context is greater emphasis on Canada's role and responsibility in using its talents and wealth to help bring about a reduction in hunger and poverty in the Third World . . . The Federal government and private organizations in Canada have made some significant contributions to international development and to the creation of a stronger, more stable economic and social order, but the country as a whole lacks the political base to establish a high priority for the kind of co-operation that would give substance to the policies of industrial nations towards the Third World. A clear commitment to this objective will not come easily or quickly, or without strong government and institutional leadership to develop a broad political base.* (Canadian Association for the Club of Rome, Brief, July 18, 1984, p. 6.)

Trade with Other Regions

Canada has traditional trading links with Australia and New Zealand. While trade relations are largely governed by GATT, for both countries there remain vestiges of the bilateral preferential arrangements first negotiated at the 1932 Ottawa Conference. The agreement with New Zealand has recently been renegotiated with a view to modernizing these preferences to bring them into line with present-day trading patterns. Similar discussions have been held with Australia. Although the remaining preferences affecting both countries are small, they remain important to individual companies in Canada and provide them with a slight competitive edge over their American and European competitors.

Australia and New Zealand have negotiated a free-trade arrangement, and its provisions are currently being put into effect. This will have some effect on the remaining preferences Canada enjoys. At the same time, if Canada and the United States should seek to forge closer economic ties, Australia and New Zealand can be expected to view these with some understanding.

Trade relations with state-trading countries will continue to make a contribution to the well-being of individual producers and regions, especially for fully manufactured products. The volume of trade is unlikely to grow significantly, but the opportunities for expansion of exports of particular product lines is significant. For the state-trading economies, exploitation of opportunities through counter-trade may prove more rewarding than traditional trade flows, requiring a more than usual element of government participation. The Soviet Union has long been a major importer of Canadian grains, and together with other Eastern European countries, might become a market for Canadian manufactured goods. Though opportunities are conditioned by East-West political realities and financial constraints, there remains adequate scope to develop broad, stable and sophisticated trading ties with the centrally planned economies.

Although a number of state-trading countries are members of GATT, their participation is anomalous. GATT assumes that trade is largely the product of private transactions which may be influenced by government policies and practices. It seeks to limit the scope for government interference in private transactions. Foreign trade is a monopoly of the state in state-trading countries and thus is conducted on a wholly different basis. The participation of these countries in GATT has little effect on their trade policies. In most instances, access results only from direct government-to-government negotiations. Bilateralism, rather than multilateralism, continues to be the main focus for trade relations with these countries.

Notes

1. The European Community or Common Market consisted in 1984 of Ireland, the United Kingdom, France, Italy, Greece, the Federal Republic of Germany, Denmark, the Netherlands, Belgium and Luxembourg. The Community was established as a result of the integration in 1965 of the separate but related communities established earlier: the European Coal and Steel Community (ECSC) was formed in 1952, the European Economic Community (EED) was established by the 1957 Treaty of Rome, and the European Atomic Energy Community (EURATOM) was established in the same year. The European Free Trade Association, consisting of Sweden, Norway, Finland, Austria, is linked to the EC by means of industrial free-trade agreements. Turkey and the Mahgreb countries are linked by association agreements, and are considered by some to be a sort of membership-in-waiting. Portugal and Spain will be joining the European Community on January 1, 1986. The former European colonies in Africa, the Caribbean and the Pacific are linked by means of the aid and trade Lomé Convention. Various institutions link the constituent elements, including the Commission, the Council of Ministers, the European Parliament and the European Court. Of these, the Commission is the most important for Canada as it is the Community's executive body, responsible for foreign commercial policy. It is supported by an army of bureaucrats in Brussels.

2. Canada, Royal Commission on Canada's Economic Prospects, *Final Report* (Ottawa: Queen's Printer, 1957), p. 72.
3. L.D. Wilgress, *The Impact of European Integration on Canada* (Montreal: Private Planning Association of Canada, 1962), p. 25.
4. Robert A. Mundell, Transcript, Toronto, December 8, 1983 [vol. 64], pp. 13342–53.
5. R.J. Wonnacott, "Notes from an Address on the Proposal for a Canada-Japan Free Trade Area", in *Canada and the Multilateral Trading System*, vol. 10, prepared for the Royal Commission on the Economic Union and Development Prospects for Canada (Toronto: University of Toronto Press, 1985).
6. The themes in this section are examined in more detail in G.K. Helleiner, "Underutilized Potential: Canada's Economic Relations with Developing Countries", and Margaret Biggs, "The Developing Countries in the International Trading System", in *Canada and the Multilateral Trading System*, vol. 10, prepared for the Royal Commission on the Economic Union and Development Prospects for Canada (Toronto: University of Toronto Press, 1985).
7. For a detailed analysis of Canada's textile-import policies, see M.M. Hart, *Canadian Development and the International Trading System: Constraints and Opportunities*, vol. 53, prepared for the Royal Commission on the Economic Union and Development Prospects for Canada (Toronto: University of Toronto Press, 1985).
8. Roger Ehrhardt, *Canadian Development Assistance to Bangladesh: An Independent Study* (Ottawa: North-South Institute, 1983).
9. Réal Lavergne, *Canadian Development Assistance to Senegal* (Ottawa: North-South Institute, 1985, forthcoming).

The Choices Before Us

The recession of the early 1980s and its aftermath deepened Canada's reliance on the United States at the expense of our trade relationships elsewhere. Current trade figures indicate that this trend will continue. In 1984, trade with the United States accounted for 76.6 per cent of Canadian exports and 72.8 per cent of imports. The positive side of this relationship is that the United States is a quality customer, and takes far higher percentages of Canada's fabricated and manufactured end products than do our other trade partners. Moreover, the United States is a good source of quality imports. The negative side of this relationship, however, is that the natural flow of Canadian manufactured exports has made Canada much more dependent on the American market-place and, more important, on the trade policies of the U.S. government, which ultimately controls access to that market-place.

A trade concentration – particularly an export concentration – can be a concern for a nation just as it can for a single firm. There is security in a wide diversity of customers. Conversely, the greater the amount of trade with any one partner, the greater the need for a certain and secure relationship with that partner. Our relationship with the United States, however, is neither certain nor secure, for while trade statistics demonstrate the importance of the United States to Canada's economy, Canada is relatively much less important to the United States. Our country is the largest of America's trading partners, accounting for 19.3 per cent of U.S. trade in 1983, but it is not perceived to be as important to the United States, in terms of international political economy, as the European Community (EC) or Japan. The real concern is that Canada might be disproportionately affected by a given American multilateral trade policy. That policy could have some effect on all the United States' trading partners, but it would have a far greater effect on Canada because of our concentration on U.S. trade.

Given that Canada has a close, even a trade-dependent, relationship with the United States, we would do well to ensure that our trade policy nurtures industries which can compete in the U.S. market, and which have access unimpeded by U.S. protection. Canada, as the smaller power, still suffers from a lack of competitiveness perpetuated by protectionism. A long-standing Canadian economic goal has been to increase the fabricated and end-product/manufacturing component in Canadian exports, but our nation is unlikely to achieve this aim while pursuing a policy of protecting secondary manufacturing. Paradoxically, strong industries result from open markets rather than protected ones because they grow stronger by responding to foreign competitive pressures.

Trade protection in Canada, as in any nation, is implemented, essentially, by two means: tariffs and non-tariff barriers (NTBs). On tariffs, the position between Canada and its major trading partners is unbalanced: by 1987, U.S. average tariffs on dutiable imports will be about 4 to 5 per cent (though on imports from Canada, it will average about 1 per cent, because of the Auto Pact and the high level of duty-free resource imports), while Japanese and EC average tariffs will be in the 5 to 7 per cent range; Canadian average tariffs on dutiable imports will stand at 9 to 10 per cent. Obscured by such averages is the fact that tariffs are much higher on some items. Average tariffs are calculated on a "trade-weighted" basis. This means that they are heavily influenced by the volume of trade in each component, and these volumes are likely to be higher for low-tariff items. For this reason, too, we tend to underestimate the significant effect of tariffs on trade. Still, it is probable that tariff protection affects the Canadian economy more substantially than it does the U.S., Japanese and EC economies, not only because of average levels of duties, but also because of the nature of the protection. One reason is that some Canadian tariffs, particularly those on machinery products, are applied only if similar goods are made in Canada. This practice can create considerable uncertainty for Canadian importers of, say, American products, and it serves to extend tariff protection automatically for newly-developed products whether that protection is needed or not. In other words, this important manufacturing sector might be presumed to need protection that it could well do without.

The tariff schedule, too, demonstrates the presumption that Canadian enterprises need protection. It is inherently difficult to compare different nations' tariff schedules, but one way to approximate a comparison is to examine "basket-category" rates of duty. Tariff schedules are historical documents designed to serve for a long time, and as they have gradually developed they have come to include "basket", or otherwise unspecified, categories that were intended to include and protect products not yet developed or classified. Basket rates thus provide a basic level of protection, which may be adjusted upward or downward when a specific product is classified.

A sample of Canadian and U.S. basket rates is provided in Table 4-3. This table demonstrates that the Canadian rates are consistently and, for some products, substantially higher than U.S. rates. Similar examples could be found for EC and Japanese tariffs. The higher Canadian basket rates are a legacy of the National Policy, and they demonstrate the assumption that Canadian manufacturing needs protection provided by Canadian trade policy. Today, however, in a much more developed industrial economy, such tariff protection only serves to insulate Canadian industries from the world marketplace, even when they do not need it in order to compete. Such tariffs penalize Canadian industrial users and consumers by allowing Canadian producers to keep their prices as high as the tariff will allow. In some sectors, foreign buyers of Canadian products pay less than domestic buyers. Protection, especially in such instances, is no longer warranted. It would be in Canada's interest to reduce such tariffs, particularly on manufactures, in any way it can.

Again, as with tariff protection, Canada's use of non-tariff barriers does not balance that of its trading partners. The United States, the European Community, Japan and Canada all make use of NTBs, but the first three countries make more prominent use of these devices than does Canada. The United States, for example, frequently resorts to countervailing and antidumping duties, administrative regulations, and preferential government

TABLE 4-3 A Comparison of Canadian and U.S. Basket-Category Mean Tariff Rates, 1983–1987

Product	Canadian Tariff Line Item	Canadian Tariff (%) 1983	Canadian Tariff (%) 1987	U.S. Tariff (%) 1983	U.S. Tariff (%) 1987	Comparable U.S. Tariff Line Item (TSUS)[a]
Manufacturers of wood, n.o.p.[b]	50600-1 MFN[c] line 46	12.1	9.2	6.6	5.1	207.00
Manufacturers of iron or steel, n.o.p.	44603-1 MFN line 29	13.9	10.2	7.6	5.7	657.25
Manufacturers of aluminum, n.o.p.	35400-1 MFN line 29	13.9	10.2	7.6	5.7	657.40
Paper and paperboards of all kinds, n.o.p.	19700-1 MFN line 46	12.1	9.2	6.9	5.3	256.90[d]
Manufacturers of glass, n.o.p.	32615-1 MFN line 29	13.9	10.2	9.6	6.6	548.05
Articles of materials of plastines,[e] n.o.p.	93907-1 MFN line 230	15.5	13.5	6.9	5.3	774.55
Machinery, n.o.p.	42700-1 MFN line 46	12.1	9.2	4.4	3.7	678.50

Source: Canada, Revenue Canada, Customs and Excise, *Customs Tariff* (Ottawa: The Department, Directives Management Division, 1984); *The International Customs Journal: United States of America* 21 (April 1983) and *Annex* (January 1984).

a. TSUS = Tariff Schedules of the United States.
b. N.o.p. = not otherwise provided for.
c. MFN = most-favoured nation.
d. In addition to paper and paperboard, the U.S. category includes articles made of pulp and papier-mâché.
e. Plastines are plastic end-products.

procurement, such as "Buy America" requirements. Such American NTBs affect Canada and, particularly, investment in Canada more seriously than our NTBs affect our major trading partners.

There are two prominent examples of the effect of American NTB practices on Canada. The first concerns countervailing duties. It occurs when the United States reserves the right to apply special import duties to foreign products that might have benefited from a subsidy supplied by a foreign government. This practice is intended as a legitimate counter-measure against unfair trade, but the practice itself is open to abuse, particularly when it permits U.S. firms to harass foreign competitors with threats of countervail lawsuits. The Canadian lumber industry recently faced a countervail suit, and while Canada won the case, the proceedings entailed a long and expensive legal battle for the Canadian industry; the industry now faces a renewed threat of Congressional action to limit access to the U.S. market for Canadian lumber. The Canadian fishing industry may be facing a similar experience, for a late-1984 report of the U.S. International Trade Commission claimed that Canada had provided subsidies to producers, particularly in the Maritime Provinces. The result of this practice is that, rightly or wrongly, Canadian exporters of goods to the United States can be subjected to, or threatened by, costly legal proceedings that are beyond their control to avoid. The effect is to make business, either Canadian or foreign, think twice about investing in Canada, particularly if the investment will result in products largely exported to the United States. Of course, such exports would be necessary to the efficient operation of any large-scale modern plant located in Canada.

Government procurement provides a second example of American NTB practices disadvantageous to Canada. The United States has a general Buy America Act, and Buy America provisions are part of various pieces of U.S. legislation that regulate procurement by either federal or state governments. These provisions have borne particularly heavily on Canada's internationally competitive mass-transit industry; indeed, to sell their products in the United States, firms like Bombardier have been required to set up plants in that country. This necessity reduces the level of investment in Canada that could be made by a Canadian industry which is truly "world class", and with this loss of investment is coupled a loss of high-quality jobs as well.

The United States is certainly not the only nation to impose foreign NTBs that frustrate Canadian exporters. Indeed, Canadian producers are most familiar with the threats inherent in U.S. practices, based on the importance of the U.S. market to their continued good health. Non-tariff barriers to other markets have been successful enough to make such markets less significant for more fully manufactured products, despite reductions in tariff barriers. Such NTBs as import quotas, subsidies, and variable import levies permeate trade in agricultural and fishery products, and act as effective shields to the EC and Japanese markets for such products. The Community continues to insist on cumbersome standards procedures and arcane procurement practices. Japan specializes in invisible barriers, difficult to document and impossible to circumvent, and effective in frustrating Canadian exporters of manufactured and agricultural products. Even with competitive products to sell, access to off-shore foreign markets is by no means assured.

Thus, from a brief examination of tariffs and NTBs, it seems plain that Canada is a two-time loser from trade protection. We suffer reduced domestic competitiveness of manufactures, of which one cause is our own tariff protection. As compared to countries with large internal markets, we suffer, too, from an uncertain investment climate and from the loss of job-creating investment. Both these disadvantages are made worse by the function of foreign NTBs.

Canada's manufacturing performance is a further cause of concern. Our country's traditional trade portfolio consisted of export surpluses in agriculture, crude materials and fabricated (that is, semi-processed) goods. Canada, however, runs a substantial deficit on fully-manufactured end products. It had such a strong surplus of raw materials and semi-processed goods, however, that our government was able to conduct an expensive policy of import substitution under the protection of the National Policy. Today, this arrangement is more difficult to justify. The real growth in international trade has been in manufactured goods: as the Economic Council of Canada has noted, "the commerce in food and raw materials among market economies today is approximately 2.5 times as great, in real terms, as it was two decades ago whereas the corresponding figure in respect of manufactured goods is about 5 times [as great]."[1] Over this period Canada, too, has increased substantially its exports of fabricated and end products, and while we still have a large deficit on manufactured end products, at least that deficit is a much smaller proportion of Canada's total trade in those products than it was in 1960.[2] Since world trade over the next decade is not expected to favour primary products, it is clear that Canada will have to increase its capacity to export manufactured products if we are to remain competitive in international trade. It is a truism that nations export in order to import the goods they want. If we fail to expand our manufactured exports over the next decade, we shall suffer a reduced capacity to import and, with that reduction, a corresponding drop in our standard of living. Britain's poor economic performance shows that the stakes are high in this matter, for with its slow productivity growth and its erosion of international competitiveness over the past 30 years, its standard of living, also, has declined: its place was one of the highest in Europe in the mid-1950s, only to become, in the mid-1980s, one of the lowest for the member countries of the European Community.

Thus, to an important extent, Canada's future trade performance will depend on our country's manufacturing performance. To achieve an improved manufacturing performance will not, however, be easy. There are major changes occurring world wide in the manufacturing sector that increase the competition for all countries. There has been a growth in world industrial capacity, producing a trend which will continue in future years as developing countries expand their manufacturing capabilities. In some areas, modern technology has brought rapid change to individual product lines that tends to shorten product-life cycles. Part of this development takes the form of process technology, such as the development of robotics, and part brings about changes in products themselves. All this puts a premium on innovation, on the capacity to increase output rapidly, and on the ability to capture market share. Finally, improvements in international transportation mean that domestic markets can more and more be serviced from abroad. The result is that firms in Canada and elsewhere must compete more effectively or else retreat before international competition. Modern developments have given firms the capacity and incentive to obtain access to foreign markets, and they have also removed some of the natural protection, such as transportation difficulties, that previously served to insulate economies. Again, the message is that there is less and less place to hide, and that Canadian well-being depends ultimately on the future competitiveness of the Canadian economy. The Economic Council of Canada has claimed that much of Canada's future competitiveness may be determined by the trade policy our country chooses to pursue in the next decade:

> *The long-term rate of growth of the Canadian economy is largely determined by improvement in its competitive productivity. Current projections suggest that such improvement will be significantly less during the 1980s than in the late 1960s and early 1970s ... one cannot discount the fact that competitive rigidities and protectionist sentiment and practices have been increasing in the economy in recent years, holding back productivity improvement.*[3]

Policy Choices

One important choice Canadians must face will be whether to pursue our nation's foreign economic goals bilaterally or multilaterally. In coming to our decision, we should do well to remember that these choices need not be exclusive. If we make wise decisions, our choices will be complementary, and one will reinforce another. Our strong preference for multilateralism, which has characterized our policies over the past 40 years, was partly a reaction to the particularism and bilateralism of the 1920s and 1930s. Some of these forces are still present, discernible, for example, in our attempts to find bilateral solutions for difficult import problems through orderly marketing arrangements and voluntary export restraints. However, Canada also makes use of positive bilateral policies and instruments, such as those which resolve issues unique to a particular relationship, or those which open markets between two countries when other nations are not prepared to take that step. Indeed, well-chosen bilateral instruments may serve as catalysts that will strengthen multilateral institutions.

Over the past 50 years, Canada has forged beneficial relationships with many trading partners on a one-to-one basis. These relationships are controlled by both multilateral and bilateral agreements so that governments, when addressing issues of mutual interest, can resort to either bilateral or multilateral commitments, or to both. Pressures on the present global institutions strongly suggest that in future, governments may rely more and more on bilateral commitments. The importance to Canada of pursuing some of our interests bilaterally, though within the framework of rules provided by the multilateral system, became a recurrent theme both in the public hearings and in the research program of this Commission. One researcher, for example, claimed that the evolving international trade environment might well make multilateralism a less effective approach to trade policy in the future than it has been in the past. In particular, a policy of multilateralism might fail to provide Canada with efficient means to build up its domestic economy and to deal effectively with growing U.S. economic nationalism and protectionism. The risk created by this potential weakness in multilateral institutions is all the more serious because, of all the changes occurring in the world economy, those relating to the increasingly defensive U.S. economic stance are probably the most critical from Canada's point of view.[4] In pursuing its economic interests over the next 20 years, Canada will do well to be sensitive to this aspect of the global environment.

As a result of our hearings across the country and our study of the numerous briefs presented to us, we Commissioners believe that there is broad consensus in Canada about the objectives of Canadian trade policy as described in the federal government's 1983 trade-policy paper.[5] We were told again and again that our government should use the instruments available to it to stimulate a stronger, more efficient, productive, competitive and growing economy, and promote a more stable and open international trading environment. We heard, too, that Canadian producers need better, more stable and more secure access to a large market. Many consider that the Canadian market is too small to achieve the economies of scale that would stimulate greater productivity and efficiency.

Canadians argue about the best way to achieve these objectives. Essentially, the arguments revolve around two sets of issues: How best are we to use trade policy instruments to achieve a stronger, more competitive economy? How best are we to promote better and more secure access to foreign markets? The two issues, of course, are not unrelated. In an era when market access is largely the product of negotiations between governments, a country must pay for improved access to foreign markets by opening up its own market, whether it pursues negotiations multilaterally or bilaterally. In Canada, as elsewhere, this fact is not always well appreciated. Even so, there are other reasons for extending or reducing protection. As we noted above, Canada's economy is open and trade-dependent, and our industrial policy has been dominated by trade policy.

Economists have long argued the advantages of free trade for small economies that have little influence over their terms of trade in world markets. A country gains by exporting those commodities which it can produce relatively cheaply as compared with the rest of the world. It should, therefore, specialize in producing those goods and use the proceeds of their sale in world markets to finance its imports. In short, comparative, rather than absolute, advantage should determine the direction of trade policy. Over the years, however, many Canadians have acquired a strong aversion to developing an economy in which we are largely producers of primary resource products, even though we have traditionally seen our comparative advantage as lying in our resource industries. As a result, much of our policy making has been devoted to strengthening and establishing an industrial base in Canada.

It is now more than ever important for Canadians to recognize the virtues of allowing greater play to free-market forces in determining the direction of our economic development. In the opinion of one informed observer:

> *It is high time as Canadians that we started to concentrate on those things we can do best, those things where we have a natural advantage, either because of our geography or our resources, and stopped trying to push water uphill all the time at great cost . . . not only [to] the taxpayers but to our standard of living. We have done too much of this . . . and we would be much better off [to] pursue goals that become natural because of our geography and our location in the world.*

(Senator Van Roggen, Transcript, Vancouver, September 7, 1983 [vol. 2], pp. 337–38.)

Only by moving in this direction will Canada achieve full benefit from its trade. Canadians must resist pressures to introduce more protection into our economy; we must, instead, slowly reduce and eventually remove our protective trade barriers as we proceed by way of bilateral and multilateral negotiations with our trade partners.

This Commission heard, however, from Canadians who advocated a course of increasing protection and encouragement for the development of secondary manufacturing through import substitution. Such an approach would use protectionist measures such as production quotas, content requirements and high tariffs as a defensive strategy to counteract the effect both of high foreign investment in Canada and protectionism in foreign markets.

In a brief to this Commission, Professor Abraham Rotstein, a leading proponent of such a defensive strategy, called for a halt to further movement toward freer trade and argued for a much greater emphasis on a more active industrial policy as a first priority.[6] The first building block of such a strategy, in his view, would be import substitution. Commissioners address the issue of industrial policy in another part of this Report. Nevertheless, without anticipating too much at this point, we wish to state that we do not recommend the type of massive intervention proposed in this alternative approach, although we do believe that it is important to co-ordinate industrial policies very closely with trade policy.

A policy of import substitution would be a reaffirmation of the techniques of the National Policy. Like that policy, it would create some industrial growth, largely by encouraging foreign companies to set up branch plants in Canada in order to avoid Canadian trade barriers. Such plants would likely be designed to serve only our small Canadian market, and as a result, they would be inefficient by world standards. This does not constitute the best strategy for attracting foreign investment to Canada. If Canada is to have foreign investment, it should be investment that has located here because of the productive opportunities available in our country, and not because of need to circumvent artificial trade barriers.

Part of the defensive strategy is to emphasize building greater strength within Canada before opening the doors further to import competition or seeking broader access abroad. There is a certain appeal to ensuring one is fit to meet the competition before entering the ring. Nevertheless, this form of preparation suffers from several drawbacks. Without foreign competition, there is no particular incentive to force new internal competitiveness. Adjustment is therefore delayed or, often, fails to take place at all. Moreover, it is not clear how countries would choose particular areas of their economies for scaling up to world standards. Another difficulty, posed by purely domestic rationalization, is that there are costs both of up-scaling and of down-scaling sectors. Where sectors are being down-scaled by whatever process (not usually spelled out) there is less chance for workers to gain alternative employment because this process does not take advantage of the benefits of broader foreign access. Sectors that are up-scaling to take advantage of a larger world market are doing so on the premise that the government will eventually negotiate freer trade. Can Canadians really expect business and labour to operate effectively under these incentives?

Commissioners think not. The benefits of domestic rationalization are far greater where they are combined with international rationalization through trade negotiations.

A policy of import substitution would cause still other problems. It is inconsistent with the trend toward freer multilateral trade that industrial nations have pursued in the General Agreement on Tariffs and Trade (GATT) for the past 40 years. Canada has traditionally viewed the development of strong multilateral institutions like the GATT to be in our interest, and consequently we have been a strong proponent of GATT efforts to liberalize trade. Import substitution would represent a sharp break with our strong support of GATT and GATT's liberalizing influence in international trade. Moreover, a policy of import substitution carried out by an already-industrialized nation like our own would surely invite retaliation and thus lead to reduced and less-secure access to foreign markets, for other nations would view the industries and jobs that Canada created through import substitution as effectively stolen from our trading partners. We depend on international trade, and we benefit enormously from our exchanges with other countries. A Canadian policy of import substitution would therefore be threatening to the multilateral trading system and inconsistent with our long-term needs and interests.

This Commission, then, rejects unequivocally a general policy of aggressive import substitution. We believe that Canada should seek, and would benefit from, more liberal trading conditions, both at home and abroad. In Commissioners' opinion, the question is not, "Should we Canadians open up our own market?" Rather, it is, "How, at what pace, and in return for what access to foreign markets are we to offer readier access to our own?" Such an approach is also consonant with the desire of many Canadians who see the need for a more stable and more open international trading environment. We heard many interesting and innovative suggestions about what could be done, but for ease of analysis and presentation we shall reduce them to three major approaches.

Canada might:

- Maintain its present policy. It might keep to the level and type of protection currently in place, but make selective efforts both to improve access abroad and to protect Canadian industry on a limited case-by-case basis.
- Participate actively in a new round of multilateral trade negotiations under the auspices of the GATT, in order to improve and secure our access to foreign markets, to open up our own market, and to strengthen the legal framework for international trade
- In addition to taking the initiative for the elimination of trade barriers at the multilateral level, open negotiations with the Government of the United States to reach an agreement on a substantial reduction of barriers, tariff and non-tariff, between Canada and the United States.

Commissioners recognize, of course, that the day-to-day choices which governments face cannot be parcelled so conveniently into three packages, for no situation is ever that neat, nor is there any reason why pursuit of one approach should exclude an element of another. Nevertheless, we believe that the distinctions among these three approaches are clear enough that we can delineate the advantages and disadvantages they would represent for Canada, both in the near future and for the rest of this century.

The first approach, then, would be to maintain a *status quo* policy. It would be politically attractive because it would not require innovative action, but it is problematic because it might leave Canada caught for too long in awkward transition between two incompatible trade strategies: the historic developmental and protectionist approach of the National Policy as opposed to the more modern, multilateral, liberalizing policy of the GATT. The problem is that this transition has now reached the stage where Canadian manufacturers are without sufficient protection to insulate them effectively from foreign competition or without sufficient access to foreign markets. To maintain this policy stance would be likely to deny Canada the future economic benefits of a more productive export sector. If Canada maintains its present policy, it risks facing a stagnating economy in the future. We could, of course, gradually reduce our current level of protection through continuing participation in future multilateral trade negotiations, but unless we aggressively pursue trade liberalization, the reduction might proceed at a pace too slow to effect the kinds of changes Canada must make to remain competitive.

It is difficult to hold onto the *status quo*: either a nation faces and overcomes new challenges, or it declines. Similarly, a *status quo* trade policy would be difficult to conduct. Protectionist demands would be hard to resist, and there are, indeed, signs that resistance may already have weakened. In June 1984, the Government of Canada passed the Special Import Measures Act, which included legislation on countervailing duties, emergency safeguard measures and other NTBs. The thrust of this legislation is to make contingency protection easier to impose in Canada. For example, injury criteria have been relaxed to make it easier for courts to find against foreign producers on the grounds of injurious imports. In addition, the range of adverse effects that could trigger countervailing and anti-dumping duties has been broadened to benefit import-competing domestic producers. Other changes have given our government more flexibility to manage trade, and this development will probably make Canada less accessible to foreign imports. The Act is an example of the kind of incremental drift toward increased protectionism in the name of "fair" trade that becomes possible in the absence of a clear policy commitment to broader trade liberalization.

Finally, as we have noted, trade policy and industrial policy are inextricably linked. Those who favour more open approaches to trade policy usually advocate a more market-minded, but supportive, industrial policy. Those who wish to place less reliance on economic forces usually advocate more government intervention in industrial policy. Commissioners believe that a *status quo* trade policy might lead very quickly, over the next few years, to calls for a planned economy. This degree of intervention, however, is inconsistent with the view of industrial policy that we have taken elsewhere in this Report. We argue that a highly interventionist industrial policy should be considered only if the world becomes a much darker place than we expect it to be in the future. Otherwise, an industrial policy emphasizing efficiency and excellence is most likely to contribute to Canada's overall goals. In general, therefore, although maintenance of the *status quo* has its attractions, it does not promise enough benefit to overcome its disadvantages.

Maintenance of the *status quo* may also prove an insufficient means of gaining for Canadian producers better and more secure access to foreign markets, especially the U.S. market. Since 1947, Canada has generally pursued multilateral trade negotiations to gain access to foreign markets. We have pursued this course because it has proved to be the most effective way to improve and secure access for our products and to instil order, stability and predictability into our trade relationships. Active participation in the multilateral system has allowed Canadians to benefit from a more efficient allocation of our nation's resources on a world-wide basis.

A second approach for Canada would be to embark on a deliberate and aggressive policy of trade liberalization in order to make our manufacturing sector more competitive and to broaden our access to foreign markets. The historic protection provided by the National Policy has left Canada with an industrial manufacturing base much of which is designed to service the small Canadian domestic market. More and more, this manufacturing base suffers from a scale of production that is too small to be competitive by world standards. The most severe problems of Canadian industry are lack of product specialization and short production runs. Other problems include the lack of product innovation, which is especially related to the branch-plant characteristics of our economy. These difficulties of Canadian production are not new: indeed, they have been referred to repeatedly in government reports and academic studies of our economy.

There is urgent need for Canada's economy to expand economies of scale and to realize greater productivity. Multilateral trade negotiations provide one way to accomplish this end. Freer trade would create a desirable restructuring and rationalization of Canadian industry as a result of increased competition from abroad. By becoming more competitive and gaining better access to world markets, Canadian manufacturers would become better able to survive in a more competitive, global trading environment. Ultimately, it is only by creating a more competitive domestic economy that Canada will be able to create the new jobs needed to reduce unemployment.

The power of freer trade has been amply demonstrated by historical examples, including many offered in our own country. Britain's repeal of the Corn Laws in 1846 ushered in the period of its greatest economic growth. The disastrous depression of the 1930s was deepened and lengthened by protectionism. The rapid economic growth of Western industrialized countries that began in the mid-1950s and ended in the 1970s was partly a product of the liberalizing influence of GATT negotiations. Although Commissioners do not wish to overemphasize the connection, we do note that the decline in economic growth that began in 1973 has coincided with the adoption of more protectionist policies and a reduction of GATT influence. Both the 1930s and the 1970s have demonstrated the "bankruptcy" of protectionist policies. In Canada, our strongest and most progressive industrial sectors are those most fully integrated into world markets: that is, those which operate under low levels of protection at home and face low barriers to export markets.

Multilateral negotiations, however, have become highly complicated and long-drawn-out affairs. Attempts are currently under way to explore whether a basis can be found for another round of GATT negotiations. A new round would focus on elaborating world trade law and reducing barriers to world trade. These developments would be in Canada's interest, but the results of a future GATT negotiation are *not* just around the corner. Initiating a new round is a complicated process, yet it would centre largely on the interests of three or four major players: the United States, the European Community (EC), the less-developed countries as a group, and Japan. Canada is an important player in the system, but our country does not set the agenda or determine the outcome. There is as yet no consensus on any issue. When negotiations are joined, they will last a long time, and they will not necessarily provide solutions for specific Canadian concerns, particularly as these relate to trade with our most important trading partner.

Exclusive concentration on multilateralism may not be able to provide Canada with better and more secure access to our most important market. The growth of our exports to the United States has been the product of proximity, close inter- and intra-corporate ties, and the relative openness of that market compared to that of our other major trading partners: the European Community and Japan. The very accessiblity of the U.S. market compared to that of the others means that the United States is unlikely to extend its multilateral policies much further unless it is satisfied that the Community and Japan are likely to reciprocate. While there are benefits to negotiating access to the U.S. market in concert with these two partners, there is also the disadvantage of being held hostage to EC and Japanese willingness to open their markets to U.S. exports.

A third approach option would be to try to reap the advantages of the multilateral approach and, at the same time, pursue complementary Canada-U.S. bilateral free trade. This would be a bold move and would elicit strong controversy. Even though there now appears to be substantial public support for freer trade with the United States, it would not be easy for Canada to negotiate an acceptable agreement. In Commissioners' view, the second and third approaches deserve to be weighed very carefully. Our own analysis follows in the next two chapters.

Notes

1. Economic Council of Canada, *On the Mend*, Twentieth Annual Review (Ottawa: Minister of Supply and Services Canada, 1983), pp. 19–20.
2. Economic Council of Canada, *The Bottom Line: Technology, Trade, and Economic Growth* (Ottawa: Minister of Supply and Services Canada, 1983), p. 99.
3. Economic Council, *On the Mend*, p. 95.
4. See John M. Curtis, "Which Way? Canadian Trade Policy in a Changing World Economy", in *Canada and the Multilateral Trading System*, vol. 10, prepared for

the Royal Commission on the Economic Union and Development Prospects for Canada (Toronto: University of Toronto Press, 1985).

5. Canada, External Affairs Canada, *Canadian Trade Policy for the 1980s: A Discussion Paper* (Ottawa: Minister of Supply and Services Canada, 1983).

6. See Canadian Institute for Economic Policy, Brief, February 1984. This brief was later published. See Abraham Rotstein, *Rebuilding from Within: Remedies for Canada's Ailing Economy* (Ottawa: Canadian Institute for Economic Policy, 1984).

CHAPTER 5

Canada and the General Agreement on Tariffs and Trade

Introduction *279*
The GATT's Achievements *280*
Difficulties Facing GATT *281*
Note *288*
The Prospect for Future Negotiations *289*
Note *295*
Conclusions *296*
Note *296*

CHAPTER 5

Canada and the General Agreement on Tariffs and Trade

Introduction

Commissioners strongly believe that a more liberal trading environment will expose Canadian producers to the beneficial effects of more world competition and will provide the framework within which our country will be able to improve its access to foreign markets. At the same time, we Canadians must also look to securing the access we currently enjoy, with the intent of removing as much uncertainty as possible from Canadian firms seeking world markets in order to develop their business. In this more liberal and secure trade environment, our exporters will be able to use improved access to exploit fully the opportunities available to Canada in the global economy.

Since 1947, the means Canada has used most frequently to improve and secure access to foreign markets and gradually to liberalize access to our own market have been multilateral negotiations under the General Agreement on Tariffs and Trade (GATT). Many Canadians are convinced that the GATT has served us well by offering wider access to export markets abroad and by providing for discipline in world trade, thus guaranteeing some security of access to international markets. GATT has also provided a basis for an orderly liberalization of our own market, thus ensuring our development into a more competitive economy. Among those who appeared before this Commission, the Canadian Chamber of Commerce made this point succinctly:

> *Because of its high level of dependence on trade and the relatively limited size of the domestic market, Canada, more than virtually any other industrial nation, is critically reliant on a liberal and open international trade environment. It is in Canada's interest that multilateral institutions such as GATT are maintained and strengthened.* (Canadian Chamber of Commerce, Brief, October 3, 1983, p. 19.)

In evaluating the trade-policy options available to Canadians in the years ahead, it is necessary to assess both the benefits we have already derived from participation in the GATT and our future prospects. How much broader access to world markets can we obtain through GATT measures? At what pace and with what degree of security?

The GATT's Achievements

The GATT inherited a legacy of high and often discriminatory tariffs reinforced by a tangle of non-tariff barriers (NTBs) that also were frequently applied on a discriminatory basis. Retaliation and counter-retaliation were the normal means of attempting to settle disputes. Seven GATT negotiating rounds have taken place since the General Agreement was signed in 1947. Canada has fully participated in these rounds. In the second to fifth rounds, the actual reductions achieved in trade barriers were relatively modest. The Kennedy and Tokyo Rounds, however, achieved significant cuts. Today, the industrial tariffs of the developed market economies are probably lower than at any time since the late 1870s and substantially lower than during the 1930s. (For example, the U.S. average tariff during the 1930s stood at 50 per cent, whereas after the Tokyo Round cuts are fully implemented, the average tariff on industrial products will be 5 per cent.) In addition, virtually all of these industrial and fish tariffs and many agricultural tariffs are "bound". They can only be increased if they are renegotiated on the basis of paying compensation or accepting retaliation. The cumulative effect of the GATT rounds has been significant, especially in establishing the habit of multilateral negotiation and practices, and in generating the momentum for further trade liberalization at each stage.

The GATT has also made progress in the removal of non-tariff barriers or, where removal is not appropriate, in bringing NTBs under better international discipline and reducing the scope for their misuse. In the early 1960s, European countries, Japan, and other nations removed thousands of quantitative restrictions. This landmark achievement resulted in the substantial liberalization of trade. The Tokyo Round agreements relating to valuation, dumping, technical barriers, government procurement, subsidies and countervailing measures, and import licensing marked a long step toward reducing the risk that such measures might be misused to restrict trade. As time passes and observers gain perspective, the agreements on technical barriers and government procurement, which, for the first time, bring these types of barriers under the GATT, probably will be seen to have made important contributions to the liberalization of trade. Trade in industrial products, most fish products, and some agricultural products has become less constrained by non-tariff barriers than at any time since before the Great Depression. Equally important, the GATT has begun the process of establishing the rule of law in the conduct of international trade relations. The system for adjudicating disputes neutralizes disparities in power between the parties in disagreement and usually results in prompt and fair settlements.

The developed market economies now offer freer access, overall, for products exported by other developed market economies than they have offered at any time since the early 1900s. Moreover, a much smaller risk exists that such access will be reduced or cancelled out by raising tariffs or imposing other barriers to trade. Since the GATT was established, the value of world trade has increased more than six times. During most of this time, most of the developed market countries, including Canada, experienced a faster rate of export growth than did their national economies. The liberalization of trade under the GATT was the necessary basis of the expansion of world trade and the growth of the industrial economies.

It is essential that Canada have stable access to foreign markets, especially the markets of the United States, the European Community (EC) and Japan, as well as opportunities to negotiate improved access to foreign markets on reasonable terms. Such access is best incorporated in a contractual framework that seeks to neutralize disparities in power. Measured by these basic interests, the performance of the GATT to date has been without historical precedent and generally satisfactory, not in any absolute sense of perfection, but in comparison with that of earlier periods. Without GATT, it is unlikely that Canadian exports would have grown at a faster pace than the national economy during the post-war years.

Difficulties Facing GATT

While there can be no question that the GATT has been instrumental in reducing trade barriers and has thus facilitated the growth in post-Second World War trade, it is now at a difficult stage in its evolution. Over time, its membership has expanded, and negotiations have become more difficult to conduct. The GATT is no longer – and appropriately so – the cosy club of 23 countries which negotiated the original General Agreement in 1947. Indeed, negotiating simultaneously with 100 or more countries is quite a different matter from negotiating with the original members, and the "lowest common denominator" seems, at times, to determine the outcome of GATT proceedings. More trade is now managed through voluntary export restraints, orderly marketing agreements have increased in number, and resort to quotas has grown more frequent. Issues of concern both to Canada and to our main trading partners have not, on occasion, been fully pursued because of our collective inability to convince all parties to the negotiations of the worth of alternative proposals.

The issue now facing Canadians is to decide how much further benefit, in the form of improved and assured access to world markets, the GATT process can offer us. Canada, like other nations, has long recognized the need to facilitate progressive movement to a more liberal trading environment. Now, however, proposals for trade liberalization are countered by demands for new restrictions on imports and for the protection of existing industries, in order to preserve employment. An international economic system based on specialization and the free flow of goods and services imposes restrictions on each country's right to pursue its own particular goals and policies. As Canadians enter the latter years of the current century, we must consider seriously whether the multilateral approach to the liberalization of trade offers broad enough prospects for our economy.

It cannot be assumed blithely at this stage that the rule of law, such as it is, and the political will underlying it will continue to be a feature of world trade and the global economic order. Many governments are intervening to a greater extent in their domestic economies; they are formulating all kinds of "strategies" for industrial and agricultural development, which, in many instances, amount simply to elaborate assistance programs that need to be defended by the imposition of controls on competitive imports. As a result, some governments, especially those of the larger countries, now tend to regard the international economic and trade rules as extensions, in essence, of particular domestic policies: regulations to be observed only when they accommodate those policies and to be changed or evaded when they do not.

The general principles enshrined in the General Agreement itself were originally intended to provide a framework for the conduct of trade relations, for periodic negotiations to reduce trade barriers, and for the introduction of a liberalizing bias into members' trade policies. Over the years, the desire to impose discipline and thus maintain the integrity of tariff reductions has been one of the influences which has gradually changed the character of the GATT. This change became especially obvious during the Tokyo Round, when members made a concerted effort to translate general principles into detailed rules and procedures. Unfortunately, it has had perverse and unintended side effects. Rather than continuing to push for the elimination of trade barriers, GATT now sanctions certain barriers as long as these are imposed in a particular manner and follow specific procedures. This development has encouraged certain member states which had not used certain types of trade barriers to arm themselves with the full panoply of GATT rights in order to defend themselves against other members. Canada has been no exception. Until 1977, Canada lacked complete procedures for imposing countervailing duties. We now have a fully developed system wholly consistent with our GATT rights, but not necessarily in our best interests. Thus, through its members' efforts to impose discipline, GATT negotiations have directly stimulated the introduction of new trade barriers in countries which previously had seen no need for them.

In general terms, the GATT has made significant progress in reducing tariff barriers. Those that remain are often the most difficult to negotiate, especially on a multilateral basis. The present problem areas of trade policy now have less to do with tariffs and more with non-tariff barriers (NTBs). These latter forms of protection are extremely difficult to identify and monitor, since they are often inseparable from a nation's domestic policies. The provisions of the General Agreement relating to NTBs deal only with broad principles and not with detailed rules. The Tokyo Round marked the first comprehensive attempt to bring such measures within a framework of rules, but the process is far from complete, and not all the applicable codes are fully satisfactory.

Closely related to the problems of NTBs are difficulties pertaining to dispute-settlement procedures in the GATT. Member countries are committed to consult bilaterally in the event of a dispute; if bilateral consultations prove unsuccessful, the parties may request a panel review. This procedure worked reasonably well as long as there was broad agreement on the value of a liberal trading environment, but of late, a number of problems have arisen. These include the absence of effective monitoring, compliance and enforcement methods; increased use of protective measures not covered by GATT rules; and non-adherence by contracting parties to GATT-panel recommendations. These problems all relate to the widening divergence of views among participants on the nature and purpose of the GATT. Since the Kennedy Round, there has been an increasing tendency for countries to settle trade-policy disputes bilaterally, outside the GATT. The trend to resort to non-GATT agreements and the consequent erosion of the GATT principle of non-discrimination has made Canadians more concerned about guarantees of continued access to world markets.

An important characteristic of the GATT system has been the desire to maintain an overall balance of advantage for all participants through application of the principle of reciprocity. If any member should consider that its interests have been adversely affected, GATT dispute-settlement procedures allow it to pursue a new balance, either on a one-to-one basis or through collective action. The GATT is thus a dynamic political institution operating within a framework of rules, none of which are absolute, and many of which are obscure and subject to diverse interpretations. Its dynamism, however, favours the more powerful members which can afford to take action that may adversely affect a smaller country, secure in the knowledge that retaliation is unlikely. If a measure is challenged, it remains in effect until the dispute-settlement mechanism runs its course. If the challenge is upheld, a recalcitrant major power can make minor adjustments and force renewed resort to dispute settlement. Conversely, great powers can readily retaliate against any trade-policy measure that is not in its interest and force a smaller power to resort again to dispute-settlement procedures.

Canada's experiences with the European Community in the matter of gaining access to the EC market for Canadian high-quality beef, lead and zinc, and newsprint have all demonstrated the truth of this perception. The newsprint case was especially educational. Following negotiations with the Scandinavian countries, the Community considered that it would be to its advantage to reduce a duty-free quota, bound to Canada, for newsprint. Canada repeatedly challenged the EC and was vindicated by a GATT panel; in the end, however, for the sake of our relations with the Community, our government, in order to resolve the issue, felt constrained to accept a lower quota than we had paid for in previous multilateral negotiations. The Community obviously considered its commitments to a free-trade agreement with the Scandinavian countries and its desire to limit the access it granted for newsprint of more importance than its relations with Canada or its obligations under GATT.

A third general problem concerns the integration of the less-developed countries (LDCs) into the full GATT system. These nations lack the capacity to influence or alter negotiations effectively in their favour. Bargaining power in GATT relates to market power. LDCs have neither had sufficient market power, nor displayed a desire, to open up their own markets and thus deploy what limited bargaining power they do possess. Their perception of the post-war trade-and-payments system is radically different from that of the developed countries, and thus their approach to negotiations is different. The future strength of the multilateral trade system, however, requires the full support and participation of all its members; without that support, its members will become obsessed with the problems of one group to the detriment of others.

The GATT does not exist independent of the will of its members, nor is it capable of arriving at decisions with which its members cannot live. It is not a judicial system, nor is it a law-enforcement body. Rather, it represents the collective will of its member states. It represents the cumulative result of many major and minor negotiations relating both to general rules and to specific trade concessions. If its discipline has eroded, the reason is that its participants have not seen fit to accept greater discipline.

The GATT system today encompasses much more than the 38 articles of the General Agreement. To these must be added:

- Detailed tariff schedules amended by seven rounds of general negotiations and many "out-of-season" individual negotiations
- The Protocols of Accession and Association which spell out precise terms and conditions applied by members at variance with the General Agreement
- The ancillary codes and agreements negotiated during the Kennedy and Tokyo Rounds, to which not all GATT members are party
- Almost forty years of experience, understandings, interpretations, panel findings, working party reports, and agreements contained in the 31 volumes (as of 1985) of *Basic Instruments and Selected Documents*
- The Multi-fibre Agreement, an organized derogation from the discipline of Article XIX, which permits its 52 participants to apply discriminatory quotas to trade in textiles and clothing
- Various other derogations and waivers, particularly those under Article XXIV, which provide for discriminatory free-trade areas, common markets and customs unions.

In short, over the years, the GATT has evolved into a highly complicated system marked by various levels of commitment and participation. It is far from representing a clear-cut code of international rules applied by all its members on a non-discriminatory basis.

The attitudes of various GATT-member governments to the purposes that the GATT system serves have devolved over the years to the point where there is no longer ready consensus about what future actions should or should not be taken through GATT. It is particularly important that we Canadians understand the attitudes toward GATT of the United States, the European Community, Japan and the LDCs as a group.

The United States has long enjoyed its role as the principal force behind the GATT. It sees this institution as the best way to manage its numerous and varied trade relations. As sponsor of many of the issues currently dominating the international trade-policy agenda, it is strongly committed to a revitalization of the GATT through a new multilateral trade negotiation. But whereas in years past, U.S. participation in GATT was as much inspired by political and strategic considerations as by trade and economic factors, the latter are now much more important. The United States sees itself as the victim of its past generosity. It views its market as more open than any of those of its trading partners, its economy as more vibrant, and its currency as stronger; it also sees its trade deficit as unacceptably large. It therefore looks forward to a future GATT round, not only in terms of reforming that institution, but also in terms of righting the imbalances that have evolved within it. The United States no longer considers that there is any strategic advantage in "going first". It is not prepared to open its market further until it is clear that other markets will be significantly more open, and that greater discipline will be imposed on unfair trade practices. An indication of the American attitude is that while the United States is pushing for an early start to negotiations, it is not seeking a tariff-cutting authority, as it did in earlier negotiations.

U.S. participation in GATT, while generally forward-looking and biased towards trade liberalization, has not always been benign. The United States has sometimes used GATT to give international legitimacy to its particular trade policies. Considering its dominance, it has generally done so successfully, whether these policies were in every member's interest or not. It was the U.S. request for a waiver from its GATT obligations in relation to agricultural import restrictions which formed the origin of GATT's inability to exercise more discipline over trade in agricultural products. It was U.S. sponsorship of the Multi-fibre Agreement which gave rise to the past 25 years of organized protectionism in trade in textiles and clothing. And it was U.S. preoccupation with rules and procedures which introduced what some observers now see as GATT's greatest danger: the complete legitimization of systems of contingency protection.

Since GATT's inception, its members have sought to instil stability, predictability and transparency into international trade relations by negotiating general rules applicable to all member states. Business confidence and investment require such order and stability in an interdependent world. Systems of contingency protection, however, have exactly the opposite effect. These systems involve elaborate rules and procedures relating both to injurious, dumped and subsidized imports and to seriously injurious (that is, politically intolerable) imports; they also allow governments to impose quotas, surcharges or penalties on such imports. These systems have now replaced tariffs in industrialized countries as the principal tool of economic protection. They allow imports to enter until such time as affected domestic producers can convince government that they should be curtailed. Nowhere is such a system more complete than in the Unites States. U.S. trade law, which is generally consistent with U.S. obligations to GATT because the United States has been the principal sponsor of the rules, gives American business interests broad scope to harass their foreign competitors and thus deter investment. The U.S. call for more rules and discipline in international trade relations, therefore, holds an ominous message for other countries.

Since its inception, the European Community has been driven by a perception of the world trading system which is fundamentally at odds with that of the United States. Its priorities are based on the development of a preference system around the European heartland that discriminates against its main competitors, the United States and Japan. Most of its trade is now governed by the terms of the Treaty of Rome and related agreements, and not by the GATT. The GATT system serves mainly to manage EC-trade relations with the United States, Japan and Canada, and these, while not unimportant, provide a decreasing proportion of EC trade. The strengthening of the multilateral system is thus of decidedly secondary interest to the Community. The EC does not perceive many of the issues on the U.S.-sponsored/trade-policy agenda as critical to its advantage; indeed, it sees some of them as a positive threat. Thus it is playing a delicate game of welcoming proposals for negotiations, but frustrating efforts to put them into operation or to define an agenda.

There are sharp differences between the EC and the American perceptions of the role of the state in the economy, and these are clearly apparent in their differing approaches to future trade negotiations. The European Community perceives the U.S. desire to revitalize the GATT and to strengthen international discipline as a threat to many of its internal policies. The United States sees a need to develop rules which will penalize governments for intervening in its economy in order to meet particular social and political goals. An issue that symbolizes this difference is the EC Common Agricultural Policy (CAP). Under the CAP, prices for farm produce are set by the state on a basis essentially unrelated to costs. As a result, even the least efficient farmer in the Community can be confident of making a comfortable living. The integrity of these prices is maintained by a system of variable levies and import quotas meant to keep more competitive foreign produce out of the EC market. Almost all producers are, in effect, subsidized and produce huge surpluses which can only be disposed of by dumping them on international markets at distress prices. To the European Community, the CAP is an expensive, but necessary, policy to bind the Community together, assure it virtual self-sufficiency in agriculture, and maintain small farmers' income at a level similar to that of urban industrial workers. Community policies, in place without interruption for some twenty years, have closed the EC market to more competitive foreign produce and have made it an unfair competitor in third markets. To the United States, the CAP is proof positive of the bankruptcy caused by too much state intervention. Such differences are not readily reconciled in multilateral negotiations, especially when they are replicated across other sectors.

The European Community is ambivalent, too, about the efficacy of the rule of law in international trade relations. It views strengthening of the rule of law and dispute-settlement mechanisms as a threat to its ability to reach bilateral and sectoral deals with those most affected by particular practices. While the United States may have invented the discrimination inherent in the rules governing international trade in textiles and clothing, the Community has perfected it and periodically tightens those rules' restrictive and discriminatory effect. It finds third-party arbitration, as called for under GATT rules, an intrusion into its own already-complicated decision-making process. It does not welcome such intrusions and generally ignores unwelcome conclusions.

Japan participates actively in the GATT and, together with the United States, is calling for a new round of trade negotiations. Nevertheless, it does not fully adhere to GATT principles, either in its export policy, where it is prepared to accommodate its trading partners in ways inconsistent with the

General Agreement, or in its import policy, where myriad subtle rules and practices seriously frustrate the more forthright Western business approach. Japan shares the perception that it is important to maintain and strengthen the integrity of the multilateral trading system, though its motives may be more closely related to a desire to divert attention from specific bilateral trade irritants than to a desire to impose greater general discipline. Although Japan can be counted on to participate fully in GATT activities, it is unlikely to provide leadership. In the long run, better access to the Japanese market is less likely to be achieved through GATT than through bilateral negotiations, particularly those patterned on the negotiations of the United States.

Less-developed countries which participate in GATT are not subject to the same discipline and obligations as industrialized countries. Over the years, GATT members have systematically waived obligations or introduced special measures that differentiate in their favour. Nevertheless, the LDCs see the multilateral trade-and-payments system as a means of establishing new dependencies through economic exploitation. They view the failure in negotiating multilateral safeguards and the perpetuation of the discriminatory provisions of the Arrangement regarding International Trade in Textiles (Multi-fibre Agreement) as evidence of the GATT's lack of response to their aspirations. They believe that the GATT needs a fundamental restructuring to the point where it requires its members to discriminate positively in their favour until such time as their economic development approaches that of the countries that make up the Organisation for Economic Co-operation and Development (OECD). Understandably, their view of the GATT is not widely shared by developed countries:

> *It is difficult to argue that developing countries, having almost unlimited rights to protect themselves against imports, could somehow be harmed by other countries keeping themselves open to trade. Even legitimate criticisms about the levels of protection established by many countries on developing country exports such as textiles and clothing are not altogether valid. Notwithstanding the protection, actual levels of market penetration of these products are substantial in many industrialized countries, although they would certainly be higher without the high level of protection these sectors enjoy. The GATT system is not a system which exploits developing countries; rather, it provides developing countries with some assurance of relatively open markets, particularly in comparison to the markets of the centrally planned countries, or to the markets of the developing countries themselves. For these reasons, it is unlikely that fundamental changes in the international trading system will be made in response to LDC demands. Any changes will be in response to more broadly based needs.*[1]

Despite these seemingly incompatible attitudes on the part of the major participants, the GATT remains a remarkably successful instrument and a symbol of multilateral co-operation. The challenge in future negotiations will be to retain that record and even improve on it. This will be a very difficult challenge to meet and will take substantial amounts of political determination, time and compromise.

The current situation, therefore, should not be overdramatized. The international trading system, though weakened, has not collapsed. While the GATT rules and norms of behaviour have been avoided or disregarded in a number of areas, they continue to govern much of the world's trade, and they remain the standard against which trade actions are measured. Overall, it appears that no country, large or small, is prepared to countenance the collapse of the existing international systems for economic co-operation for fear of the consequences. Many proposals have been made for reforming and re-energizing the international trading system. These range from the suggestion that a new GATT round be initiated later in this decade, to the statement that the GATT should, instead, pursue trade liberalization and the extension of the rules governing international trade through one or several approaches, including bilateral, regional or functional arrangements.

The GATT was the product of the uneasy compromise between the perfectionists and the protectionists. U.S. ratification of the Havana Charter foundered on the dissatisfaction both of those who wanted the International Trade Organization (ITO) to be a perfect embodiment of the economic principles of free trade and of those who believed that any international rules would prevent the United States from protecting its market from unwanted foreign competition. Although the GATT emerged as the interim compromise, the tension between perfectionists and protectionists has animated its existence ever since. That tension will be a major force in future negotiations.

Note

1. M.M. Hart, *Canadian Economic Development and the International Trading System*, vol. 53, prepared for the Royal Commission on the Economic Union and Development Prospects for Canada (Toronto: University of Toronto Press, 1985).

The Prospect for Future Negotiations

Multilateralism has formed the basis of Canadian trade policy since the Second World War. Overall, Canada has adhered to multilateral principles, while accepting the need for complementary bilateral initiatives in areas where it has relatively more strength and hence occupies a better bargaining position. This tendency has rested primarily on the belief that all countries – especially a relatively small economic power – can make greater gains in this kind of forum than in any other. It has been argued that the multilateral approach to trade policy results in a situation where the Canadian interest is likely to be consonant, on any given trade issue, with that of one or other of the major economic powers.

The evolution of international rules in economic areas, to the extent that this development will continue over the next decade or so, will have important implications for domestic economic and foreign trade legislation in the countries concerned. As an outcome of the Tokyo Round, for example, significant changes were made in Canadian and U.S. trade legislation. Cynics may argue that the international rules are written by the larger countries simply to accommodate their own laws and policies. Although this argument is valid to some extent, it is not entirely so. If the international rules are to have any authority, they must necessarily win agreement through a process of negotiation in which the interests of a significant group of countries are also accommodated, and they must also be interpreted and observed in ways which, over a period of time, will command the respect of the system's members. That they have eroded over the past few years does not mean that the whole system must be discredited.

Prospects for a new GATT round in the late 1980s are still uncertain, but the United States and Japan are pursuing the initiative, and Canada is giving its strong support. The European Community appears to remain largely unenthusiastic. Nevertheless, the probability of a new round now appears to be good, although neither the scope nor the timing is easy to predict.

The impetus behind widening international consensus in favour of new negotiations is to be found in:

- A desire to curtail protectionist pressures that are seriously threatening multilateral trade co-operation
- The resurgence of the view that GATT members either move towards further liberalization or regress to the beggar-your-neighbour policies of the 1930s
- A desire to strengthen existing international rules which constrain government fiscal practices and thus reduce budgetary deficits now frustrating growth and adjustment
- A desire to improve and to clarify existing rules to make the trading environment more predictable
- A desire to broaden the scope for international trade co-operation to cover more areas not now subject to international disciplines including, for example, trade in services

- A desire to look for a more closely co-ordinated framework that effectively takes into account the linkages between trade policy, industrial policy and international financial relations
- A desire to bring the developing countries more effectively into the multilateral framework on the basis of some reciprocity of benefit. There is growing awareness that the real solution to developing-country indebtedness lies in improved trade flows between developed and developing countries, arising from better access to developed markets.

Important as these general desires may be, real impetus is more likely to result from events in the United States, as it did for the Tokyo Round. The United States has long been, and will continue to be, the world's most attractive single market. In retrospect, the United States' devaluation of its dollar and its introduction of an import surcharge in August 1971 were crucial to launching the Tokyo Round. The present U.S. budget deficit, strong dollar, and trade and current-account deficits could precipitate another 1971-type crisis. The number of protectionist bills being readied for consideration in Congress is similarly ominous. Despite its differences with the United States, the European Community may find such threats easier to contain within the context of a general trade negotiation. The Japanese have already reached this conclusion. Experience during the Tokyo Round demonstrated that U.S. Congressional protectionism is more easily managed and held off in such a setting. The Administration shares this perception and will use it as an effective tool to advance U.S. interests.

While the impetus for a new round of multilateral trade negotiations may be fear of developments in the United States, a successful negotiation will require that participants spell out their objectives, that these objectives be reasonably compatible or susceptible to compromise, and that the major players display sufficient flexibility and political will to drive the negotiations to a successful conclusion. For its part, Canada, as one of the more important players, will have to advance its interests, pursue its objectives, and make its contribution. Broadly stated, Canada's objectives would include:

- A more ordered world trading environment, promoted by the introduction of sufficient stability, predictability and transparency in international trade relations to inspire business confidence and thus lead to job-creating investment
- More secure access to its major markets, particularly the U.S. market
- Improved opportunity for the further processing of our natural resources before export, by reducing barriers to manufactured goods
- Improved access and trading conditions for agricultural and fishery products
- An improved framework of rules that will encourage orderly adjustment in the Canadian economy.

Our trading partners share some of these objectives; there is, however, little consensus on the means of achieving them.

A new round would establish much of the international trade-policy agenda for the remainder of this century. The overall agenda would probably cover negotiations in a number of areas, including the following.

Safeguards. Participants will examine new constraints on the use of emergency measures of protection against injurious imports of particular products – the "escape-clause" provisions – covering matters such as the action on steel and lumber threatened by the United States, Canadian action on footwear, and negotiated export restraints on motor vehicles. This general issue has been subject to discussion and negotiation for more than ten years, and no resolution is in sight. The contention has come to symbolize the erosion of GATT discipline, especially for LDCs. Progress on this issue will be very difficult, but failure to make progress will further discredit the GATT system. Canada has long expressed strong support for discipline in this area.

Agriculture. Negotiations will be designed to liberalize trade in agricultural products, to limit or eliminate the use of subsidies, and to limit the trade-distorting effects of domestic support measures. Of particular concern is the problem of competitive export subsidies used to dispose of surpluses generated behind high levels of protection. Negotiations would largely revolve around U.S.-led efforts, strongly supported by Canada and Australia, to reduce the distorting effects of certain types of domestic policies. Again, progress is likely to be difficult.

Developing Countries. Members will examine the scope for liberalizing trade for the benefit of developing countries in terms of their economic development requirements, while at the same time securing increased obligations from the newly industrialized countries that continue to maintain high levels of protection. This is another very difficult issue which will require a high level of political will and U.S. leadership, and a willingness on the part of LDCs to differentiate among themselves and thus allow the more advanced among them to assume more obligations.

Government procurement. Negotiations have already commenced regarding the broadening of the existing GATT Agreement on Government Procurement. This undertaking introduces the concept of national treatment to, and non-discrimination among, parties to the Agreement in the matter of purchases by governments. Work will continue, but it is unlikely to be completed in isolation from broader multilateral negotiations which will offer the scope for the trade-offs required to strike a comprehensive deal. Negotiations, however, will not be truly multilateral in that most LDCs do not participate in the Agreement and have shown little inclination to join.

Trade in services. International rules might be developed respecting trade in those services that lend themselves to the negotiation of a general framework of rules. So far, only the United States is convinced of the need to negotiate rules; other members are prepared to examine the issues involved. "Services" in this context applies to a whole range of economic activities, including insurance, consulting, banking, accounting, advertising, transportation, communications, art, design, education, legal and health services. For a number of these activities there already exist various bilateral and multilateral agreements, such as the many bilateral air agreements and the framework of the International Civil Air Organization; for others, there are virtually no international rules. In some areas, there are many impediments to international commerce; in others, none. Many of the issues relating to trade in services are closely associated with rules about investment, such as the right of establishment. Whether such diverse economic activities are susceptible to general rules is an open question. Whether such general rules are desirable is a question at the heart of the debate.[1]

Textiles and clothing. This issue is of key interest to developing countries in view of the scheduled expiration of the GATT Multi-fibre Agreement (MFA) in July 1986. Many LDCs see U.S. and EC commitment to phasing out the MFA over the rest of the decade as a pre-condition for agreement to broader multilateral negotiations, a view these two members find hard to accept. The issue is closely related to safeguards negotiations and, together with these, symbolizes for LDCs their view that the GATT is an instrument which the more powerful countries use to legitimize their economic exploitation of the weak.

Tariffs. Members might negotiate further reductions in tariffs which continue to have important effects on trade in certain markets, such as Australia and Japan, in certain products, such as petrochemicals. At least in its early stages, a new round is likely to concentrate on harmonizing tariff structures and levels rather than on tariff cutting. Only if much progress is made on other issues is the U.S. Administration likely to seek a tariff-cutting authority from Congress.

Non-tariff measures. This is a very broad category of issues and is likely to be the main focus of the agenda. The issues involved will need to be more clearly defined before participants are likely to commit themselves to negotiations.

Resource industries. Participants might examine the possibility of further liberalizing trade in a broad range of unprocessed, semi- and fully-processed, and related machinery products of interest to primary-resource industries such as agriculture, forestry, the fishery and non-ferrous metals and minerals. This is one of Canada's chief negotiating objectives, but it is not widely shared.

Strengthening the multilateral system. An examination might be made of the scope for strengthening the institutional framework for trade co-operation (that is, the GATT processes and procedures including those related to dispute settlement) and for closer co-ordination of international trade and financial institutions. This issue touches on many others and could be identified as the theme underlying the whole of the negotiation.

The list of issues to be addressed in future negotiations is long and comprehensive, and many of the issues are extremely difficult. For none is there yet sufficient consensus to be able to indicate the likely outcome. Even though there appears to be growing political will to begin serious preparations for commencing formal negotiations, the lack of agreement on most topics suggests that the preparatory process will be prolonged. For example, LDCs are insisting that industrialized countries provide verifiable evidence that they are prepared to begin dismantling their protectionist textile- and clothing-import regimes, and this requirement may prove a stumbling block for a number of years. The reservations of the European Community about the perceived attack on its agricultural policies will make it a reluctant participant. LDC concerns about the American call for discipline in trade in services, which they consider to be aimed largely at them, will not readily be overcome.

Even when such reservations have been removed, it will not be easy for participants to reach agreement. As we noted earlier, to reach consensus among 100-odd participants is extremely difficult, especially when the dominant players are sharply divided. The European Community sees little need to strengthen the multilateral system or to reach agreement on many of the issues on the agenda. The United States may consider dismantling its textile- and clothing-import regime too high a price to pay if results in other areas do not achieve its objectives. The more advanced developing countries may find partial progress on safeguards and textile and clothing issues insufficient incentive to persuade them to accept more discipline on trade in services, particularly since they find the United Nations Conference on Trade and Development (UNCTAD) a more suitable forum than the GATT for discussing such trade.

Despite all these difficulties, progress will eventually be made, since no country is prepared to see the system collapse, and lack of progress would eventually lead to its demise. Compromises, therefore, will be made and partial solutions accepted. This stage, however, may not be reached for another decade. Each successive GATT round has taken longer to prepare and to conclude than the previous round as the numbers of issues and participants have proliferated. The Tokyo Round took five years to prepare and six years to conclude. Indeed, there are some observers who see the next round as the final one, in the sense that it will usher in a period of continuous negotiation. The number of issues is now so large and the items for negotiation are so varied that it will scarcely be possible to wrap them all into a final package which can bring negotiations to a conclusion.

For Canada, such a state of affairs has serious implications. Canada is more dependent on the international trade system than are most other GATT members and thus relies more on progress in negotiations than do most other major players. Canada, however, as already mentioned, lacks unimpeded access to a large market. What access we have is the product of, and guaranteed by, GATT negotiations. Prolonged negotiations with an uncertain outcome thus do not meet the first and most important of Canada's objectives: a more ordered world trading environment capable of stimulating job-creating investment.

Finally, if multilateral negotiations were to proceed with more dispatch than appears to be likely, and if they were to achieve more than Commissioners anticipate, would such an outcome address Canada's most important trade policy challenge: better and more secure access for three-quarters of our exports? In other words, would even the most optimistic outlook for future multilateral trade negotiations be sufficient to meet our objectives for our most important market? Commissioners think not. Take, for example, government procurement: U.S. "Buy America" provisions are a major obstacle for a number of Canadian industries, including urban transport, steel, and telecommunications equipment. The GATT Government Procurement Agreement, negotiated during the Tokyo Round and now in process of expansion in its coverage, opens up a U.S. procurement market estimated to be worth about $25 billion. This represents less than 5 per cent of the total U.S. federal and state procurement market. Current GATT negotiations may increase this proportion to 10 per cent or even 15 per cent. Canadian industry, however, would benefit greatly from application of the principle of national treatment, that is, full participation in the U.S. market equivalent to the access enjoyed by U.S. suppliers. Many business enterprises would be prepared, on this basis, to share the total Canadian market of some $50 billion. The entrepreneurs have done their sums. Even 5 per cent of the U.S. market is worth more than 50 per cent of our market. It is an objective well worth pursuing.

Similarly, during the Tokyo Round, Canada's petrochemical industry showed itself prepared to share the Canadian market in return for better access to the U.S. market. Canada pursued this objective, but it foundered on the objections of the U.S. industry to sharing that market with their EC and Japanese counterparts. Similar disappointments are likely to occur during the next multilateral negotiations. There are, as we have stated, benefits to negotiating in concert with others. The price paid, however, is that progress is sometimes held hostage to the offer of the least liberal of the major participants. Thus a country prepared to proceed further towards liberalization must scale down its sights to that of its multilateral partners.

Canada cannot, however, afford to forgo active participation in forthcoming multilateral negotiations. Rather, we must approach such negotiations realistically. Multilateral negotiations have proved of immense value in the past. They are likely to be of significant value in the future. The GATT will remain the major forum for trade liberalization and for the gradual consolidation of a rule-oriented system for conducting trade relations, but it should no longer be seen as an exclusive and sufficient forum.

Note

1. See Rodney de C. Grey, "The Service Industries: A Note of Caution About the Proposal to Negotiate Rules About Traded Services", in *Canada and the Multilateral Trading System*, vol. 10, prepared for the Royal Commission on the Economic Union and Development Prospects for Canada (Toronto: University of Toronto Press, 1985).

Conclusions

Commissioners believe that multilateral trade negotiations under the GATT should remain a central theme of Canadian trade policy. As noted in the federal government's 1983 discussion paper, *Canadian Trade Policy for the 1980s*, "given Canada's large stake in trade, Canada must in the first place seek to preserve and enhance the multilateral trading system, in fair weather or in foul. This is not a matter of choice, but one of practical necessity . . ."[1] We are unconvinced, however, that Canada should continue to pursue the multilateral route to trade expansion to the exclusion of opportunities which can best be realized bilaterally. Indeed, we believe, given the state of international consensus on reform of the multilateral system, that it would be naïve for Canada to put all its eggs in the multilateral basket. A major reform of the trading system, important as it is, does not devolve on Canada. We can play our part, but we cannot lead. Fresh opportunities await Canadians if we are willing to explore pragmatically all possible avenues to better and more secure market access, and if we view the pursuit of both the bilateral and the multilateral routes to trade liberalization as desirable, joint and complementary means to the same end. Indeed, we are of the view that multilateral trade negotiations should be seen as representing long-term possibilities largely related to a broad framework of concerns, while bilateral opportunities may be seized in the nearer future and might lead to direct benefits. This is a position shared by many intervenors who appeared before Commissioners, or who provided us with briefs. For example:

> *While continuing to give the fullest support to the maintenance and improvement of the multilateral trading system, Canada should look carefully at the means by which bilateral arrangements could be put in place to supplement our multilateral rights and obligations, and to serve as a substitute should the international support for the multilateral system begin seriously to be eroded.*
>
> (Canadian Export Association, Brief, October 23, 1983, p. 2.)

Note

1. Canada, External Affairs Canada, *Canadian Trade Policy for the 1980s: A Discussion Paper* (Ottawa: Minister of Supply and Services Canada, 1983), p. 37.

CHAPTER 6

Freer Trade with the United States

Introduction *299*

Notes 301

A New Canada-U.S. Framework for Trade *302*

The Negotiating Format 304

Substantive Provisions 310

Anti-Dumping and Countervailing Duties 313

Safeguard Action 314

Other Non-Tariff Measures 315

Adjustment Assistance and Transitional Measures 316

Implementation 318

Institutional Arrangements and Dispute Settlement 320

Notes 322

Costs and Benefits of Freer Trade with the United States *323*

Access to Markets and Canadian Competitiveness 323

Benefits to Incomes and Output 327

Regional Considerations 330

Problem Areas 331

Notes 334

The Effect of Freer Trade on Canadian Industry *336*

Sector Analysis 336

Diversity of Industrial Performance 337

Diversity of Protection 338

Diversity of Adaptation to Freer Trade 342

Conclusions from Sectoral Analysis 347

Notes 349

Political Issues *350*

Indirect Implications: The Symbolic and the Real 350

Direct Implications: Political Demands and Policy Constraints 357

Notes 367

Federalism and Achieving National Consensus *368*

Note 373

The Prospect of Freer Canada-U.S. Trade *374*

American Attitudes 376

Note 377

CHAPTER 6

Freer Trade with the United States

Introduction

In a seminal article published late in 1984, Canadian journalist Anthony Westell examined what had gone wrong with the "Third Option". This was the trade policy by which the federal government sought to strengthen the domestic foundations of the Canadian economy, diversify trade relations, and reduce Canada's vulnerability to the United States. After reviewing the problems of the "Third Option", Westell suggests that over the years, our government had, in fact, drifted gradually into the "first option": a fairly steady maintenance of the *status quo* in our relationship with the United States. What our government should have done and can still do, he argues, is to pursue the "second option": to move deliberately toward closer integration with the United States. He concludes his examination:

> *The basic argument being made here is that Canadians, both as individuals and as a political nation, are more likely to prosper and fulfill themselves in free association with Americans than they are by seeking to protect themselves from US competition and influence. The desire to escape from US influence, the desire to put distance between Canada and the United States, arises in large measure from fear of absorption by the US and from jealousy of US wealth, power and vitality. But fear and jealousy are corrosive in national as in personal life; they feed the Canadian sense of inferiority, encourage parochial attitudes, and give rise in politics to nationalist policies that are bound to fail because they are against the tide of events and against the private aspirations of most Canadians who wish to enjoy the maximum freedom to trade, invest, travel and exchange ideas.*[1]

Relations with the United States have consumed Canadian energies from our country's very beginning. Most Americans live their whole lives only dimly aware of Canada and its people, but Canadians in all provinces have always fretted about our neighbour to the south. It is not easy to live next door to the most powerful, energetic and wealthy nation in the world. One reason why Americans are wealthier than we are is that they comprise an economic union of 240 million people, while our economic union is made up of only 25 million people. In an age of specialization, a difference of such scale matters a great deal.

Whether our association with our neighbour is easy or not, we "need" the United States. It buys about a fifth of what we produce, and it sells us many of the products which make our own lives rich and varied. We watch American television, drive American cars, eat American vegetables, drink American orange juice, and wear American clothes. The United States, however, also needs us. It needs our iron ore to make cars, our paper to print newspapers, our subway cars to travel to work, and our lumber to build homes. We are not only their best customer, but also their principal supplier.[2]

The extent of our links is demonstrated by the fact that every day of the year, thousands of cars, planes, trains, trucks, people and ideas flow back and forth across the Canada-U.S. border: more traffic than between any other two nations on earth. The closeness of this relationship offers both tremendous benefit and risk of harm. We Canadians are wealthier because of the Americans, but we are also vulnerable to changes in their fortunes. In 1972, this vulnerability caused our federal government to find deliberate ways to differentiate ourselves and to strengthen our links with other trading partners. Our vulnerability, however, can also be reduced by strengthening the links we have with the United States. Canadian business has reached a stage where our domestic market can no longer assure our continued growth, and where our access to foreign markets is no longer perceived to be secure enough to stimulate long-term, job-creating investment. One senior corporate executive has pointed out:

> *We, manufacturers, are caught in a catch 22 situation. On one hand, the tariffs in Canada are no longer high enough to offset the higher costs of producing solely for the Canadian market. On the other hand, even modest tariffs into the U.S. can make it difficult, if not impossible, to set up production in Canada to export into that market. When dealing on the location of a new production facility, why locate it on the small market side of the border especially when it's dependent on exports and faces the problems of the Non-Tariff Barriers. We need to be inside those safeguards.*
>
> *Unless we can negotiate increased and assured access to the U.S. market, Canadian industry will be unable to take the risks involved in making the substantial investments required to operate on a North American basis. Whether the strategy chosen to take advantage of the U.S. potential is specialization, rationalization, or whatever, secure access to the American market is mandatory.*[3]

In Chapter 5, Commissioners examined the prospects for gaining more secure and better access to foreign markets through multilateral trade negotiations. While we are convinced that such negotiations are important to Canada's future well-being, we are not persuaded that they will address our immediate problems quickly and thoroughly enough. Nor do we believe that they are likely, in this century, to provide the best foundation for our relationship with our principal trading partner.

We turn, in this chapter, to an examination of the advantages and disadvantages of forging closer economic links with the United States. While such a relationship has often been described as one of free trade, it is both much more and much less. The economic concept of free trade (that is, trade which is unfettered by government-imposed trade restrictions), is unlikely ever to be achieved between two sovereign countries. Indeed, after 120 years of internal economic union, it does not now exist among Canada's ten provinces. Thus, trade between Canada and the United States will always be subject to more restrictions than the economists envisage. At the present time, however, and in present circumstances, it should represent more than the historic concept of free trade (that is, the removal of all tariff barriers), for even if all tariffs were to be removed, trade would still be restricted by the many other types of barriers governments have devised. What kinds of barriers, then, can be brought down bilaterally? If these barriers were removed, what would be the political and economic consequences of such a development? And what effects might that development have on Canadian industry? An examination of these issues should clarify what may be available to Canadians down the bilateral route. To avoid what Commissioners believe is a sterile debate, we shall use the terms "free trade" and "freer trade" interchangeably.

Notes

1. Anthony Westell, "Economic Integration with the USA", *International Perspectives* (November/December 1984), p. 22. For a discussion of the "Third Option", see Mitchell Sharp, "Canada-U.S. Relations: Options for the Future", *International Perspectives* (Special Issue, Autumn 1972).
2. A general review of Canada-U.S. relations can be found in Frank Stone and Carol Osmond, "Institutional Arrangements for Managing Canada-U.S. Bilateral Economic and Trade Relations", in *The International Legal Environment*, vol. 52, prepared for the Royal Commission on the Economic Union and Development Prospects for Canada (Toronto: University of Toronto Press, 1985).
3. J.E. Newall, Chairman, Du Pont Canada Inc., "Canadian Trade Challenges", an address to the Conference Board of Canada International Conference, Toronto, February 6, 1985, pp. 10–11.

A New Canada-U.S. Framework for Trade

A satisfactory analysis of the economic and political consequences of Canada-U.S. free trade should be based on some concrete notions of what a free-trade arrangement might involve, and how it would work in practice. Commissioners' purpose in this section is to analyse Canada's major options for the conduct of bilateral trade relations over the next 25 years. We are not attempting to offer advice on the most appropriate short-term negotiating agenda. Rather, our purpose is to formulate broad negotiating objectives and procedural frameworks to give direction and focus to future bilateral efforts towards freer trade.

Three basic components of a possible free-trade agreement deserve careful consideration. The first of these components is the format, or procedural framework, for conducting bilateral negotiations. Should talks, for example, focus on particular industrial sectors? Alternatively, should they aim at across-the-board liberalization? Again, should certain industries or sectors be exempt from consideration in any negotiations? The second component consists of those substantive provisions of a treaty that govern the elimination or limitation of trade barriers. Should a free-trade arrangement cover all non-tariff barriers (NTBs), including instruments of contingent protection? Should it include production or employment safeguards? The third, and perhaps most important, basic component comprises the procedures and legal mechanisms for implementing and enforcing a free-trade agreement. Should such an agreement be implemented as a formal treaty under U.S. law, a move which would require Senate ratification? Should Canada and the United States adopt a dispute-settlement procedure that incorporates the possibility of binding arbitration, a feature not fully developed in the existing enforcement system of the General Agreement on Tariffs and Trade (GATT)?[1] Another prime issue impinging on the legal organization of Canada-U.S. economic relations is the choice of a process for managing federal-provincial conflicts arising from trade-policy issues. The successful outcome of any negotiations will depend on the design of a structure to promote federal-provincial consensus and co-ordination.

These three general features of a free-trade agreement must be analysed in the context of certain broad policy objectives and constraints for North American trade liberalization. The first, and most important, concern is for Canadian producers to obtain barrier-free market access under a negotiated arrangement which ensures that access is dependable and secure from future political and legal challenges. Only if entrepreneurs and investors are confident of the arrangement's permanence and effectiveness will Canadian industry be likely to make the necessary adjustments and long-term commitments required to maximize the economic benefits of freer trade.

U.S. trade policy is created and applied through political and legal processes which decentralize decision-making power and enhance the political influence of relatively small and narrowly based interest groups such as unions and trade associations. The most notable examples of this fragmentation of power within the U.S. system are the legal mechanisms that afford producers contingent protection from import competition. These mechanisms usually involve countervailing duties, anti-dumping duties and emergency protection for U.S. producers suffering serious competitive injury from imports. U.S. legislation gives domestic producers the right to launch costly lawsuits against foreign rivals, with little risk of loss if the claims of unfair and injurious import competition are proved groundless. Since these U.S. lawsuits are initiated by private firms, it is seldom possible to predict when they will be launched. Thus the threat of harassment they pose deters Canadian investment in new plants and equipment when the future profitability of such facilities depends on uninterrupted access to the North American market. Since free trade would be of primary importance to Canadian industrial development, the federal government would need to anticipate potential problems and to spell out, as fully and precisely as possible, the rules and procedures governing any bilateral arrangement.

A second broad concern in this same area of negotiation must be the maintenance and strengthening of the GATT, the International Monetary Fund (IMF) and other multilateral economic institutions. Commissioners recognize the substantial benefits that have accrued to Canada from the GATT multilateral system. We perceive that this system will continue to serve Canada well, in part by managing Canadian relations with our most important trading partner. If North American free trade were to jeopardize or undermine the stability of the GATT system, it would be a steep price for Canadians to pay in order to secure improved access to the U.S. market. There is no inconsistency in principle, however, between continued support for the GATT and a Canada-U.S./free-trade arrangement. GATT law authorizes the creation of free-trade areas under certain conditions, and it is particularly important that any Canada-U.S. agreement be designed to comply with that treaty's legal requirements. Basically, Article XXIV of the General Agreement states that in order to qualify as legally valid, a free-trade agreement must require the elimination of all barriers or restrictions on "substantially all trade" among the signatories. A review of cases involving the application of Article XXIV indicates that if parties to an arrangement free 80 per cent, by value, of the commodities they trade, they will be deemed to have satisfied the GATT's "substantially all trade" standard. While it seems probable that Canada and the United States could negotiate a mutually acceptable agreement that satisfied this test, Article XXIV imposes somewhat flexible constraints on the terms of any treaty used to create bilateral free trade.

Finally, it is important that any formal arrangement be designed to mitigate the inevitable tensions that it would create for Canadians. On the one hand, we have a natural desire for closer trade relations with the United States; on the other hand, we are determined to preserve our national autonomy in social, economic and defence policies even when this choice requires that we chart a policy course different from that adopted by our closest partner and ally. Free trade will intensify competition for many Canadians, whether they work in export-oriented businesses or in firms concentrating on our domestic market. Stronger competitive pressures, in turn, will further political initiatives aimed at modifying such federal and provincial policies that put U.S. firms at a disadvantage in relation to our tax and regulatory measures. Moreover, closer trade relations will increase the force of U.S. political influence at both levels of Canadian government. In future bilateral disputes unrelated to trade in goods and services as GATT would traditionally define it, the American government might be tempted to threaten the suspension or unilateral alteration of any existing free-trade agreement, in order to persuade Canada to accept a compromise that was relatively more favourable to U.S. interests. Canada would hold larger economic stakes in preserving an effective bilateral free-trade agreement than would the United States, and it is therefore important to negotiate a legal arrangement which incorporates strong safeguards. These limitations must constrain the power of either nation to use the trade relation to influence other public policies that are functionally unrelated to trade in goods and services.

The Negotiating Format

Canadian Trade Policy for the 1980s[2] indicated that the Canadian government would study options for achieving freer trade with the United States. One plausible strategy it suggested was to negotiate bilateral free-trade agreements that are limited to a number of specific industries. In early 1984, Canada's International Trade Minister Regan and U.S. Trade Representative Brock announced a joint national study of the prospects for liberalizing trade in four product areas: steel, farm machinery, urban transit equipment, and computer services. These recent expressions of interest in a sectoral negotiation might well be attributed to several advantages of an industry-by-industry approach to freer trade. To negotiate on a sectoral basis limits the scope of potential problems of economic adjustment which might, in some circumstances, entail higher public expenditures. Moreover, a piecemeal or incremental approach focuses the issues in ways that encourage both bilateral negotiations and public debate: that is to say, it gives the free-trade initiative a concrete set of objectives that can be analysed and discussed quite readily.

A sectoral negotiating approach, however, is open to several serious objections. An agreement to remove tariff and non-tariff barriers in only a few industries or sectors might violate GATT Article XXIV, which requires that a free-trade agreement remove barriers to "substantially all" the trade between the signatories in order to qualify as a valid preferential arrangement. Canada and the United States could answer a legal challenge under this regulation by maintaining that bilateral trade has already been freed enough to justify future step-by-step reductions. This defence against a charge of using bilateral trade restrictions would be a strong one if only tariff barriers were considered, but if NTBs were also taken into account, the factual support for this defence would be weaker. The U.S. Administration sought and obtained an explicit waiver of compliance with the provisions of Article XXIV when the Auto Pact was negotiated in the mid-1960s. Such a waiver requires the consent of two-thirds of the GATT contracting parties, and Commissioners believe that it would be politically difficult to employ this procedure to validate a series of sectoral agreements in the mid-1980s.

A second disadvantage of sectoral bargaining is that it offers an unwieldy format for dealing with the critical issue of contingent protection. Sectoral bargaining would make it necessary, for example, to negotiate industry-specific exemptions from U.S. and Canadian laws regulating unfair trade practices, and industries that are not accorded exempt status might perceive such exemptions as unjust.

A third objection applies to the practical politics of the sectoral approach to free trade. An industry-by-industry approach limits inter-sectoral trade-offs during free-trade negotiations and makes it more difficult to organize effective political coalitions in support of trade liberalization. Canadian and U.S. firms operating in sectors targeted for negotiation are likely to support or oppose freer trade according to their assessment of prospects for their particular industry or firm. The problem is that investors and employees in industries unaffected by the bargaining are unlikely to provide much support for freer trade in other sectors. Moreover, if negotiations are limited to only a few sectors, there is unlikely to be sufficient public support to overcome the inevitable resistance to the withdrawal of protectionist measures. A further disadvantage would be the possibility of more severe trade distortions in sectors such as textiles, where producers might lobby for imposing more restrictive import quotas on third countries if imports from the preferred trading partner increase. Distortions could also arise if end products are traded free of barriers, while trade in primary products or intermediate goods remains subject to restrictions. For example, free trade in wine might not be sustainable without free trade in grapes if U.S. growers enjoyed substantial cost advantages over their Canadian rivals.

In contrast to a sectoral approach, negotiations aimed at securing a broader, more general, free-trade area would be consistent with GATT principles; they would also avoid many of the political and economic disadvantages of a piecemeal strategy for trade liberalization. Again, a general or "across-the-board" approach would be more likely to promote productive bargaining on the critical issue of contingent protection and on the elimination of other non-tariff barriers which affect many sectors. This Commission is firmly of the opinion, therefore, that a limited sectoral/free-trade arrangement with the United States would go only a short way towards meeting Canada's negotiating objectives. The need is for a broader or comprehensive free-trade arrangement.[3]

Three basic types of across-the-board arrangements have been discussed as feasible options for North American economic integration: a common market, a customs union, and a free-trade area. It is important to distinguish among these three possibilities because much of the public debate on the general issue of "free trade with the United States" has been confused by a failure to do so.

A common market calls for:

- Free movement of goods and services among member countries
- Common tariffs and harmonization of protected-trade policies applied to the outside world (that is, to non-members)
- Free movement of labour and capital among member countries.

This arrangement is the most complete form of economic integration in current use that maintains the political sovereignty and formal independence of member countries. It is not, however, the most complete form of integration *per se*. A common market need not, for example, form a monetary union where the member countries share a single currency that is subject to a single central bank's monetary policy. To form a common market is the primary objective of the European Community (EC), and its member countries have made great strides in harmonizing their economic policies, even though much remains to be done.

For two major reasons this Commission rejects the common-market form of free trade as inappropriate in the North American context. A common market requires that a uniform set of trade and allied commercial policies be applied to all non-member countries. In the past, Canada has not always wished to follow U.S. initiatives on trade with the outside world: for instance, Canada maintained trade relations with China and Cuba after the United States ceased to do so. If we Canadians are to preserve our autonomy in foreign political and economic policies, our government cannot accept a common market's legal restrictions on its capacity for independent action. Again, a common market would require the co-ordination of other policies besides those concerned with foreign trade, since it involves the "free movement" of both labour and capital among member states. Control over foreign immigration is a basic and very important national policy, and the obvious need for Canada to maintain control in this field is sufficient reason to rule out a common market. Moreoever, in Commissioners' view, it will be desirable for Canada to reserve the right to exercise some controls over the movement of U.S. capital into this country. Such reservations to enable Canada to deal with specific problems arising from the operation of U.S.-controlled firms in our country would be impermissible under a common market.

In a customs union, Canada and the United States would have to agree to remove all barriers to their trade in goods and services, and to impose a single set of commercial policies on imports from third countries. Since Commissioners have already argued that a common external trade policy would be unacceptable to Canada, we must also reject the option of a customs union with the United States. Because of the relative size of the two countries, Canada could not hope to exercise equal influence in establishing a common set of tariff and tariff-related policies; thus the commercial policy of both nations would be made, by and large, in Washington. For example, a customs union would not allow Canada to reduce protection against third countries unless it could persuade the United States to take the same action. Given the possibilities for conflict that inevitably lie in such a high degree of policy co-ordination between two countries, a less ambitious form of association is desirable. Any such tight co-ordination is likely to be politically unacceptable to both nations, nor would it be required to achieve most or all of the economic benefits of Canada-U.S. free trade.

A free-trade area is the form of across-the-board arrangement most often suggested for Canada and the United States. In such an area, each country may impose its own restrictions on movements of capital and labour between partner countries. Each nation has the right, also, to levy its own taxes and to stipulate its own regulations for goods entering from third countries. All that the free-trade agreement guarantees is that for the most part, goods and services originating in a member country may enter other member countries free of tariff and non-tariff restrictions. A process of elimination leads Commissioners to regard this form of arrangement as more advantageous than either a common market or a customs union. Any less broadly encompassing form of agreement threatens to leave Canadian investors and employees handicapped by the constraints of a relatively limited domestic market. Any more comprehensive arrangement is unacceptable because of the constraints it would place on Canada's ability to pursue its own social and economic policies.

Several additional considerations suggest the choice of a bilateral free-trade agreement. Since each member would be free to reduce its tariffs against third countries, a free-trade arrangement might lead to fewer global trade restrictions than would a common market or a customs union. On the other hand, each member could pursue import-substitution policies sanctioned by the GATT against products from non-member countries, without the need for practising complete consistency with its partner's policies. Moreover, it is relatively easy to bring new nations into a free-trade area because its expansion avoids the costly and time-consuming process of policy harmonization that must accompany the two more comprehensive forms of free-trade arrangement.

What, then, would be the nature of a Canada-U.S., bilateral, free-trade agreement? And how would it work? The answer to the first question need not be speculative, for there are international models of free-trade agreements that could guide any Canada-U.S. action. One example appears in the 1983 Trade Agreement between New Zealand and Australia, which is designed to eliminate mutual trade restrictions and to create a free-trade area. This agreement provides that for most products, New Zealand and Australian tariffs on each other's exports will fall to nil by the mid-1990s. Some products are excepted, of course, to take account of special circumstances. On the non-tariff side, there is a series of Articles that curtail the right of each country to apply non-tariff barriers, such as countervailing duties or safeguard measures, against the other country's exports. To administer the accord, the Trade Agreement provides that the ministers concerned meet annually to review the arrangement, and, further, that if difficulties arise, consultations be undertaken promptly, at the written request of either partner. If such a consultative mechanism were used in North America, it would be wholly consistent with the ordinary flow of government business between Canada and the United States.

Canadian public opinion has occasionally seen the operation of a Canada-U.S./free-trade agreement as enormously significant. To assess how a free-trade agreement might actually work, however, let us consider the Canadian manufacture of ordinary lead pencils and crayons, which, in 1984, carried a Canadian tariff of 14.6 per cent of their value. Under the Tokyo Round concessions already accepted, that tariff is designed to fall to 11.3 per cent by 1987, and this projected move will promote adjustment to world-wide competition in this Canadian industry. Under a Canada-U.S./free-trade agreement, the tariff on these products might be further reduced to nil; the reductions might be phased in, for example, between 1987 and 1997. This arrangement would mean that during the ten-year adjustment period, Canadian producers of pencils and crayons would see the products of their American competitors becoming cheaper at the rate of approximately 1.1 per cent per year. The falling Canadian tariff would lower consumer prices in Canada and stimulate competitiveness and productivity as well, but its effects would hardly be sudden, nor would they be devastating to the Canadian economy. Moreover, any negative effects on Canadian business that did result would have to be balanced against the compensating benefits in other areas, where Canada would gain from falling U.S. tariffs. What both sides in such a debate need, above all, is a sense of proportion: bilateral free trade would be neither a panacea for Canada nor a disaster. On balance, however, it would help our country.

Within the framework of a general free-trade agreement, it would still be possible to exclude certain sectors or industries from the scope of bilateral negotiations. Article XXIV of the GATT has been interpreted to authorize the exclusion of up to 20 per cent of the total trade in goods among the members of a legitimate free-trade area. Moreover, since trade in services lies outside the jurisdiction of the GATT, Canada and the United States are not legally constrained to remove all barriers affecting it. There is, therefore, no legal impediment to the negotiation of a limited number of exclusions on a case-by-case basis. Several Canadian industries might, in fact, have special needs or problems that would justify their total or partial exclusion from a general free-trade regime. While Commissioners do not believe that any industry should automatically be excluded from consideration, nevertheless, we recognize that as negotiations proceed, it may prove necessary to make exceptions. Such a development would be entirely consistent with our understanding of a free-trade agreement.

Both Canada and the United States use import quotas to restrict trade in some agricultural products.[4] Both nations impose quotas on poultry, dairy and some meat products, in support of their domestic supply-management programs. Canada also imposes seasonal tariffs on fresh produce in order to support farm incomes. The removal of these quotas and tariffs would necessitate a co-ordinated approach to the supply-management and other agricultural support policies currently maintained by both countries. The task of harmonizing these policies through extensive negotiations with the United States is likely to be technically complex and politically difficult. These potential problems may justify deferring free trade for agricultural products to which import quotas currently apply, at least until detailed agreements can be worked out concerning supply-management and other subsidy policies.

The U.S. Administration has recently stressed the need for liberalizing trade in services, principally transportation, communications, banking, insurance, engineering and construction, and business consulting. It has indicated that the reduction of barriers to trade in services will be one of its top-priority negotiating objectives in any future GATT round. Trade in service industries will probably figure prominently in any Canada-U.S. trade talks.

Several of Canada's service industries, such as banking, insurance and allied financial activities, would appear to be capable of substantial export successes in the U.S. market. The removal of existing Canadian restrictions on the entry of U.S. firms in some fields could result in significant penetration of Canadian markets by U.S.-based competitors without conferring comparable benefits in the other direction. Overall, it is likely that the United States has more to gain from the reciprocal reduction of barriers to trade in services than has Canada. For this reason, perhaps, Canada might reasonably expect that in return for its willingness to provide more open access to its services market, the United States might offer guarantees of improved access for goods exported from Canada.

Despite U.S. enthusiasm for rapid progress in trade in services, several difficulties might lie in the way of a broad across-the-board approach to liberalizing bilateral trade in many types of services. Although both governments have recently undertaken exploratory research, there is still insufficient objective information on the economic consequences of existing national regulatory barriers to trade in services. Both Canada and the United States maintain entry controls and similar regulations which exclude foreign-controlled enterprises or limit their allowed share of the domestic market in many service sectors such as banking, transportation and communications; other barriers, too, operate in particular sectors. Any useful analysis of service-trade issues must focus, therefore, on the national regulatory arrangements specific to each particular type of service. For example, government-procurement preferences for local suppliers are a major impediment to trade in engineering and construction services, while restrictions and cost-increasing regulations on the trans-border transmission of business data are a major irritant to those who trade in financial and business-consulting services. The negotiations on this diverse set of problems will be further complicated by considerable differences in the national regulatory policies that currently apply in many service sectors. Free trade in transportation or in financial services, for instance, will require the harmonization of diverse national rules governing price competition, service quality, consumer protection and other equally contentious matters. The fact that each particular service industry is affected by regulations that are virtually unique suggests that future negotiations on services should be conducted on a sectoral basis. While it may be desirable to establish some general rules applicable to all service sectors, such as a code for government procurement, it seems clear that more detailed standards and the settlement of future disputes will have to be handled by specialized bilateral bodies responsible for particular service industries.

Cultural activities may also require special treatment under a general free-trade agreement. Canada provides both import protection and subsidies for cultural activities, because of the widely held view that our domestic market is not large enough to support these activities. Current policies aimed at creating and disseminating more Canadian cultural products, such as the so-called "Canadian content" rules imposed by the Canadian Radio-television and Telecommunications Commission (CRTC), discriminate against U.S. firms in the cultural industries and might therefore be inconsistent with a general free-trade scheme. Talks with the United States might show that many existing policies would be compatible with the maintenance of an acceptable free-trade regime; those that did cause substantial competitive distortions could be replaced by more-or-less equally effective substitute measures. In any event, Canada could insist on explicit treaty provisions that would authorize public funding of its cultural activities and permit affirmative discrimination for Canadian producers, in order to compensate for the handicap of our small domestic market. The examples of the European Free Trade Association (EFTA) and the European Community demonstrate that substantial subsidization of cultural activities is possible within an effective free-trade framework.

Finally, there may be a need for special rules to govern bilateral trade in energy and other natural resources. Canadians' principal concern regarding natural resources is whether a free-trade arrangement would constrain our ability to impose production quotas, taxes and export controls, to further national security and industrial policy objectives. The GATT specifically provides for such controls, unless they are discriminatory or act as disguised restrictions on international trade. National tax and subsidy policies governing petroleum products will need to be harmonized to some extent. The most difficult negotiating problems are likely to centre on the potential use of export controls covering non-renewable commodities such as oil and perhaps, in the future, water. It is possible, for instance, that the United States may seek to negotiate some legal assurance of access to future Canadian resource supplies. Any guarantee to U.S. resource consumers must, however, preserve Canada's authority to limit exports in order to meet anticipated domestic requirements for such resources. Article XX(g) of the GATT permits signatories to maintain non-discriminatory measures "relating to the conservation of exhaustible natural resources if such measures are made effective in conjunction with restrictions on domestic production or consumption." A similar provision could be included in any general agreement covering trade in non-renewable resources.

Commissioners have described these areas of economic activity, not because we doubt there is substantial scope for removing obstacles to trade in these sectors, but because we recognize that these are among the most difficult areas in which to achieve full free trade. The United States undoubtedly has similar concerns. Our view, however, is that such obstacles should not stand in the way of agreement. While we believe a sectoral approach to be unwise, the temporary or even permanent exemption of certain sectors might be a prudent or even a necessary means to reach agreement.

Substantive Provisions

As we have noted, Article XXIV of the GATT directs that the parties to a general agreement eliminate all barriers to substantially all their trade in goods as a prerequisite to the creation of a valid free-trade area. A Canada-U.S./free-trade agreement should regulate the three general types of barriers that currently restrict trade between the two nations: tariffs, contingent-protection measures, and other non-tariff barriers (NTBs). Canada must certainly negotiate for effective restraints on American contingent-protection measures and other NTBs; an agreement aimed only at phasing out tariffs would not provide the security of access required by Canadian producers. Since both national legal systems sharply differentiate the legal instruments and procedures used to implement these three types of trade barriers, it will be necessary to draft specific treaty rules applicable to each one.

When the Tokyo Round tariff cuts are fully implemented in 1987, it has been estimated that some 80 per cent of Canada's exports to the United States will enter that country duty free; a further 15 per cent will enter at duties of 5 per cent or less, and only 5 per cent will enter at higher duties. These figures are somewhat misleading, however, as they mask the fact that certain commodities are not traded because of U.S. tariffs that effectively neutralize the comparative advantage of Canadian producers. In other words, an exclusive focus on our current sales to the United States obscures the fact that our exports tend to flow through duty-free holes in the U.S. tariff wall that are open to such Canadian exports as resources and autos. In 1987, a significant number of manufacturing firms in Canada will still be deterred from exporting goods by remaining U.S. tariffs. In certain resource sectors, U.S. tariffs set at 2 or 3 per cent are still high enough to discourage new investment in Canadian mines and plants. From the U.S. standpoint, the removal of Canadian tariffs is likely to confer substantial benefits on many manufacturing industries. Nevertheless, while the overall incidence of the Canadian tariff is likely to be lower than 5 per cent by 1987, the average tariff on dutiable goods will stand at 9 to 10 per cent, and some tariffs will remain as high as 25 per cent. An appropriate procedure for cutting both nations' tariffs to zero will need to be spelled out clearly in any free-trade agreement. GATT Article XXIV permits a "reasonable" amount of time for gradual implementation of free-trade arrangements. There are a number of options available for tariff elimination which are worthy of careful consideration.

One possibility is to eliminate tariffs completely on a particular date, which might be announced two or three years in advance. This would give firms a deadline around which to plan the rationalization of their operations in order both to meet new competition and to enter the U.S. market. This adjustment could well require considerable new investment in capital equipment and in the training of workers in new skills.

Another possibility would be to agree to phase in the tariff cuts over a number of years. The rate at which Canadian and U.S. tariffs were cut could differ. As it is widely acknowledged that greater industrial adjustments will be required in Canada, a case might be made for a slower phase-out of Canadian tariffs to ease the adjustment process, say over a period of ten years, while the United States would eliminate tariffs in five years. This arrangement would provide Canadian producers with better access to the U.S. market while they still retained some temporary protection in the Canadian market.

The choice of a method of tariff removal will hinge on an evaluation of the ensuing adjustment process. Whatever method is chosen, Commissioners expect that an extensive program of adjustment assistance will be desirable to achieve the benefits of freer trade with the least cost. We shall review this question in Parts III and V of this Report.

In contrast to a customs union and a common market, which impose common external tariffs, a free-trade area retains differences in national tariff levels and tariff policies where these measures affect third parties. Since each member of a free-trade area sets its own external tariff, third countries have an incentive to get their exports into the free-trade area by first shipping them into the member country with the lower external tariff and then sending them into the other member's market duty free. To prevent such "deflections of trade", Canada and the United States would have to establish "rules of origin", stipulating that imports from a third country must satisfy national-content requirements in order to qualify for free entry. A rules-of-origin system may be liberal or strict. A liberal system allows a substantial proportion of the value of "free-trade/area products" to originate in non-member countries. The European Free Trade Association, for example, has adopted a liberal set of rules of origin which generally provide that a product qualifies for duty-free treatment if at least 50 per cent of its export price originated in activities conducted within the free-trade area. EFTA countries initially feared that sizeable deflections of trade to lower-tariff members of the free-trade area would occur unless relatively strict rules of origin were adopted; these suggested rules required that 70 per cent of a product's export price originate in the free area. The disadvantage of a strict regime is that if other free-trade/area members are not the least-cost suppliers for semi-processed and raw-material inputs, export-oriented industries may find themselves priced out of third-country markets because of their input-cost disadvantage. The EFTA's liberal rules of origin have, however, worked reasonably smoothly, and there has been relatively little of the trade diversion that was anticipated. One factor considered important to this successful result was that in EFTA countries, tariff levels on raw materials and semi-processed goods were low or non-existent. Since the same general situation prevails for Canadian and U.S. customs duties, it is likely that a liberal origin system would provide adequate protection from harmful trade deflection.

In addition to a phased withdrawal of tariffs and effective rules of origin, the Canada-U.S./free-trade agreement would also have to deal with a range of NTBs that have substantially impeded trade between the two countries. As events of recent years have demonstrated, Canada's exports of goods to the U.S. market are vulnerable to several different types of barriers. The policy rationales and procedures governing these NTBs must be taken into account in designing a free-trade arrangement. U.S. non-tariff barriers affecting Canadian exports can be separated into two basic categories:

- Measures of contingent protection, principally anti-dumping duties, countervailing duties and safeguard or "escape-clause" actions
- Laws or regulations which, either explicitly or through administrative practice, impose discriminatory burdens on goods of foreign origin through

government-procurement practices, product-quality and safety standards, quantitative restrictions on agricultural products, and similar measures.

Measures of contingent protection can be further subdivided into those governing "fair" trade (such as safeguard actions), and those regulating certain "unfair" trading practices (such as anti-dumping and countervailing duty proceedings). This "fair/unfair" distinction arises from the GATT rules which authorize nations to retaliate with compensatory duties on imports benefiting from foreign subsidies and on imports that are "dumped", that is, sold for export at prices lower than those prevailing in the exporter's home market. U.S. firms that can prove material or non-negligible commercial injury by way of lost sales or declining profits caused by subsidized or dumped imports are legally entitled to demand the imposition of retaliatory customs duties calculated to offset the unfair competitive advantage favouring the imported products. Of course, the main problem with these contingent measures aimed at unfair practices is that they may be employed by U.S. competitors to harass Canadian exporters for technical or extremely minor infractions of the rules or even for perceived infractions resulting from different laws or practices.

Safeguard or escape-clause action differs in several important respects from these defensive unfair-trade measures. The GATT provides that temporary protection against imports which cause "serious injury" to the sales or profit levels of domestic producers is legitimate, provided that the retaliatory duties or quotas are imposed on a most-favoured-nation (MFN) basis, and that agreement is reached with exporting nations which are adversely affected by the safeguard action. (Agreement usually involves compensation or guarantees concerning the duration of, or other limitations on, the protective measures imposed.) Proceedings for safeguard protection can be initiated by private individuals or groups, but the final arbiter in the United States is the President, who is given broad legal discretion to grant or deny safeguard relief. In Canada, Cabinet is the final arbiter in this matter. In the past decade, American Presidents have adopted the practice of providing safeguard protection by negotiating "voluntary export restraints" or "orderly marketing arrangements" with the exporting countries whose firms were principally responsible for the injurious imports. While this U.S. Administrative practice probably violates the GATT requirements for valid safeguard action, it is highly beneficial to Canada, whose exporters have rarely been the principal sources of commercial injury to their U.S. competitors. Given the existing structure of U.S. foreign-trade regulations, how should a Canada-U.S. agreement deal with these existing and contingent impediments to North American free trade?

Anti-Dumping and Countervailing Duties

It is improbable that any U.S. Administration would agree simply to exempt Canadian goods from the possible application of anti-dumping or countervailing duties. Such an agreement would seem possible only if Canada were prepared to accept stringent obligations to prevent subsidies or dumping which resulted in serious disruption of U.S. markets. It would not be necessary for Canada to promise that its governments would never provide subsidies, or that its exporters would never dump, but rather to agree that both parties should accept a binding obligation to ensure that neither subsidies nor dumping caused an unreasonable degree of disruption in their respective markets. Under such a broad legal principle, questions of interpretation and enforcement would determine the efficacy of the agreement.

Another option would be to alter U.S. federal law to provide that Canadian goods would not be included with the products of other countries for the purpose of determining whether a U.S. industry had suffered "material injury", a prerequisite for the imposition of both anti-dumping and countervailing duties. In other words, dumped or subsidized imports from Canada could only be restrained if it were established that they were exclusively responsible for creating a material level of injury to U.S. competitors. Canada has won most significant countervailing duty cases in which Canadian goods were the alleged principal source of injury because U.S. producers have been unable to prove the existence of a *material* level of lost sales or reduced profits caused by Canadian imports, such as softwood lumber and urban transport equipment. The six cases where countervailing duties were imposed by the United States, between 1975 and 1979, on Canadian exports were all terminated in 1980, when the American government introduced the injury test, and American producers were unable to prove material injury.

A third option for limiting the impact of U.S. unfair trade-practice regulations is to shift their enforcement from a national administrative tribunal (that is, the United States International Trade Commission) to some new intergovernmental body established under the free-trade arrangement. On this basis, the agreement could contain provisions establishing a standing tribunal to adjudicate on anti-dumping and countervailing duty complaints originating from private industry or labour groups in either country. The tribunal would, in effect, assume the administrative and executive decision-making functions that are currently performed in Ottawa and Washington. This strategy for improving security of access would place principal reliance on the neutrality of an essentially judicial panel composed of appointees from both nations and a neutral chairperson possibly selected from third countries or chosen by agreement of the national appointees. An effective panel system would probably also require the creation of an administrative support staff possessing commercial, economic and legal expertise. The staff might be assembled from government officials seconded from departments with responsibility for trade, economic development and external affairs. A panel and staff composed in this way should ensure the even-handed application of existing national rules on dumping and subsidized imports.

Safeguard Action

A modest Canada-U.S. agreement was signed in February 1984, to provide for advance notification of safeguard proceedings initiated in either country.

The agreement provides for at least 30 days' notice before restrictions are imposed; consultations on measures to minimize any adverse effects; and a declaration that short-term tariff relief is preferable to quantitative restraints as the instrument for providing safeguard protection. It is clear that any agreement which would provide more secure market access for Canadian and U.S. exporters would have to impose more substantial constraints on the use of U.S. and Canadian safeguard action. The rules discussed here governing safeguards against fairly traded, but politically intolerable, imports should be distinguished from the adjustment or transitional measures that may be used to implement a free-trade agreement. The parties to such an arrangement might agree to permit safeguard protection in specified circumstances during, for example, a ten-year period following the signing of the pact. The problem raised here is whether safeguard action should ever be available to the parties after the adjustment or transition period expires.

One can argue that the preferred solution would be the complete dismantling of safeguard protection applicable to goods originating in either country. The main purpose of a free-trade arrangement's guarantee of market access may well be to create positive incentives for the parties to undertake industrial restructuring. In this instance, the continued availability of safeguard protection to firms injured by imports would substantially undermine the economic goal of the signatories. On the other hand, a free-trade agreement which offered no prospect of escape for injured domestic industries would probably attract substantial political opposition in both nations. An alternative to a complete dismantling of protection is to draft a rule providing that only if Canadian exports were found to be the primary cause of serious injury to U.S. competitors would the safeguard action apply to Canadian producers. Another possibility would be to retain safeguard measures, but to transfer the responsibility for their enforcement (that is, for determining whether a domestic industry had, in fact, suffered serious injury) to a transnational panel or tribunal created by the free-trade agreement. Therefore, as with anti-dumping and countervailing duties, the choice of a negotiating strategy on safeguards depends, in part, on designing appropriate institutions for implementing the free-trade arrangement.

Other Non-Tariff Measures

The remaining major non-tariff measures which now limit Canadian exports to the United States are:

- Discriminatory federal- and state-government/procurement practices
- Federal and state product standards that conflict with prevailing Canadian standards
- Federal customs-classification rules and administrative procedures that impose unreasonable cost burdens on exports from Canada.

It is essential that any proposed free-trade agreement provide some effective mechanism for removing or limiting the protectionist effects of these U.S. laws and policies. The major drafting problem relating to these NTBs derives from their resistance to control through the enforcement of detailed rules. A prime example of this difficulty appears in government-procurement practices. North American governments employ dozens of strategies for discriminating in favour of domestic suppliers in the tendering processes. While explicit statutory discrimination, such as the federal and state "Buy America" laws, would be repealed under a free-trade agreement, the attempt to write specific rules to eliminate discrimination in government contracting would create strong incentives to invent new ways to circumvent that agreement. This problem of detailed rules is related to a second impediment to the predictable regulation of these NTBs. Some non-tariff measures may be justifiable on national policy grounds, in spite of their trade-limiting effects. Consumer-product/safety standards covering lawnmowers, for example, may specify the installation of certain protective devices when these items are offered for sale in the U.S. market. If Canada did not require the use of similar devices, would Canadian manufacturers be justified in arguing that the U.S. safety standard imposed an unreasonable burden on imports from Canada? This may seem an isolated example, but there have been many instances in which it has been difficult to determine whether divergent national product standards were motivated by legitimate differences in safety or consumer-protection policies, or by a desire to discriminate against foreign goods. (One instance of the latter motive appeared in the Canada-U.S. metal can-grading dispute.) In short, reasonable people will frequently have differences of opinion concerning acceptable justifications for limiting or restricting trade among nations.

A Canada-U.S./free-trade agreement should, then, contain detailed codes of national conduct controlling government procurement, product standards and customs procedures. Yet the experience with similar codes of conduct under the GATT indicates that highly detailed rules are relatively easy to circumvent, and that effective implementation of such an agreement requires the application, on a case-by-case basis, of general standards prohibiting unnecessary or unjustified protection against imports. Thus problems exist both in finding means to prevent evasion of the proposed agreement and in managing what are likely to be difficult questions of legal and political judgement in interpreting the agreement's provisions. These problems suggest that the design of an effective institution for implementing the agreement would be the primary determinant of the treaty's future success in regulating non-tariff measures.

Adjustment Assistance and Transitional Measures

Commissioners' assessment of the economic costs of free trade indicates that Canadian investors and employees are likely to bear relatively larger adjustment burdens than their U.S. counterparts. A free-trade agreement should therefore incorporate explicit provisions that reflect the proportionately greater costs of adjustment that Canadians will face. It should provide for transitional safeguards which permit temporary limits on the speed of adjustment, and it should operate to smooth out the dislocation and re-employment of workers and physical capital. One legal mechanism that can be employed to provide temporary relief from import competition is the system of "trigger points" used in the Sweden-EC/free-trade agreement. Basically, this mechanism establishes a temporary safeguard scheme that is triggered if imports flood in at higher-than-anticipated rates after the free-trade agreement is put into effect. This scheme would allow more-severely affected industries to delay meeting the general tariff-cutting schedule established by the treaty. The agreement should clearly establish, however, that these authorized delays in the removal of protective measures are nothing more than short-term transitional safeguards. The history of these provisions, as they relate to permanent employment or value-added guarantees, suggests that the more specific the attempt to protect existing Canadian employment patterns, the greater will be the administrative and political difficulties of enforcing the agreement. Many of the problems encountered with the Auto Pact guarantees, for example, including the long-standing dispute concerning their intended duration, are inherent in this form of contractual undertaking. Similar problems are likely to surface if such provisions are included in the free-trade agreement.

Other trade-liberalization experiences, such as the formation of the European Community and EFTA, and the initiation of the Kennedy Round, suggest that adjustment costs resulting from the removal of trade barriers have turned out to be smaller than expected. Moreover, two institutions already exist that should help to reduce the costs of short-term adjustment. The flexible Canadian exchange rate should provide some braking mechanism against a rapid influx of imports and a loss of employment in Canada. Moreover, the presence of U.S. multi-nationals in Canada may also make our adjustment easier, since they already have facilities for distributing throughout the United States any newly specialized output of their Canadian plants. Despite the aid of these natural balancing forces, there is widespread anxiety about the severity of adjustment burdens which particularly import-sensitive industries might have to bear as a result of Canada-U.S. free trade. Commissioners are certain that an extensive adjustment-assistance program will be needed as an integral part of any free-trade arrangement, both to assist factors of production leaving declining industries and to promote their rapid absorption into expanding sectors. Since investors, workers and managers will begin to plan their strategies for adjustment even before a final agreement is reached, it is essential that both nations accept an overall adjustment-assistance framework well in advance of concluding a formal treaty.

Transitional assistance could take many forms: government-backed loans, special research and development (R&D) grants, or accelerated depreciation for Canadian firms which are rationalizing in order to expand into the U.S. market.[5] Commissioners' preference, however, is for programs designed to support displaced workers and to speed up their retraining or re-employment. Much of what Commissioners will have to say in Parts III and V about the design of effective and equitable adjustment programs (including the proposed Transitional Adjustment Assistance Program) is directly applicable to managing the process of industrial change that will result from free trade. Any adjustment subsidies would have to be authorized explicitly by the agreement and would therefore be exempt from U.S. countervailing duties.

Finally, Commissioners have been intrigued by the suggestion, made in 1984 by an "old hand" experienced in negotiating trade agreements with the United States. Speaking to a conference on U.S.-Canadian economic relations sponsored by the Brookings Institution, Simon Reisman suggested that one way to ensure stability in a free-trade arrangement would be to establish a Canada-U.S. Trade Disruption Insurance Program (TDIP). Under such a scheme the two governments would establish and, initially, support a fund in proportion to the exports of each to the other; later the fund would be maintained by a small premium on exports. It would insure exporters against damages resulting from trade-disrupting measures adopted by either government. A board of directors would consider claims and assess either government for damages. Mr. Reisman went on to say:

> *A program of this kind would go a long way toward removing fears about commercial policy instability that inhibit investment and trade. It is put forward on the assumption that actual restrictive measures would be infrequent, an assumption not inconsistent with recent experience. Because a trade restriction would be costly, the obligation to replenish the fund would itself serve as a deterrent to its use.*[6]

While Commissioners see no need to develop such a scheme in detail in these pages, we are confident that measures such as this can and should be developed to add to the integrity of any Canada-U.S./free-trade agreement.

Implementation

In order to be legally and politically effective, any free-trade agreement requires independent governing institutions and implementation procedures. These arrangements are needed to ensure that the legislation and regulations of both member nations be brought into full compliance with the treaty's provisions. Canada's need for dependable market access suggests that an effective intergovernmental body should be established to administer the agreement, and that a legally binding process should be designed for resolving disputes over the proper interpretation of its obligations. Because there would likely be opposition from those groups of investors and workers who would bear the costs of adjusting to freer trade, it is equally important that a Canada-U.S./free-trade arrangement should be implemented through legal processes which would ensure its political durability and provide safeguards against subsequent national laws or regulations that would detract from its essentials.

To implement the free-trade arrangement under U.S. domestic law, the agreement could be structured as a formal treaty, or it could be put into effect through conforming federal and state legislation. The primary advantage of a treaty is that its provisions would clearly take precedence over any state statute which legislated trade barriers; its existence would also impose procedural constraints on subsequent federal legislation. Thus, implementation through a formal treaty would provide Canadian exporters with a strong legal guarantee of future market access. The disadvantage of this strategy is that under U.S. constitutional law, a treaty must be ratified by a two-thirds majority of the Senate. Past experience with this ratification procedure indicates that it would be difficult to secure the required margin of Senate approval for the kind of comprehensive and detailed free-trade agreement that would best serve Canadian interests. The major risk in attempting to obtain Senate ratification at this time of highly protectionist sentiments in Congress is that the process might generate a series of amendments designed to weaken the treaty to the detriment of Canadian producers.

The second option is to implement the free-trade agreement by obtaining the enactment of U.S. federal and, if necessary, state legislation that conforms to its major obligations. Although it would be useful to have conforming state legislation in all instances, the practicality of this solution is less certain, and it is not entirely clear from a constitutional point of view. This option entails a less secure form of legal arrangement, since the implementing statutes could be amended by subsequent legislation. The main advantage of the statutory approach is that it would allow implementation through simple-majority voting procedures, both in the Congress and, if necessary, in State legislatures. Moreover, the risk of the agreement being watered down or otherwise renegotiated at the legislative-approval stage could be reduced if the President were to seek advance negotiating authority from Congress, spelling out in detail the content of a free-trade arrangement acceptable to the United States. The U.S. Congress implemented the recent Tokyo Round agreements through the enactment of conforming legislation under a so-called "fast track" procedure. This process requires that Congress pass implementing legislation within 90 days of the President's formal declaration that he intends to sign an international agreement binding the United States; it also limits the introduction of amendments to the implementing legislation during the latter's passage through Congress. Commissioners believe that it would be desirable to encourage the U.S. government to employ the fast-track process when seeking approval of any Canada-U.S./free-trade agreement.

Canada's parliamentary form of democracy virtually guarantees that a majority government will succeed in securing legislative implementation of any international agreements it signs. Canada, however, shares with the United States a federal constitutional structure, and both nations have the same basic problem of accommodating local and regional interests in the conduct of foreign economic relations. Since Canadian provinces possess more extensive constitutional authority to tax, subsidize and regulate economic activities than do the American States, the problem of securing consensus between the two levels of government would be relatively more difficult to manage in Canada than in the United States. It is clear that if the provinces and States are to be bound by the rules of the proposed federal free-trade agreement, concerning such matters as government procurement and industrial subsidies, then their governments should be consulted in advance of, and during, the bilateral negotiating process.

Institutional Arrangements and Dispute Settlement

The question of appropriate institutional arrangements for a Canada-U.S./free-trade agreement is, to a large extent, predetermined by choices made on other important issues, such as the scope of the barriers and commodities to be covered and the desired generality of the legal standards in the treaty. Moreover, virtually any form of free-trade framework would require some minimal arrangements to support a number of essential functions: making basic executive and administrative decisions; providing technical-staff services; and adjudicating on complaints and appeals made under the agreement. The scope for choice in the design of an effective institutional structure is, therefore, limited by other decisions and by the need to satisfy basic functional requirements. The questions that would remain involve two basic design choices: Will the key decisions taken under the proposed free-trade agreement be made by the two national executives? Or will they be made by a standing body comprised of appointed representatives, with long fixed terms and formal legal independence from their home governments? Will a governing institution, regardless of its form, have the authority to issue legally binding directives to the national, state and provincial governments? These questions are interrelated, since choices about the structure and composition of a decision-making body are likely to be influenced strongly by the legal consequences of its official actions.

An intergovernmental arrangement to carry out administrative functions, provide technical advice, conduct economic research, and assist in the conciliation of disputes arising under a free-trade agreement would be essential, but there is no convincing argument for creating an elaborate supra-national structure independent of national, state and provincial government departments. It will, however, be essential to involve executive officials at the highest level of government in the implementation of a free-trade arrangement. All major decisions concerning the interpretation and implementation of the agreement should be made by a committee of national officials at the ministerial level. For example, this committee could consist of the Ministers of External Affairs, Finance, International Trade and Regional and Industrial Expansion. On the U.S. side, it could include the Trade Representative and the Secretaries of Commerce, State and Treasury. Since each nation would have equal voting representation in the "Committee of Ministers", each would retain a *de facto* veto power over all aspects of the agreement's implementation. Most modern free-trade arrangements employ intergovernmental bodies consisting of ministerial-level officials from each member government. Decisions are taken on virtually all important issues only on a unanimous vote of national ministers. Because Commissioners believe that the effective implementation of a free-trade agreement will involve difficult questions of political, as well as legal, judgement, it is essential that politically accountable officials of both nations accept responsibility for the enforcement of any agreement's obligations.

The size and composition of the administrative staff required to support a ministerial committee structure would depend on the choices made concerning several important options discussed earlier. If, for example, the enforcement of anti-dumping and countervailing duties, and safeguard measures is to become a responsibility of the Committee of Ministers, it will be necessary to create a panel with appropriate staff support to adjudicate on private complaints. Under this option the Ministerial Committee could exercise appellate review over specific decisions of the panel.

Since any workable agreement is likely to contain rules and standards framed in broad and indefinite terms, conflicts would probably arise over the appropriate interpretation of the treaty's provisions. While this Commission believes that the Committee of Ministers should take final responsibility for resolving disputes arising under the treaty, (subject to the arbitral procedure proposed below), it might be expedient for the Committee to appoint a consultative council whose members could engage in fact-finding and conciliation to further dispute resolution. A council might be composed of private experts such as retired public servants, business executives, union leaders, professionals, and academics; the members would be assigned to panels created to rule on specific complaints. Panels of council members would investigate complaints of non-compliance, originating from either government, and try to facilitate negotiated settlements at the departmental level. If negotiations resulted in a stalemate, the panel would be required to make recommendations to the Committee of Ministers concerning the appropriate resolution of the dispute. A consultative council could also assist the ministers and their departments with formulating and bargaining on amendments to the free-trade agreement, either extending its coverage or changing its major rules.

While there is no compelling need for a permanent executive body independent of the two national governments, the creation of a standing arbitral tribunal to resolve disputes concerning the proper interpretation of the proposed free-trade agreement would be desirable. The option of binding arbitration as a last-resort solution, in cases where the standard fact-finding and conciliation processes failed to resolve a serious dispute, would strengthen the stability and predictability of North American free trade. In future disputes over the meaning of the treaty's provisions, Canadian interests might be better served if the conflict were resolved through binding arbitration by a tribunal with strong bi-national representation. Such an arrangement might be preferable to a bargaining process involving a strong adversary with comparatively less to lose from the weakening or abrogation of the agreement. An accord to submit future disputes to binding arbitration at the instance of either nation would send a strong message to private investors concerning the durability of Canada's guarantee of access. An effective court or tribunal would, of course, require neutral members in order to ensure that a body comprised of equal numbers of national representatives would not be paralysed by deadlocks. Moreover, an arbitral panel would safeguard Canadian political autonomy by operating as a check on unfair or insensitive demands backed by threats of non-compliance with the agreement. A five-member standing body consisting of two Canadians, two Americans and one neutral member would appear to Commissioners to form a satisfactory arbitral panel. Decisions could be taken on the basis of simple-majority voting, and members could serve for five-year renewable terms. The selection of the neutral voting member would be a matter of great importance: it would be essential that the person chosen possess the skills and diplomatic experience required to perform capably this sensitive function. The panel's jurisdiction could be limited to the resolution of disputes arising from conflicting interpretations of the agreement. It is probable that serious disputes of this type would arise rather infrequently. In fact, we anticipate that most disputes would be resolved through bargaining at the administrative and ministerial levels of the organization proposed in this Report, if only to avoid resort to binding arbitration.

Notes

1. See John J. Quinn, "The International Legal Environment: An Overview", in *The International Legal Environment*, vol. 52, prepared for the Royal Commission on the Economic Union and Development Prospects for Canada (Toronto: University of Toronto Press, 1985).
2. Canada, External Affairs Canada, *Canadian Trade Policy for the 1980s: A Discussion Paper* (Ottawa: Minister of Supply and Services Canada, 1983).
3. For a more detailed discussion of the sectoral approach, see Michael Hart, *Some Thoughts on Canada-United States Sectoral Free Trade* (Montreal: Institute for Research on Public Policy, 1985). For an assessment of U.S. attitudes, see Gary C. Hufbauer and Andrew J. Samet, "U.S. Response to Canadian Initiatives for Sectoral Trade Liberalization, 1983 to 1984", in *The Politics of Canada's Economic Relationship with the United States*, vol. 29, prepared for the Royal Commission on the Economic Union and Development Prospects for Canada (Toronto: University of Toronto Press, 1985).
4. See Thorald K. Warley, "Issues in Canadian Agricultural Trade Policy", in *Canada-United States Free Trade*, vol. 11, prepared for the Royal Commission on the Economic Union and Development Prospects for Canada (Toronto: University of Toronto Press, 1985).
5. Ronald J. Wonnacott, "Potential Economic Effects of a Canada-U.S. Free Trade Agreement", in *Canada-United States Free Trade*, vol. 11, prepared for the Royal Commission on the Economic Union and Development Prospects for Canada (Toronto: University of Toronto Press, 1985). This subject has also been discussed in a paper published by the Ontario Economic Council: *Canada/United States Free Trade: Problems and Opportunities* (1985).
6. Simon S. Reisman, "The Issue of Free Trade", in *U.S.-Canadian Economic Relations: Next Steps?*, edited by Edward R. Fried and Philip H. Trezise (Washington, D.C.: Brookings Institution, 1984), p. 50.

Costs and Benefits of Freer Trade with the United States

We Commissioners based our decision to consider bilateral free-trade negotiations with the United States on our assessment of Canada's current economic position, the global environment, and the advantages which would accrue over time from such a step. The key to our thinking was the extent of Canada's trade with the United States, compared to that with other countries. Canada's trade with the United States has continued to grow, even during the last few years. This concentration of trade, particularly in Canadian exports, clearly reflects the benefits Canada receives from trading with the United States. Obviously, the more extensive the trade, the greater the need for a certain and secure relationship between the traders.

Trade makes the United States important to Canada's economy, but Canada is perceived to be less important to the United States. Our nation is the United States' largest trade partner, yet we accounted for less than 20 per cent of U.S. trade between 1980 and 1983. U.S. observers often perceive our country incorrectly, as less important to the United States than is the European Community (EC) or Japan. Indeed, many Canadians are deeply concerned that because trade with Canada is quantitatively less important to Americans than is their trade with us, the United States might implement protective trade measures harmful to Canadians and be relatively unaware of, or unconcerned by, the consequences. Although the U.S. Administration might believe that these measures would apply equally to all U.S. trade partners, the protection might, in fact, have much the greater effect on our country because of our high degree of concentration on U.S. trade. Since the United States is by far our most important trading partner, managing our U.S. trade, whether through bilateral or through multilateral arrangements, is central to our foreign economic policy. Furthermore, because our trade has involved us so thoroughly in the U.S. economy, loss of access to U.S. markets constitutes a danger for Canada against which we Canadians must guard.

It is imperative that Canada reduce both the uncertainty of our access to U.S. markets and the adverse effects that might result from any trade-restrictive measures.

> *We must face the world as we find it. Canada should act with all possible speed to establish firm and secure access to at least one world-scale market since Canada can only achieve its objective of [attaining] economic efficiency if producers are able to utilize all available economies of scale. Given Canada's geographical proximity to and historical linkages with the United States, [these intervenors] recommend that Canada should regard better access to that market through free-trade arrangements as its primary trade objective.*
>
> (Royal Bank of Canada, Brief, August 1, 1984, p. 55.)

Access to Markets and Canadian Competitiveness

Canada would gain several advantages by negotiating a free-trade agreement with the United States. In the first place, freer trade would reduce the exposure of Canadian exporters to American non-tariff barriers (NTBs) such as countervailing duties and, hence, increase our *security* of access to the U.S. market. Of all the major economies in the developed world, Canada is unique in its lack of a large internal market like that of the United States or Japan and of access to a market of over 100 million people through a bilateral or other free-trade arrangement. Many years ago, the major European countries negotiated such an arrangement and formed the European Community (EC). The smaller European countries, in turn, negotiated similar arrangements among themselves to set up the European Free Trade Area (EFTA), and they have subsequently negotiated further access to the European Community. By contrast, Canada's access to foreign markets depends largely on the outcome of multilateral trade negotiations in the General Agreement on Tariffs and Trade (GATT). The multilateral trading system has its advantages, and our continuing involvement in those negotiations would offer Canada potential gains. Nevertheless, the benefits of access to our largest market, the United States, are critically dependent on our maintaining secure access.

Even if access is not actually withdrawn, insecurity of access imposes costs. The chance that access might be withdrawn as a result of the application of safeguard measures or countervailing duties imposed by the United States substantially restricts the ability of Canadian firms to take advantage of increased trading opportunities. Only if our access is secure, will firms be willing to make the necessary long-term investments in plant, technology and human resources that are needed to secure fully those gains which accompany access to a larger market. Improved security of access and improvements in the terms of access themselves would therefore be equally important to Canada as part of a free-trade arrangement with the United States.

The global environment within which Canada operates is becoming increasingly insecure. Over the last two years, there has been discussion in the United States of the possible aggressive use of reciprocal trade measures as a means of forcing major American trading partners to open their markets to U.S. suppliers. According to the extreme form of such proposals, the U.S. Administration would impose trade barriers against other countries at levels equal to the trade barriers which the U.S. faces on a market-by-market and product-by-product basis.[1] Although, at the present time, such U.S. legislation still seems a remote possibility, there is no doubt that widespread change in opinion on trade policy is currently developing in the United States. American thinking now accepts the aggressive use of trade-policy instruments to gain increased access to foreign markets in U.S.-supplier countries. The dangers posed to Canada by the use of these instruments and our difficult experience, in recent years, in the steel, lumber and copper industries strongly suggest the benefits of improving our security of access to U.S. markets. A free-trade arrangement would reduce the hazard that Canada, as an innocent party in a wider trade conflict, could lose part of its access to its largest market.

Another advantage of Canada-U.S. free trade is that it would *improve* our access to the U.S. market in areas where that country now employs tariff and non-tariff-barrier (NTB) protection. While the U.S. economy has less tariff protection than Canada, there are important areas where American tariffs restrict the potential for increased Canadian exports. Certain steel products would fall into this category, as well as the petrochemical sector. This sector is especially important to producers in western Canada, but Canada's capacity to achieve improved access for petrochemicals in the multilateral Tokyo Round was circumscribed by the implications of this deal for U.S. trade with the European Community. In a bilateral agreement, Canada could negotiate for improved access to the U.S. market, in sectors like petrochemicals, without being constrained by the relations between the United States and its other trading partners. Although Commissioners believe that improved access is important for the export of certain commodities and services, Canada's goals should not be interpreted as a desire to become even more dependent on trade with the United States. Paradoxically, we believe that improved and secure access to that market will, in the long run, be the best means to achieve greater diversity of our economic and trade relations. To clarify this contention, we turn to the third advantage.

The most important advantage to Canadians of a free-trade agreement with the United States would be its effect on productivity and thus, in particular, on the competitiveness of our manufacturing sector. Improved and more stable access would create opportunities for Canadian business and increase the tendency toward specialization and rationalization of Canadian production.

As we noted above, the historic protection provided by the National Policy has left Canada with an industrial manufacturing base too small to be competitive by world standards. Government reports and academic studies of the Canadian economy have referred repeatedly to these difficulties. In 1961, for example, the Royal Commission on the Automotive Industry (the Bladen Commission) reported its extensive examination of the Canadian auto industry.[2] That industry was then suffering from chronic underproductivity, and the Bladen *Report* identified low-volume production as the main cause of that condition. The *Report* provided the theoretical analysis that eventually led to the Canada-U.S. Auto Pact and to the rationalization of the Canadian automobile industry in the larger North American market. That rationalization promoted longer production runs and a greater degree of product specialization in the Canadian sector of the industry, and these factors, along with sharply increased investment in Canada by U.S. multi-nationals, produced a more than twelve-fold increase in Canadian auto exports between 1965 and 1981.

The concerns addressed in the Bladen *Report* in 1961 are now relevant to much of Canada's manufacturing industry. Our industry urgently needs to increase economies of scale in order to realize greater productivity. Establishing freer trade with the United States is one important way to accomplish this end. Freer trade would create desirable restructuring and rationalization in Canadian industry that would evolve from increased competition with U.S. industry. By becoming more competitive with American firms, Canadian manufacturers would also increase their ability to survive in a more competitive, global trade environment. Ultimately, it is only by creating a more competitive domestic economy that Canada will be able to produce the additional jobs needed to reduce unemployment.

As the Economic Council of Canada stated in its first submission to this Commission:

> *Many appear to believe that freer trade and expanded trade with the United States precludes expanded trade with other countries. There is no logical basis for this view; in fact, expansion of our export sector to serve U.S. customers could well facilitate the economies of scale needed to reach more distant markets.* (Economic Council of Canada, Brief, November 28, 1983, p. 28.)

As a result, then, of a Canada-U.S. free-trade agreement, we could lower unit costs of production, at home and abroad. This advance would enable Canadian firms to concentrate on their most efficient product lines, thus lengthening production runs and further lowering costs. The resulting expansion of trade would increase the variety of products available to Canadian consumers, for even though our own economy might produce fewer types of each product, more types overall would be available to consumers because of increased trade.

As an example of the kind of restructuring that freer trade would promote in Canadian industry, consider the Strategic Plan developed by Canadian General Electric (CGE) in 1978.[3] For most of its existence, CGE was, in effect, a mini-General Electric operating in Canada and producing, behind high tariff walls, a wide range of products, essentially for the Canadian market. In the late 1970s, however, in response to the challenge of Tokyo Round tariff cuts, CGE assessed its capacity to restructure through the specialization, rationalization and internationalization of its operations. The company's objective was to turn out products that could be manufactured in sufficient volume to compete against imports on the Canadian market. To this end, CGE meant to seek niches in international markets that would enable it to produce the volume of goods needed to reduce its manufacturing costs. The company invested in world-class, high-technology products (such as pulp and paper machinery) in which it had a competitive advantage, and it sought "world product mandates" from its parent firm in order to market its products internationally. At last count, CGE listed 22 product mandates earned, which accounted for 31 per cent of its manufactured-product sales. The type of restructuring represented in the CGE Strategic Plan benefited the company and helped, as well, to make our national economy more resilient. Freer trade would serve to stimulate a similar restructuring in other Canadian industries. Moreover, as CGE itself noted, the current low value of the Canadian dollar against the U.S. dollar will give Canadian business a five- to ten-year "window of opportunity", and its duration will afford time for firms to restructure to meet international competition. That this window of opportunity exists now makes the present time all the more advantageous for establishing freer trade while Canadian business has the breathing room to adjust and restructure.

Improved and more secure access to a larger market would further promote Canada's relative advantage over third countries, both in the U.S. market and in head-to-head competition in those third countries' markets. Numerous briefs submitted to this Commission have stressed the importance to Canada of establishing trading preferences in the U.S. market. A general bilateral free-trade agreement could establish such preferences across the board; this action would produce a substantial increase in the opportunities that Canadian business would enjoy in export sales.

A free-trade agreement with the United States must not be allowed, however, to harm Canada's trade with other countries to any significant degree. When countries reduce trade restrictions on a bilateral basis, the effects are usually twofold: new trade is created, but trade is also diverted from third countries. Under a Canada-U.S. agreement, significant diversions on the Canadian side are unlikely because a large portion of our trade already takes place with the United States. The chief effect of such an agreement, in Commissioners' view, would be that Canada's North American trade would take place on terms more beneficial to Canadians. The arrangement would, in fact, create trade, rather than substantially divert it from Canada's non-U.S. suppliers.

Benefits to Incomes and Output

If the success of arguments in favour of free trade with the United States hinges on the benefits to be obtained from increased and more secure access to American markets, it becomes highly important to assess the potential net benefits to Canadians, in terms of lower costs, higher wages and incomes, and increased output of the economy in general.

The conclusion reached on the basis of this assessment should strongly influence the Canadian decision on whether or not to proceed to negotiations. Commissioners have carefully considered studies of this issue, along with reports by our research staff.[4] Our conclusion has been that in the long run, Canada would benefit substantially from bilateral free trade with the United States, particularly from access to the expanded unrestricted market and from economies of scale. Many studies have confirmed this view, and among Canadian economists it now seems a mainstream opinion. The consistency expressed in this area of intellectual debate over the last 30 years has impressed us in our deliberations, and we therefore base our case, in part, on these studies. We would also emphasize, however, that the studies concentrate on only one component of the potential gains, that of reduced trade barriers in both Canada and the United States. They do not address the additional arguments of improved security of access and of the potential enhancement of Canada's multilateral negotiating abilities. Hence, while we accept these studies' general consensus on potential benefits from reduced barriers, we also argue that other benefits, too, must be weighed into an evaluation of free trade. These further strengthen the case.

As early as 1957, economist John Young sought to quantify the effect of a move by Canada towards freer trade through the complete elimination of the Canadian tariff. In his study for the Royal Commission on Canada's Economic Prospects,[5] he estimated the cost to Canadians of our tariffs. Using 1954 data covering 13 categories of goods, Young compared Canadian prices with the prices of foreign (generally U.S.) goods. On this basis, he estimated the cost of the tariff at between \$0.6 and \$0.75 billion: the equivalent of 3.5 to 4.5 per cent of gross private expenditure net of indirect taxes (such as excise and sales taxes). He considered that the inclusion of other factors, such as the higher costs of goods purchased by governments as a result of the tariff, would have increased the cost to about $1 billion. Young concluded:

> *The principal result of this analysis can be summarized in a sentence. In general and over the long run, increases in protection can be expected to lead to economic losses and decreases in protection to economic gains for the country as a whole. This follows not only from the direct effect the Canadian tariff has on the Canadian economy, but also from the effect Canadian commercial policy has on the treatment accorded this country's exports.*[6]

In 1967, Ronald and Paul Wonnacott produced the first major study of the possible effects of Canada-U.S. free trade.[7] Using 1958 data, the authors found that the total cost to us of Canadian and U.S. trade barriers represented a little more than 10 per cent of Canadian gross national product (GNP); 4 per cent of this amount the authors attributed to Canadian trade barriers, and 6 per cent to U.S. barriers. They have since periodically reviewed and updated their study, refining their findings in the light of changing circumstances. Writing in 1982, they noted:

> *Essentially, the case for free trade has remained the same over the past decade or two, although the gains we measured would be somewhat reduced because of the trade liberalization that has already occurred. These gains would come from increased productivity in manufacturing . . .*[8]

In 1971, Ronald Shearer, John Young and Gordon Munro produced one of a number of studies on the estimated results of free trade on one or more regions of Canada. They considered the effects on British Columbia of the removal of tariffs among the North Atlantic countries. Using a method similar to the concept in Young's 1957 study, the authors suggested that British Columbians might stand to gain an amount ranging between 4 and 7 per cent of their incomes from free trade. They concluded further:

> *Western Canada – and specifically British Columbia – suffers from being in a customs union with the rest of the country; the central provinces suffer from not being in a customs union with the rest of the world . . .*
>
> *North Atlantic free trade would raise incomes in the industrialized regions of Canada relative to incomes in areas like British Columbia, although incomes would rise absolutely in both places. Free trade would be less of a stimulus to economic expansion in British Columbia than in the industrialized central part of the country.*[9]

A later work published by James Williams in 1978 concentrated specifically on Canada-U.S. free trade.[10] Williams approached the problem of calculating the cost of Canadian and U.S. tariffs by estimating the maximum value of consumption that could be generated by the Canadian economy under both bilateral free trade and a situation of unchanged trade policies. The difference between these two values, that is, the amount of additional consumption possible under bilateral free trade, comprised the estimated gains to Canada from such an arrangement. By Williams' reckoning, the elimination of Canadian tariffs would produce a 1.36 per cent increase in consumption; elimination of U.S. tariffs would provide a 2.03 per cent increase; and elimination of both tariffs would give a 3.97 per cent increase.

Roma Dauphin's study,[11] also published in 1978, used Williams' results to estimate the effect of unilateral free trade (that is, the elimination of Canadian tariff and some non-tariff barriers) on the regional distribution of income in Canada. On the basis of 1971 Canadian data, Dauphin calculated that real incomes would increase in the Atlantic region, the Prairies and British Columbia; little change would occur in Ontario and Quebec, although a larger increase in real wages would occur there. All regions would therefore gain from free trade.

In the most recent work in this tradition, Richard Harris and David Cox have developed a micro-economic simulation model of the Canadian economy, which they have used to analyse Canada's trade policies. In work published in 1983, and in subsequent work summarized in this Commission's research publications, Harris and Cox have used their model to estimate the effects of unilateral free trade, full multilateral free trade, bilateral free trade with the United States, and sectoral Canada-U.S. free trade.[12] The authors divide the Canadian economy into 29 industries, 20 of them in the manufacturing sector. In their model, the removal of Canadian tariffs increases domestic competitive forces, and compels rationalization of our domestic industry. The removal of foreign-trade barriers facilitates Canadian penetration of foreign markets, permitting economies of scale to be more fully exploited. In their 1983 study, they reported results for the effects of unilateral and multilateral free trade on the Canadian economy. Under unilateral free trade, they estimate that Canada's GNP will rise by about 3.5 per cent. Multilateral free trade would raise GNP by about 7 per cent.

In his summary article for this Commission, Harris[13] reports results for bilateral and sectoral Canada-U.S. free trade. His analysis of sectoral free trade takes account of the effect of the bilateral elimination of trade barriers in textiles, steel, chemicals, urban transportation equipment, and agricultural machinery. He examines this hypothetical situation both with and without export subsidies, most of them provided by the U.S. government. Where sectoral free trade continues to be supported by export subsidies after a bilateral agreement is struck, an aggregate welfare gain occurs, amounting to a 1.9 per cent increase in base Gross National Expenditure (GNE).

The corresponding analysis, presented in the same paper, of full bilateral free trade involves the elimination by both partners of tariffs and non-tariff barriers (NTBs), including export subsidies, in all industries studied. The author estimates gains significantly larger than those under sectoral free trade. These amount to 9 per cent of national income, a higher figure than that achieved under multilateral free trade. Even though the gains from bilateral free trade depend on the joint removal of trade restrictions on only about 70 per cent of Canada's trade (as compared with 100 per cent in the multilateral case), preferential access to U.S. markets more than compensates Canadians for the difference. As a number of analysts, including the authors themselves, have warned, the results of this analysis must be accepted cautiously. Nevertheless, the broad thrust of its conclusions supports those of earlier studies. Gains to Canada from Canada-U.S. free trade would be significant and widespread. As a nation, we stand to benefit a good deal from such an arrangement.

All economic analyses of possible effects of changes in Canada's trade policies examine unobservable situations; inevitably, therefore, their results are uncertain. Analysts must make a range of simplifying assumptions, and supportive data are frequently unavailable. In evaluating these studies and working their results into our deliberations, Commissioners have noted the differences among researchers' estimates of the gains to be made from free trade. In many instances, these differences are the result of the different methods and data employed by the researchers, and this variety makes it impossible to predict with absolute precision the effects of free trade. Nevertheless, the results of the analyses have convinced us that such disagreements as exist are quantitative and not qualitative. The debate concerns the *size* of long-term gains that free trade has to offer Canada, not whether such gains will occur.

We Commissioners do not see our role as one of arbitrating differences of opinion among individual researchers, but of using our analyses to help Canadians reach the best judgement about the appropriate course for Canada to follow. These studies have helped to convince us that there is a high probability that Canada would experience significant gains from free trade with the United States. The long-term gains suggested by these studies lie in the range of 4 to 10 per cent of Canadian GNP. Considering that tariffs will be lower by the end of the Tokyo Round tariff cuts than the levels used in these studies, this range might perhaps be lowered to 3 to 8 per cent of GNP. These are still substantial gains, and they exclude other factors such as the contingent protectionism and other non-tariff barriers which create uncertainty for Canadian producers. They therefore provide strong support for our proposal of freer trade with the United States.

Regional Considerations

Since Confederation, trade policy and regional interests have been closely linked. Both our eastern and western provinces have long considered that central Canada has used the tariff to its own advantage by forcing itself on them as a trading partner, rather than leaving them the option to trade with more competitive foreign suppliers. They see the tariff largely as an instrument for protecting manufactured products, which are produced in central Canada. The tariff supposedly forces hinterland regions to pay higher prices for manufactured imports, produces large volumes of interprovincial trade and smaller volumes of international trade, and transfers income to central Canadian manufacturing industries from hinterland consuming regions.

Irrespective of whether or not this perception is true, it has proved over the years to exercise subtle influence over the conduct and formation of our trade policies. It has generally been assumed that western and eastern provinces would welcome any move towards freer trade, whether this be unilateral, through a negotiated arrangement with the Americans, or multilateral, through GATT negotiations. Equally, it has been assumed that both Ontario and Quebec would oppose any such moves.

During the course of this Commission's hearings, however, we have been impressed by the degree to which this traditional heartland-hinterland view of Canadian trade policy is now being challenged from several quarters. Both the very concept of a region and the notion of how regions are affected by changes in trade policies are central to any discussion of interregional effects of those policies. If factors of production are mobile between regions, however, as they now appear to be, how can it be determined whether a given region gains or loses from a change in trade policies? Some of the residents will be affected, but if workers move in and out of regions in response to changes in trade policy, the size of a region is not fixed, and interregional effects of trade policies become hard to "nail down".

Again, who owns interregional assets? And how does their ownership affect analysis of interregional effects of trade policies? Through pension funds, stock ownership, and other forms of financial intermediation, for instance, residents (say, of Ontario) will own assets that are located in other provinces (say, Alberta). Interregional effects of trade policies, measured in terms of the impacts on factors of production located in particular regions, will be different from the results for residents of a region. Thus the interregional effects of our tariffs or other trade-policy measures may have quite different results from what is often supposed when they percolate through to the ultimate recipients of the returns to factors used in particular regions.

Observers often fail to appreciate that our own trade barriers and those we face abroad typically affect Canada's regions in opposite ways. To the degree that the traditional view of interregional effects of Canadian protection is correct, the interregional effects of trade barriers abroad, especially when they are higher for manufacturing than for non-manufacturing products, operate in the opposite direction. Moreover, the threat from contingent protection in the United States applies to industries in all regions, and the estimates of benefits from bilateral free trade with the Americans seem to suggest that the advantages will be spread broadly throughout our economy.

Commissioners therefore believe that the regional divisions on the free-trade issue that have been prominent in the past should not occur in the same way today. While some regions may anticipate adverse effects from free trade, we believe that the likelihood is that all regions will benefit, and that Canadians everywhere will be able to enjoy a higher standard of living. To put an even finer point on this conviction, we believe that freer trade with the United States would make a major contribution to Canada's regional development and to national competitiveness and overall confidence.

Problem Areas

While the economic benefits of Canada-U.S. free trade hinge largely on the gains Canadians would enjoy from increased and more secure access to a larger market, Commissioners recognize that there are also potential economic costs. One argument commonly raised against free trade is that it might induce significant amounts of investment to leave Canada. Protection has encouraged foreign firms to invest here: once tariffs are in place, these firms benefit from producing in Canada, rather than servicing our market from abroad. What, then, would happen to the level of investment in Canada under free trade?

If Canada were to remove its protection unilaterally, investors entirely dependent on the Canadian market might well withdraw. The net effect on investors of bilateral free trade is less clear. It is true that investors attracted to Canada by our protection would have less incentive to remain, but firms previously discouraged from investing here by the presence of U.S. trade barriers could enter Canada and produce for both a foreign (U.S.) and a domestic market. The possibility of penetrating the U.S. market from a secure Canadian base, unimpeded by U.S. trade barriers that inhibit competition from Canada, could well encourage investment and job creation here to a much greater extent than elimination of protection would discourage them.

Commissioners are strongly of the opinion that attempts either to stimulate or to restrict foreign investment in Canada by using domestic trade barriers as levers are inappropriate. Whatever the desired level of foreign investment in Canada, it is more fitting to achieve it through tax and subsidy policies toward domestic and foreign firms and the regulatory stance of Investment Canada. Trade barriers are unsuitable instruments with which to control foreign investment. It strikes us as ill conceived to refrain from negotiating free trade with the United States because of Canadian concern that unprotected trade between the two countries could discourage investment here. Canada should meet these concerns and achieve its objectives by using instruments other than protective barriers.

Some Canadians see protection as a stimulus to our manufacturing industries, and are concerned that without protection, disruptive adjustments would be required. It is true that a unilateral move towards free trade, involving the elimination of Canadian trade barriers only, could well reduce the size of our manufacturing industries. Rodrigue Tremblay, an economist at the Université de Montréal and a former Quebec Cabinet Minister, told Commissioners:

> *Unilateral disarmament [of trade barriers] is of less interest [because it] would create major problems of industrial reorganization, since certain industries would completely disappear from Canada [and this would have] serious regional consequences. This does not hold when one speaks of a reorganization that applies [only] to North America because, in the latter case particularly, the reorganizaton occurs on an industry-by-industry basis.*
>
> (Rodrigue Tremblay, Transcript, Montreal, May 31, 1984 [vol. 2], p. 361.)

Bilateral free trade would probably produce a different situation. Elimination of foreign-trade barriers would stimulate manufacturing industries, including those likely to be diminished by the disappearance of Canadian protection. Studies on this matter suggest the likelihood of a net increase in our manufacturing production: the stimulative effect of increased penetration of markets abroad would more than offset the reduction caused by removal of our own protection.[14] Adjustment may therefore be less difficult under bilateral free trade, especially if it tends to take the form of reallocation among firms within industries, rather than simple changes across industries, as Canadian production becomes rationalized.

However, in evaluating short-term adjustment costs under any Canada-U.S./free-trade arrangement, Canadians must consider many elements. We must identify the industries which would expand and those which would contract, and the extent of the changes for each. We must assess disruptions in the markets for labour and other factors of production, calculate the length of unemployment periods for workers affected, and evaluate the costs of forgone opportunities in terms of lost production. We must determine the length of adjustment periods and separate the factors listed from all the others taking place at the same time in our economy. Because there are so many factors involved and the data are so limited, it is difficult to assess the possible adjustment costs of a Canada-U.S./free-trade agreement.

Studies made in other countries where data are more plentiful have compared the relative size of the long-term gains from expected higher real incomes with the shorter-term costs of adjusting to the new situation. These adjustment costs consist of temporarily higher unemployment and forgone production as productive resources move from one firm to another or from one industry to another. The ratio of the long-term gains to the short-term costs of trade liberalization range between 25:1 and 80:1. An American study in 1978 estimated the effects on a number of countries, including Canada, of a 60 per cent multilateral tariff cut from pre-Tokyo Round levels.[15] If the tariff cut excluded textiles, but eliminated all tariffs of less than 5 per cent, the adjustment costs to Canada were estimated at $286.8 million (in 1974 U.S. $). The present value of the long-term gains was estimated at $17.8 billion (1974 U.S. $). Thus the ratio of the adjustment costs of the estimated long-run benefits to Canada was 62:1. This figure falls within the same range as those offered in other studies.

Commissioners recognize that adjustment difficulties in Canada could well be somewhat more costly than those assessed elsewhere. Our economy is spatially more diverse than that of most other developed economies, and Canadians would be entering a free-trade agreement with a country much larger than our own. Nevertheless, even if we multiplied the estimated short-term adjustment costs by factors of, say, five or even ten, the net balance in favour of free trade would still be great and unmistakable.

This Commission's view is that on balance, long-term gains from bilateral free trade would almost certainly heavily outweigh short-term adjustment costs. Some Canadians will say that a policy judgement such as this should be based on total certainty. Commissioners believe, however, that uncertainties about effects will always remain the very nature of debate about policy, even after decisions have been made; nor is there any need to presume that maintenance of the *status quo* is always the appropriate operating principle. We are convinced that on this important issue, the weight of evidence lies in the direction we have stated. Consequently, the importance of improving and securing Canadian access to export markets has convinced us that change is the better choice, but we look forward to further discussion of these matters in the debate which will undoubtedly follow. We fully acknowledge that that debate would clearly be advanced by the availability of more precise data on this issue.

A third argument sometimes raised against free trade is the risk that it could reduce Canada's ability to negotiate multilaterally for access to export markets. It would be ideal if Canada could expand and secure its access to export markets in the United States through multilateral, rather than bilateral, negotiations. A multilateral trading system based on clear rules and transparent trade barriers now has a proved track record of almost forty years. Indeed, the advantage of multilateralism has been one of the major themes in Canadian trade policy since the Second World War.

Free trade with the United States would not pose major legal problems under the General Agreement on Tariffs and Trade (GATT) if its Article XXIV were respected. Legal aspects, however, may be less important than other factors. Some Canadians who oppose free trade argue that while Canada is not a dominant force in multilateral negotiations, our presence there is important. They believe that major bilateral negotiations between Canada and the United States could further fracture the multilateral system which has served us well. Commissioners believe, however, that the converse is more likely. The formation of the European Economic Community in 1958, for instance, helped to accelerate multilateral negotiations under the GATT's Dillon Round, in 1960–61, as the larger powers sought to deal with the new trade group. The entry of the United Kingdom into the Community in 1971 helped to launch the Tokyo Round. A similar situation could well evolve over the next few years if Canada were to negotiate a bilateral trade arrangement with the United States.

Commissioners do not deny that Canadians must make a delicate judgement on this issue. Canada is a relatively small country, and any bilateral arrangement we made with the United States might serve to accelerate multilateral negotiations. Alternatively, it could harm the multilateral trading system. While this Commission believes that the former outcome is the more likely to occur, unequivocal evidence of one view or the other is hard to find. Commissioners repeat that multilateral and bilateral negotiations are not mutually exclusive: they can be engaged in jointly, and they can be mutually reinforcing. Canadians clearly stand to benefit from increased access to foreign markets and increased security of that access. The method is less important than achievement of the objective. We think both routes worth exploring, and bilateral negotiations especially so.

Notes

1. For a full explication of this proposal, see R.J. Wonnacott, *Aggressive U.S. Reciprocity Evaluated with a New Analytical Approach to Trade Conflicts* (Montreal: Institute for Research on Public Policy, 1984).
2. Canada, Royal Commission on the Automotive Industry, *Report* (Ottawa: Queen's Printer, 1961).
3. See Canadian General Electric Company Limited, Brief, November 21, 1983, pp. 10–11.

4. See, for example, the research papers in *Canada-United States Free Trade*, vol. 11 (co-ordinated by John Whalley), prepared for the Royal Commission on the Economic Union and Development Prospects for Canada (Toronto: University of Toronto Press, 1985).
5. John H. Young, *Canadian Commercial Policy* (Ottawa: Queen's Printer, 1957).
6. *Ibid.*, p. 160.
7. Ronald Wonnacott and Paul Wonnacott, *Free Trade Between the United States and Canada: The Potential Economic Effects* (Cambridge, Mass.: Harvard University Press, 1967).
8. Paul Wonnacott and Ronald J. Wonnacott, "Free Trade Between the US and Canada", *Canadian Public Policy* 8 (Supplement, 1982): 412–27. See also Ronald J. Wonnacott, "Potential Economic Effects of a Canada-U.S. Free Trade Agreement", in *Canada-United States Free Trade*, vol. 11, prepared for the Royal Commission on the Economic Union and Development Prospects for Canada (Toronto: University of Toronto Press, 1985). This subject has also been discussed in a paper published by the Ontario Economic Council: *Canada/United States Free Trade: Problems and Opportunities* (1985).
9. Ronald A. Shearer, John H. Young, and Gordon R. Munro, *Trade Liberalization and a Regional Economy: Studies of the Impact of Free Trade on British Columbia* (Toronto: University of Toronto Press for the Private Planning Association of Canada, 1971), p. 203.
10. James R. Williams, *The Canadian-United States Tariff and Canadian Industry: A Multisectoral Analysis* (Toronto: University of Toronto Press, 1978).
11. Roma Dauphin, *The Impact of Free Trade in Canada*, study prepared for the Economic Council of Canada (Ottawa: Minister of Supply and Services Canada, 1978).
12. Richard G. Harris with David Cox, *Trade, Industrial Policy, and Canadian Manufacturing* (Toronto: Ontario Economic Council, 1983); and see also the research papers in *Canada-United States Free Trade*, vol. 11, prepared for the Royal Commission on the Economic Union and Development Prospects for Canada (Toronto: University of Toronto Press, 1985).
13. Richard G. Harris, "Summary of a Project on the General Equilibrium Evaluation of Canadian Trade Policy", in *Canada-United States Free Trade*, vol. 11, prepared for the Royal Commission on the Economic Union and Development Prospects for Canada (Toronto: University of Toronto Press, 1985).
14. See Harris, *Trade, Industrial Policy, and Canadian Manufacturing*, p. 115; and Williams, *The Canadian-United States Tariff and Canadian Industry*, p. 34.
15. See William R. Cline, Noboru Kawanabe, T.O.M. Kronsjö, and Thomas Williams, *Trade Negotiations in the Tokyo Round: A Quantitative Assessment* (Washington: D.C.: Brookings Institution, 1978).

The Effect of Freer Trade on Canadian Industry

Canada's business and labour communities remain uncertain about freer trade, as is natural about any major initiative of government. Governments cannot foretell precisely the effects of a new policy. They can act, however, on the basis of available facts and good judgement. To determine the facts and reduce uncertainty, this Commission undertook sectoral studies of the probable effect of freer Canada-U.S. trade on Canadian industry.[1] Commissioners emphasize that these studies represent a preliminary analysis, and that the Canadian government stands in need of more detailed information before it negotiates freer trade with the U.S. Administration or any other government.

Some critics have charged that the costs of freer trade would be excessive, and they have raised the spectre of large-scale transfers of labour among sectors of our Canadian economy, with consequent high increases in unemployment. Such events are unlikely. Freer trade would chiefly affect our manufacturing sector, and this sector now accounts for less than 20 per cent of Canadian employment. Thus, at most, freer trade would directly affect only one-fifth of our country's labour force. It is important to maintain a balanced perspective when analysing Canada's trade and not to overstate either the costs of freer trade or its benefits.

In hearings held in 1980, before the Standing Senate Committee on Foreign Affairs, the Canadian Manufacturers' Association (CMA) stated that a survey of 1031 Canadian firms indicated that only about one-third anticipated contraction as a result of Canada-U.S. free trade. About half the remaining companies expected expansion, and half foresaw no change. Recent informal soundings indicate that as few as 20 per cent of CMA members anticipate contraction from bilateral free trade. The growth anticipated by other members would offset this contraction. Overall, Canadian business seems to judge that freer trade would be in its best interests.

Sector Analysis

To analyse the probable effect of freer trade on Canadian industry, this Commission separated Canada-U.S. trade into workable subdivisions or sectors. These sectors appear in Table 6-1, together with figures recording Canada's trade with the United States and other nations for 1978 and 1983. The data suggest Canada's weakness in all manufacturing sectors except automotive products. In general, our trade balances in manufacturing are negative: in 1983, Canada had a negative trade balance of over $1 billion in each of a group of sectors: textiles, machinery, electronics, electrical machinery, scientific equipment and consumer products. As partial compensation, however, there were strong export increases in such sectors as machinery and equipment. Between 1978 and 1983, our trade balances improved in most manufacturing sectors. This is particularly true for trade with the United States, which showed improvement in all manufacturing sectors except electronics and scientific and medical equipment. In 1983, Canada had an unusually high export surplus, over the United States, of more than $4 billion-worth of automotive products. This surplus accrued largely because of the resurgence of U.S. sales of medium-sized to large autos, a Canadian specialty.

Table 6-1 also confirms that most of Canada's exports are resource based. We continue to have large export surpluses in sectors such as agriculture and food processing, forestry products, metals and minerals, and energy. The most dramatic change occurred in the energy sector, with increased sales of electricity, natural gas and petroleum derivatives to the United States, and increased coal exports to other countries. We achieved a net increase in these exports of over $5 billion (in 1983 $) between 1978 and 1983. During these same years, agricultural exports showed strong growth; wheat sales outside North America represented the largest proportion. Exports of forestry products and metals and minerals, declined, however, between 1978 and 1983; while these sectors remain important to Canadian trade, they may not grow much in future.

The study next examined the sectors themselves. Table 6-1 generally confirms the traditional picture of Canada as an exporter of resource-based products and an importer of manufactured goods. Consequently, the sector studies might well have reflected consistent underlying strength in resource sectors, and consistent weakness in manufacturing industries operating behind uniformly high tariff walls. Reality proved to be quite different. Instead of weakness, we found substantial areas of great strength in Canadian manufacturing. Instead of sameness, we found great diversity in industrial performance, patterns of protection, and patterns of adaptation to the prospect of freer trade with the United States.

Diversity of Industrial Performance

There is substantial import-export Canada-U.S. trade in all manufacturing sectors; in most of these, Canadian exports have grown faster than have imports. No manufacturing sector is unequivocally weak. For instance, Canada's imports of electrical machinery from the United States are over four times greater than our corresponding exports to that country, but even that sector has areas of substantial export strength. In textiles, clothing and footwear, Canada has a large overall deficit in U.S. trade, but we ran surpluses in 1983 in clothing and footwear.[2] Canadian quotas on imports helped to produce the surplus in footwear. Although we ran a sharp deficit in the processing of fruits and vegetables, we had a large surplus in the processing of meat and poultry; surpluses in alcoholic beverages tended to offset deficits for fresh fruits and vegetables. Our furniture sector has been historically weak; in 1978, it ran a deficit with the United States of nearly $109 million (in 1983 dollars); however, it posted a surplus of $185 million in 1983. Most of this growth occurred in office furniture, yet household furniture, despite a continuing deficit, recorded a four-fold export increase.

The earliest and most striking evidence of the diversity of Canada's trade performance was the difference apparent from firm to firm. The most important variable in industrial performance is quality of management, which occurs at the level of the firm, and not of the sector. Thus, in the generally weak electronics sector, the Canadian multi-national Northern Telecom is a world leader in telecommunications technology. Our imports in hand tools and farm equipment are seven times greater than our exports, but the efficient Canadian branch of Black and Decker has acquired, through world product mandates, a flourishing U.S-export trade. Finally, in scientific and medical products, where Canada ran a $1 billion deficit in 1983, the Canadian firm of Madson Electronics delivers only 8 per cent of its sales in this country and could not survive without the American market.

The list could be expanded almost indefinitely, but the point is clear: Canada has proved its industrial capacity at the level of the individual firm and sub-sector, even in sectors that normally run a deficit in U.S-trade. If these firms or industries can successfully meet direct U.S. competition, others can do so, as well. Thus Canada would be likely to achieve substantial benefits from more open trade even in our weakest manufacturing sectors.

Diversity of Protection

Again, this Commission's sector studies show diversity in Canada's pattern of economic protection. As Commissioners noted earlier, most Canadian tariffs are higher than corresponding U.S. tariffs, but the United States makes more extensive use of non-tariff barriers (NTBs) than does Canada. Yet certain exceptions to this generalization have an important bearing on the process of adjustment to freer trade. Some Canadian sectors, for example, are already operating effectively without tariff protection. These include automobiles, where trade is governed by a bilateral agreement; fish products, where Canada has an unquestioned comparative export advantage; and aircraft, where trade is governed largely by a multilateral sectoral-free/trade agreement. In these sectors, freer trade with the United States would make little difference to Canada. Even in fishery products, where the United States maintains some protective measures, availability and quality of the resource influence trade flows to a greater degree than does the level of trade barriers. Nevertheless, a high tariff protects some Canadian sectors: for example, furniture enjoys tariff protection of about 15.5 per cent of value, and textiles and clothing are protected at rates that average about 20 per cent. While freer trade might entail higher adjustment costs in these sectors, in certain others, such as furniture, the current strong position of exports suggests that parts of the sector could bear the adjustment costs.

Canadians make few complaints about generally lower U.S. tariffs, but the few sharp exceptions to this general observation tend to confirm Commissioners' views that Canada would gain if access to the U.S. market were improved by means of bilateral tariff reductions. Canada could gain, for example, from reduced U.S. tariffs on agriculture and food processing and on textiles, clothing and footwear. Furthermore, Canada applies tariffs selectively on strategic goods, a practice that can greatly increase the effect of a tariff on foreign producers. Thus, in 1983, methanol, a primary petrochemical, had a U.S. tariff of 18.0 per cent and a Canadian tariff of 10.0 per cent; plywood, an important intermediate product in domestic construction, carried a U.S. tariff of 20 per cent and a Canadian tariff of 15 per cent.

TABLE 6-1 Canadian Trade Balances by Sector, 1978 and 1983[a]

(Canadian millions $; 1983 dollars)[b]

	Exports				Imports				Balance of Trade					
	1978		1983		1978		1983		1978		1983		Change from 1978-83	
	U.S. 1	R.O.W.[c] 2	U.S. 3	R.O.W. 4	U.S. 5	R.O.W. 6	U.S. 7	R.O.W. 8	U.S. 9[d]	R.O.W. 10[e]	U.S. 11[f]	R.O.W. 12[g]	U.S. 13[h]	R.O.W. 14[i]
Agriculture and Food Processing	1 536	5 135	1 980	6 907	2 802	2 742	2 493	2 062	(1 266)	2 391	(514)	4 845	752	2 454
Fish and Fish Products	866	670	960	612	221	171	237	182	645	449	724	429	79	(20)
Sundry Crude & Fabricated Materials, n.e.s.	373	1 355	465	1 031	1 242	477	1 026	372	(871)	876	(560)	659	311	(217)
Forestry Products	11 132	3 999	9 466	3 729	1 258	213	1 204	198	9 874	3 785	8 263	3 531	(1 611)	(254)
Metals & Minerals	8 378	5 421	7 465	4 834	4 247	2 385	4 790	2 056	4 132	3 099	2 674	2 778	(1 458)	(321)
Energy	8 110	1 427	11 400	1 373	2 200	4 816	1 932	3 232	5 908	(3 389)	9 468	(1 860)	3 560	1 529
Textiles, Clothing and Footwear	343	398	408	306	1 437	2 383	1 200	2 482	(1 092)	(1 985)	(792)	(2 176)	300	(191)
Chemicals & Petrochemicals	2 508	929	2 908	1 663	3 261	1 064	3 587	1 120	(785)	288	(679)	544	106	256

TABLE 6-1 (con'd.)

(Canadian millions $; 1983 dollars)[b]

	Exports				Imports				Balance of Trade					
	1978		1983		1978		1983		1978		1983		Change from 1978-83	
	U.S. 1	R.O.W.[c] 2	U.S. 3	R.O.W. 4	U.S. 5	R.O.W. 6	U.S. 7	R.O.W. 8	U.S. 9[d]	R.O.W. 10[e]	U.S. 11[f]	R.O.W. 12[g]	U.S. 13[h]	R.O.W. 14[i]
Machinery and Equipment	2 726	934	2 471	960	7 206	1 691	5 291	1 355	(4 478)	(757)	(2 820)	(395)	1 658	362
Automotive Products	18 268	1 614	20 986	733	19 110	1 927	16 916	2 334	(842)	(311)	4 070	(1 600)	4 912	(1 289)
Urban Transportation	36	8	125	0.9	41	3	66	0.2	(5)	5	59	0.7	64	(4.3)
Ocean and Marine Industries	190	213	152	183	242	144	184	602	(52)	70	(32)	(419)	20	(489)
Aircraft	853	417	1 390	427	1 231	96	1 727	87	(376)	321	(337)	339	39	18
Electronics	1 419	605	2 461	1 018	3 256	1 296	5 130	1 857	(1 838)	(691)	(2 668)	(839)	(830)	(148)
Electrical Machinery and Equipment	375	270	512	192	2 377	627	2 127	688	(2 001)	(357)	(1 614)	(495)	387	(138)
Furniture	180	33	373	34	288	134	188	146	(109)	(101)	185	(112)	294	(11)
Scientific and Medical Equipment Products	196	130	294	140	1 084	275	1 346	318	(888)	(145)	(1 052)	(179)	(164)	(34)

Miscellaneous Consumer Products	368	187	582	135	1 672	1 340	1 680	1 237	(1 304)	(1 154)	(1 098)	(1 102)	206	52
Other End Products and Special Transactions	1 110	515	1 913	501	2 760	1 364	2 936	1 148	(1 649)	(849)	(1 024)	(647)	625	202
Total[j] – All Sectors	59 067	24 990	66 333	24 631	56 003	23 194	54 103	21 483	3 065	1 796	12 229	3 148	9 164	1 352

Source: Gilbert R. Winham, "Canada-U.S. Sectoral Trade Study", working paper prepared for the Royal Commission on the Economic Union and Development Prospects for Canada (Ottawa, 1985).

a. Data supplied by Statistics Canada, External Trade Division. For additional information, including further breakdown within sectors, see Canada-U.S. Sectoral Trade Study, Royal Commission on the Economy, April 1985.

b. GNE Deflator: 1971 = 100; 1978 = 193.8; 1983 = 290.5. Reference: Statistics Canada Catalogue #13-001, Table 21.

c. Rest of World.

d. Column 9 equals Column 1 minus Column 5.

e. Column 10 equals Column 2 minus Column 6.

f. Column 11 equals Column 3 minus Column 7.

g. Column 12 equals Column 4 minus Column 8.

h. Column 13 equals Column 11 minus Column 9.

i. Column 14 equals Column 12 minus Column 10.

j. Total includes small residuals for each trade category.

Another example of tariff disparity comes from the area of clothing. Canada has a competitive edge over the United States in the manufacture of high-fashion garments. The United States, however, maintains tariffs on "ornamented" clothing that average about 10 per cent higher than duties on non-ornamented clothing, which stand at about 35 per cent. This distinction effectively reduces the U.S. market for Canada's exports. Our exports would have a new "window of opportunity" if these strategic tariffs were removed.

Four types of U.S. non-tariff barriers particularly affect Canadian exports, though some products, such as furniture, hardware and hand tools, face none. One commonly applied NTB is the safeguard provision (an "Article 201 action") established under the U.S. Trade Act of 1974. It authorizes the U.S. Administration to impose quotas or additional duties on foreign imports deemed to be causing injury to competing U.S. producers. The American government recently attempted such an action against Canadian copper exports, but pressure from domestic users of imported copper persuaded it to desist.

Customs-classification procedures cause a particular problem in textiles, clothing and footwear. There are many U.S. tariff items in this sector and officials have considerable leeway in choosing among these items in applying duties. The choice factor itself creates uncertainty for Canadians.[3] Again, U.S. legislation pertaining to countervailing duties particularly affects Canadian resource-based sectors that might have been subsidized. Perhaps the most troublesome forms of NTBs, however, are the U.S. Administration's preferential procurement practices. These are especially disadvantageous for sectors exporting large capital goods such as electrical machinery, electronic equipment and non-electric machinery. They also touch more consumer-oriented sectors: the Berry Amendment covers the purchase of textiles by the U.S. Department of Defence, and extensive state and local legislation sets domestic preferences for purchases of clothing and footwear.[4]

Canada, too, makes use of non-tariff barriers, although some of these actually harm our own interests. Most provinces showed preferences for local or Canadian production in their government purchases. Quebec, for example, in many instances allows only Quebec firms to bid for contracts, and may favour those tenders offering higher Quebec content. Ontario gives a 10 per cent preference to its own companies. Provincial governments often buy from "domestic" producers on a non-competitive basis, shunning lower bids from outsiders. These policies have fragmented the Canadian market and reduced the ability of Canadian companies to collaborate in bidding on large foreign projects. They have also led, in some instances, to undue competition among Canadian companies operating in foreign markets. Obviously, Canada would benefit from removal of this sort of protection under a wider Canada-U.S./free-trade arrangement.

Diversity of Adaptation to Freer Trade

There is no single common denominator which reflects the way that different sectors, or even different firms, might respond to the stimulus of freer trade. To simplify our sectoral analysis, however, Commissioners chose to consider the likely response in three different categories: strong exporting sectors, resource-based sectors, and weaker exporting sectors.

Strong sectors. Urban transit constitutes a strong sector. It covers a diverse range of products, from complete vehicles and vehicle-control and -communication systems, through fare-control, traction-power and track systems, to passenger-distribution and maintenance systems. The sector includes five major transit-vehicle producers, 25 significant manufacturers of components and materials, a number of consulting and engineering firms, and about 200 firms peripherally involved in urban transit. Though rapidly growing in Canada, it is not so strong in the United States.

Despite the weakness of the U.S. urban-transit sector, the Canadian industry faces stiff NTB protection in the U.S. The major NTB consists of the "Buy America" provisions of the Surface Transportation Assistance Act (STAA), which provides the major source of funding for new U.S. urban-transit projects. The Buy America provisions have forced Canadian firms seeking U.S. contracts to establish plants in the United States. For example, both Bombardier and Ontario Bus Industries have established permanent U.S. production facilities, while other Canadian firms are prepared to sub-contract final assembly work to American companies. It has been noted in our sector study that, "a major reason for negotiating freer trade would be to prevent the outflow of capital investment which the Buy America provisions have encouraged."[5]

Freer trade would strongly promote the interests of Canada's urban-transit sector, but not without cost. Removal of Canadian barriers would expose our producers to domestic competition from the more efficient European and Japanese subsidiaries which have located in the United States as a result of Buy America regulations. However, free trade would reduce the incentive for Canadian industry to locate in the United States, to the benefit of our own economy and labour market. Thirty years ago, an influential article[6] on Canadian trade policy noted the capacity of U.S. tariff protection to discourage domestic manufacturing in Canada, to the detriment of Canadian labour and Canadian developmental aspirations. Today U.S. tariff protection is much weaker and no longer has this effect, but the argument is still valid for U.S. NTBs. Thus freer trade and reduction of these less visible American barriers would facilitate the future growth and security of the stronger areas of our Canadian economy.

Forestry products form another strong sector of Canadian trade. Here adjustment to meet world competition often requires massive capital investments to realize economies of scale. However, uncertainties created by the use or threatened use of NTBs make companies reluctant to commit the necessary assets. Freer trade, particularly in pulp and paper, might make Canadian production more competitive internationally. To establish conditions that encourage investment can thus improve trade. The fact that about half of the paper-making machines in Canada were made before 1950, as compared to about 25 per cent in the United States and 5 per cent in Scandinavia, suggests that there is considerable scope for gains through new investment.

Resource-based sectors. Discussions of freer trade often treat its effect on resource-based sectors as a matter of secondary importance. They assume that manufactured goods are the principal focus of concern in a free-trade arrangement, and that the major costs and benefits will occur in that area. This generalization may be correct, but it obscures some important aspects of the situation. Canada's resource-based trade, to take one instance, involves more fabricated goods than raw materials. In the metals and minerals sector, for example, the proportion of crude-material exports has been dropping over the past 20 years and as compared to fabricated or semi-manufactured products, represented only 18 per cent of Canadian exports to the United States in 1983. Crude materials provided only 1 per cent of total forestry sector exports in the same year.

While tariffs are relatively low on fabricated products as compared to end products, the effect of lower tariffs on resource-based exports should not be dismissed lightly. Low tariffs can affect a nation's profitability of processing, and thus influence investment decisions that determine the location of processing facilities. Moreover, even low tariffs must be administered by customs brokers and customs officials and this necessity represents a cost passed on to the foreign exporter that duty-free treatment does not impose. Thus Canada's resource-based industries could make small but significant gains under freer trade.

The cost factor of foreign trade barriers becomes much more important, however, in the area of NTBs. Canada's resource-based industries have been one of the principal targets of U.S. contingency protection; it follows that an agreement on freer trade could give our industries a stronger guarantee of access to U.S. markets. Recently, Canada has faced countervail action against its west-coast lumber industry, and the U.S. Administration has launched investigations into our hog-slaughtering and fishing industries. Copper imports, including those from Canada, were investigated in 1984, but although they were found to be injurious, the U.S. Administration has not imposed restrictive measures.

These NTBs strike at an area of great strength in Canada-U.S. export trade. They harm, in particular, our non-industrial regions. If these regions are to develop further manufacturing potential, they must increase the fabricated content of resource-based products. Abolition of NTBs directed at these products might well represent the largest benefit such regions would obtain from freer Canada-U.S. trade. The importance of a move in this direction is obvious, for as Canada's non-industrial regions develop economically, they will probably export more fabricated and resource-based products to the United States. As this growth occurs, the risk of future U.S. protection – and of the disadvantages it represents to our resource sector – is likely to grow.

Many Canadians have argued that our historic policy of protection has benefited our industrial heartland, but, by contrast, has forced higher prices on the rest of the country. Protection will probably exacerbate any such problem because it will add to the expenses of resource-producing regions, since resource-based industries are most likely to suffer retaliatory U.S. measures. In Commissioners' view, this possibility constitutes another reason for Canada to negotiate freer trade with the United States.

Weaker sectors. The weaker exporting sectors should be of major concern in any move toward freer trade with the United States. These sectors exist principally in secondary manufacturing: the production of textiles, clothing and footwear; machinery and equipment; electronics; electrical machinery and equipment; furniture; scientific equipment; and consumer products. As we have seen, however, it is difficult to determine the areas of weaker performance in Canada's export trade. Where there has been protection, industries or firms tend to protest if that protection is removed and to predict that the change will produce dire consequences. This reaction can create an impression that a sector is weak overall, though as experience in the furniture sector testifies, such an impression is not always accurate. In assessing the effect of free trade on weaker sectors, we Canadians should not ignore areas of strength even within those sectors. Let us examine, for instance, two of these sectors: furniture and electrical machinery and equipment.

The effect of Canada-U.S. free trade on our furniture sector would be uneven and multi-dimensional, and would impinge in different ways on the household-furniture industry and the office-furniture industry. Free trade would affect productivity, competitiveness, labour-market structure and, to a lesser extent, investment patterns. Overall, producers of household furniture would have to make significant structural adjustments to reap production benefits from freer trade, redirecting their marketing strategies from the smaller, domestic, consumer base to the larger and more competitive North American market. Firms that manufacture office furniture would need to make fewer adjustments: many are already oriented toward the North American market, since the majority are American owned. Increased production, therefore, would represent a less demanding challenge for this sub-sector.

It is difficult to assess the effect of free trade on the furniture industry's ability to meet competition. Asian furniture-producers are already challenging Canada's household-furniture sub-sector, although North Carolina, Virginia and Tennessee still produce much of North America's wooden furniture. Ten large firms operate in those States' furniture sectors, and five of them produce more than the entire Canadian household-furnishing industry. The prospect of lowering tariff barriers to these "giants" intimidates Canadian producers.

Many Canadian household-furniture firms, fragmented and operating in single plants, are in a poor position to diversify, to expand marketing networks, and to finance higher transportation costs. Larger firms would be better able to compete with the United States on a free-trade basis. Bauhaus, of Toronto, for example, has established several plants and exports a substantial portion of its product. Some firms, oriented toward the high-income luxury market, export most of their products. Smaller firms would find a foothold in the market because of the continuing need for regional manufacturing, since most furniture is not easily transported. The quality of Canadian design would appear to be an important factor in determining the ability to compete in the U.S. market. The picture, however, is not entirely rosy. The furniture sector employs some 50 000 employees, half of them in the household sub-sector, and the industry estimates that as many as 10 000 jobs could be lost under free trade as smaller and less efficient firms closed down.

The manufacturers of office furniture could meet American competition without making as many adjustments. Despite tariffs, many firms within this sub-sector are oriented to a continental market. Still, a good number of U.S.-controlled Canadian firms hold significant mandates for research and development (R&D) or for design, and they would appreciate elimination of tariffs which add to their product costs.

The electrical machinery and equipment sector produces equipment that generates and distributes electricity or that uses this form of energy. It covers six major sub-sectors: industrial electrical equipment to generate and transmit electricity; electrical wire and cable; major household appliances, such as stoves and refrigerators; small appliances, such as toasters and tea-kettles; miscellaneous electrical products, including conduits and fittings, lamp bulbs, wiring devices and lighting fixtures; and batteries.

The sector generally consists of mature companies with an output of well-established products, and these circumstances suggest that it should seek and exploit new markets in order to re-establish growth. Although employment has fallen in recent years from a peak of 78 268 in 1981 to 70 862 in 1984 – a marked recovery from the trough of 1983 – it is still one of Canada's largest manufacturing employers and therefore of major economic significance. While the majority of firms in the sector are Canadian-owned, American-owned companies account for most of the industry's shipments, revenue and employment (about 60 per cent in 1975). To underscore this reality, one only need think of such industry giants as Canadian General Electric (CGE) and Westinghouse Canada. Intra-corporate trade is extensive and growing as many larger multi-nationals rework their production strategy to cover the North American continent. CGE is a trend-setter in this endeavour.

If Canada and the United States were to move toward freer trade, large American-owned multi-nationals would benefit. Free trade would promote North American rationalization and hence facilitate greater economies of scale. Foreign firms might obtain access to the larger American market through their Canadian subsidiaries, although those with American operations might close their (probably smaller) Canadian branches unless they could be converted to single-product facilities. The effect of free trade on Canadian-owned firms would vary by sub-sector, but as a rule, firms producing relatively customized products, such as electricity-generating equipment, would benefit from increased market access. Firms producing off-the-shelf items such as distribution transformers for the Canadian market might, on the other hand, face strong competition from American producers.

In general, then, free trade would usher in a period of substantial adjustment for both Canadian and foreign-owned firms. The sector has little growth potential beyond exploitation of new market opportunities. Ultimately, free trade would make it necessary for Canadian firms to "bite the bullet", but with a reasonable expectation of long-term increases in employment and sales.

One issue that arises in assessing the effect of free trade on Canada is whether multi-nationals would continue to use their Canadian facilities and would include Canadian operations in their rationalization plans. The example offered by CGE and evidence from the rationalization strategies of other multi-nationals suggest to Commissioners that these large firms are planning to grant specific product mandates to their Canadian facilities. Such an outcome could yield another important benefit to Canada: increased R&D activity, as multi-nationals move projects related to a given product mandate to the appropriate production facility. At present, branch plants producing full product lines on a small scale for the Canadian market undertake little or no R&D; that aspect of their operation is carried out by the parent firm in the "home" country, with consequent loss to Canada.

Conclusions from Sectoral Analysis

Examination of the furniture and electrical machinery sectors can help focus Canadian concerns about free trade: Would individual firms "go under"? Would whole industries or sectors disappear? Would foreign multi-nationals that have located in Canada and provided productive capacity and jobs return home? Perhaps most important: Would Canadian unemployment increase? These questions relate to economic adjustments. Where such adjustments result from change induced by government policy, they create special responsibilities for government, which must manage the consequences of that change.

The results of this Commission's analysis answer the question: Might free trade eliminate any of Canada's manufacturing sectors? Canada has strength in all sectors of its economy. Indeed, free trade would benefit, and not harm, parts of every sector. Even in weaker industries, there are strong and internationally competitive firms. At the level of the individual firm, however, some companies might not withstand increased competition and would probably go under. For example, Canadian firms in the household appliances sub-sector now receive tariff protection that gives them an approximate 15 per cent cost advantage over their U.S. competitors. Firms unable to forgo that advantage would not fare well against increased foreign competition.

Could management in individual firms, and management and labour working in concert, set levels of productivity consistent with North American standards? A good deal depends on the answer, but empirical studies have already shown that a significant amount of routine adjustment takes place in any dynamic economy.[7] Since the end of the Tokyo Round in 1979, Canadian sectors affected by trade have already made adjustments. The adjustments in weaker sectors more often take the form of declining "birth rates" of firms than of rising "death rates". This reality suggests that the popular image of adjustment through plant closings is inaccurate. Commissioners expect that adjustment to Canada-U.S. free trade would be similar to that following the Tokyo Round. Free trade would stimulate entrepreneurial initiative and boost the birth rate of new businesses in areas where Canada is competitive (such as office furniture), and retard the birth of new businesses in less competitive areas (such as household appliances).

Would multi-nationals leave Canada in reaction to free trade? One argument is that multi-nationals originally located here to circumvent our tariffs and would therefore leave if those tariffs were reduced. Some multi-nationals have already left Canada in reaction to Tokyo Round tariff cuts, but there has been no exodus. For several reasons, such a move would be an unlikely consequence of Canada-U.S. free trade. It is not easy to move capital investment. If there are productive opportunities here, foreign investment will pursue them regardless of trade restrictions. If free trade increased access to the U.S. market and made it more secure, opportunities for productive investment in Canada would increase rather than decrease.

While Canadians need expect no general withdrawal of investment, freer trade would probably increase capital and labour mobility between Canada and the United States. Sectoral analysis indicates that Canada would experience gains and losses in a more fluid situation, but that, in general, we would hold our own. Canadian shipbuilding is competitive with that of the United States, and investment would likely increase that sector. The same forecast applies to pulp and paper. In other areas, such as housewares and sporting goods, the results of freer trade would be mixed. Some net "disinvestment" would probably occur in Canada's tire industry and our medical equipment sub-sector, where foreign firms have established themselves in order to supply a small domestic market. In fact, disinvestment has already occurred among manufacturers of medical equipment – a reminder that the *status quo* does not necessarily offer security for our Canadian economy.

Finally, would freer Canada-U.S. trade affect the level of Canadian employment? Commissioners believe that other forces affecting employment dwarf those that would flow from free trade. Among these is the restructuring of industry which has occurred as Canadian firms attempt to meet increasing world competition. Restructuring could reduce labour in individual firms. For example, the recent restructuring at Canadian General Electric resulted in a drop in employment, and reductions in labour occurred for similar reasons at Westinghouse Canada. Freer trade would increase the trend toward restructuring and a reduction in the number of workers per firm: as noted in an analysis of the chemicals sector, "a restructured sector is likely to be more capital intensive."[8] These employment losses probably could not be avoided; in fact, however, the losses would be greater if firms did not modernize and develop greater efficiency. This reality again emphasizes Canada's need to develop a competitive economy which will stimulate the birth of new businesses. Employment gains are more likely to come from new investment than from protecting existing jobs through trade restrictions. They will also derive from the higher real wages made possible by a more productive economy and, by encouraging Canadian consumers to buy more goods, will create more jobs.

Freer trade may also produce a movement toward larger firms, a trend that could have positive effects for labour as well as business. For example, in the ocean and marine sector, "smaller firms would face the largest adjustment problems."[9] A similar trend might occur in many other sectors, such as electrical machinery, chemicals, scientific and medical equipment, forestry and furniture. Smaller firms, especially those producing a wide range of products mainly for local consumption, generally lack the economies of scale required to compete in a wider North American market.

Commissioners believe that on balance, the decision should be made in favour of wider national benefits as against the costs borne by those in weaker and adversely affected industries. Equally, however, we believe that the Canadian government must help to cover the costs of adjustment within declining sectors and industries, for all Canadians will have either to tolerate the decline of some industries or to accept poorer performance overall from our economy. In recommending freer trade between Canada and the United States, Commissioners also recommend that the Canadian government provide a Transitional Adjustment Assistance Program, directed particularly toward retraining displaced employees. We consider details of such assistance in Part V of this Report.

Notes

1. Gilbert R. Winham, "Canada-U.S. Sectoral Trade Study", working paper prepared for the Royal Commission on the Economic Union and Development Prospects for Canada (Ottawa, 1985).
2. Data and tables on sub-sectors (such as footwear) are presented in Winham, "Canada-U.S. Sectoral Trade Study".
3. Canada, Textile and Clothing Board, *Study of the Impact of Potential Free Trade in Textiles and Clothing Between Canada and the United States: Final Report* (Ottawa: The Board, 1984), p. 36.
4. *Ibid.*, p. 35.
5. Winham, "Canada-U.S. Sectoral Trade Study".
6. Clarence L. Barber, "Canadian Tariff Policy", *Canadian Journal of Economics and Political Science* 21 (November 1955): 513–30.
7. Economic Council of Canada, *The Bottom Line: Technology, Trade, and Income Growth* (Ottawa: Minister of Supply and Services Canada, 1983), chapter 9.
8. Winham, "Canada-U.S. Sectoral Trade Study".
9. *Ibid.*

Political Issues

The economic case for freer trade with the United States is strong. It is obvious, of course, that any change of this extent in economic policy is bound to entail a measure of risk, and Commissioners recognize that the consequences of a more open Canada-U.S. trading relationship cannot be predicted in every detail. We are convinced, nonetheless, that the potential economic benefits to Canada of freer trade with the United States far outweigh the costs, and that the principal hazards can be met by instituting appropriate policies of adjustment. Given Canada's increasingly isolated position in the international economy at large, it is difficult, in any case, to conceive of a genuinely effective alternative trade policy.

Nevertheless, we Canadians must also recognize that traditionally, we have been preoccupied as much with the political, cultural and social implications that could result from continental free trade as with its potential effect on our economy. The former concerns are legitimate and important, and obviously, they must be addressed in any serious and responsible evaluation of the bilateral free-trade option. This task, however, is unusually difficult because the issues involved relate to intangibles, and because they raise questions of value. In matters of this kind, unambiguous cause-and-effect relationships are hard to establish and sometimes impossible to verify. Political, cultural and social changes, even when they are profound, often develop only gradually, and at first they may pass unnoticed. They can be as difficult to define as they are awkward to measure. Certainly their scope and character are difficult to guage in advance.

Changes in political, cultural and social behaviour, and in the values that such behaviour reflects, are influenced by a variety of different factors, and not by one factor alone. This reality, of course, further complicates the problem. To identify the particular effect of a single element among many – in this instance, the nature of Canada's trade relationship with the United States – thus presents a challenge capable of defeating even the most sophisticated of modern social scientists' analytical methods. Science can help, but in the end, the answer must come from preference and judgement, subtly combined. Room for disagreement, and hence for public debate, is bound to remain. The question itself, however, is of central importance and warrants a prominent place on the agenda for any discussion of Canada-U.S. trade relations.[1]

Indirect Implications: The Symbolic and the Real

Commissioners are aware that in considering these complicated issues, we are dealing as much with the symbolic as the "real". The problem, of course, concerns the way in which a freer-trading arrangement with the United States would *actually* influence the play of forces affecting Canada's political, social and cultural life. It is just as much concerned, however, with the way that Canadians, Americans and third parties, too, *perceive* the Canada-U.S. relationship. Perceptions are important for two reasons. They can have a potential psychological significance, an effect, for example, on the human sense of "identity" and hence on feelings of psychic well-being. They also affect the individual's own and others' expectations. These expectations, in turn, influence personal conclusions about the nature of reasonable aspirations and the judgements others form about those conclusions and their results. Canadians' goals and capacities are thus determined, not merely by our values and assets, but also by the way in which we perceive ourselves and by the way in which we are perceived by others.

If a bilateral free-trade area were negotiated, would it have a symbolic effect, no matter what its practical economic implications, powerful enough to persuade Canadians that they had finally abandoned (in substance, if not in form) their traditional objective of maintaining a genuinely independent political community culturally and socially different from the United States? It is possible, after all, to argue that this general purpose has underlain the Canadian political experiment throughout its history. Certainly, much of Canadian public policy in such areas as transport and communications, resource and revenue sharing, cultural affairs, broadcasting and constitutional law has been designed, in part, to preserve a separate and distinctive political community, despite the North-South pull of natural market forces. These policy initiatives have exacted an economic and even, perhaps, a political price. Would an announcement that Canada had successfully negotiated a free-trade arrangement with the United States ultimately reduce Canadians' desire to "pay the piper" and hence impel us to move to other forms of integration, as well? Would a formal meshing of the two markets lead to the view that the differences remaining between the two countries are so insignificant, so trivial or so ancillary that they are not worth defending?

Though this concern may be legitimate, few Canadians seem to hold it. Rather, this Commission's public hearings discovered a sense of political confidence which may not have existed just a few years ago. This sense of assurance is evident both in an aura of confidence about the distinctiveness of Canadian political values and in lucid assessments of political reality and of the particular role that Canada might play in international affairs.

Canada's trade, both import and export, is already extremely closely linked to the United States. A free-trade area would help to secure our access to the U.S. market over the longer term and would gradually increase the efficiency of our industrial structure. Presumably, it would also increase the volume of trade between the two countries and ultimately make Canadian products more competitive in markets overseas, besides. Overall, however, there is no reason to assume that the nature of Canada's existing trade dependency on the United States would change significantly. We might conclude, therefore, that a free-trade area would be unlikely to induce psychological or symbolic side-effects that Canadians are not already experiencing.

Nevertheless, it could still be held that this conclusion underestimates the symbolic impact that a formal declaration of Canada-U.S. free trade would have on the Canadian side of the border. To declare a free-trade area after formal intergovernmental negotiations as a concerted act of political will is a procedure very different from the incremental process that has led to the current Canada-U.S. trade relationship. At the very least, a declaration is much more dramatic. In symbolic terms, therefore, its effect might be substantially greater than the resulting change in real economic relations would appear, on the surface, to warrant. Indeed, Commissioners believe that this is part of the reason that the present participants in the free-trade debate are searching for palatable terms to replace "free trade".

To put the issue in perspective, we should, perhaps, consider that much more elaborately integrative economic arrangements have been negotiated elsewhere without causing harmful side-effects. The European Community (EC) is the commonly cited example. The analogy is not entirely persuasive, however, and certainly it will hardly reassure the sceptical. The Community constitutes a multilateral, not a bilateral, arrangement, and the distribution of power among its principal members is far less disparate than that within the Canada-U.S. relationship. In addition, the EC countries differ far more profoundly from one another, in language, in culture and, often, in historical experiences of conflict, than do Canada and the United States.

The concerns of Canadians about the United States are clearly of a different order: they stem, not from preoccupation with the prevention of war and the maintenance of peace, but from a fear of complete assimilation. More persuasive examples are afforded by the free-trade arrangements forged on an individual basis, between the European Community and members of the European Free Trade Association (EFTA): Norway, Sweden, Finland, Portugal, Austria and Switzerland. None of these countries has a population larger than ten million, while the EC population stands at 240 million. Yet no one would suggest that the EFTA members are no longer distinctive, or that they have felt constrained to mirror the Community in their foreign policy or other areas of activity. Certainly there has been no effort to effect political integration. Similarly, the free-trade arrangement between the United Kingdom and Ireland before they both joined the Community did not dispose the Irish to become more like the English; nor have we seen any evidence that New Zealanders are becoming more like Australians as a result of their bilateral free-trade agreement.

Arguments drawn from the experiences of the European Community, EC-EFTA and Australia-New Zealand and reassurances based on the present scope of the Canada-U.S. trade relationship may not be conclusive enough, in themselves, to comfort those concerned that the creation of a formal free-trade area would profoundly weaken that distinctive political will that has inspired Canada's development. Other considerations, however, lead this Commission to conclude that this anxiety can be safely put to rest. The first of these considerations stems from the very disparity of power that is the source of the problem. Traditionally, Canadians have assumed that American influence is so overwhelmingly pervasive that it has left Canada, politically and socially, permanently vulnerable. Some Canadians have even argued that it will be impossible, in the end, to avoid the loss of our distinctive political, social and cultural values. One of the consequences of permanent vulnerability, however, is the tendency to defend oneself by adopting a posture of permanent vigilance. Some scholars have argued quite cogently that in bilateral contexts of this kind, the smaller of the two countries is bound to be especially protective of its distinguishing characteristics. It has often been observed that nothing has made francophone Canadians so determined to preserve the distinctive ingredients of their culture as the fact that they are surrounded by 250 million anglophones. Much the same phenomenon, Commissioners believe, applies to Canada as a whole, in relation to the United States. We do not think, therefore, that a more visible integration of Canadian and American economic markets will lead Canadians to abandon the defence of indigenous political and social norms. Such a development might, in fact, have precisely the reverse effect.

Many of the most distinctive features of Canada's political culture are securely rooted in a historical experience that not only differed from that of the United States, but was, in some respects, deliberately opposed to it. It is a commonplace that Americans established their independence by revolution, whereas Canadians acquired theirs by a succession of relatively peaceful steps. Our evolutionary political development, strengthened by the influence of the United Empire Loyalists, originated in a counter-revolutionary tradition that was deeply embedded in both anglophone and francophone communities. It has produced a markedly different concept of the role of government in society and has profoundly affected the priorities that Canadians attach to various political values. We consider order highly important, for example, to the pursuit of political ends; this is not because we think decorum more attractive than liberty, but because we believe that true liberty, which can be found only in communities where civility is highly valued, cannot be enjoyed without it. Our accommodative approach to the resolution of political conflict, both at home and abroad, reflects a similar conviction. Such attitudes, vital as they are to the survival of the distinctive features of Canadian political life, are deeply ingrained in our society. Certainly it would take more than a change in trade policy to dislodge them.

Commissioners' conviction on this matter is reinforced by our view that in recent years, Canada's linguistic duality has been gaining wider and wider internal recognition and acceptance, and that over time, bilingualism in English and French will become a more prevalent – indeed, a prominent – feature of Canadian life. Canada's accommodation of a large and lively francophone community and culture has always served to distinguish our society from that of the United States, and the need to secure and promote the welfare of our francophone element has led us to adopt policies and conventions that have strengthened our accommodative political culture. The importance of this characteristic as a source of differences between Canadians and Americans is bound to increase as bilingualism becomes more common and is viewed, not as an inconvenience, but as a matter of national pride.

This Commission has been profoundly impressed by the confidence that Canadians have come to show in themselves as individuals and in their country as a political community. The evidence obtained through our public hearings, as well as from personal observation and other sources, has led us to conclude that as a people, we Canadians are no longer victim to that enervating sense of uncertainty that derives from self-perceived "colonial" status, whether that status be formal (as in the days of French sovereignty or of the British Empire) or informal (as some have considered it more recently, in relation to the United States). Our country has matured, and our literature, art, theatre, music, dance and scholarship more and more reflect its vitality. This same spirit can be found, as well, in the imaginative renovation of our cities; in the calibre of our professions; in our adaptations to technological change; in the mix of realism and compassion that is demonstrated in our social policies; in the cosmopolitan flavour of our urban communities; in the determination to protect our natural environment that is central to the Canadian experience; and even in the variety, style and quality of our restaurants and places of popular entertainment. These indicators may be subjective: certainly they must be subjectively read. Yet they all seem to point in the same direction. The day of the apologetic Canadian is gone, and there is no reason to suppose that our present confidence will be undermined by an arrangement designed only to secure a continuing exchange of goods and services with the United States. On the contrary, it seems probable that a free-trade arrangement would actually strengthen our national assurance by providing clear evidence that Canadians can prosper in a highly competitive market, without the aid of artificial protection. From the psychological, as from the economic, point of view, protective barriers may seem, on the surface, to offer a measure of security in a harsh and uncertain environment. We must also recognize them, however, as unmistakable confessions of weakness. Until these barriers are gone, the exhilaration that can come from a true sense of maturity will remain beyond our nation's reach.

Finally, Commissioners are persuaded that we Canadians are perfectly capable of mentally separating our trading activities in the North American market-place from the other aspects of our national way of life. Motives of protection aside, the concerns of Canadians who have traditionally opposed free trade with the United States have been founded on the premise, whether explicit or not, that among the basic determinants of our political, social and cultural habits and values are the prevailing patterns of economic exchange. This proposition should not, of course, be confused with a complex argument sometimes advanced by political theorists. The essential tenet of this contention is that our political beliefs, social norms and cultural practices ultimately reflect the way in which we organize and conduct our system of economic production. How we *produce* our economic goods and services is not ground for argument in the Canada-U.S. free-trade debate. The point at issue is the manner in which those goods and services are *traded*. The assumption underlying the fears of the hesitant observer is that this trade is or, if further expanded, could well become the principal connection through which Canadians will be exposed to, and eventually transformed by, the values and the behaviour of a society both different from and more powerful than our own.

Clearly this is not a proposition that is new to Canadians, nor is it confined to the Canadian context. The free movement of goods and services has often been viewed as an instrument of political, social and cultural change. Its presumed effects have sometimes been regarded as positive (when thought, for example, to be an encouragement to peace) and sometimes as negative (when perceived, for instance, as a vehicle of empire). Whatever its intellectual history, however, free trade constitutes a thesis that cannot lightly be dismissed. At a general psychological level, however, it does not seem to this Commission that the development of such a system would have an automatic "spill-over" effect on the way we Canadians perceive ourselves in political, social or cultural terms. We surely tend to differentiate these other ingredients of our lives from the way in which we market that portion of our gross national product that we export. Digby scallop fishermen are no less Digby scallop fishermen because more of their catch is sold in Boston than in Montreal. If free trade is to reduce our political, social and cultural sovereignty, it must work in ways far more definite and concrete than the psychological.

It is less certain, however, that reactions outside Canada will be as varied, and this is a matter to which Commissioners have given considerable attention. Social scientists often observe that human beings tend to perceive communities other than their own – national communities included – as oversimplified stereotypes. This tendency increases when the observers are at a distance, and when their detailed knowledge of the external group is limited. Distinctions obvious to Canadians may thus be invisible abroad, and accordingly, our participation with the United States in a free-trade area may lead both Americans and nations overseas to assume that Canada and its neighbour are homogeneous, not merely in our marketing arrangements, but in other essential respects, as well. Consequently these external observers may expect that Canadian and American policies and behaviour will be the same, and this disposition may be enhanced by their perception of other similarities between the two societies.

In the United States, persons with a special interest in Canadian affairs would probably make less obvious presumptions of this sort than would the population at large, since the former would be more fully acquainted with the details and complexities of Canadian life. Nevertheless, the preoccupations even of these especially interested sectors are often very narrow. The executives of construction firms along the border may focus with genuine expertise on Canadian cement production, but pay little attention to any other aspect of Canadian life. In fact, ignorance of Canada, even among occupants of important government offices in Washington, understandable though it may be, is nonetheless regarded by knowledgeable observers as a recurring and pervasive problem. Is it possible, then, that the creation of a formal Canada-U.S./free-trade area would lead influential Americans to assume that we Canadians had allied ourselves even more fully than in the past with American objectives and "the American dream"? If so, would these American leaders expect Canadian public policies and pronouncements – especially in foreign affairs – to follow suit? And if they did, would a Canadian government that disagreed with an American position and adopted an independent view risk generating greater resentment in the United States than under present conditions? Further, would that complication, in itself, make Ottawa even more reluctant than it is now to deviate from American preferences?

To some extent these possibilities have already, for some time past, assumed a degree of reality in Canada's foreign-policy environment. The danger, therefore, would be more a result of changes in degree than of changes in kind. Nevertheless, it is certainly possible that after concluding a free-trade agreement, Canada's foreign-policy community would have to deal with expectations of co-operative Canadian behaviour that would be much more deeply rooted in American perceptions than they are now. We should therefore have to make a considerable and continuing effort to prevent policy makers in Washington from assuming that the free-trade arrangement included integration in other policy fields as well. This requirement is part of the ground on which this Commission has based its conclusion, stated in Chapter 2 of this report, that Canada should pursue an actively "internationalist" role in world affairs, giving particular priority, for example, to assisting less-developed countries to resolve their economic problems. Nothing will more quickly dispel the notion that Canadian foreign policy has followed our trade policy than convincingly concrete demonstrations that it has not. To provide this evidence may not prove overly difficult, since Canadians will probably become more aware of our wider foreign-policy capabilities as economic benefits from free-trade with the United States provide us with a new sense of "clout" in the international community. In the words of one study, "a persuasive case can be made that, if a formal bilateral free-trade agreement strengthens the Canadian economy, Canada's ability to pursue an independent foreign policy would be strengthened, not weakened."[2] Thus the cultivation of Washington's respect for Canada's complete sovereignty in the conduct of our external affairs could help to preserve the measure of independence that Canadians have come to expect.

The need for our diplomatic missions overseas to demonstrate this reality, as well as to deploy aggressive public-education strategies would be all the greater because nations elsewhere in the world might be even more prone than Americans to assume that Canada and the United States, once linked under a formal free-trade agreement, would speak and act in unison. This assumption already creates a problem for Canadian diplomats. Foreign-service officers who have worked in Europe, for example, constantly complain that European statespersons and officials fail to distinguish Canada from the United States, in responding to what they take to be a common North American interest. It seems highly probable that this tendency would be increased by the announcement that a Canada-U.S./free-trade area had been established. Even where the tendency to "homogenize" Canada and the United States derived more from tactical calculation than from thoughtless assumption, the very existence of the arrangement would give third-party governments ammunition with which to defend their positions against Canadian complaint. Only with the greatest difficulty, indeed, was Canada able to negotiate a largely innocuous and ultimately ineffective "contractual link" with the European Community. The reluctance of the European governments most concerned, Britain and Denmark prominently among them, would have been even easier to justify if a Canada-U.S./free-trade area had been in place. The problem for Canadian negotiators would have been complicated if the Americans had insisted, as they probably would have done, on "pass-through" safeguards to ensure that they were not deluged with European goods imported by way of Canada. Such circumstances would have provided the Europeans with a ready-made rationale for their resistance, even if their real motive had lain elsewhere.

These situations, real and hypothetical, demonstrate that Canada must make a vigorous and persistent effort to ensure that foreign powers and their interested publics understand the intended limits of any Canada-U.S. agreement. Unfortunately, the very circumstance that would strengthen the necessity for this effort could also make it more difficult to exercise. The free-trade area itself would be visible, lasting and concrete. Equally impressive characteristics would be harder to detect in the exhortations of Canadian diplomats bent on public education abroad or in their sporadic displays of independence of American policies. The challenge to Canada's foreign-policy community would thus be a serious and demanding one, calling for determined and imaginative responses. For internal as well as international purposes, that challenge would have to be met.

Direct Implications: Political Demands and Policy Constraints

It is probable that the most significant and long-term effect of free trade would be the strengthening of national unity and the removal of one of the most persistent and corrosive sources of regional alienation in Canada's political history. The resentment generated by protectionist policies has been especially acute in the West, but it has also been a nagging cause of irritation in Atlantic Canada and in the agricultural communities of Ontario and Quebec. Although, in recent years, multilateral negotiations through the GATT have lowered tariffs a good deal, Canadians elsewhere in the country still believe strongly that the manufacturing and industrial economy of central Canada is being maintained at their expense. To conclude a free-trade agreement with the United States would remove this long-standing cause of dissatisfaction at a single stroke. It is difficult to think of any other act of Canadian public policy that would have so comparably healing an effect. This act could be expected, in time, to contribute enormously to our national sense of Canada as a single community and could regenerate our previous store of general good will. It would correspondingly reduce the level of federal-provincial conflict and increase our capacity to work together for common purposes. Commissioners have concluded that this positive political consequence of a bilateral free-trade agreement represents one of the strongest arguments in its favour. This result would embody long-term advantages for all Canadians as individuals and for the whole of Canada as a political and social community.

It is still possible, of course, that Canada-U.S. free trade would constrain aspects of Canadian public policy in certain specific areas not immediately related to free trade *per se*, but perhaps linked to it indirectly. Though such constraints would count for little, compared to the improvement in national harmony already described, they should nonetheless be taken into account. They could be expected to materialize in one or the other of two general contexts: the first of them a source of pressure from the United States; the second, a source of pressure from Canadians themselves.

The first of these two contexts would derive from fields of activity which, in Canadian eyes, required a measure of state intervention, but where the Americans would regard such intervention as violating the spirit, if not the letter, of the free-trade arrangement. The most obvious sources of this kind of disagreement would be Canadian policies designed to protect or promote indigenous cultural activities, along with measures intended to encourage local, regional or sectoral economic development. As in so many of the situations where difficulty might arise from Canada-U.S./free-trade proposals, these sources of friction would not be entirely new in relations between the two countries. Students of the dispute over transborder broadcasting, for example, will attest to this observation. The problem can result, not merely from initiatives undertaken by the federal authorities in Ottawa, but from those instigated by provincial and municipal governments as well. It has, in fact, appeared not merely in relation to economic strategies at the national level, as with the National Energy Policy, but also in the context of policies of little more than local significance. An example of the latter sort of intervention appears in American reactions to Canadian incentives given to Michelin tire producers or to the builders of fishing boats in Nova Scotia.

While this problem, then, would not be new, it might certainly expand to less tractable dimensions. A free-trade arrangement would heighten free-market expectations in the United States and correspondingly reduce the range of what the Americans would consider appropriate standards of "fair play". It would, in essence, strengthen the conviction of offended American interests that in protesting Canadian governments' intervention in support of our own economy, they were acting from just cause. This conviction would increase American determination to press for changes in Canadian policy and at the same time, make U.S. arguments more difficult for Canadian authorities to resist. In short, if the problem of American influence on our Canadian economy is already serious, the establishment of a bilateral free-trade area could make it more serious still.

Since encouragement to regional economic development is among the most central of the public policy expectations of Canadians, no government properly concerned with the maintenance of national unity and with its own survival in office will be prepared to give up its latitude of decision in this field. Moreover, the case for assisting those engaged in Canadian cultural activities may well be strengthened, rather than weakened, by a bilateral free-trade arrangement, since many Canadians will insist that free trade is "safe" only if other facets of Canadian life are properly protected. It follows that any agreement negotiated with the United States would have to be accompanied by specific exclusions designed to preserve the capacity of Canadian governments at all levels to pursue these important objectives. Undoubtedly, this proviso would increase both the technical and the diplomatic complexity of free-trade negotiations. Certainly it would prolong them, and it could ultimately generate opposing forces in the American Congress. Even after an agreement had been concluded and put into place, it could be expected to lead to recurring disputes over the implementation of the "exclusion" provisions.

There can be no easy solution to this problem, and Canadians should realize from the beginning that coping with it will be part of the price of any Canada-U.S./free-trade agreement. In the past, however, the Canada-U.S. agenda has been crowded with "functional" issues of this kind, and it will continue to be crowded with them in the future. But we cannot avoid these issues simply by perpetuating our current policies. On the contrary, there is good reason to assume that in the absence of an explicit agreement, they will create ever more difficult problems for Canada-U.S. relations. These problems will arise as the Americans become both more aware and more resentful of Canadian policies which, in times of economic hardship, they are bound to perceive as unfair. Therefore, the wisest course for Canada, notwithstanding obstacles along the way, might well be to pursue a free-trade agreement in which exclusions could be clearly defined. It would have the practical effect of removing important Canadian public policy initiatives in the nation-building field from the direct line of American fire.

There is, however, a second context in which a bilateral free-trade agreement might lead to significant change in the configuration of political forces confronting Canadian decision-makers. It would be characterized by constraints emanating, not from the United States, but from within Canada itself. Such constraints, of course, are always present in the political system, but as a specific by-product of free trade, they could be expected to arise primarily in relation to government policies that had the effect of "artificially" increasing the production costs of Canadian enterprises over those of comparable and competing firms in the United States. Cost increases of this kind are sometimes the indirect result of regulatory activity designed to serve other public objectives; for instance, labour codes, safety requirements, environmental regulations and product standards might increase production costs. Increases can also appear more directly as a consequence of any of a number of different forms of taxation. In either situation, the costs are ultimately reflected in product prices, and if those borne by Canadian companies are out of line with those faced by corresponding businesses in the United States, a decline in competitive position can result. The natural disposition of an economic sector which is disadvantaged in this way — and if corporate taxation is a cause, the disadvantage could extend to a very large proportion of the business community — is to protest what it will regard as an unfair handicap and to press for an appropriate relaxation of government requirements.

Again, this is a phenomenon with which governments are already very familiar. Some might argue, therefore, that a bilateral Canada-U.S./trade arrangement would bring very little change in this respect. Nevertheless, political authorities might find such expressions of discontent more persistent and more difficult to resist under a bilateral free-trade regime. The problem might intensify because the new agreement would place businesses in a position to invoke the same standards of "fair play" as Americans are likely to cite in their attacks, for example, on subsidies to support regional economic development. Moreover, Canadian regulations are sometimes more expensive to implement than are American regulations because the former demand a higher standard of performance. To the extent that this difference applies, there could well be a decline in public welfare as previously defined by the internal political process.

Whether such a pattern of policy change would actually develop on a significant scale is hard to predict. Ultimately, the extent of its development would depend on the degree to which Canadians were genuinely committed to the objectives supported by the regulations in question and to the particular distribution of tax obligations that might also be involved. Canadians at large, for example, are increasingly conscious of their plight as victims of acid rain. It seems improbable, therefore, that they would very readily support a relaxation of air-pollution controls simply because the industries affected were complaining that the pertinent regulations were placing them at a competitive disadvantage in the American market. This is an unusually dramatic example, however, and it is not inconceivable that in many other areas, a free-trade arrangement would generate political forces which, over time, would bring Canadian taxation and industrial regulation much closer to the American pattern than they are at present. In some instances, this development might result in an improvement. In others, however, it would not, and a public authority determined to resist what might be considered a change for the worse could find itself in confrontation with opposing forces stronger than those it had faced in the past.

Furthermore, under a bilateral free-trade agreement with the United States, Canadian governments, both federal and provincial, would find themselves subject, even more than they are now, to conflicting demands arising from competing principles or interests. A government might be tempted, for instance, to relax or abandon a particular policy either because interests in the American private or public sector (perhaps aided by Canadian allies) pressed it to do so in the interests of freer trade, or because Canadian entrepreneurs had argued their need to compete on an equal footing in the American market. If it gave way to the temptation it could face a strong backlash from constituents who disapproved. To the extent that the change in policy could be traced directly to American pressure or even to the logic of the free-trade agreement, such a reaction would probably be fuelled and strengthened by nationalist sentiments. This, in fact, is precisely the syndrome supporting the "posture of permanent vigilance", which is one of the bases of Commissioners' confidence that Canada-U.S. free trade could be safely instituted without damaging Canadians' sense of political, social and cultural independence. It does not, however, create a situation which governments would necessarily welcome, since it would force them to deal with incompatible demands. Administrators could be pardoned for thinking that they have enough of this to do even now, without the addition of further complications to their task.

This problem of "cross pressures" could be particularly acute in matters bearing on foreign affairs. In those areas, it could even arise as a result of foreign-policy decisions taken in Washington, without any reference whatever to Canadian interests or concerns. Unpopular foreign-policy behaviour on the part of the United States could cause angry Canadian constituents to charge authorities with a kind of "guilt by association" firmly established by the creation of the free-trade area. During the Vietnamese War, for instance, the Canadian government was accused of complicity in American policy. This accusation was based, in part, on the practical implications of the Defence Production Sharing Arrangement, and Canadian firms known to be exporting military materiel to the United States under this arrangement became targets of vigorous demonstrations. A sectoral trading agreement that seemed to make good sense at a time of general consensus among the Western powers on "Cold War" issues thus came to be regarded in some quarters as totally unsatisfactory when consensus broke down. Canadians who have shared a more general belief that our foreign policies in the politico-security field have been too closely linked with those of the United States have argued for years that the problem, as they see it, is ultimately rooted in our heavy dependence for our prosperity on our links with the American economy. Once a Canada-U.S./free-trade area had been formally established, this sort of complaint could be expected to recur, and discontent might become a particularly difficult problem if the United States were to embark on controversial military interventions in Latin America or elsewhere. It is possible, indeed, that concerns about such issues are well-founded, for a Canadian government, in circumstances of this kind, would be tempted, at the very least, to moderate its criticisms in order to preserve the amity of the all-important bilateral Canada-U.S. relationship.

Once again, this problem of cross pressures is not new in Canadian politics. It comes down, therefore, to a question of whether or not a free-trade arrangement would appreciably enhance its importance with the United States. In practice, the answer would depend, in part, on the nature of American policy and on political conditions in the entire international community. It is certainly possible that the formation of a Canada-U.S./free-trade area would increase, at least moderately, the potential for controversy over foreign-policy issues of this kind. At the same time, however, we should recognize that Canada is already closely linked with the United States through a variety of associations, and that some of these are far more directly related to international political and security matters than a free-trade arrangement would be. Since 1949, Canada and the United States have been members of the North Atlantic Treaty Organization (NATO), a formal institutionalized alliance. Moreover, the technical requirements of military operations in this nuclear age have compelled both nations to integrate many of their practical preparations for continental defence, an arrangement that is most visible in the North American Aerospace Defence Command (NORAD) arrangement. In such circumstances, it seems unlikely that a bilateral free-trade agreement would have more than a marginal effect on complications which are already very much in evidence, and which cannot, in any event, be avoided.

Some Canadians may be concerned with the broader possibility that a Canada-U.S./free-trade agreement would lead in time to an erosion of the distinctive characteristics of Canada's "political culture". These characteristics include such fundamental matters as the way we Canadians view our political system and the political process; how we assess the proper role of the state in relation to individuals; the manner in which we approach the resolution of our internal political conflicts; and the overall objectives that we think it appropriate for our various levels of government to pursue. While our collective attitudes on questions of this sort are not always clearly expressed, they are nonetheless centrally important determinants of our style of political life and our expectations of public policy. If, under the influence of an American example strengthened by free-trade connections, they were fundamentally to change their character, a subtle but significant transformation of Canadian political practice would result.

Commissioners have already indicated that there are powerful reasons for concluding that bilateral free trade would not, in fact, jeopardize Canadians' perceptions of the ways in which our political culture differs from that of the United States. Our politico-cultural distinctions are too well secured by our historical experience, our linguistic duality, and other factors. The issue is sufficiently complex, however, to warrant further discussion, if only because our political values are difficult to define, and because the question of what they are, both in theory and in practice, is open for argument.

At the broadest level of political philosophy, there is little, if any, reason to anticipate a noticeable change in Canada's political norms. Canadians subscribe, in general terms, to the principles and practices of liberal democracy as sustained by representative parliamentary institutions; to the concepts of responsible government and of government through political party; and to the rule of law. We share the essential values of the liberal democratic position with the citizens of the United States, and to the extent that Canadians differ from Americans in putting these values into practice, the difference arises from distinctive institutional arrangements that are now firmly embedded in constitutional history and practice. In recent years, some analysts have argued that the Canadian style of political leadership in the executive branch of government has become similar to that of the American presidential system. Others have suggested that Canada's new Charter of Rights will eventually help us to become much more "rights-conscious" than we have been in the past. This change, they suggest, will make us more "American" in our view of the way in which individuals and groups ought to react to the exercise of authority. If this process occurs, it may "Americanize" the role played by Canadian courts. Given our system of "parliamentary sovereignty" as modified by the federal-provincial division of powers, Canadian courts have traditionally interpreted their functions much more narrowly than have their counterparts in the United States, where a constitutional arrangement of "checks and balances" applies. Cases arising from the Charter, however, may compel our Justices to adopt a more typically American view. It has also been argued, however, that the particular characteristics of the Canadian Charter, including the various caveats attached to its provisions, will combine with the conservatism of our courts to produce a uniquely Canadian constitutional jurisprudence. In these matters, certainty comes only with hindsight, but if our courts are changing in the direction of American practice, the changes are originating in forces that appear to be operating quite independently of the American example. Certainly, in this Commission's view, it would be difficult to argue convincingly that such changes are the result of the American orientation of

Canadian trade. Neither is there any intrinsic element in the proposal for a formal bilateral free-trade area that would accelerate Canada's constitutional "Americanization", even if our current political evolution is taking us in that direction.

The nature of Canada's constitutional processes would thus be unaffected by the new trade relationship *per se*. The consequences could be very different, however, in relation to Canadians' concept of how and for what purpose the powers of the state ought to be used. Americans, for example, have been attracted to the principle – if not always to the policy – of free trade, not merely because they have thought that principle to be in their overall economic interest, but also because it appeals to the *laissez-faire* values of free enterprise that have been so prominent a feature of their particular interpretation of liberalism. At the admitted risk of overgeneralization, it can be argued that one of the basic differences between the political cultures of Canada and the United States appears in the greater willingness of Canadians to encourage direct state intervention in the operations of the economy to attain those objectives of society that they consider more important than maintaining economic efficiency. This difference, of course, is a matter of degree, and not every example fits the general pattern.

In some quarters, changes would doubtless be welcome, but welcome or not, it seems clear that they would eventually make Canadian society less distinguishable from that of the United States. Of course, processes of this sort would be influenced by a great variety of different factors, and if they materialized at all, they would do so over a long period of time. It is not obvious, therefore, that a bilateral free-trade regime would make the most significant contribution to change, either directly, through its effect on the distribution of real political forces, or indirectly, by way of its influence on Canada's public philosophy. As Commissioners have already argued, it seems probable that countervailing reactions would quickly emerge. Yet the issue is no less important because it is relatively subjective and its outcome uncertain. Indeed, a judgement concerning it must be part of any responsible calculation of the possible costs and benefits to Canada of a bilateral free-trade agreement.

Another possible political implication of a Canada-U.S./free-trade arrangement is of the possibility that it would influence the structural distribution of power within the Canadian political system. Some analysts have suggested, in particular, that such an agreement might enhance the power of the executive branch of government at the expense of the legislative branch – a phenomenon commonly described by political scientists as "executive dominance" – and that it might also increase the powers of the federal government in relation to those of the provinces.

The European Community certainly offers evidence that common market arrangements can amplify the executive's role. It is important to remember, however, that the Community is just that: a common market, and not merely a free-trade area. Moreover, its operations extend into an impressive range of regulatory activities under the administration of an elaborately developed, supranational, public service. It has a directly elected parliament and an intricate system of intergovernmental meetings. In short, it is a much more ambitious, and certainly much more highly institutionalized, arrangement than Commissioners contemplate for Canada and the United States. The founders of the Common Market set about deliberately to encourage economic and political integration and, if anything, are disappointed at its slow pace. There seems to be no reason to assume, therefore, that the European pattern would be replicated automatically in any Canada-U.S./free-trade arrangement.

Conversely, many of the non-tariff barriers (NTBs) that would be negotiated in discussions leading to a bilateral Canada-U.S./free-trade regime clearly fall within the jurisdiction of our provinces rather than of our federal government. Thus these NTBs reflect provincial rather than federal policies. For this reason, Canada could not pursue a free-trade agreement with the United States without extensive discussions between our federal and provincial authorities. Since it would be difficult for either the federal or the provincial legislative branches to play an active role in this process, and since the successful conclusion of a free-trade agreement would confront both levels of government with a *fait accompli*, it is clear that "executive federalism" would be reinforced at least temporarily. That is to say, important public policy issues would be settled through behind-the-scenes bargaining by executives at both levels of government, to the effective exclusion of the legislatures. Trade policy has always been conducted in this manner, and will continue to be managed in this way, whether we Canadians pursue our interests bilaterally or multilaterally.

A free-trade agreement would require the provinces to give up some of their latitude in the use of public policies that made use of NTBs. This constraint would certainly deprive them of some of their freedom of political and governmental manœuvre. In fact, the prospect could represent one of the most difficult obstacles in the way of a successful agreement between the federal governments of the United States and Canada. Provincial opposition to some of the specific provisions that the Americans would expect to have included in a free-trade arrangement could seriously impede the progress of negotiations. Presumably, this difficulty could be overcome only if provincial authorities were satisfied that their interests, including their jurisdictional rights, were being adequately protected. It is conceivable, nonetheless, that in the long run, a free-trade arrangement would reduce the power of the provinces in relation to that of the federal government and of the market, as well. Such a process, however, appears to Commissioners to be in prospect for multilateral negotiations also, given the issues on the GATT agenda.

Finally, it is possible that a bilateral free-trade agreement would raise the general level of conflict in Canadian politics. Our trade policy in relation to the United States has always been a major source of domestic political controversy. Canadians have commonly assumed, for instance, that our tariff structures have been designed to serve the interests of the industrial heartland at the expense of the rest of the country. Debate on this issue is bound to revive with any proposal for radical policy change, and such conflicts could persist after an agreement was established if the distribution of its costs and benefits was perceived in some quarters to be inequitable. The problem could be complicated if economic hardships later developed from other causes, but were attributed to the workings of the free-trade agreement. In effect, that agreement could become the scapegoat for economic difficulties, the origins of which were located elsewhere. If these difficulties were concentrated in particular regions or industrial sectors, as seems likely, significant cleavages over the merits of the arrangement could easily occur, and they could seriously complicate our political process.

Whether or not some such sequence of events would actually occur over the longer term is impossible to determine in advance, since the eventuality would depend on conditions which cannot now be predicted. The critical question, in any event, is whether the intensity of the problem would be significantly greater under bilateral free trade than it is at present, or under another trade-policy option. There is a sense, of course, in which conflicts of this kind are endemic in liberal democracies everywhere, and it would be utopian to expect them to disappear. Such conflicts are therefore an overriding cause for concern only if they become so severe that they exceed the capacity of normal political processes to resolve them. The conclusion of this Commission is that they will not reach this level. On the contrary, Commissioners are sufficiently confident of the economic rewards that would come from the establishment of a bilateral free-trade area that we believe a Canada-U.S./free-trade agreement would ultimately reduce, rather than increase, the general degree of disaffection within Canadian society. A far more serious danger would result from persisting in our present course which, under current conditions of international trade, is certain to isolate our economy further and to cause Canadians significant hardship.

Although these arguments represent this Commission's point of view, we recognize that the questions we have raised in this section of our Report are ultimately matters of judgement. We realize, too, that there are few political (as contrasted with economic) arguments that can be mounted in favour of the bilateral free-trade option, except for those rooted in regional harmony and in the economic prosperity that a free-trade area would help to promote and maintain. The question, therefore, is whether the political arguments that can be deployed against a Canada-U.S./free-trade agreement should be regarded as decisive. Since we find many of these arguments unpersuasive, and since we are convinced that in cultural and other fields they can be countered by aggressive public policy responses of a kind with which Canadians are already very familiar, we do not consider them compelling. Under a free-trade arrangement, problems would doubtless remain, but there are problems even now, and it does not seem to us that their weight would be greatly increased by the conclusion of a formal free-trade agreement with the United States.

Commissioners wish to make it clear that our reference here to the need for "aggressive public policy" in cultural and other fields as a concomitant of a bilateral freer-trade initiative is not merely incidental to our main argument. We are convinced that freer trade with the United States, whether achieved multilaterally or bilaterally, is the only sound choice for Canada in the years ahead, and we are persuaded that in the end, it would serve to strengthen our economic policy at home and thereby enhance our effectiveness abroad. Given the economics of Canadian cultural activity, however, it is clear that in this field, active government support will still be required.

This support should not, in Commissioners' view, take the form of restrictions on the flow into Canada of cultural, intellectual and informational communications from the outside world. Barriers of this kind are increasingly impracticable to administer and enforce, as broadcasting regulators would be the first to agree. More important, they come dangerously close to violating the basic principles of a free society, and for this reason they are properly resented by Canadians who wish to maximize their own freedom of choice in such matters. They tend, in addition, to protect our artists, writers, entertainers and educators from the "quality control" that results from exposure to international standards of performance. Inevitably, perhaps, they also cause irritation abroad.

What Canadians do require, however, is a willingness on the part of public authorities to provide support for those forms of indigenous cultural expression that would otherwise give way to the impersonal forces of the market. It has not been the function of this Commission to examine these matters in depth. (They are considered at length in the 1982 *Report* of the Federal Cultural Policy Review Committee.)[3] It does, however, seem to us essential that programs designed to encourage both the production and the dissemination of Canadian contributions to the visual, applied and performing arts, to creative and academic literature, and to quality enterprises in film, broadcasting and musical recording, should be maintained and, indeed, expanded. Our opinion is reinforced by the obvious success of the Canada Council and other granting agencies in stimulating the extraordinary growth, over the past 20 years, of a thriving Canadian community of artists, writers and scholars, many of whom have international reputations of which all Canadians can be proud. The Canadian Radio-television and Telecommunications Commission (CRTC), the Canadian Broadcasting Corporation (CBC), the National Film Board, various programs in support of book publishing and film and record production, the maintenance of national and provincial museums and archives – all these and more, with varying degrees of success, have contributed to the overall objective of sustaining and promoting the indigenous cultural and intellectual creativity of Canadians, despite almost overwhelming pressures from abroad and, most notably, from the United States. The need for their activities persists. If a bilateral free-trade agreement is successfully negotiated, it will become even more acute.

Different Canadians are certain, of course, to have different views on all these various matters, interrelated as they are. Given the importance to Canada's future of the issues involved, it is critical that Canadians articulate those views in the debate to come. Commissioners believe that for a public body, we have been unusually frank concerning matters that are often left just below the surface of official – but not private – debate. Indeed, if we have erred in our political analysis, it has been towards the negative viewpoint, and yet we are confident that the balance of argument comes down on the side of further trade liberalization. This is particularly so when our contentions are weighed against the other options. Slow progress towards multilateralism or a drift towards a more protectionist stance would, we believe, cause further deterioration of our economic foundation and unleash even greater political dangers than we have addressed above. To maintain the *status quo* on the political front, as well as within the economy, is not without risk.

Notes

1. Denis Stairs and Gilbert R. Winham, "The Politics of Canada's Economic Relationship with the United States: An Introduction", in *The Politics of Canada's Economic Relationship with the United States*, vol. 29, prepared for the Royal Commission on the Economic Union and Development Prospects for Canada (Toronto: University of Toronto Press, 1985).
2. Canada, Senate, Standing Committee on Foreign Affairs, *Canada's Trade Relations with the United States*, vol. 3 (Ottawa: Minister of Supply and Services Canada, 1982), p. 107.
3. Canada, Communications Canada, Federal Cultural Policy Review Committee, *Report* (Ottawa: Minister of Supply and Services Canada, 1982).

Federalism and Achieving National Consensus

To understand fully the politics of Canada's external economic policies requires some knowledge of the workings of our federal constitutional system. Although it is doubtful whether the Fathers of Confederation intended to create such legally powerful provincial governments, the present constitutional strength of the provinces in economic matters is generally accepted by most Canadians. Each provincial government has the authority to tax, subsidize and otherwise regulate economic activities which are carried on primarily within the province. Provinces also hold ownership rights over their land and natural resources. These areas of authority provide provincial governments with strong levers for shaping the development of their regional economies.

The federal government, for its part, is responsible for regulating both inter-provincial and foreign commercial activities, and for coping with problems of national policy. In the field of foreign economic relations, there was little possibility for jurisdictional conflict between the federal and provincial governments until the 1960s. Before that time, the only significant legal instrument employed in the conduct of Canada's external economic relations was the customs tariff, which the Constitution reserves exclusively to the federal government. Since that government also holds the exclusive right to conduct Canada's foreign affairs, which includes the power to bind Canada to international agreements, it was under no legal necessity to consult with the provinces on matters of international trade and commercial policy. This situation changed in the 1960s and 1970s, when trade-liberalization initiatives under the General Agreement on Tariffs and Trade (GATT) came to focus increasingly on various non-tariff barriers (NTBs) to trade. Many of these NTBs arise from laws and regulations adopted by provincial governments, such as government procurement practices, subsidies to local industries, and consumer-product regulations.

During the Tokyo Round of GATT negotiations, Canada's federal and provincial governments consulted on the prospects for mutual commitments to limit discriminatory procurement practices and trade-restrictive product standards. They agreed that it would not be advantageous to offer specific provincial promises to implement the codes governing these NTBs. Rather than offer a binding legal commitment on behalf of the provinces, our federal government promised the other GATT signatories to use its "best efforts" to promote provincial compliance with the NTB agreements.

The expansion of international law-making activity into areas of provincial jurisdiction has coincided with an expansion of provincial government programs and regulations covering such economic activities as agriculture, manufacturing and resource development, which are closely linked to external trade and investment flows. This steady growth in provincial regulatory and promotional activities expands the provinces' ability to control inward flows of goods and capital, as well. There is a risk that jurisdictional disputes may arise if provincial economic or social policies conflict with federal initiatives to remove, or reduce the restrictive effects of, laws and regulations which limit access to the Canadian market. This risk is heightened by the legal uncertainty about the locus of powers to regulate international trade and commerce. For example, do provincial subsidies which either increase exports or reduce imports amount to an unlawful invasion of federal jurisdiction over foreign trade? Similar questions arise concerning provincial purchasing practices that discriminate against foreign suppliers, and provincial product standards that increase the cost and price of imported products.

Some Canadians argue that the existing uncertainty about the scope of federal authority creates serious impediments to the effective management of our external economic policies. Foreign nations might well be reluctant to conclude agreements with Canada if our government cannot assure them of provincial compliance. The legal necessity to obtain provincial agreement to proposed treaty obligations would mean that even a single dissenting province could block major portions of an arrangement that would confer substantial net benefits on our entire nation. This may become a serious problem because our regionally diverse economy will inevitably create some national-provincial conflict over foreign economic issues. Those who argue for expansion, or at least clarification, of federal legislative powers to implement foreign economic agreements also contend that there are strategic reasons for managing foreign economic relations differently from internal economic policies. Matters of timing and of bargaining strategy may be crucial to Canada's success in negotiating with other nations. Therefore the necessity to hold elaborate federal-provincial consultations before concluding an agreement might seriously handicap Canadian negotiators. It might, for example, force the disclosure of strategically valuable information or prevent a swift response to last-minute initiatives.[1]

While these concerns about jurisdictional conflicts seem warranted, the recent history of federal-provincial co-operation on trade and foreign-investment policies has been relatively satisfactory; in general, it does not justify a pessimistic forecast for future relations in these fields. The single exception – and it may indicate a need to examine existing mechanisms to promote co-operation – is the liquor-pricing dispute which arose several years ago between the federal and Ontario governments. At the time of the Tokyo Round, British Columbia, Ontario and Quebec all maintained pricing policies for alcoholic beverages that discriminated against foreign products. Federal officials proposed an end to higher mark-ups for foreign beverages in return for improved access for Canadian liquor exports to the European and U.S. markets. After an extensive process of consultation, a joint "statement of intent", endorsed by all ten provincial governments, gave assurance that the discriminatory mark-up practices would be withdrawn or, at least, that existing mark-up differentials would be frozen at current levels. Shortly after the negotiations, however, the Government of Ontario imposed new "handling charges" which, in effect, discriminated against foreign products. When the European Community (EC) and the United States complained about these charges, the Ontario government withdrew them, but it soon levied new "minimum reference prices" that imposed equivalent discrimination. The Government of Ontario has insisted that the Tokyo Round "statement of intention" was only that, and not a legally binding commitment.

The stage has thus been reached at which provincial involvement in issues affected by the international trading system must be dealt with as a matter of course. Provincial governments wish to be involved – indeed, they are demanding a voice in those aspects of foreign economic policy which affect their interests. Although our federal government has been reluctant to encourage too much involvement, hesitant first steps have been taken. Official machinery has been developed to exchange information and co-ordinate positions on matters including trade relations, negotiating objectives and major developments in off-shore markets. Since 1982, there have been periodic federal-provincial trade ministers' conferences that have significantly increased the level of communication among governments. Close intergovernmental co-operation is likely to become an increasingly important dimension of foreign economic policy making. It will be especially important in any future free-trade negotiations.

Commissioners have considered several possible options for reducing federal-provincial jurisdictional conflicts in the field of international economic relations. One solution would be to adopt a constitutional amendment giving the federal government the legislative authority necessary to implement international economic agreements. Many federal nations, such as Australia and the United States, have enacted constitutional provisions which give their central governments broad and plenary powers to implement treaties. In Canada, such a constitutional amendment would require the consent of at least seven of the provinces, and, of course, would be subject to the opting-out procedure. In order to secure the required margin of provincial support, it would probably be necessary to provide some explicit, judicially reviewable standard to protect the provinces against abuse or restraint exercised by means of any broad federal treaty-making power.

Rather than depend exclusively on the courts to strike an acceptable balance between the two levels of government, Canadians might also consider possible arrangements for the representation of provincial or regional interests in the federal process of formulating international economic policies. One possibility would be to assign a role in the conduct of foreign economic affairs to a new elected Senate redesigned to give greater weight to regional representation. An elected Senate could be given responsibility for approving or ratifying international agreements before their implementation by the federal government. This arrangement would require a constitutional amendment to provide that treaties approved by a majority of the Senate be self-executing: that is, such treaties would prevail over conflicting provincial legislation.

A third option, one which Commissioners describe at greater length in Part VI of this Report, would be to apply the general constitutional amending formula to sections of a treaty imposing obligations on provinces. A variation of this option would be to establish a joint federal-provincial commission on international agreements. Before the implementation of any international agreement dealing with matters within provincial jurisdiction, the federal government would apply for approval to a commission composed of federal and provincial representatives. A voting rule specifying a two-thirds majority would protect provincial interests and, at the same time, limit the potential problem of one or two dissenting provinces exercising a *de facto* veto over new international agreements. This arrangement might give the provinces more responsibility for foreign economic matters than they have exercised in the past, but it would also place them under a legal bond to implement treaties approved by the joint commission. Its implementation, however, would require an amendment to the Constitution, since it would limit existing provincial legislative powers.

A complement to any of these three options would be the creation of a permanent consultative committee, consisting of federal and provincial representatives. This committee would provide an established forum for the discussion of both pending international negotiations and the implementation of agreements concluded by the federal government. It would not exercise any formal constitutional authority concerning treaty implementation, nor would it possess the legal power to issue binding directives to either level of government. Both the federal and the provincial governments have strong incentives to compromise their differences over treaty implementation rather than to pursue the risky process of constitutional litigation. Nevertheless, in the matter of the division of legislative powers governing foreign economic relations, recourse to the committee would be optional for all parties. This non-binding process of consultation has worked well in Australia, for instance. A federal-state agreement, concluded in 1977, provides for prior consultation with the states when the treaty to be implemented affects matters which would otherwise be within their sphere of legislative competence. The Australian process also gives the states the first chance to enact legislation implementing international treaties which affect their areas of constitutional jurisdiction.

In choosing an option to recommend, this Commission considers it essential to ensure that the division of powers inherent in Canada's federal system should not impose undue constraints on Ottawa's ability to conduct foreign economic relations. As a principal power dependent on foreign markets, Canada cannot permit federal-provincial conflicts to dissipate its bargaining power in bilateral and multilateral negotiations. If the provinces desire deeper involvement in Canada's foreign economic affairs, they will need to demonstrate a willingness to assume obligations and make concessions. Ontario's administration of its commitment on liquor-pricing is not likely to convince the United States and the European Community of the value of similar commitments on government procurement or industrial subsidies. Over the past 20 years, the tendency of our provincial governments to open offices abroad has raised concern in some foreign capitals as to who speaks for Canada. The scope for intergovernmental rivalry is increasing, and such rivalry could seriously impede the effective management of our foreign economic relations. An effective federal-provincial partnership in matters of foreign economic policy will require that information, participation and co-operation be reciprocal, and that it be based on a clear understanding of accountability.

Commissioners have considered the various arguments for a constitutional amendment governing the implementation of economic treaties, but we are not convinced that any fundamental legal reforms are required *at this time* to safeguard against future federal-provincial conflicts. We do, however, foresee some risk of heightened conflict in future years if the federal government aggressively pursues trade-liberalization both multilaterally and bilaterally. For example, the easing of existing restrictions on trade in services and agricultural products will require more closely co-ordinated federal and provincial policies affecting these industries. Trade negotiations will probably focus on the restrictive effects of provincial policies concerning government procurement, on industrial subsidies that substantially increase exports, and on discriminatory product standards. These future trade talks will provide Canada with major opportunities to improve our access to export markets. In order to take advantage of these opportunities, both levels of government must co-operate and agree to accept the binding commitments likely to be demanded by our major trading partners.

Canada has no established or permanent intergovernmental mechanism for mediating and ultimately co-ordinating combined federal and provincial policies on foreign economic relations. While periodic federal-provincial trade ministers' meetings are helpful, Commissioners favour the commitment of additional resources to ensure the efficient co-ordination of government policies in this field. We recommend sustained and continuous consultation by federal and provincial ministers on foreign economic policies. Before Canada begins multilateral or bilateral negotiations, there should be close consultation between ministers about provincial, as well as federal, objectives and the binding commitments required to achieve them. During international trade negotiations, provincial representatives should be on hand to counsel the federal delegation. The delegation should also keep provincial governments informed and request their advice on specific proposals advanced during the bargaining process.

During trade talks, there should be continual consultation between the private sector, provincial officials and federal representatives. Commissioners recommend as a model the discussions and meetings organized by the federal government during the GATT Tokyo Round. These meetings, chaired by a senior official with extensive experience in trade policy, took place both at regular intervals and as need arose during the more intensive periods of negotiation, and canvassed systematically the views of all interested parties. Moreover, after the conclusion of a trade agreement, federal and provincial governments should continue to work together for effective implementation of treaty commitments. We believe it essential for the federal government to employ a similar process of consultation as a complement to future bilateral and multilateral trade initiatives. This co-ordinating role has implications for the structure of federal departments, and it may be that a special trade negotiator for a Canada-U.S./free-trade arrangement should be appointed and should report directly to the Prime Minister.

Primarily, we Commissioners base our view of achieving federal-provincial consensus in international economic relations on pragmatic considerations. These matters have not caused major conflict in the past. Thus, in the short term, we recommend that modest improvements be made in federal-provincial mechanisms for consultation. This strategy, we believe, should also be satisfactory in the context of our recommendations for negotiation of a Canada-U.S./free-trade arrangement if that negotiation should be undertaken soon. We are of the opinion, however, that over the long term, pressures will grow as a result of the constitutional gap in treaty making. For this reason, we have treated this problem in more detail in Part VI of this Report, where we recommend a constitutional solution.

Note

1. See George J. Szablowski, "Treaty-Making Power in the Context of Canadian Politics: An Exploratory and Innovative Approach", in *Recurring Issues in Canadian Federalism*, vol. 57, prepared for the Royal Commission on the Economic Union and Development Prospects for Canada (Toronto: University of Toronto Press, 1985).

The Prospect of Freer Canada-U.S. Trade

Geography, combined with similar cultural and ethnic backgrounds has given rise to an interrelationship between the industry, energy, agriculture, fisheries and intercorporate relationships characteristic of Canadian and U.S. economies. This interconnection is immeasurably more extensive than Canada's relationship with any other country or group of countries. Canadian economic well-being thus depends substantially on our relations with the United States. There is significant scope for the reduction or removal of barriers to cross-border trade and for improving the management of bilateral issues in a variety of areas. More fundamentally, Canada needs to engage the United States directly and formally in the fight to resist new trade barriers, eliminate the old barriers, and generally place cross-border trade on a more secure footing. Many of our industries are competitive and prepared to grow, but they cannot do so in the face of protectionist barriers to their most important market. They are prepared to invest and create new jobs, but they need to be assured that their efforts will not be frustrated by old or new barriers.

Existing barriers to trade, including tariffs, are real. The rosy expectation of 80 per cent duty-free trade by 1987 masks the fact that trade takes place through "holes" in the tariff. While a tariff of 5 to 10 per cent may not prevent trade, it will deter investment beyond that necessary to service the Canadian market. Futhermore, non-tariff barriers, especially in the form of contingent protection, are most effective in denying exporters the kind of security they need to make large-scale, job-creating investment. On the Canadian side, our tariff remains significant and, in addition to protecting producers, raises costs to consumers and producers, and thus retards development of a more competitive economy.

Successive rounds of GATT negotiations have traditionally provided Canada and the United States with the main opportunities to liberalize cross-border trade. Future negotiations could well offer new oportunities to liberalize and secure Canada-U.S. bilateral trade. Such negotiations, however, are unlikely to take place soon enough or to be thorough enough or provide the kind of environment Canadian producers will need by the end of the decade and beyond. We need, therefore, to engage the United States more directly in bilateral free-trade negotiations.

Commissioners' review of the various elements of what would be involved in developing an effective new framework for Canada-U.S. free trade leads us to conclude that a successful agreement would include the following arrangements:

- It would establish a free-trade area, rather than a customs union or common market.
- It should be a broad agreement, covering substantially all trade between the two countries, rather than a collection of sectoral agreements.
- Some sectors could be excluded from the agreement's coverage.
- It should be consistent with Canada's continued participation in GATT.

- It should apply to tariffs, contingency protection and other forms of non-tariff barriers.
- The elimination of tariffs should be phased in over a period of several years. In recognition of the relatively greater effect on the Canadian economy, the phase-in period of the elimination of the Canadian tariff should be longer than that for the United States.
- Non-tariff barriers should be neutralized or reduced by means of common procedures and controlled by codes of conduct; these codes should provide for decision making and implementation by a joint tribunal.
- It should provide for agreed measures of transitional adjustment assistance and safeguards.
- It should include effective dispute-settlement procedures whereby national politicians jointly arrive at final decisions; compulsory arbitration by a neutral panel should be stipulated as a procedure of last resort.
- It needs to be guaranteed by national laws, and it should provide adequate room to involve provincial and state interests.

A bilateral agreement constructed along these lines would make our manufacturing sector competitive by encouraging a process of restructuring and rationalization of Canadian industry to serve the North American market and, from that base, to penetrate overseas markets. It would also increase the security of our access to our most important market, a condition essential for growth and new investment, given the relatively small domestic Canadian market. Finally, it would improve the access we now enjoy in the U.S. market and thus allow Canadian industries presently shut out of that market to grow and invest with renewed confidence. Overall, such an arrangement would make Canadians richer. How much richer is a question best left to the specialist, but on the basis of analyses made for this Commission by competent professionals, we are prepared to say that it would be in the order of a 3 to 8 per cent increase of our national income.

Despite this assurance, a bilateral free-trade agreement would not operate without cost. The new circumstances would inevitably require adjustment, but that is an ongoing process which will affect Canadians whether we move to free trade or not. Again, on the basis of studies done by competent professionals, Commissioners are confident that long-term gains will be many times greater than short-term adjustment costs. Such costs, moreover, can be cushioned by the introduction of appropriate transitional adjustment assistance.

Finally, our review of the political consequences of a move toward free trade has convinced Commissioners that even here there are benefits. Free trade will strengthen Canada's economic fabric; it will reduce regional differences concerning the conduct of trade and industrial policy; and it will contribute to our growing sense of national confidence. Any adverse consequences can be managed by pursuing deliberate policies to strengthen cultural and other aspects of Canadian identity. Our government should also strengthen the objectives and administration of our foreign policy to reflect a more activist internationalist stance to the world community.

American Attitudes

It is only natural to question, as some Canadians have done, why the United States might be interested in concluding a bilateral free-trade arrangement with us at this time. After all, if successful negotiation is not assured, why raise this idea now, given all the debate which will follow in Canada? The answer is that there are good reasons to anticipate that the United States might respond favourably. Commissioners see both trade-policy and wider foreign-policy objectives for the United States that would make a favourable response likely. The United States has clearly indicated that any overtures toward free trade would, of necessity, have to come from Canada. Canadians have the largest interests at stake, but the Americans, we believe, would welcome a first approach from Canada. Recently the United States has indicated clearly its willingness to deal with its trading partners on a bilateral basis, not only through their trade arrangements with Caribbean countries and Israel, but in their declarations of broader trade-policy objectives.

In March 1985, the United States signed a bilateral free-trade agreement with Israel. This treaty calls for the phased-in abolition of all tariffs, export subsidies and other barriers to trade over a ten-year period. The American interest was to increase U.S.-Israel trade and also to show other countries, reluctant to open their markets, how much benefit there can be from freer trade. Trade Representative William Brock recently told the American Chamber of Commerce:

> *The failure of the [world trading] system to move has put the U.S. in the position where we have to contemplate defending our own vital interests. One of the ways we can do that is to take one or more countries and setting up (*sic*) a complete process by which we remove all trade barriers between us as an example of how good the world can be.*
>
> *The U.S. has to operate in its own self-interest and that means that priority has to be building up a global system . . . I would not be in the least reluctant to have several examples for those countries which seem to have chosen a different path for the moment.*[1]

The U.S. interest in freer bilateral trade with Canada is not casual or recent. It is not only based on the so-called "demonstration effect" noted by Brock, but it is also of interest in its own right. Better and more secure access to its most important market is not an advantage to be taken lightly. Since the mid-1970s, U.S. trade law has contained a provision authorizing the President to explore bilateral free trade with Canada. The United States welcomed the federal government's sectoral initiative in 1983, although both sides have since agreed that the scope for bilateral liberalization on a sectoral basis is limited.

The latest expression of U.S. interest appeared in the Declaration on Trade issued by Prime Minister Mulroney and President Reagan at the end of their March 17–18, 1985 meeting in Quebec City. In that document, the two leaders made a strong political commitment to consider all available means to liberalize trade between the two countries. As an indication of the seriousness of their interest, they adopted a specific work program and schedule to negotiate a number of particular agreements that will reduce barriers to the freer flow of trade and investment while the two governments consider whether to take the broader step. The interest of the American Administration in a full free-trade agreement is therefore clear.

The attitude of Congress is more problematic. While the U.S. Administration generally favours freer trade, Congress, influenced by individual lobbyists and interest groups, tends to be biased towards protection. Certain Senators and Congressmen have expressed support for Canada-U.S. bilateral free trade; nevertheless, the attitude of Congress as a whole would be greatly influenced by the interests of the American business community and by the sectoral costs and benefits assessed by individual firms. In making this assessment, both Congress and the American public would probably take longer-term considerations into account and not allow themselves to be overly influenced by such shorter-term circumstances as the current trade balance with Canada. Thus the Administration realizes that progress towards bilateral free trade requires a coalition of interests that expect overall benefit from such an arrangement. The American situation, in fact, is not all that different from our own.

A process of bilateral and multilateral negotiations would dampen protectionist initiatives, especially in the United States, and this development could damage important Canadian interests in the U.S. market. An ongoing process of negotiations focusing, during the coming years, on bilateral trade and trade-policy issues would direct attention to Canadian economic and trade problems, and to the important U.S. stake in the Canadian economy. In addition, by opening bilateral negotiations now, the two countries would encourage broader international agreement to begin a new round of tariff and trade negotiations within GATT. Finally, it seems strategically essential to launch such a process of negotiations in a period when the two governments have both been given new and strong electoral mandates, and before attention in the United States is diverted to mid-term Congressional elections.

An approach of the kind suggested represents recognition that there exists between Canada and the United States a closer, broader and more intricate economic and trade relationship than either country has with any third nation. Arising from this relationship and from changes in the international trade environment are unique trade problems that require bilateral solutions complementary to those provided within the multilateral framework: that is, bilateral solutions which have been worked out in the past to deal with special problems of trade in automotive products and defence arms procurement. Most important, a combination of bilateral and multilateral approaches, carried forward in parallel, could, in the end, prove to be the most effective way of moving towards freer trade between Canada and the United States.

Note

1. See Jennifer Lewington, "U.S. Free Trade Strategy Both Means and an End", *Globe and Mail*, March 6, 1985, p. 11.

Conclusions and Recommendations

The global environment presents Canada with enormous challenges and opportunities. Rapid growth of imports from the developing countries, a changing trade-policy environment and domestic pressures on our trading partners for new protection imperil Canadian jobs. By contrast, growth and technical progress abroad offer us new export opportunities and chances to benefit from access to cheaper and higher-quality products than we can produce. As Commissioners noted at the beginning of this Part, the challenge is one of change, adaptation and adjustment; the opportunities may be unlimited. In light of these developments, however, the choices Canadians must make are difficult.

We Commissioners have been frequently reminded, in the course of our task, that Canada's domestic economy is largely defined by its relationship to the wider global economic system. Canada's last Royal Commission on our economic prospects captured this point:

> *Something of Canada's essence is defined by its external relations. Much of its economic structure can be explained only in terms of its external trade . . .*
>
> *The ships loading lumber on Vancouver Island or aluminum ingots on the Saguenay are reminders of how deeply our material well-being is involved in the prosperity of other countries, even outside the boundaries of North America.*[1]

Canada's economic development, then, as well as our government's economic development policies, are significantly affected by conditions beyond our borders. As a relatively small, "open" economy, Canada is particularly vulnerable to outside influences on its trade and economic performance. In order to foster stability and predictability in some of these external forces, successive Canadian governments have sought to develop formal rules for conducting relationships with our trading partners. The pursuit of this objective has always involved an essential problem: How are we to reconcile conflicting priorities among national objectives and the requirements of a stable international economic system? To resolve inherent conflicts has required a continual process of negotiation and compromise at both the domestic and the international level. Governments have often had to adjust and put to positive use the constant tension between the forces of economic protection and trade liberalization.

For almost forty years, Canada has pursued a largely multilateral approach to its foreign economic policy; indeed we have been one of the strongest supporters of the multilateral system centred on the GATT and the International Monetary Fund. This approach was the most effective way to improve and secure access for our products and to instil order, stability and predictability into that process. Even on the import side, we have found that we must negotiate multilaterally to open our own market, in exchange for access to foreign markets. This action has proved a useful tool of industrial policy and has allowed for orderly adjustment of the economy through foreign competition.

To a great extent, Canadian trade policy has been, and will continue to be, developed as a trade-off between the business objective of securing improved access to foreign markets, the economic need to promote efficiency and competitiveness in the domestic economy, and the political need to maintain our sovereignty and freedom of action. The international trade and payments system largely determines the design and use of particular policy instruments. For Canadian producers and investors, there are several tests of this international system. Can our government successfully improve market access for those sectors where Canadian production is, or can be, competitive in world markets? Will it maintain current access available to Canadian producers? Will it protect producers from unfair or injurious foreign competition? Because private sector investment is necessary for growth and job creation, Canadian producers need to be confident that their access is secure, and that foreign governments will not move to frustrate the efforts to market Canadian goods abroad.

The multilateral system of rules is intended to facilitate decisions favouring adjustment and to penalize decisions favouring protection, but it needs political will to make it work. Between 1973 and 1979, the Tokyo Round of trade negotiations provided a framework for organizing political will. The negotiators sought to reduce trade barriers and to move the ongoing management of trade relations in the direction of freer trade. For the past six years, however, there has been no such framework.

A new round of GATT negotiations may be initiated, to concentrate on elaborating world trade law and removing remaining barriers to world trade, and to provide a basis for organizing political will to resist protection. The results of a future GATT negotiation are not certain, however, nor are they just around the corner. A new round of negotiations requires complex co-ordination and revolves largely around the interests of three or four players: the United States, the European Community, the less-developed countries (LDCs) as a group, and, perhaps, Japan. Canada can make an important contribution, but we cannot control either the agenda or the outcome. Even to influence the outcome requires adroit negotiators. The Community is reluctant to come to the table. The United States is eager, but as yet has no negotiating authority. The LDCs are willing, but insist on some problematic pre-conditions and do not agree on the agenda. Japan is willing, but largely because a new round would facilitate management of its trade relations with the United States and the European Community.

Canada's economic growth is critically dependent on secure access to foreign markets. Our most important market is the United States, which now takes up to three-quarters of our exports. More, better and more secure access to the U.S. market represents a basic requirement, while denial of that access is an ever-present threat. We are extremely vulnerable to any strengthening of U.S. protectionism. Early bilateral negotiations with the United States could provide opportunities for the two countries to negotiate reduction or elimination of tariff and other barriers to cross-border trade, at a pace and on a scale not likely to be achieved multilaterally in a further GATT round. Such negotiations could also be used to win agreement on rules designed to deal with special or unique problems affecting cross-border trade; they would provide a more secure shield against a U.S. policy of protection.

The pursuit of Canada-U.S. free trade is not at odds with efforts to strengthen and improve the existing multilateral framework. Rather, Commissioners see it as a complementary approach, involving concentration of our efforts and scarce resources on our most important market. We see multilateral negotiations proceeding in parallel. In our view, such a two-tiered approach is the best way to ensure that Canadian industry will win sufficient access to foreign markets to invest and grow with confidence. At the same time, it will allow us to open our market in an orderly fashion and thus ensure that trade policy does its part in encouraging the development of a more competitive and more productive economy.

Commissioners see negotiations with the United States as neither panacea nor disaster, but as a prudent course which will help to make us richer and, by making us richer, strengthen the fabric of our country and increase our self-confidence. While this course may initially make Canada more dependent on the U.S. market, it will offer our nation a more secure relationship and thus make us less vulnerable. Ultimately, it should strengthen and diversify our economy, achieving for us goals that we have long sought, but which have eluded us, largely because our domestic manufacturing sector has been too weak to attain them.

Negotiations leading to freer trade, whether pursued bilaterally or multilaterally, will be of little use if they are not supported by the right domestic policies. Our support for freer trade, therefore, depends in no small way on the recommendations Commissioners develop later in this Report. These recommendations should contribute to strengthening the competitiveness and productivity of Canada's domestic economy. Trade policy alone will not be enough.

Commissioners, like others who have enquired into Canada's relations with developing countries, see a need for Canada to take more positive action to help these countries through aid and trade measures. We have reached this conclusion, not only on humanitarian grounds, but also on the basis of our perception of Canada's own interest. Development of stronger links with these countries through aid and trade will pay dividends to future generations of Canadians, by contributing to a more stable world environment and by nurturing future trading partners.

We believe that the approaches we recommend below will help to strengthen our country. They will allow Canadians to pursue the gradual transition from a staple economy to a fully-industrialized modern economy, living in harmony with, but distinct from, our friends and allies.

Recommendations

■ Having carefully considered the analyses presented above, Commissioners make the following general recommendations.

- Canadians have benefited from and contributed to the multilateral system of trade and payments developed primarily in the last 40 years, and we should continue to support that system as the mainstay of our foreign economic policy. Canada is sufficiently strong and independent, however, to pursue bilateral intitiatives, including better economic relations with the United States, within the framework of multilateral relations.

- Canadian import policy in general should be based on a recognition of its costs to consumers and the costs of delaying adjustment. Canada should minimize any new protection, reduce protection gradually as part of bilateral or multilateral negotiations, and accelerate adjustment processes.
- Export promotion should be pursued aggressively and with greater reliance on private sector mechanisms, but the degree of subsidization this may involve should be within internationally accepted rules and practices.

International Trade

International trade is the life-blood of the Canadian economy. It is a major contributor to Canadian growth, jobs and real incomes. In view of the changing nature and patterns of international trade, Canadians are now confronted with several options in formulating trade policy. This Commission has identified three major approaches, each of which has several variations. Canada might:

- Maintain its present policy. It might keep to the level and type of protection currently in place, but make selective efforts both to improve access abroad and to protect Canadian industry on a limited case-by-case basis.
- Participate actively in a new round of multilateral trade negotiations under the auspices of the GATT, in order to improve and secure our country's access to foreign markets, to open up our own market, and to strengthen the legal framework for international trade
- In addition to taking the initiative for the elimination of trade barriers at the multilateral level, open negotiations with the Government of the United States to reach an agreement on a substantial reduction of barriers, tariff and non-tariff, between Canada and the United States.

This Commission rejects any generalized move toward greater protection or toward import substitution as a general policy to insulate Canadian producers from the international economy. This approach, while perhaps the most comfortable in the short term, would lead, in the longer term, to major inefficiencies in the national economy, a loss of jobs and lower incomes, and would contribute to an erosion of the multilateral system. In our view, a policy of maintaining the *status quo* would carry the serious risk of taking Canada backwards to a more protectionist position.

■ Commissioners recommend that multilateral trade negotiations under the GATT remain a central theme of Canadian trade policy; thus Canada should move quickly to define its objectives for the forthcoming round. The GATT has served Canada well, and our nation's participation in further strengthening this international system of co-operation is a general insurance policy for the future. Broadly stated, Canada's objectives should include:

- A more ordered world trading environment: that is, sufficiently stable, predictable and transparent international trade relations to instil a degree of business confidence that will lead to job-creating investment
- More secure access to our major markets, particularly the U.S. market
- Improved opportunity for the further processing of our natural resources before export, by reducing foreign barriers to manufactured goods
- Improved access and trading conditions for agricultural and fishery products
- An improved framework of international rules which will encourage orderly adjustment in the Canadian economy.

■ Commissioners recommend that the Government of Canada, at the same time it undertakes an initiative at the multilateral level to eliminate trade barriers, open negotiations with the Government of the United States to reach agreement on a substantial reduction of barriers, tariff and non-tariff, between Canada and the United States. Such an agreement would have to stand within the terms of Article XXIV of the GATT, and it would provide for a reduction of barriers between the two countries, but would leave each country with freedom of action to maintain separate trading policies with other economic partners. We do not recommend a more intensive arrangement such as a common market or an economic union, where even closer integration would take place between these two economies.

- Commissioners recommend that Canada negotiate a legal arrangement with the United States which incorporates strong safeguards to limit spill-over from the arrangement and thus to protect substantive policies, such as those pertaining to culture and defence, which are functionally unrelated to trade in goods and services. Indeed, a policy that creates no linkage should be explicitly confirmed in order to avoid surprises if the Government of Canada, as we recommend, were to pursue a more aggressive policy of support for indigenous cultural expression as a concomitant of a bilateral trade initiative.
- Commissioners recommend that this legal arrangement attempt to regulate three general types of barriers that currently restrict trade between the two countries. We recommend that:
  - Tariffs be phased down to zero over a period of perhaps ten years. Effective rules of origin must be developed.
  - An approach should be developed to use measures of contingent protection as follows:
    - For measures governing "fair" trade (such as safeguard action) and "unfair" trading practices (such as anti-

dumping and countervailing-duty proceedings), enforcement would be shifted from national administrative tribunals to a new Canada-U.S. intergovernmental body established under the arrangement; this body would be known as the "Canada-U.S. Trade Commission" (CUSTC).

– Detailed codes of national conduct would be required to govern resort to other non-tariff measures such as discriminatory federal and state-government/procurement practices, product standards and federal customs, classification rules and administrative procedures. Again, these matters should be subject to review of the CUSTC.

- This Commission holds that a free-trade arrangement should incorporate explicit provisions which reflect the proportionately greater costs of adjustment that Canadians will face. The Canadian economy needs more time for adjustment than does the U.S. economy. We therefore recommend a two-track approach to phasing in the tariff cuts to allow U.S. rates of duty generally to be reduced either at a faster rate or earlier than Canadian tariffs. The Canadian government should quickly develop strategies for adjustment which are compatible with the framework of adjustment assistance proposed in Part V of this Report, that is, the new Transitional Adjustment Assistance Program. The emphasis of government programs should be on assisting workers to adjust to new employment opportunities. In addition, a reoriented industrial policy, as set out in Part III, will encourage the flexibility and growth orientation required by a freer-trade environment.
- This Commission recommends that the Government of Canada urge the Government of the United States to implement the free-trade arrangement by amending U.S. federal and, if necessary, state legislation to conform to the arrangement, and that they do so under a "fast track" procedure which would require Congress to pass implementing legislation within 90 days of the President's formal declaration that he intends to sign an international agreement binding the United States. We also recommend, however, that a formal treaty eventually be struck once both governments have had sufficient experience with the arrangement.
- This Commission recommends that negotiations in Canada proceed on the basis of a broadly based, federal-provincial consensus, and that provinces be prepared to give legislative assent to the provisions of the arrangement, in keeping with the high degree of consultation that will be required to achieve federal-provincial consensus. We also recommend that in the longer term, Canadian governments establish a federal-provincial constitutional procedure: sections of the treaty that impose obligations on provinces would come into effect across

Canada when two-thirds of provincial legislatures, representing at least half of Canada's population, passed resolutions in support of the treaty.

- This Commission recommends the formation of a three-tiered Canada-U.S. intergovernmental institution to provide basic executive and administrative decisions; technical staff services; adjudication of complaints and appeals under the agreement. We further recommend the following mechanisms:
  - A committee of national officials at the ministerial level to be responsible for the enforcement of the agreement's obligations
  - A supporting body of officials known as the "Canada-U.S. Trade Commission" (CUSTC) to manage non-tariff barriers, but subject to appellate review by the Ministerial Committee
  - A standing arbitral panel with binding powers as a board of last resort, to resolve disputes arising from conflicting interpretations of the agreement. Such a panel would consist of two Canadians, two Americans and one neutral member to be chosen by the members of the panel.
- International trade and industrial policy are inextricably linked. In Canada, there is the added dimension of cultural and social implications. To undertake successful negotiations on freer trade with the United States will require an extraordinary management effort by the Government of Canada. Commissioners, while making no specific recommendation on how best to prepare the way for the negotiations, wish to express concern that the current federal departmental structure does not appear to provide the degree of integration required to carry out a major negotiation of this kind. It may be that an Office of the Special Trade Negotiator should be established, and that the incumbent should report directly to the Prime Minister.

Development Assistance

■ The motives of altruism and long-term national interest coincide in this Commission's recommendations for Canadian objectives pertaining to Canada's relations with developing countries. In pursuing these objectives, Canadians should be aware that the primary responsibility for development rests with the nations in question, and that although greater international efforts are required, difficult intranational, social and institutional issues are often the fundamental impediments to progress, just as they are in all nations. Commissioners recommend:

- An improvement in both the quantity and the quality of Canada's aid performance. Canada should advance to the Lima target of 0.7 per cent of GNP, not by 1995, but by 1990, and aim to achieve 1 per cent of GNP by the year 2000. The Canadian government should reduce the fraction of our aid which is tied, and to facilitate this reduction, we should rely more on multilateral than on bilateral aid.

- That Canada work within global institutions to improve the receptivity of these bodies to proposals helpful to developing countries. Canada should, for instance, systematically seek ways to involve developing countries more fully in a future round of GATT negotiations.
- That the Canadian government be ready to consider proposals for mitigating some of the more harmful effects of the international debt crisis on developing countries. Canadians should resist pressures for economic protection that would apply to exports from these countries. A more constructive and conciliatory approach to developing countries and their problems will not only help these countries, but also yield longer-term dividends for all countries. □

Note

1. Canada, Royal Commission on Canada's Economic Prospects, *Final Report* (Ottawa: Queen's Printer, 1957), p. 17.